ORA WILLIAMS

American Black Women in the Arts and Social Sciences

Third Edition, revised and enlarged

by
ORA WILLIAMS

The Scarecrow Press, Inc.
Metuchen, N.J., & London
1994

Previously published:

American Black Women in the Arts and Social Sciences: A Bibliographic Survey. Metuchen, N.J.: Scarecrow Press, 1973.

American Black Women in the Arts and Social Sciences: A Bibliographic Survey, revised and expanded edition. Metuchen, N.J.: Scarecrow Press, 1978.

British Library Cataloguing-in-Publication data available

Library of Congress Cataloging-in-Publication Data

Williams, Ora.
    American Black women in the arts and social sciences /
by Ora Williams. —3rd ed., rev. and enl.
        p.   cm.
    Includes index.
    ISBN 0-8108-2671-2 (acid-free paper)
    1. Afro-American women—Bibliography.   I. Title.
Z1361.N39W56   1994
[E185.86]
016.30548'896073—dc20   93-33079

Dedicated to

the Augusta Bakers,
the Miriam Matthewses,
the Dorothy Porters,
the Charlemae Rollinses,
and other African-American librarians
on whose shoulders we stand

CONTENTS

PREFACE

Phillis Wheatley

The child died. And then you died.
Your husband burned your poems
And tried to forget he was an African.
It happened so easily—in America. Overnight
One day, you were a slave-girl poet,
Society curio, and the next—nothing.

The children keep dying. Husbands die.
You wonder why you keep coming back to your poems.
It is the mystery that built Kangaba.[1]
It has something to do with living—
Maybe *everything*. Night after night,
You keep at it.

—Anthony Grooms[2]

Anthony Grooms' tribute to Phillis Wheatley, one of the earliest female and authentic Black influences on American literature, speaks to Wheatley and to American Black women poets. Since Wheatley, whose dates were *c.* 1754 to 1783, was the second American female to have a book of poetry published, and the first acknowledged Black American to have a literary volume published, she is more than a literary progenitor of American and women's literature. She, Lucy Terry, whose "Bars of Flight" appeared in 1746, and Jupiter Hammon, whose poem "An Evening Thought, Salvation by Christ, with Penitential Cries," appeared in 1760, are titular heads of American Black women's, Black, American women's, and yes, of all American literature. Thus, this poem also speaks to all American writers.

Grooms' tribute to Wheatley and American Black women poets also establishes major themes in this essay and in this edition of *American Black Women in the Arts and Social Sciences:*

ix

A Bibliographic Survey. Wheatley and other cultural contributors, such as Black women poets and other Black female and male artists, have always been poets, writers, artists. They have kept at it—have continued to create and to invent in spite of the forms of slavery they have experienced.

But, a bit of history is needed to ensure an understanding of the purposes of this work and of its importance at this time. This history is also essential to establishing the extent to which racism, sexism, and ageism have influenced all levels of the Black experience. Each has impacted on the ways in which Blacks perceive and are perceived. In 1972, when this writer began compiling lists of works by Black women, in most circles—Black or White—American Black women were not considered valid or positive research subjects. It was a time of heightened Black-woman bashing.

Black heroes of the day were Black males associated with the waning civil rights struggles. Black studies courses were high-lighting the works of Booker Washington, W. E. B. DuBois, Malcolm X, James Weldon Johnson, Frederick Douglass, and Richard Wright. Black women, not White men and women, were asked and expected to "take a back seat, so that deprived Black men could advance." Therefore, with the exception of the negative public attention being given Angela Davis, any attempt to focus on the cultural contributions of Black women in our society fell on deaf and unsympathetic ears.

When women's literature was introduced *c.* 1970 on this writer's campus, some of her White male colleagues, wishing to include at least one Black woman in their courses, asked her for the name of "a Black woman poet," and later for the name of "a Black woman writer." The works of Phillis Wheatley, although included in American literature textbooks, had been forgotten or were declared not militant enough to appeal to the predominantly liberal White audiences enrolled in women's studies classes. The works of contemporaries Gwendolyn Brooks and Lorraine Hansberry were not known in the halls of White academe.

The inquiries prompted this writer to make a short and then a longer checklist of Black women writers. Most of her colleagues viewed her focus on American Black women with considerable amusement. Research and grant committees rejected her proposals for subsidies to underwrite modest typing costs on her reseach. When the first edition of *American Black Women in the Arts and Social Sciences* appeared, one Black administrator questioned her, for he thought that this bibliography, a small list of works by and about African-American women—not racism or sexism—created a schism between Black males and females.

Two years later, in about 1972, when this writer proposed a course on the literature of Black women, greater skepticism surfaced. Some wondered how substantive such a course could be. Others declared such would be "the briefest course ever taught." Still others expressed concern about a "college" course that consisted of works by Lorraine Hansberry, Nella Larsen, Jessie Fauset, Margaret Walker, Zora Neale Hurston, Paule Marshall, Kristin Hunter, Ann Petry, Alice Dunbar-Nelson, Georgia Douglas Johnson, and Maya Angelou, just a fraction of the works that could have been taught at that time. No one seemed to correlate the need for existing and developing women's studies courses with a need for this one course in Black women's literature.

Superficially, much has changed since the second edition of *American Black Women* was published in 1978. In need of highly marketable works, publishers are finding that some books by African-American women are publishers' dreams. Not only are publishers and the media willing to promote a limited number of Black women writers, but established journals and periodicals are focusing on works by American Black women writers. New publications, such as *Sage, A Scholarly Journal on Black Women* and *The Zora Neale Hurston Forum,* have emerged. Conferences on all phases of Black women's experiences are being convened, and panels addressing these varied experiences are part of heretofore all-White professional meetings. Artists, curators, and photographers throughout the country have mounted whole shows on African-American women and their contributions, marvelling at their endless achievements.

For these reasons and because of legislative nudging due to an influx of new ethnic groups, a handful of this writer's colleagues, the Doubting Thomases of the seventies, now find it the "in thing" to include Walker's *The Color Purple,* Morrison's *Beloved,* and Wanda Coleman's *Mad Dog Black Lady* in American literature courses or the "in thing" to take charge of ethnically oriented literature courses. The latter is being done without the usual expertise required for teaching non-ethnic courses, for instance, Victorian Literature or American Drama.

Although it appears that Black women have only now made significant breakthroughs in terms of equal opportunities, and that they have only now broken all barriers, American Black women are doing what they have been doing for centuries,—what one panelist at a recent Claremont College conference described as "reinventing the wheel." Indeed, their cultural accomplishments may be unparalleled when compared to those of other American ethnic groups or to other Americans.

We are reminded that when in 1772, Phillis Wheatley attempted to have a volume of her poetry published, she had to convince a group of White males (in a country which has discouraged Black literacy) of her ability to write those poems.[3] In 1892, one hundred and twenty years later, Anna Julia Cooper was compelled to reinvent the wheel with *Voice from the South,* in which she recorded the cultural contributions American Black women had been making. She used such phrases as "muffled strain" and "mute and voiceless note" to call attention to the general invisibility of these women.[4]

In 1894, two years later, Mrs. N. F. Mossell made the same point when she published *The Work of the Afro-American Woman,* an anthology about the achievements of Black women in the arts and sciences. In 1926, thirty-two years later, Hallie Q. Brown also reinvented the wheel when she published her *Homespun Heroines,* recording achievements of American Black women from the mid-eighteenth century to the early twentieth century.

For years, some scholars of African-American studies have presented the cultural contributions of American Blacks and Black women as they should be, on the same type of continuum used for other Americans. The results are such classics as *The Negro Caravan,* by Arthur P. Davis, Sterling Brown, and

Ulysses Lee; *The American Negro Reference Book,* edited by John Davis; *To Make a Poet Black,* by J. Saunders Redding; *Black Voices,* edited by Abraham Chapman; *They Also Spoke: An Essay on Negro Literature in America, 1787–1930,* by Kenny Jackson Williams; *Invisible Poets: Afro-Americans of the Nineteenth Century,* by Joan Sherman, the six volumes of *Afro-American Writers,* edited by Trudier Harris and Thadious Davis; *The Schomburg Library of Nineteenth-Century Black Women Writers,* General Editor, Henry Lewis Gates, Jr.; *American Negro Art,* by Cedric Dover; and *Black Artists on Art,* by Samella Lewis and Ruth Waddy.

Virtually all of the resistance to acknowledging the accomplishments of African-American women in the arts can be traced to racism and sexism in society and in the arts. Whites and few, if any, African-American men remain empowered. Now, with the successes of feminist groups, White women and other non-Black women are making substantial gains, seemingly at the expense of both African-American men and women. The attention given sexual harassment has replaced any concern with racism. Indeed, there is a concerted effort to delete the word "racism" from the American vocabulary. College and university class schedules provide "sexual harassment" information, but make no references to racial harassment, a growing problem on most campuses. The lack of concern for racism among many White women is reflected in a recent action ballot of the National Organization for Women which lists eleven critical issues, not one of which is racism.[5]

Yet, Black women's groups treat global problems. In April 1989, the Intercollegiate Department of Black Studies and The Claremont Colleges led a consortium of departments and related colleges in a conference "Embodied & Engendered: A Conference to Vision and Revision Sexuality, Gender, and Selfhood in Africa and Its Diaspora," focusing on racism and sexism. In the summer of 1989, the concerns of the National Political Congress of Black Women (NPCBW) were racism and sexism. With others being empowered, Black women's invisibility in other arenas is becoming the accepted norm.

Because of racism, sexism, and ageism, the purposes of the 1978 edition of the *American Black Women in the Arts and Social Sciences* were to:

□ Show that thousands of American Black women have
made significant cultural contributions to the United
States,
□ Give easy access to works by and about American Black
women,
□ Establish the diversity among American Black women as
a means of refuting the general stereotypes,
□ Reaffirm and celebrate American Black women to whom
society often ascribes its major pathologies.

This 1993 revised and enlarged edition of *American Black
Women* does not purport to have undertaken the impossible
task of listing all cultural contributions of American Black
women. For instance, popular and classical musicians and
many writers of contemporary literature with adult themes
have not been covered adequately. Such research as that
suggested below might be undertaken by others. Because
little has changed in our society, this work seeks to reiterate
and reinforce the purposes of the 1973 and 1978 editions. In
addition, it intends, among other things, to:

□ Illustrate how long African-American women have made
positive contributions to their country;
□ Make visible and bring together a more comprehensive
listing of the cultural contributions of American Black
women than appeared in the previous two editions;
□ Herald sung and unsung African-American women who
have made contributions;
□ Give easy access to less familiar Black women in the arts
and social sciences and their works, possibly establishing
a network for some;
□ Direct much-needed attention to West Coast Black
Women in the arts and social sciences;
□ Re-emphasize that American Black women have a long
cultural history and that their works must be viewed on
the same type of continuum as that used for the works of
other American artists;
□ Give American Black women the rare opportunity of
seeing themselves as a positive and major part of rich and
diverse national/global cultural traditions;

☐ Suggest new areas for scholarship by calling attention to some of the gaps in available works by and about American Black women, for instance, in the culinary arts, quilting, religious writings, film making, ceramics, and dance.

This volume and other works since the 1970s answer the question, "What have American Black women ever done?" Here are refutations to old and newly surfaced myths that African-American women *are not* intellectuals, *do not* write essays, biography, science fiction; *do not* paint or write about flowers; *are not* chroniclers; *do not* sing opera; *are not* ceramists; *are not* technicians; and *cannot* relate "warmly" to their fathers, mothers, sisters, brothers, sons, or daughters. Here is proof that these women have been far busier making positive contributions to society than society dares to admit.

This occasional poem by Bertha Davis, an English teacher in the Houston Public Schools, illustrates the positive manner in which African-American women are represented in this resource:

The Two of You

So it's your birthday,
it's also mine.
for your coming to me
was the first time,
i really knew about
love.
you see
it was the beginning
of a new life for me.
from a world of
fun,
frivolity,
foolishness,
selfishness,
you ushered me into
a new world of
thinking carefully
caring,
sharing,
sacrificing,

responsibility,
and an awareness
i never knew before.
aware
of your every accomplishment.
i heard you awaken
before it happened
heard your cry, before it was
uttered,
knew when you were happy
and felt sad when your desires
        were unsatisfied
i prayed that you would always
        be healthy and happy
and it was hard to let you out
        of my sight.
to me,
it was impossible to love more.
and then when you were two
your sister came and that doubled

my caring	love
and loving and sharing.	and my heart
as the years passed by with all the	could hardly contain
pain,	the happiness
joy,	and the pleasure
tears,	that you two have given me.
woes,	happy birthday!
i watched	i'm enjoying my birthday, too
both of you grow along with my	all because of the two of you.
	bed[6]

This volume has other purposes. For most individuals, media attention is fleeting. At the moment great attention seems to be given a few African-American women, but like others before them, these too may soon be forgotten. This edition will help immortalize the contributions of the women included here and may inspire scholars to search out other artists whose works are not listed.

Many obvious changes have been made in this edition. The 1978 edition had three major divisions: "Reference Works," "Comprehensive Listings," and "Selected Bibliography." This edition has four major sections: "Reference Works," "Comprehensive Listings," "West Coast Black Women in the Arts and Social Sciences," and "Other Resource Lists." Part II: "Comprehensive Listings" has been reorganized with five major sub-headings: "Literary Arts," "Performing Arts," "Visual Arts," "Culinary and Other Arts," and "Critical Issues."

A few categories have been eliminated from this work and others created. For instance, Part III: "West Coast Black Women in the Arts and Social Sciences" replaces "Selected Individual Bibliographies" for a number of reasons, one being to direct much-needed attention to the burgeoning cultural contributions of West Coast Black women. (The West Coast listings include women who were born or lived in this region.)The sub-categories within this new division are similar to and similarly arranged as those within the comprehensive category. Whereas the last section in the 1978 edition consisted of three sub-divisions, the last section in this edition, Part IV, consists of six important resources.

Another major change is the many additions. Some sections (for example, the chronology, reference, autobiography and biography lists) have more than doubled. In the first and

Bertha E. Davis, who signs her poems "bed".

second editions, the bibliography sections had 21 and 42 entries. This edition has about 189 entries in the two bibliography sections. In the first and second editions, the autobiography and biography sections had 64 and 136 entries. The current edition has approximately 268 entries. The first edition listed 51 novels, the second 67, and this one, almost 138. These marked contrasts reflect the increased productivity of Black women and the increased accessibility of their works.

As with many of the traditional written and visual arts, audio-visual materials by and about African-American women have literally quadrupled since 1978. The increased numbers of audio-visual materials and of critical and historical works made it feasible to conclude each of the arts categories with the related critical, historical, and audio-visual materials.

Profiles on two of our mature women emphasize how much ageism may also contribute to one's invisibility . The first profile on the contributions of octogenarian Dr. Dorothy Porter Wesley introduces "References." The other, an overview of the music career of Dr. Eva Jessye (who died as this work went to press), introduces "Performing Arts."

African-American women in dance have had a very definite impact on the dance globally; therefore, the choreography section merely suggests the work that these women are doing and reminds us that the written word is not always a complete portrayal of what exists. Thus, all artists are obligated to keep records and share them.

Considering that a true picture of any group must include the perspectives of all segments of our society, this edition includes more works by non-Black women than the previous editions. In the former editions, as a way of playing catch-up, the focus was primarily on what Black women were doing. Now that some records have been set straight, it seems essential to include the points of view of African-Black men, of whom Maya Angelou has said, "We have always been together, at Jamestown, at the auction block. . . . "[7] Despite these added perspectives, the emphasis remains on African-American women.

Although W. E. B. DuBois, Alain Locke, and Carter G. Woodson were among many Black male writers who recognized the roles Black women had in the American experience, lately many Black men have seen their sisters in victimization as oppressors. Anthony Grooms' tribute to Phillis Wheatley and to "Black women poets in general" captures our forefathers' understanding and reflects the respect some American Black males have always had for their sisters, mothers, and daughters. This poem also places the plight of these women in a broader context, perhaps encouraging and heralding a change in attitude of non-Black women toward both women and American Black women.

While emphasizing the continuity among African-American women's works, this work also highlights some of the gaps, one of which is in the culinary arts. Although many of the early recipes may not have been recorded by Blacks, hundreds of Black secular and religious organizations have published cookbooks, some based on oral history. These cookbooks have been difficult for this compiler to come by. Such works should be collected and made available because cookbooks, in expository and narrative form are, as Dr. Agnes Moreland Jackson, English Professor at Pitzer College, says, a composite of many of the arts: literary, visual, folk art, and for some people, music.[8] Mrs. Gladys Garvin, formerly of Pomona, confirms the place of cookery in *Food and Nutrient for All Ages,* when she writes, "Just as paint and oils, and musical notes are all about us, so there are, at every hand, wide varieties of food products which one may fashion into dishes which, too, are works, of art." She mentions the "fine art of cooking," the "Art of Baking," and compares the "fundamental laws of painting and music" to those involved with cooking.[9]

The importance of food-related activities is spelled out by some compilers of cookbooks. Norma Jean and Carole Darden see working on their cookbook as a means of collecting family history and memories. Pearl Bowser, Joan Eckstein, and Edna Lewis speak of family bonds being created at the kitchen table.[10,11] Others describe the nurturing that comes from preparing and eating favorite foods and special meals. So significant are food, recipes, food preparation, eating, and accompanying narratives, that these are constants in a large body of Black literature.

Educator and critic Frances Smith Foster notes that recipes

in African-American imaginative literature are an unexplored field. [12] We see food as a major image in Paul Laurence Dunbar's "Christmas Is a Comin'," "When De Con' Pone's Hot," and "The Party"; Alice Dunbar-Nelson's "Big Quarterly in Wilmington"; Maya Angelou's *I Know Why the Caged Bird Sings*; Joyce Carol Thomas's *Bright Shadows*; Paule Marshall's "Reena"; and Ntozake Shange's *Sassafrass*. The kitchen, the table, and food are extremely important in August Wilson's *Joe Turner's Come and Gone*.

The section on musical conductors and directors touches on the enormous impact that the Black female has had on the musical heritage of this continent. The predecessor and in some instances counterpart of these directors has been the Black female music teacher, who turned her home into a studio or who each week walked to the homes of her twenty to sixty private pupils. Among such institutions were Rachel Washington (1880s), Boston; Bessie Doans (violin), Lorenza Jordan Coles (piano), Los Angeles; Gladys Childress Jackson (piano, Southern University and Los Angeles); Genevieve Lewis, and Alma Hightower (piano), Los Angeles. There were Adah Killian Jenkins(voice and piano) and Mary Josephine Turner (piano), Baltimore; Leota Apple Palmer (piano, Oberlin and Philadelphia); Mildred McGowan (piano, Montclair, NJ., Atlanta, and Southern University); Barbara E. Williams (piano and string), Lakewood, Trenton, and Hopewell Valley, NJ; and Thelma O. Williams (piano), Lakewood, Englewood, and Teaneck, N.J. These women ought to be counted as important nurturers of our youth and among major shapers of American culture.

This volume reminds us that more research must be done on the influences of Black artists on each other. For instance, we think it essential to know the influences of Papa Haydn on his pupils Wolfgang Mozart and Ludwig Beethoven, of Mark Twain on most American writers, of Leo Tolstoy on an assortment of European and American writers, of Nathaniel Hawthorne on William Faulkner. Many Black writers establish their legitimacy by tracing their literary kinship to the Feodor Dostoyevskys, Gustave Flauberts, Victor Hugos, and the Robert and Elizabeth Brownings. We know of the blood relationships of artists, William Sidney Porter to Katherine

Anne Porter and Sir Leslie Stephen to Virginia Woolf (father and daughter).

We might continue exploring influences among artists listed here and try to determine the significance of the various teacher-student relationships and of the multi-talented families included in this work. For instance, at least four members of the Arthur P. Davis family are listed: Dr. Arthur Paul Davis, educator and author, Dr. Charles Davis, educator and author, Dr. Jean Morrow Granger, educator, and Thulani Davis, writer. Dancers Janet Collins and Carmen de Lavallade are first cousins. Another member of their family, Yvonne de Lavallade, is an important dance figure in Los Angeles. Musicians and scholars Geneva Southall and Antoinette Handy are sisters. Essie Jones Handy was the mother and grandmother of Jewell Gresham, educator and writer, and Joi Gresham, dancer and educator, respectively. Consuela Lee Moorehead, Director of the Snow Hill, Alabama, Institute for the Performing Arts, musician, and Spike Lee, movie director, are the Greshams' cousins.

Thelma and Barbara Williams, music educators and performers, are sisters of this writer and Dorothy Stallworth, composer, music educator, classical and jazz artist. Aunts of Ntozake Shange and Ifa Bayeza, actress, writer-producer in television, theater, film, and former writer for *Different Strokes,* all are cousins of entrepreneurs Carol Poindexter Brown and Mary Francis Winters, Anthony Grooms, Professor of English, University of Georgia, Athens, and Bertha E. Davis, teacher of English, Houston. Sara Lightfoot, educator and author, and Margaret Lawrence, child psychiatrist and author, are mother and daughter. Author Ruth Graham was married to the late author Lorenz Graham, brother of Shirley Graham DuBois. Former librarian and writer Pauline Young was the niece of author Alice Dunbar-Nelson.

Perhaps the best way to show the overall contributions of African-American women is for scholars to study African-American women by genre, by specific locales, by individual states, and then, by geographic regions. As a few of the titles show, some scholars have been pursuing inter-disciplinary or comparative studies of all the arts. Now, much broader studies may be undertaken.

A fitting closing to this preface is the poem of Judith Still-Headlee, one of the West Coast Artists included in this volume. Still-Headlee's occasional piece can be seen as a companion to Grooms' poem in that it addresses the hardships and suffering of African-American artists. Hers is to William Grant Still, her father, a pioneer in African-American and American music and famous composer and conductor. By the same token, both works are companions to Bertha Davis's poem of tribute to her daughters, printed earlier in this preface. All write omitted history, disprove some commonly held myths about Black women, and present positive images of familial relationships. All demonstrate an ability to express aesthetically deep and/or restrained emotions:

The Hungry Guest of Honor

He often dreamed he was the hungry guest
Of honor at a splendid feast, or that
He stood on steps of arched facades, not dressed
Too well—his shoes too thin, the heels worn flat.
Because the doors were locked to him, he crept
Close in to hear cathedral sounds, in walls
Where deep winds (swelling with percussion) swept
Polished pews and marble-vaulted halls.

The music called, but though he knocked, no host
Would come to lift the iron bar, or swing
The gates outward to his advance. The most
That came was song, and his own will to sing.

His final sleep took him inside to find
The music his, played by all humankind.

Judith Still-Headlee

Notes

[1]Kangaba was the capital of Ancient Mali, the cultural center of Black Africa and was in the general area of Senegal from which Wheatley came.

[2]Anthony Grooms, Professor of English, University of Georgia,

TOP: Judith Still–Headlee. BOTTOM: William Grant Still (Headlee's father) to whom she dedicated her poem, *"The Hungry Guest of Honor,"* pictured with his family.

Athens, GA, is the author of *Ice Poems,* Poetry Atlanta Signature Series, Poetry Atlanta Press, 614 Page Avenue, Atlanta, GA 30307.
[3]Henry Louis Gates, Jr., "Forward, In Her Own Write," *A Voice from the South,* Anna Julia Cooper. With an introduction by Mary Helen Washington. *The Schomburg Library of Nineteenth Century Black Women Writers* New York: Oxford Press, 1988, vii, viii.
[4]*A Voice from the South,* II.
[5]National Organization for Women, *An Initiative Action Ballot,* 1988–89.
[6]bed, signature for Bertha Elizabeth Davis, retired teacher of English, Houston Public Schools.
[7]Maya Angelou, *Phil Donahue Show,* 26 July 1989.
[8]Agnes Moreland Jackson, telephone conversation, 10 July 1989.
[9]Gladys Garvin, *Food and Nutrient for All Ages* (Pomona, CA.: The Little Informant, P.O. Box 1663), ix.
[10,11]Norma Jean and Carole Darden, *Spoonbread and Strawberry Wine* with line drawing by Doug Jamieson (New York: Fawcett Crest, 1980), introduction; Edna Lewis, *The Taste of Country Cooking* (New York: Alfred A. Knopf, 1986), xv.
[12]Frances Foster, "The Afro-American Literary Tradition: Women Writers." Lecture given at the Afro-American Museum of Art, 10 August 1986.

ACKNOWLEDGMENTS

Many persons have helped me with this work. Among those who have made suggestions, contacted resource persons, submitted entries, and proofread copy are Mrs. Renee Anderson, Mrs. Sue Belles, Mrs. Helen Britton, Dr. Roland Bush, Dr. Hansonia Caldwell, Miss Beverly Coleman, Mrs. Bette Cox, Mrs. Bertha Branch Davis, Dr. Jacqueline DjeDje, Dr. Frances Foster, Mr. Roy Garrott, Ms. Norma Graeves (Caribbean Union College), Professor Anthony Grooms, Mrs. Marcia Hampton, Mrs. Catherine Lewis-Ida, Dr. Agnes Jackson, Mr. C. Bernard Jackson, Mrs. Hermia Justice, Dr. Pinkey Gordon Lane, Ms. Charlene LaForge, Mr. Chris Leonti, Miss Miriam Matthews, Dr. Claudia Mitchell-Kernan, Dr. Yvonne Meo, Miss Marilyn Moy, Dr. Jewell Gresham Handy Nemiroff, Mr. George Ouendijk, Mrs. Jayne Senegal, Ms. Maria Sugranes, Mr. Oscar Sims, Mr. James G. Spady, Mrs. Willie Smith, Mrs. Leslie Swigert, Mrs. Cynthia Tucker, Dr. Terrence Wiley, Dr. Dorythea Cooley Williams, Miss Thelma O. Williams, Mrs. Lucy Wilson, Dr. Richard Yarborough, and Mr. Marwan Zeineddine. My deepest appreciation goes to these persons and to any who assisted me but whose names were inadvertently omitted.

Ora Williams

CHRONOLOGY:
SOME SIGNIFICANT DATES IN THE
HISTORY OF AMERICAN BLACK WOMEN

1619   The first Black slaves landed at Jamestown Harbor, Virginia.

1746   Lucy Terry, whose poem "Bars of Flight" appeared this year, was the first Black American to have a poem published.

1770   Phillis Wheatley's poem "An Elegiac Poem on the Death of the Rev'd Mr. George Whitefield—1770" was published.

1777   Vermont abolished slavery, the first territory to do so.

1783   The second published volume of poetry by an American woman and the first volume of poetry by an American Black person was Phillis Wheatley's *Poems on Various Subjects, Religious and Moral*.

1786   The New York African Free School was begun.

1780   Massachusetts declared all men to be born free and equal.

1790   All Blacks in Boston, Massachusetts, were freed.

1797   Sojourner Truth is said to have been born around this time in Ulster County, New York.

1816   The first independent Black church, the African Methodist Episcopal Church, was founded in Philadelphia.

1820   This date is the approximate birthdate of Harriet Tubman, Eastern Shore, Maryland.

1821   The African Grove Theater, the first Black theatrical company, was organized in New York City.

1831   The first convention of "people of color" met in Philadelphia.

1837   The American Friends founded the Institute for Colored Youth in Philadelphia.

        A national convention of Negro women met in Philadelphia to promote the abolition of slavery.

1843   Sojourner Truth was a popular traveled abolitionist speaker.

1848   William and Mary Ellen Craft escaped from slavery.

1849   Harriet Tubman escaped from slavery in Maryland.

1850   Lucy Sessions earned a degree from Oberlin, possibly becoming the first Black woman in America to receive a college degree.

        The Narrative of Sojourner Truth as told to Olive Gilbert appeared.

1853   Rachel Parker, who won her freedom in a Maryland state court, is thought to have been the first Black freed by a slave state court.

1853/4 Elizabeth Taylor Greenfield ("The Black Swan"), a soprano with a remarkably sweet voice and exceptionally wide range—G in the bass clef to E in the treble clef—gave a highly successful appearance in England, including a performance in Buckingham Palace before Queen Victoria.

1854   *Poems on Miscellaneous Subjects,* by Frances Harper, was published.

1856   Wilberforce College, said to be the first Black College in the U. S., was founded by the African Methodist Episcopal Church in Xenia, OH.

1861   President Abraham Lincoln read first draft of Emancipation Proclamation.

1862   Mary Jane Patterson received a bachelor of arts degree from Oberlin College.

        Harriet Tubman served as a spy, scout, and guerrilla leader for the Union Army.

1864   Fannie Jackson Coppin was one of forty students selected to teach preparatory classes at Oberlin.

        Edmonia Lewis, first American Negro woman sculptor to

achieve distinction in this art, exhibited her work in Boston.

Mary Ellen Pleasant, civil rights advocate and abolitionist, sued the San Francisco Street Car Company for rude treatment to her and two other Black women.

Sojourner Truth was appointed counselor to freed Blacks in Arlington Heights, VA.

1866   Fisk University opened in Nashville, TN.

1867   Dr. Rebecca J. Cole was the first Black woman graduate of the Women's Medical College of Pennsylvania and the second known Black woman in the United States to become a doctor.

Howard University was established in Washington, D.C.

1868   Hampton Institute was established in Hampton, VA.

1871   Edmonia Lewis received acclaim in Rome for her exhibit of sculpture.

Sarah Parker Remond, abolitionist and medical doctor, earned her medical degree from a medical school in Florence, Italy.

1872   Charlotte Ray earned a formal law degree and was the first Black woman to be admitted to the District of Columbia bar.

Biddy Mason, pioneer, laundry woman, philanthropist, was one of the founders of the first Black church in Los Angeles, the First A.M.E. Church.

1876   Edmonia Lewis exhibited her sculpture, "Death of Cleopatra," in the Centennial Celebration, Philadelphia. She was the only Black to exhibit.

1884   *The African Methodist Episcopal Church Review* was published.

Ida B. Wells sued the Chesapeake and Ohio Railroad Company for assault.

1886   The Alpha Home for Aged Colored Women, perhaps the first of its kind, was opened in Indiana.

Lucy Laney founded Haines Institute in Augusta, GA.

1889   Emma Azalia Hackley, author, composer, performer,

teacher, choir director, was graduated from the College of Music, Denver, CO.

Ida B. Wells, one of the first Black newspaper women in the country, became one of the editors of the *Memphis Free Speech and Headlight.*

1890   Ida Gray became the first known Black woman to earn a doctorate in dental surgery when she graduated from the University of Michigan School of Dentistry.

1892   Frances Harper, abolitionist, feminist, lecturer, poet, published a novel, *Iola Leroy or Shadows Uplifted.*

1893   Georgia E. L. Patton Washington, an ex-slave who became a medical doctor, was the first female graduate from Meharry Medical College.

Ida B. Wells expanded her anti-lynching crusade with a lecture tour in England.

1895   Black women from 20 Black women's clubs formed the National Federation of Afro-American Women.

1896   The National League of Colored Women and the National Federation of Afro-American Woman joined, becoming the National Association of Colored Women (NACW).

1897   Dr. Matilda Arabelle Evans was graduated from Women's Medical College in PA.

Victoria Earle Matthews, author and teacher, founded the White Rose Home Mission in New York City, similar to the Travelers' Aid Society, but for Black women.

1898   Ida B. Wells led a group of women and congressmen to discuss with President William McKinley the lynching of a Black postmaster.

1902   Charlotte Hawkins Brown founded Palmer Institute in Sedalia, NC.

1903   Maggie L. Walker opened the St. Luke Penny Savings Bank in Richmond, VA, becoming the first woman bank president in the United States.

1904   Mary McLeod Bethune founded the Daytona Educational and Industrial Training School, later known as Bethune-Cookman College.

Mary Church Terrell addressed the Geneva International Congress of Women in Berlin, speaking in several languages.

1905   Eva Bowles accepted a position at the Harlem Branch of the YWCA, becoming the first Black woman on the YWCA staff.

Madame C. J. Walker invented the straightening comb. Walker, described in the *Guinness Book of World Records* as "the first American woman to become a millionaire through her own efforts," revolutionized cosmetology for Black—and perhaps White—women, when she began selling Madame Walker hair products from door to door and when she sent many of her agents to a national convention to lobby for her products made by the Mme. C. J. Walker Manufacturing Company.

1908   National Association of Colored Nurses was created.

Janie Barrett was made president of the newly-formed Virginia State Federation of Women.

Alpha Kappa Alpha, the first African-American women's sorority, was founded at Howard University, Washington, DC.

1909   Nannie Burroughs founded the National Training School for Women, Washington, DC.

1912   Dr. Mary M. Bethune, founder of Bethune-Cookman College, and Mme. C. J. Walker, entrepreneur and inventor, defied the leaders of the National Negro Business League, who determined these women could not speak at the convention. Madame Walker walked up to the podium and presented her business credentials as the manufacturer of hair goods and preparations and as one who had built a factory on her own land.

Charlotta (Spears) Bass, civil rights fighter and politician, became the owner, editor, and publisher of *The Eagle* (*The California Eagle*), the first Black newspaper in Los Angeles.

1913   Delta Sigma Theta Sorority was founded at Howard University.

1918   Dr. Vada J. Somerville, noted clubwoman and community leader, was the first African-American woman to graduate from the University of Southern California School of Dentistry. Dr. Somerville ranked 28th in a class of 95 White males.

Dr. Ruth Temple, the first woman graduate from the Loma Linda Medical College, was the first African-American woman to practice medicine in the state of California.

1919   Alice H. Parker patented a gas-heating furnace.

1920   Lillian Evanti was hailed as the first Negro to sing operatic roles in Europe.

Zeta Phi Beta Sorority was founded at Howard University.

1921   Alice Dunbar-Nelson and Robert Nelson founded the Wilmington *Advocate,* a weekly newspaper, in Wilmington, DE.

Vivian Osborne Marsh, founder of Delta Sigma Theta in the West, founded the first Western chapter, Kappa.

1922   The name of Frances Ellen Harper, poet, novelist, lecturer, was placed on the *Red Letter Calendar* at the World's Meeting of the Women's Christian Temperance Union.

1923   Bessie Smith, famous blues singer, made her first recording, *Down Hearted Blues.*

Opportunity: Journal of Negro Life was published.

Phi Delta Kappa, a teachers' sorority, was founded in Jersey City, New Jersey.

1924   Harpist Princess Mae Richardson, trained by Cheshire, by Madame Van Der Berg, and at the New England Conservatory of Music, gave her first professional recital at Ebenezer Baptist A. M. E. Church, Washington.

1926   Florence Mills appeared in *Blackbirds,* a Broadway show.

Lorenza Jordan Cole, concert pianist and public school teacher, won Juilliard Musical Foundation Scholarships.

1929   Fay M. Jackson, first American Black woman foreign news correspondent, co-founded *Flash,* a weekly news magazine.

Vivian Osborne Marsh—founder of Delta Sigma Theta on the West Coast.

Miriam Matthews, librarian, stimulated interest in the celebration of Negro History Week when she sent articles and book reviews to local newspapers, city schools, and community organizations.

Sigma Gamma Rho Sorority was founded at Butler University.

1930   Lorenza Jordan Cole, internationally known concert pianist, studied in London, England, with "eminent pedagogue," Tobian Matthay.

Historian Ida Tarbell named Mary McLeod Bethune as one of America's 50 leading women.

Thomas Dorsey, composer of gospel songs, and Sally Martin, gospel composer and singer, founded the National Gospel Convention of Choirs and Choruses.

Sally Martin helped form Martin and Morris Music Studio at 4312 S. Indiana Avenue, Chicago, IL.

1932   Ella Baker, Civil Rights Activist, founded the Young Negroes Cooperative League in order to address consumer issues, such as consumer buying power.

1933   George Gershwin invited Eva Jessye to become the choral director of his first *Porgy and Bess* production.

1935   Mary McLeod Bethune, educator, founded the National Council of Negro Women.

1936   Sculptor Beulah Ecton Woodard received national attention through the Associated Press when she completed and presented the bust of Los Angeles County Supervisor John Anson Ford to the County of Los Angeles.

1937   Journalist Fay M. Jackson covered the coronation of King George VI. She was the only African-American woman seated in Westminster Abbey. The former managing editor of the California News and co-founder of *Flash,* a weekly news magazine, she also made a special presentation before the French Parliament for the Associated Negro Press.

Sculptor Beulah Woodard helped form the Los Angeles Negro Art Association to develop public appreciation for the work of local African-American artists.

The Association's first event "was an exhibition at Stendahl Galleries, Wilshire Boulevard." More than 2,500 persons visited the exhibit in one week.

Lambda Kappa Mu, a business and professional sorority, was founded in New York City.

1939   Music educator, politician, and civic worker, Fay Allen became the first African-American to be elected to the Los Angeles Board of Education.

Bernice Bruington became the first Black high school principal in Los Angeles.

The Daughters of the American Revolution denied Marian Anderson the right to sing in Constitution Hall, Washington, D.C.

Hattie McDaniel won the Academy Award for her role in "Gone With the Wind."

1940   Sallie Martin, gospel singer, organized the Sallie Martin singers and began a separate career.

Katherine Dunham made her dance debut in New York.

Pearl Primus received a scholarship from the New Dance Group.

1941   Choreographer Ruth Beckford founded the African Haitian Dance Company.

1942–5 Sculptor Beulah Ecton Woodard was selected to appear on the television program *Magazine of the Week,* a program "which presented the work and activities of outstanding individuals in many fields."

1943   Estelle Massey Osborn, a nurse and educator, and the first Black woman appointed to the faculty of New York University, was honored when Fisk University established the Estelle Massey School in her honor and in 1946 when she received the Mary Mahoney Award for her contributions to nursing.

Dr. Ruth Temple organized and founded the Community Health Association, Inc., a health study club, in Los Angeles.

Concert pianist Lorenza Jordan Cole became the first Black person to teach in Belvedere Jr. High School, Los Angeles. She taught instruments, started the school orchestra, and eventually became Chairperson of the Department of Music.

Ruth Acty became Berkeley's first Black school teacher.

Katherine Dunham, dancer, was guest artist for the San Francisco Symphony.

1945   *Mademoiselle* Magazine selected Gwendolyn Brooks as one of the ten women of the year.

Dr. Ruth Temple developed the concept of Community Health Week, now proclaimed a permanent institution in California by the California Legislature.

1946   Mary Lou Williams, once a leading jazz instrumentalist who composed and arranged music for a number of big bands, played her work *Zodiac Suite* with the New York Philharmonic Orchastra.

1948   Alice Coachman was the first Black American woman to win a gold medal in the Olympic games.

Charlotta Bass, editor of the California *Eagle,* and a founding member of the Progressive Party, became the National Co-Chairman of Women for Henry Wallace.

1949   M. Ashley Dickeson, recorded as the first Black female attorney in Alabama, filed one of her first cases on behalf of an African-American woman who had her children and possessions taken because she left "the plantation" without permission of the owners.

1950   Classical pianist Margaret Bonds, who earned her bachelor and Master's degrees in music by the time she was 21 years of age, made history in 1933 when she became the first Black to appear with the Chicago Symphony Orchestra and again in 1950 when she was the first Black to perform with the Scranton Philharmonic.

Zelma George performed in the Broadway production, *The Medium,* by Gian Carlo Menotti.

Gwendolyn Brooks won the Pulitzer Prize for her volume of poems, *Annie Allen.*

Beulah Ecton Woodard, sculptor, was appointed director of the Eleven Associated Gallery, Los Angeles.

1951   The National Association of Colored Graduate Nurses

officially dissolved, voting to merge with the American Nurses Association.

Janet Collins, ballerina, became the first Black dancer to perform with the Metropolitan Opera Company.

1952   Gladys Simmon Sewell, music educator and performer, founded the Sewell Piano Studio/Sewell Music Conservatory in Washington, DC.

Charlotta Bass became the first Black woman to run for the second highest office in the land, as Vice Presidential candidate on the Progressive Party ticket.

1953   Vivian Ayers Allen, artist and writer, was nominated for the Pulitzer Prize for poetry.

Beulah Ecton Woodard, sculptor, won a blue ribbon at the All-City Art Festival, Los Angeles, for her woodcarving of Korean heads titled "Travail."

Civil Rights Activist Mary Church Terrell won her long struggle to desegregate restaurants in Washington, DC.

1954   Leontyne Price, world-renowned opera singer, whose singing talents were described as "a priceless gift," gave her Town Hall debut recital and made her operatic debut with the NBC-TV Opera Company.

1955   Marian Anderson pioneered again when she sang the role of Ulrica in Verdi's *Masked Ball* at the Metropolitan Opera House.

Rosa Parks, a Black seamstress in Montgomery, AL, was arrested on December 1 for refusing to move to the back of the bus. Her arrest led to the Montgomery Bus Boycott.

1956   Ann Arnold Hedgeman, sociologist, educator, civil rights leader, became the first Black woman to run for city-wide office in a major party primary election in New York City.

Authurine Lucy was admitted, then suspended from the University of Alabama.

1957   Daisy Bates directed students in their efforts to integrate schools in Little Rock, AK.

Althea Gibson won the women's singles tennis championship at Wimbledon, England.

Charlemae Hill Rollins (1897–1979), distinguished librarian, noted author, dedicated humanitarian, and crusader against stereotypes. (Photo courtesy of the Collection of Miriam Matthews)

Charlemae Hill Rollins, educator, children's storyteller, reading guide, pioneer against stereotypes of Black youth in children's literature, and librarian, became the first African-American librarian to be president of the Children's Services Division (now ALSC), of the American Library Association.

1959   "Raisin in the Sun," written by Lorraine Hansberry, became a Broadway hit and won the Drama Critics' Award.

Marian Anderson was appointed American Lady of Goodwill, Human Rights Committee, U. S. Delegation to the United Nations.

Juanita Stout, former educator, was elected judge of the Municipal Court of Philadelphia, making her the first Black woman to be elected a judge in Philadelphia.

1960   Wilma Rudolph, track and field, won three Olympic gold medals, the first American woman to win that distinction.

1961   Leontyne Price was given a 42-minute ovation when she made her debut at the Metropolitan Opera.

Leontyne Price was given the title role in a Metropolitan Opera production.

Wilma Rudolph, track and field, was the third woman to win the AAU's annual Sullivan trophy for her outstanding contribution to sportsmanship.

1961/2   Mahalia Jackson won the Grammy Award.

1962   Marjorie Lawson, author and lawyer, became the first Black woman appointed to a judgeship by a president when President John F. Kennedy appointed her Judge of the Juvenile Court, District of Columbia.

The California Legislature resolved that Community Health Week, a concept designed by Dr. Ruth Temple, be held the third week in March.

Ruth Waddy founded the West Arts Associates, Inc.

1963   On June 9, Fannie Lou Hamer, June Johnson, and Carla Dunlap were beaten and arrested for working for democratization of the South.

1965   President Lyndon Baines Johnson signed the Voting Rights Act.

Patricia Roberts Harris was appointed Ambassador to Luxembourg by President Lyndon Johnson.

Aileen C. Hernandez was appointed to the Equal Employment Commission (EEOC).

1966   Artist Ruth Waddy, who entered the art world when she was 53 years old, was one of eight artists selected to visit and exhibit in the Soviet Union.

Barbara Jordan was the first African-American to be elected to the Texas Senate since 1882.

Constance Baker Motley, appointed a federal judge by President Lyndon B. Johnson, was the first woman and the first Black woman to sit on the bench of the United States District Court for the Southern District of New York.

Harpist Ann Hobson joined the Washington National Symphony.

Margaret Walker, educator and poet, published *Jubilee,* a historical novel, after researching her subject for 34 years. The heroine was Mrs. Walker's great-grandmother.

Yvonne Brathwaite Burke won a seat in the California State Assembly.

1967   Katherine Dunham, dancer-anthropologist-author-educator, founded the Performing Arts Centre at Southern Illinois University's East St. Louis campus.

Dr. Jean Cooke Wright became Associate Dean of New York Medical College.

Aretha Franklin, popular rhythm and blues singer, had four gold singles.

Zelma Lipscomb, Long Beach, California, became the first woman, and to date, the only woman to serve as president of the Long Beach NAACP.

1967–9 Dr. Edith Francis, administrator, author, educator, administered and supervised educational seminars for underprivileged children under the auspices of the New York City Housing Authority.

1967–70 Dr. Edith V. Francis, author, civic worker, educator, school administrator, organized two scholarship funds and administered the grants for the Education Foundation of Zeta Phi Beta Sorority and the Memorial Fund for Clara Ruth Reid at the Hunter College of the City of the University of New York.

1968   Margaret Burroughs founded the DuSable Museum of Afro-American History in Chicago.

Charlayne Hunter-Gault ran the *New York Times* Harlem Bureau.

Marian Wright Edelman founded the Washington Research Project, a forerunner of the Children's Defense Fund.

Gwendolyn Brooks became Poet Laureate of Illinois, succeeding Carl Sandburg.

Diahann Carroll starred in the television show *Julia*.

Shirley Chisholm became the first Black woman elected to the Congress of the United States.

Ella Fitzgerald was given the New York City Cultural Award.

Elizabeth Koontz was elected President of the National Educational Association.

Margaret Ann Shaw (Mrs. Leslie N. Shaw) visited England, Russia, Hungary and Czechoslovakia as a member of a delegation of "outstanding American women" at the invitation of the Institute of Soviet-American Relations and the Women's Soviet Committee in a "woman-to-woman diplomacy program."

Agnes Wilson was named "Teacher of the Year" by the state of South Carolina, becoming the first Black to win that award in South Carolina.

1969   Lorraine and Clara Hale founded Hale House, now Hale House Center in Harlem for children of addicted mothers.

Margaret Douroux, composer, choral director, counselor, teacher, received the best song award from the James Cleveland Academy of Gospel Music for her composition "Give Me a Clean Heart," and she received the A.C.C. Pauline Musician Achievement Award.

1971   Cheryl White became the first African-American female jockey.

Educator and one of a growing number of scholars of African-American women's literature, Barbara Christian was the first Black woman hired by the Department of English, University of California, Berkeley, and the first African-American woman to join the Department of Afro-American Studies at Berkeley.

Natalie Hinderas received rave notices when she performed the piano concerto of Alberto Ginastera with the Philadelphia Orchestra under the baton of Eugene Ormandy. Subsequently, she was invited to appear on "The Today Show."

1972   Celestine Shambrey formed the Shambrey Chorale in Los Angeles, CA.

Naomi Long Madgett, educator, poet, publisher, established her own publishing company, Lotus Press, in Detroit, MI, because white publishing houses were not enthusiastic about Black poetry.

Yvonne Brathwaite Burke became the first Black woman to serve as Vice Chairman of the Democratic National Convention; and she was the first Black woman from California to be elected to Congress.

Shirley Chisholm, the first Black woman to serve in Congress, was also the first Black woman from a major political party to announce her candidacy for the Presidency of the United States.

Barbara Jordan was the first Black woman to be elected to Congress from a Southern state and from Texas.

The National Association of Black Women Attorneys was founded.

1973   Yvonne Braithwaite Burke gave birth to a daughter, becoming the first member of Congress to have a child while in office.

Cicely Tyson, actress, won the Emmy Award for her role in *The Autobiography of Miss Jane Pittman*.

Marian Wright Edelman founded the Children's Defense Fund.

1974   The Reverend Alice M. Henderson was commissioned a chaplain in the U. S. Army, the first woman Army chaplain.

The National Council of Negro Women honored its founder, Mary McLeod Bethune, by dedicating a memorial to her. This statue is said to be the only memorial to a woman and the first to a Black person on public land in Washington, D.C.

Betty Gadling, Director of the Voices of Evergreen Radio Choir, the Director of Music at the Evergreen Baptist Church, and a member of the San Francisco School of Music and Drama School in the Performing Arts Department, choreographed and wrote a musical sketch called "Reflection," presented at the Oakland Auditorium Theatre.

1975   Gloria Dean Scott became the first Black to be elected president of the Girl Scouts of America.

Marva Collins, Chicago educator, founded the Westside Preparatory School to transform "unteachable" children into accomplished readers.

Ruby McKnight Williams, real estate broker and first Black kindergarten teacher in Topeka, KA, was named "Citizen of the Year" by the Pasadena Human Relations Commission.

Shirley Verrett opened the Metropolitan Opera season with her performance in Rossini's *The Siege of Corinth*.

1976   Ntozake Shange won worldwide acclaim for her choreo-poem, "For Colored Girls Who Have Considered Suicide/When the Rainbow Is Enuf'."

V.U.U.W.G., the Virginia Union University Women Graduates, held its first International Congress, which had as its theme: "The V.U.U. Women Graduates: an Untapped Resource." The meeting, held at the Virginia Union University, was coordinated by Uvelia Bowen.

Celestine Shambray, founder and director of the Shambray Chorale, was named the Bicentennial Woman of the Year by the Los Angeles Human Relations Commission.

Clara Stanton Jones became the first Black to be elected president of the American Library Association.

1977   Patricia Roberts Harris, former Ambassador to Luxem-
         bourg and Dean of the Howard University Law School,
         became the first Black woman to serve in the Cabinet
         when President Carter appointed her Director of HUD
         (Housing and Urban Development).

         The city officials of Lafayette, AL, proclaimed a special
         memoriam for Essie Jones Handy, civic worker, mother,
         and teacher, who had served the community and sur-
         rounding areas for 52 years.

         Charlayne Hunter-Gault, journalist, joined the PBS
         news program, "The MacNeil-Lehrer Report."

         Miriam Matthews, librarian, African-American historian,
         consultant, and recipient of numerous awards, was ap-
         pointed to the California Heritage Preservation Commis-
         sion by Governor Edmund G. Brown.

         Carol Poindexter Brown, owner of Carol Lee Imports:
         Infant Wear, Montclair, NJ, was named Montclair
         Woman of the Year.

1978   Ella Fitzgerald received an honorary doctorate from
         Boston University.

         Dr. Hansonia Caldwell, Choral Director and Dean of the
         Humanities and Fine and Performing Arts, California
         State University, Dominguez-Hills, CA, founded the
         Dominguez-Hills Jubilee Summer Camp for youths wish-
         ing to learn African-American music and about a Black
         celebrity whose life and works were being studied at the
         camp. Thus far, Paul Robeson, Lena Horne, Katherine
         Dunham, and Jester Hairston are among the artists
         studied and on whom presentations have been based.

         Dr. Adelaide Gulliver, Professor of Sociology and the
         Director of Afro-American Studies at Boston University,
         was appointed to the Massachusetts Board of Library
         Commissioners by Governor Michael Dukakis.

         Toni Morrison, novelist, won the National Book Critics
         Circle Award for *Song of Solomon.*

         Dr. Hansonia Caldwell, Choral Director and Dean of
         Humanities and Fine and Performing Arts, California
         State University, Dominguez-Hills, founded the Domin-
         guez-Hills, CA, Jubilee Singers, a group performimg
         African-American music.

Faye Wattleton became the director of the nation's leading family-planning agency, Planned Parenthood Federation of America.

1979   Amalya L. Kearse was appointed to the United States Court of Appeals, and at the time is the only African-American woman on the court. She is also said to be the first woman to be named to the court in New York.

Barbara Chase-Riboud won the Janet Heiding Kafka Prize for her novel *Sally Hemings,* declared the "best novel written by an American woman."

1980   Osceola Davis, coloratura, made her Carnegie Hall debut in a concert performance of Wagner's *Rienzi.*

1980–2   Dr. Edith Francis, who has received over 100 keys to cities, was the recipient of the following honors during this two-year period: the National Council of Women of the United States, Inc., "Woman of Conscience Award"; a citation from Black Media, Inc., "Refocusing the Minds and Actions of Black Americans for the Greater Benefit of All Americans"; the National Black Monitor "Hall of Fame Award"; and the NAACP Life Membership Award for "Dynamic Leadership, Service and Concern."

1981   Dr. Alexa Canady, at 30, became the first African-American female to become a neurosurgeon.

1982   Bette Cox established the BEEM Foundation for the Advancement of Music in Los Angeles to promote appreciation of contributions made by Black composers and performers.

1983   Gloria Naylor won the American Book Award for her first novel, *The Women of Brewster Place.*

Alice Walker's novel *The Color Purple* won a Pulitzer Prize for fiction.

Singer Jessye Norman won the "Outstanding Musician of the Year Award."

1984   Former Congresswoman Shirley Chisholm founded the National Political Congress of Black Women (NPOW), a bi-partisan political organization.

Lula Washington, choreographer and founder of Los

Angeles Contemporary Dance Theater, produced the Black Dance Festival at the Olympic Arts Festival.

1985   Mayor Wilson Goode, Philadelphia, ordered the bombing of women and children who were part of the Move Organization on Osage Street.

Sherian Grace Cadoria was made brigadier general, becoming the highest ranking African-American woman in the armed services.

California State University, Long Beach, hosted the Eva Jessye Symposium in which twelve institutions participated, September 14–October 4, 1985.

The City of Long Beach, CA, declared September 15, 1985, Eva Jessye Day.

Leontyne Price, whose singing has been widely acclaimed for its "technical and artistic skill," was awarded the First Medal of Arts by President Ronald Reagan.

1987   Carol Poindexter Brown, Montclair, NJ, was elected to the National Nominating Committee of the YWCA.

Beulah Mae Donald won a $7 million judgment against the Ku Klux Klan for the beating death of her son.

Famed classical pianist Natalie Hinderas succumbed to a lengthy illness.

Dr. Johnnetta Cole became the first Black woman president of the all-female Spelman College.

LaQuita Carr, selected as one of the 100 most promising graduates of 1987 by *Good Housekeeping,* was featured in the July issue of this magazine.

The Rosa and Raymond Parks Institute was established in Detroit to honor Rosa Parks, whose courage helped to spark the Montgomery, AL, bus boycott.

Mrs. Eunice Johnson, of Johnson Publications, was honored by the Boys and Girls Clubs of Chicago for her contributions.

Dr. Edith V. Francis, educator and Superintendent of Schools for Ewing Township, NJ, received the following awards: the New Jersey State Department of Education Achievement Award for Meritorious Service, the Ewing

Township Citizen of the Year Proclamation, the Junior Achievement Award for Outstanding Commitment in Preparing Students for the World of Work, and proclamations for outstanding service from the County of Mercer, Board of Chosen Freeholders and Mayor, Ewing Township.

Houston-Tillotson College, Austin, TX, received a $600,000 grant from the United States Department of Defense to "explore ways to increase the number of minorities and women who pursue careers in math, science, and engineering."

The California State University, Long Beach women's basketball team, largely composed of Black women, was the only college team to defeat the U.S.S.R. National Women's Olympic Basketball Team.

Civil rights activist, Marnesba Tillmon Tackett, was honored at the Equal Justice Awards Dinner by One Hundred Black Men of Los Angeles. Mrs. Tackett was a former member of the Board of Commissioners of the Housing Authority, Los Angeles, former director of Greater Los Angeles, and one of the founders of the Committee for Representative Government.

1988   Emma R. Gresham was elected the first mayor of Keysville, GA, in 50 years. Serving without pay, Mayor Gresham is committed to improving the community of 400.

Gospel singer Willie Mae Ford Smith was honored for being an outstanding American folk artist by the National Endowment for the Arts.

Former Olympian Anita De France was one of two Americans who served on the ILC for the 1988 Olympic Games.

Barbara Chase-Riboud was named "best American poet" and was given the Carl Sandburg Prize for her volume of poems, *Portrait of a Nude Woman as Cleopatra*.

Mary-Frances (Smith) Winters, wife, mother, founder and owner of the Winters Group research consulting company based in Rochester, New York, board member for Girl Scouts of America, United Way, and Trustee of the University of Rochester, won another in a series of prestigious awards, the Minority Businessperson of the Year Award given by the Minority Enterprise Development Committee.

On September 14, Eva Jessye, famed choral conductor, received an honorary doctorate from Glassboro State College, Glassboro, NJ.

Michele Denise Decoteau, who majored in materials science and engineering at the University of California, Berkeley, won a Rhodes Fellowship. Decoteau is said to be the second woman to win the prestigious award for Berkeley.

Dionne Warwick released the song, "That's What Friends Are For," which has raised more than one million dollars for AIDS research.

Miss Warwick was named Ambassador of Health by the Department of Health and Human Services to help fight the spread of AIDS.

Extra Change, a 28-minute dramatic film, written, produced, directed, and edited by Carmen Coustaut, won seven awards in 1988 and won one award a year from 1985 to 1987.

Louisiana State University and several of its colleges and schools presented a program of the music of Dinos Constantinides and the poetry of Pinkie Gordon Lane. Constantinides, from the LSU School of Music, composed musical settings for eight of Lane's poems. Lane, a professor emerita and former head of the English Department at Southern University, is the author of three volumes of poetry and many individual poems.

More than a month after 525 Anglican Bishops attended the Lambeth Conference at the University of Kent, England, affirming the right to elect women bishops, the Boston Episcopal Diocese elected the church's first woman bishop, the Reverend Barbara C. Harris, a Black Episcopalian priest from the Philadelphia Diocese.

Dr. Lenora Fulani ran for the office of President of the United States on the New Alliance Party ticket.

Author Toni Morrison's novel *Beloved* won her the Pulitzer Prize for fiction.

Charlayne Hunter-Gault, one of the two first Black students to be admitted to the University of Georgia in 1961, was the first Black to deliver the commencement address at the University.

In June, the Oprah Winfrey Show won the Emmy for the best talk show for two years in succession.

Dr. Edith V. Francis, administrator, author, educator, won the National Alliance of Black School Educators' "Pioneer in Education Award."

Mildred Thornhill McGowan, music educator and accomplished pianist, received the Governor's Award for the Arts in a ceremony attended by 500 persons and sponsored by the Delaware State Arts Council.

January 31: Black American Cinema Society honored Billy Dee Williams when it promoted "Held Black Talkies On Parade" film festivals. The goal was to raise funds for the Mayme A. Clayton Collection, the largest and most substantial compilation of rare books, documents, music, films and memorabilia on Black American culture in the Western United States, 2nd largest of its kind in the world—second to Schomburg Collection.

California State University, Dominguez Hills, established the Miriam Matthews Award in honor of the distinguished librarian, historian, collector and community activist, Miriam Matthews. The award will be presented annually to individuals who have made significant contributions to the field of African-American history and culture.

Florence Griffith Joyner and Jackie Joyner-Kersee, sisters-in-law, won gold medals and set world records at the Olympics held in Seoul, Korea.

1989   Joy Hall was named Easter Seal Child.

Johnson Publishing Company established a writing contest in honor of the founder's mother, Gertrude Johnson Williams.

Christine M. Lee, an Oberlin graduate and a second-year Harvard University law student, engaged in legal research at the Southern Poverty Law Center, Montgomery, AL.

The Reverend Joan M. Salmon-Campbell became the first Black woman to be moderator for the 3-million member Presbyterian Church, U.S.A.

Mrs. Anna Perez, Press Secretary to Mrs. George Bush, is the first Black woman to serve as Press Secretary at the White House.

Dr. Pinkie Gordon Lane, former Chairperson of the Department of English, Southern University, Baton Rouge, and first Black woman to earn a doctorate from Louisiana State University, was named Poet Laureate of Louisiana by Governor Buddy Roemer.

Gwendolyn S. King was appointed Commissioner of the Social Security Administration.

1990   Sharon Pratt Dixon was elected mayor of Washington, DC.

Actress Jayne Kennedy and her husband produced the play *The African American*.

Sharon McPhail was voted president-elect of the National Bar Association.

Marjorie J. Vincent, the fourth Black woman to be so crowned was made Miss America 1991.

Joyce E. Tucker was appointed Commissioner of the U. S. Equal Opportunities Commission by President George Bush.

1991   Aurelia Erskine Brazeal was assigned U.S. Ambassador to the Federated States of Micronesia.

BETSEY BROWN, a musical by Ntozake Shange (author of FOR COLORED GIRLS), Emily Mann, and Baikida Carroll, opened at McCarter Theatre, Princeton, NJ.

Singer Patti LaBelle was inducted into the Philadelphia Hall of Fame.

Professor Anita Hill, University of Oklahoma law professor, advanced the cause of sexual harassment when she testified against Judge Clarence Thomas, Supreme Court nominee.

1992   Dr. Eva Jessye, choral director, died in Ann Arbor, MI, February 21.

The National Women's Theatre held its first annual festival at UCLA and featured some multi-cultural and theatrical forms of interest to African-Americans.

Georgia Atkins Ryder, first African-American Dean of the School of Arts and Letters, Norfolk State University, was named Laureate of Virginia. Ryder was also named as one of four new trustees to Virginia Wesleyan College.

While delivering the University of Michigan commencement address, internationally known journalist Carole Simpson, announced that she had established a scholarship fund for minority students.

The Department of Music, Tufts University, featured the music of Betty Jackson King during its celebration of African-American music.

Mary Frances Winters, founder and president of the Winters Group (a Rochester-based market-research firm) received an enterprise award at the Waldorf Astoria from Avon Products and the U. S. Small Business Administration for creating a major business.

PART I: REFERENCE WORKS

Dorothy B. Porter (Dorothy Porter Wesley). (Reproduction courtesy of Roy Lewis, Photographer, Washington, DC)

DOROTHY PORTER WESLEY:
A BIO-BIBLIOGRAPHIC PROFILE

by
Helen H. Britton

Copyright © by Helen H. Britton

In a period of forty-three years, 1930–1973, Dorothy Louise Burnett Porter Wesley, librarian, administrator, curator, scholar, lecturer, author, consultant, and now curator emerita, dedicated her professional life to building a foundation for development of what in 1973 officially became the Moorland-Spingarn Research Center, Howard University. The Center, an independent university entity since 1973, consists of the Moorland Collection, the Spingarn Collection, the Howard University Museum, the Howard University Archives, the Black Press Archives, the Ralph Bunche Oral History Collection, and the Manuscript Collection.[1] This center, a bellwether repository and working laboratory for "scholarly reconstructive excursions into Negro history and literature" represents the accomplishment of an objective Dr. Wesley stated in her 1933 annual report.[2] Dr. Wesley's legendary accomplishments, which are highlighted in this profile, give her peers reasons to bestow special titles upon her. They refer to her as "Dean of ethnic-collections librarians,"[3] "Dean of Black Research Bibliographers,"[4] and the "doyenne of black bibliography."[5] Three universities have conferred upon her honorary doctorate degrees: Susquehanna University in Selinsgrove, Pennsylvania, June 1971; Syracuse University, May 1989; and Radcliffe College, February 1990.

3

During her slightly more than four decades at Howard University, Dr. Wesley successfully fostered the expansion of the collections of ethnic materials, which grew from 5,788 cataloged items in 1932[6] to 70,098 cataloged items in 1973.[7] Within this span of years, the name of the ethnic collections at Howard University changed to reflect additional major collections and to reflect the nature of the services. Beginning in 1932, Dr. Wesley promoted the use of the name "Moorland Foundation, a Library of Negro Life," often referred to as the Moorland Library. The Board of Trustees of Howard University established the name "Moorland Foundation" in 1915 in honor of Jesse E. Moorland, who donated an extensive ethnic collection to the university in 1914. In 1958, the name of the library became the Moorland-Spingarn Collection in recognition of two additional major collections, the Negro Authors Collection and the Negro Music Collection, acquired from Arthur Barnett Spingarn. The next frequently used popular name was the Moorland-Spingarn Research Library. In 1973, the name was officially changed to the Moorland-Spingarn Research Center.

During the years of growth between the 1930s and the early 1970s, the amount of uncataloged material was substantial because of the limited funds for processing expenses and for adequate staff to process the quantity of materials that Dr. Wesley aggressively acquired. One type of resource material in abundance in the uncataloged category prior to 1973 was manuscripts. In spite of this less than desirable bibliographical control of materials, the quality and vastness of the cataloged and uncataloged material on African-Americans, others of the African diaspora, and Africans attracted such renowned visitors as Benjamin Brawley, Alain Leroy Locke, Paula Giddings, Benjamin Quarles, John Hope Franklin, Horace M. Bonds, Howard Thurman, John Blassingame, Edmond Franklin Frazier, Rayford W. Logan, Charles H. Wesley, Lerone Bennett, and Maya Angelou.

Dr. Wesley's professional accomplishments are undergirded by strong family support and a commitment to formal educational preparation for her chosen career. Family relationships for Dr. Wesley began in Warrenton, Virginia, when

Hayes Joseph Burnett, M. D., and Bertha Ball Burnett, a professional tennis player, welcomed their daughter into the world on May 25, 1905.[8] Both parents taught their daughter early in life to be proud of her heritage and nurtured her affinity for history and literature by and about African-Americans. Adding to strengths from her family heritage, home life, and elementary and secondary education in Montclair, New Jersey, where she grew from childhood into early womanhood, Dorothy Porter Wesley eagerly earned undergraduate and graduate degrees in preparation for a successful life. In 1925, she received a diploma from Miner Normal School, Washington, District of Columbia, and in 1928 she received a bachelor of arts degree with honors from Howard University, entitling her to Phi Beta Kappa membership in later years. At Columbia University, she continued her formal training and earned a bachelor's degree in library service in 1931. In 1932, she earned a master's degree in the same field from Columbia University. She became one of the first of two African-American women to be awarded the master's degree in library service from Columbia University. Dr. Wesley says that she is not sure whether she or Mollie Dunlap, former librarian at Wilberforce University, was the first to receive in-hand the degree.[9] In 1957, she earned a Preservation and Administration of Archives Certificate from American University. In subsequent years, she has completed several courses at Howard University and at American University.

Contributing to Dr. Wesley's training in preparation for her career have been her experiences as a part-time library assistant in the Division of Negro Literature, History, and Prints of the 135th Street Branch Library of the New York Public Library and her experiences with one of her mentors, Edward Christopher Williams. While working in the 135th Street Branch Library during her summers as a student at Columbia University, she expanded her knowledge of African-American writers and their works. She attributes much of what she learned to Williams. Williams, who was chief librarian and a romance language professor at Howard University, was a staff member of the 135th Street Branch Library during the summer months. His primary duty at the branch was the organization of the Alphonso Schomburg Collection. He gave Dr. Wesley guidance in exploring the wealth of material in the department as she assisted him with the Collection. Dr. Wesley recalls that at Howard University during the academic year she attended the Wednesday evening meetings that Williams had with students and faculty to discuss "Negro literature," as well as other literary works and their authors. Dr. Wesley expresses her esteem of Williams, who is reported to be the first professionally trained African-American librarian, with the statement that he was "the most scholarly librarian that I have ever known."[10]

Along with Dr. Wesley's zealousness for her work, she kept a balance in her life between work and family: parents, spouses, and a daughter, who admired her accomplishments and encouraged her as she pursued her work. With her marriage to James Amos Porter (1905–1970) she had a professional and cultural companion and a sharing of love for their daughter, Constance Porter Uzelac, a librarian and business women, who continues to assist her mother with her bibliographical and biographical studies. Porter was an authority on African, African-American, and European art; a book collector; a distinguished artist and an art historian, whose *Modern Negro Art,* published in 1943, remains a standard reference on African-American art; and a former chairman of the Arts Department, Howard University.[11] On November 30, 1979, Dorothy Porter married another man of prominence, Charles Harris Wesley, Ph.D. (1891–1987). Wesley was an educator, a historian, a minister, and an administrator, having served as head of the History Department and dean of the Graduate School, Howard University. He also served as president of Wilberforce University and as president of Central State University. At the time of his death, he was President Emeritus of the Association for the Study of Afro-American Life and History. Charles H. Wesley's prolific authorship began in the twenties and continued through the eighties. Among his works are *The History of Alpha Phi Alpha: A Development in College Life* (1929); *The Collapse of the Confederacy* (1937); *Negro Labor in the United States, 1850–1925* (1937 and reprinted in 1968); *The Quest for*

Equality (1968); *Henry Arthur Callis: Life and Legacy* (1977); and *The History of the National Association of Colored Women's Clubs; A Legacy of Service* (1984).[12]

Going from the general and personal aspects of Dr. Wesley's life to the highlights of her career means turning the focus toward her work with the collections in the Moorland-Spingarn Research Library, which is one of the most comprehensive and renowned collections of its kind in the world. The initial work for Dr. Wesley following her appointment in 1930 was the assemblage and location of several scattered ethnic collections for public use in one reading room with adjacent stacks in the university's Carnegie Library Building. This task meant bringing together materials about the abolitionist movement and the Civil War that were acquired shortly after the chartering of the university in 1869; the Anti-Slavery Collections of more than 1,600 books, pamphlets, newspapers, letters, pictures, clippings, and periodicals given in 1873 by Lewis Tappan, a noted, wealthy New York abolitionist and one of the organizers of the American and Foreign Anti-Slavery Society; and the collection of 3,000 books, pamphlets, and other items given in 1914 by Jesse E. Moorland, a minister, an alumnus, and a trustee of Howard University from 1907 to 1940. In 1939, Dr. Wesley and all materials in the Moorland-Foundation, a Library of Negro Life, moved from the Carnegie Library Building to the new Founders Library Building.[13]

The schedule of activities in which Dr. Wesley engaged included publicity about the collection, preparation of bibliographies, assistance to users of the resources, and refinement of processing methods and procedures. She refined and expanded a classification and a subject analysis scheme for classifying and describing the types of special items in the Moorland Library. For this project, Dr. Wesley consulted with the Dewey Decimal staff at the Library of Congress. She also planned her work to include searches for special materials that would significantly enhance the collections. She worked fervently to build a library that would become internationally known and respected for its invaluable resources for the study of interdisciplinary and cross cultural aspects of the African diaspora. Dr. Wesley not only fulfilled her stated objectives to acquire rarities, to preserve and exhibit them, and to make them available to scholars and students, but she also fulfilled an objective to study and analyze the materials collected. A comment about Dr. Wesley's scholarly accomplishments made by Werner Sollars, acting director of the W. E. B. DuBois Institute in 1988, appearing on page 5 of the October 14, 1988, issue of the *Harvard University Gazette*, supports the claim that she fulfilled the latter objective. He is quoted as saying that she "has contributed as much as any living individual to the critical analysis . . . of Afro-American source material."

Among the personal acquaintances of Dr. Wesley were a number of bibliophiles who supported her professionally. One of these was the well-known book collector, Arthur Alphonso Schomburg, whom she met in New York shortly after he was appointed curator of what was then the Negro Department of the New York Public Library and is now the Schomburg Center for Research in Black Culture. She maintained communications with Schomburg until his death in 1938. Another was Henry Proctor Slaughter, a Louisville, Kentucky, avid collector, who sold his famous ethnic collection to Atlanta University in 1946. Slaughter was the godfather of Dr. Wesley's daughter, Constance. A third bibliophile who was extremely helpful to Dr. Wesley was Arthur Barnett Spingarn, a Caucasian attorney with extensive knowledge about African-American literature and the owner of a collection that in the mid-forties was regarded as the most comprehensive collection by and about African-Americans developed by a single individual. Dr. Wesley's relationship with Spingarn is best described in her reference to him, "Spingarn . . . was my most helpful mentor from 1932 . . . until his death on December 1, 1971."[14]

As Dr. Wesley grew in stature among collectors and scholars, she acquired a reputation as a bibliographic detective for locating and procuring unique and valuable material. She constantly searched dealers' catalogs for items to purchase from the limited funds of the Moorland Foundation. She methodically sought donors and donors who desired that their gifts would be carefully organized, preserved, and made available for public use sought her. Because of her reputation,

book dealers frequently initiated communication with Dr.
Wesley when they procured items likely to be of interest to
her. In her "Fifty Years of Collecting," an autobiographical
essay, she recalls the special relationship she developed with
Charles Egbert Tuttle, a famous bookseller and publisher in
Rutland, Vermont. Through him she purchased an extensive
collection of fugitive materials on slavery and African-
American history at nominal costs for the Moorland Collection. She remembers that on many occasions Tuttle sent her
packages of books, pamphlets, manuscripts, prints, and documents with an enclosed note of two words, "no charge."

In 1946, the resources of the Moorland Library soared with
the university's purchase of the extensive library of "Negro
authors" from Arthur Barnett Spingarn, one of the bibliophiles referred to earlier in his study. Spingarn's interest in
collecting this material began during World War I in his
efforts to provide evidence that demonstrated the intelligence and accomplishments of African-Americans, an ethnic
group he came to know and respect during his years in
military service. He witnessed the discrimination against
African-Americans not only in the military but also in other
areas of American life.[15] Following his military experiences,
he continued collecting and became an outspoken defender
of African-Americans, serving as chair of the legal committee
of the National Association for the Advancement of Colored
People (NAACP) from 1911 to 1939 and as president of the
NAACP from 1940 to January 2, 1966. His election to the
presidency on October 31, 1939, came in succession to the
presidency of his brother, Joel Spingarn, who was president of
the NAACP from December 8, 1930, until his death on July
26, 1939.[16]

The Spingarn collection includes African, Afro-American,
Afro-Brazilian, and Caribbean writers. Several items in the
collection are from the sixteenth, seventeenth, and eighteenth
centuries. Among these rare items is *Ad Catholicum Pariter et
Invicitissimum Philippum dei Gratia Hispaniarum Reguem,* a
volume published in 1573 by the former black slave, Juan
Latino, an outstanding Latinist and professor at the University
of Grenada, Spain. Another is Jacobus Elisa John Capitein's
Dissertation on Slavery, a defense of slavery, written in Latin

and in Dutch and published in Leyden in 1742. Capitein's *Sermons* published in Dutch in the same year is also another rarity in the collection. Other items, perhaps the rarest pieces of early Americana, are two works by Phillis Wheatley: "An Elegiac Poem on the Death of the Celebrated Divine . . . George Whitefield," a 1770 broadside, and *Poems on Various Subjects, Religious and Moral*, 1773.[17]

In keeping with the wishes of Spingarn, the Spingarn Collection is housed separately from the Moorland Collection. In 1958, Spingarn's "Negro Music Collection" became an addition to the Moorland Collection. This music collection at the time of its acquisition had the distinction of being the largest in the world, encompassing the gamut of American composers and including many foreign composers, such as Brazil's Antonio Carlos Gomes, Haiti's Justin Elie, France's Joseph Boulogne, and Cuba's Amadeo Rolden.[18] After Spingarn's death and in accord with Spingarn's will, the Spingarn Lincoln Collection was added to the other Spingarn items. While the Spingarn Collection is now a frozen collection, the Moorland Collection remains open for continuous growth.

The publication of bibliographies and anthologies was an inevitable endeavor for Dr. Wesley, who possesses "impeccable intellectual standards and . . . passion to preserve the record of the Afro-American past."[19] Two of her major reference compilations are bibliographies: *A Catalogue of the African Collection in the Moorland Foundation, Howard University*, 1958, and *Afro-Braziliana: A Working Bibliography*, 1978. In 1971, she published the anthology, *Early Negro Writings, 1760–1837*. Dr. Wesley has a penchant for writing biographies. The 1982 edition of the *Dictionary of American Negro Biography*, edited by Rayford W. Logan and Michael R. Winston contains Dr. Wesley's brief biographies of Maria Louise. Baldwin, Pauline E. Hopkins, Mary Edmonia Lewis, Patrick Henry Reason, Charles Lenox Remond, Sarah Parker Remond, David Ruggles, Henry Proctor Slaughter, Joshua Bowen Smith, Edward Christopher Williams, and Monroe Nathan Work. *Notable American Women, 1607–1950*, published in 1971, has Wesley's biographical notes on Maria Louise Baldwin, Mary Edmonia Lewis, and Sarah Parker Remond. The biographical sketches of Daniels Sanders and

Harriet Tubman appearing in the 1936 *Dictionary of American Biography* are those of Dr. Wesley.

The variety of conference papers delivered by Dr. Wesley gives insight into her multifaceted research. Dating back to 1951, she read a paper at the International Colloquium on Luso-Brazilian Studies at the Library of Congress. Others of her innumerable papers are "The Remonds of Salem: A Forgotten Nineteenth Century Family," Howard University, March 30, 1973; "The Religious Activities of Black Women in Antebellum America," Princeton Theological Seminary, February 16, 1979; "Non-federal Records in the Study of the History of the District of Columbia," Mid-Atlantic Regional Archives Conference, May 16, 1980; and "Collecting Afro-American Historical Materials," Philobiblio Club, Philadelphia, Pennsylvania, November 1980. On March 24, 1988, Dr. Wesley traveled to Claremont Colleges, Claremont, California, to deliver the "Sojourner Truth Lecture, 1987–1988: In Honor of American Black Women." In 1988–89, she presented several lectures on the Remond Family during her residency as a Senior Visiting Scholar at the W. E. B. DuBois Institute of Afro-American Research, Harvard University. At the African Meeting House, Boston, Massachusetts, on September 28, 1989, Dr. Wesley was one of three speakers on a program that she initiated to commemorate William Cooper Nell, 1816–1874, an African-American abolitionist and a pioneer historian, who was "one of Boston's most illustrious figures," says Dr. Wesley.

The records indicate that Dr. Wesley did not limit her travels for professional, cultural, and social concerns to the United States. She frequently traveled to foreign places for conferences, research, and consultations. A few of her travels are now recounted. In 1962, she attended the First International Congress of Africanists in Accra, Ghana; in 1966, she attended the first World Festival of African Arts in Dakar, Senegal; and in 1971, she attended the Luso-Brazilian Congress in Bahia, Brazil. Other places of her travels abroad include the islands of Trinidad and Tobago and of St. Thomas; the cities of Quebec, Montreal, Havana, Mexico, London, Paris, Rome, Florence; and several locales in Scotland, Ireland, Chile, Uruguay, Argentina, Nigeria, and the Ivory Coast.

The curriculum vitae of Dr. Wesley lists the names of at least twenty organizations and societies in which Dr. Wesley has had or has membership and the names of a few committees and commissions to which she received appointments. Some of the organizations are the Bibliographical Society of America, Society of American Archivists, Boston Public Library Associates, Black Academy of Arts and Letters, Library Company of Philadelphia, Association of Afro-American Museums, Association for the Study of Afro-American Life and History, American Antiquarian Society, Phi Beta Kappa, and Delta Sigma Theta Sorority. Her appointments include one to the President's Committee on Employment of the Handicapped and another to the National Trust for the Preservation of Historic Sites.

Consulting is a service that attracts Dr. Wesley. She accepted invitations to serve as consultant for the Black Women's Oral History Project, Radcliffe College; for the Women's History Sources Survey, University of Minnesota; for the National Gallery of Art Exhibition: Black Presence in the American Revolution; and for the *Dictionary of Notable Women*. She also served on the Frederick Douglass Papers Advisory Board, Yale University; on the D. C. Historical Records Advisory Board for the Historical Publications and Records Commission; and on boards for the Black Abolitionists Papers and the Booker T. Washington Papers.

G.K. Hall, the prestigious Boston publisher of voluminous and authoritative bibliographies, selected Dr. Wesley as one of the editors of its Black Studies Series. Continuing with her publication activities, she currently engages in research to complete two manuscripts that will be published within the next year or two. One manuscript is on the life of William Cooper Nell, 1816–1874, an African-American abolitionist and pioneer historian, referred to earlier; the other manuscript in progress is on the Remonds of Massachusetts, an African-American family of historical significance.

In reward for her accomplishments from the 1930s to date, Dr.Wesley has garnered scholarships and grants, numerous awards, honors, and testimonials of appreciation. She received a Julius Rosenwald Scholarship for study toward the master's degree in library service at Columbia University,

1931–32; a Julius Rosenwald Fellowship for research in Latin American Literature, 1944–45; a Ford Foundation Grant for research on the Remond family in England, Scotland, Ireland, and Italy, 1973; and a Charitable Foundation Grant from the Prince Hall Masons for research on the Remond family, 1977. The number of awards and public honors that this extraordinary librarian and curator possesses totals over twenty. In this number are the three honorary degrees referred to earlier; a bronze, distinguished achievement plaque presented by the D. C. Chapter of the National Barristers Wives, August 2, 1968, for outstanding service in the area of human relations; the dedication of the Dorothy B. Porter Room in Founders Library, Howard University, as a tribute to her "outstanding contributions to the University and the world of scholarship" upon her retirement, June 8, 1973; an alumni award for distinguished achievements presented during Howard University's annual Charter Day program on March 1, 1974; a bicentennial award presented by Delta Sigma Theta Sorority, August 11, 1976; a cultural achievement award in recognition of significant contributions to the preservation of America's cultural resources given by the U. S. Department of Interior, Heritage Conservation and Recreation Service, November 19, 1976; and a set of resolutions for achievements presented by the Pennsylvania Historical and Museum Commission, April 3, 1985.

The recognitions continue with an inclusion of her photograph in a presentation of "fifteen great Afro-Americans of the Century" in the Schomburg Center's 1986 exhibition, "O, Write My Name," which was a collection of photogravures made from original negatives by Carl Van Vechten; an appointment as a Senior Visiting Scholar in the W. E. B. DuBois Institute of Afro-American Research, Harvard University, 1988–89; a silver plaque presented by the Library Company of Philadelphia on April 15, 1989, at the Symposium "Turning the World Upside Down," in commemoration of the 150th anniversary of the Anti-Slavery Conventions of American Women, 1837–1839; and the establishment of the Annual Dorothy Porter Wesley Lecture at Howard University, the first of which was held April 13, 1989. On October 27, 1989, Ethnic Studies, University of Utah, awarded Dr.

Wesley the "Olaudah Equiano Award of Excellence for Pioneering Achievements in African-American Culture." The Black Caucus of the American Library Association honored this bibliographer and information specialist on June 24, 1990, with a Trailblazer Award presented at a program during the celebration of the twentieth anniversary of the Black Caucus at the 1990 Annual Conference of the American Library Association held in Chicago.

The author of this bio-bibliographic profile and compiler of the following selected list of publications by Dr. Wesley, became so overwhelmingly impressed with the information she discovered about Dr. Wesley and her career that she adds another title, "The First Lady of Ethnic Bibliography," to the list of those deemed appropriate for Dr. Dorothy Porter Wesley.

Selected Publications of Dorothy Porter Wesley

All entries in this list appear in publications under the surname "Porter," except the third entry in the section, "Parts of Books." This third entry appears under the surname "Wesley," as given in this specific entry.

Books

Afro-Braziliana: A Working Bibliography. Boston: G. K. Hall, 1978.

A Catalogue of Books in the Moorland Foundation. Comp. workers on projects 271 and 318 of the Works Progress Administration. Margaret R. Hunton and Ethel Williams, supervisors. Dorothy B. Porter, director. Washington, DC: Howard University Library, 1939.

A Catalogue of the African Collection at Howard University. Comp. students in the Program of African Studies. Ed. Dorothy B. Porter. Washington, DC: Howard University Press, 1958.

Early Negro Writing, 1760–1837. Selected and introd. Dorothy Porter. Boston: Beacon Press, 1971.

Howard University Masters' Theses, 1918–1945. Washington, DC: Howard University, Graduate School, 1946.

Journal of Negro Education: Index to Volumes 1–31, 1932–1962. Comp. Dorothy B. Porter and Ethel M. Ellis. Washington, DC: Howard University Press, 1963.

The Negro in American Cities: A Selected and Annotated Bibliography. Prepared by Dorothy B. Porter for for the National Advisory Commission on Civil Disorders. Washington, DC: Howard University Library, 1967.

The Negro in the United States: A Selected Bibliography. Washington, DC: Library of Congress, 1970.

Negro Protest Pamphlets: A Compendium. Selected and ed. with the pref. by Dorothy Porter. New York: Arno Press, 1969.

North American Negro Poets: A Bibliographical Checklist of Their Writings, 1760–1944. Hattiesburg, MS: The Book Farm, 1945.

A Working Bibliography on the Negro in the United States. Ann Arbor, MI: Xerox, University Microfilms, 1969.

Parts of Books

"Africana at Howard University." In *Handbook of American Resources for African Studies.* Ed. Peter Duignon. Stanford, CA: Stanford University, Hoover Institution on War, Revolution and Peace, 1967. 33–37.

"A Bibliographical Checklist of American Negro Writers about Africa." In *Africa Seen by American Negroes.* Pref. by Alioune Diop. Introd. by John Aubrey Davis. Paris: Présence Africaine, 1958. 79–99.

"Black Antiquarians and Bibliophiles Revisited, with a Glance at Today's Lovers of Books and Memorabilia." By Dorothy Porter Wesley. In *Black Bibliophiles and Collectors: Preservers of Black History.* Ed. Elinor Des Verney Sinnette, W. Paul Coates, and Thomas C. Battle. Washington, DC: Howard University Press, 1990. 3–20.

"Fifty Years of Collecting." Introduction. By Dorothy B. Porter. In *Black Access: A Bibliography of Afro-American Bibliographies.* Comp. Richard Newman. Westport, CT: Greenwood Press, 1984. xvii-xxviii.

"The Librarian and the Scholar: A Working Partnership." In *Proceedings of the Institute on Materials by and about the American Negro.* Atlanta: Atlanta University, School of Librarianship, 1967. 71–80.

"The Water Cure—David Ruggles." In *The Northampton Book.* Northampton, MA: Northampton, Massachusetts, Tercentenary History Committee, 1954? 121–26.

Articles

"African and Caribbean Creative Writing: A Bibliographical Survey." *African Forum* (Spring 1966): 107–11.

"The African Collection at Howard University." *African Studies Bulletin* 1 (Jan. 1959): 3–5.

"Bibliography and Research in Afro-American Scholarship." *Journal of Academic Librarianship* 2 (May 1976): 77–81.

"The Black Role during the Era of the Revolution." *Smithsonian* 4 (Aug. 1973): 52–58.

"David Ruggles, 1810–1849: Hydropathic Practitioner." *Journal of the National Medical Association* 49 (Jan. 1957): 67–72; 49 (Mar. 1957): 130–34.

"Documentation on the Afro-American: Familiar and Less Familiar Sources." *African Studies Bulletin* 12 (Dec. 1969): 293–303.

"Early American Negro Writings: A Bibliographical Study." *Papers of the Bibliographical Society of America* 39 (Third Quarter 1942): 192–268.

"Early Manuscript Letters Written by Negroes." *Journal of Negro History* 24 (Apr. 1939): 199–210.

"Family Records: A Major Resource for Documenting the Black

Experience in New England." *Old-Time New England* 63 (Winter 1973): 69–72.

"Fiction by African Authors: A Preliminary Checklist." *African Studies Bulletin* 5 (May 1962): 54–66.

"A Library on the Negro." *American Scholar* 7 (Winter 1938): 115–17.

"The Negro in the Brazilian Abolition Movement." *Journal of Negro History* 37 (Jan. 1952): 54–80.

"Negro Women in Our Wars." *Negro History Bulletin* 7 (June 1944) 195–96+.

"Organized Educational Activities of Negro Literary Societies, 1828–1840." *Journal of Negro Education* 5 (Oct. 1936): 555–76.

"Padre Domingos Caldas Barbosa, Afro-Brazilian Poet." *Phylon* 12 (Third Quarter 1951): 264–71.

"Phylon Profile XIV: Edward Christopher Williams." *Phylon* 8 (Fourth Quarter 1947): 315–21.

"Preservation of University Documents: With Special References to Negro Colleges and Universities." *Journal of Negro Education* 11 (Oct. 1942): 527–28.

"The Remonds of Salem, Massachusetts: A Nineteenth-Century Family Revisited." *Proceedings of the American Antiquarian Society* 95 (Apr. 17–Oct. 16, 1985) 259–94.

"Research Centers and Sources for the Study of African History." *Journal of Human Relations* 8 (1960): 854–63.

"Sarah Parker Remond: Abolitionist and Physician. *Journal of Negro History* 20 (July 1935): 287–93.

Notes

The basic resources for this bio-bibliographic profile are letters from Dr. Dorothy Porter Wesley to the author, a personal interview and several telephone interviews with Dr. Wesley by the author, and Dr. Wesley's curriculum vitae. Only in a few instances does the author make specific citations to these sources. Citations of the secondary sources are in the notes that follow.

The Selected Bibliography at the end of this chapter includes a few sources the author consulted for a general overview of and sensitivity to the subject of this profile but not for specific citations.

****

[1]Thomas C. Battle, "Moorland-Spingarn Research Center, Howard University." *Library Quarterly* 58 (Apr. 1988): 148–49.

[2]Moorland Foundation, Howard University. Report, Oct. 1932 (Washington, DC, photocopy of typescript), n. pag.

[3]E. J. Josey and Marva L. DeLoach, dedication, *Ethnic Collections in Libraries.* ed. E. J. Josey and Marva L. DeLoach (New York: Neal-Schuman, 1983) iii.

[4]"Porter, Dorothy Louise Burnett." *In Black and White,* 3d ed., vol. 2, by Mary Mace Spradling (Detroit: Gale Research Co., 1980) 775.

[5]Thomas C. Battle, introduction, *Black Bibliophiles and Collectors: Preservers of Black History,* ed. Elinor Des Verney Sinnette, W. Paul Coates, and Thomas C. Battle (Washington, DC: Howard University Press, 1990) xv.

[6]Moorland-Spingarn Research Center, Howard University, Report, Oct. 1932 (Washington, DC, photocopy of typescript) n. pag.

[7]Moorland-Spingarn Research Center, Howard University, Annual Report, 1973–74 (Washington, DC, photocopy of typescript) 106.

[8]Dorothy Porter Wesley, telephone interview with author, 27 July 1989. Information from this telephone interview confirmed that Washington, DC, was not the place of birth of Dorothy Burnett Porter Wesley as stated in ' *Living Black American Authors: A Bibliographic Directory,* by Ann Allen Schockley and Sue P. Chandler (New York: R. R. Bowker, 1973) 128; and as stated in *Black American Writers Past and Present,* by Theresa Gunnels Rush, Carol Fairbanks, and Esther Arata Spring, vol. 2 (Metuchen, NJ: Scarecrow Press, 1975) 598.

[9]Dorothy B. Porter, "Fifty Years of Collecting," introduction, *Black Access: A Bibliography of Afro-American Bibliographies,* comp. Richard Newman (Westport, CT: Greenwood Press, 1984) xxiv.

This introductory essay is Dr. Dorothy Porter Wesley's most important autobiographical statement to date.

[10]Betty M. Culpepper, "Moorland-Spingarn Research Center: A Legacy of Bibliographies," In *Black Bibliophiles: Preservers of Black History,* 107; Dorothy B. Porter, "Phylon Profile, XIV: Edward Christopher Williams," *Phylon* 8 (Fourth Quarter 1947): 315–16, 320; Porter, "Fifty Years of Collecting," xix-xx.

[11]"James A. Porter: Art Historian, Painter." *Negro Almanac: A Reference Work on the Afro-American,* 4th ed., comp. and ed. Harry A. Ploski and James Williams (New York: Wiley, 1983), 1029; "Porter, Dr. James Amos," Spradling, 2: 776.

[12]"Wesley, Charles H." *Who's Who among Black Americans,* 4th ed., 1985; "Charles Wesley; Historian," *Negro Almanac 1000–01;* "Wesley, Dr. Charles Harris," *Spradling, vol. 2: 1023.*

[13]Battle, "Moorland-Spingarn Research Center" 143–45. Culpepper 104. Culpepper's account of 6,000 items in the collection donated by Moorland to Howard University far exceeds Battle's account of "some 3,000 books, pamphlets, and other historical items." Perhaps Culpepper's account is more inclusive of other historical items, such as portraits and artifacts. To resolve this discrepancy, further research into primary source records at Howard University becomes a future task.

[14]Porter, "Fifty Years of Collecting," xxiii.

[15]Arna Bontemps, "Special Collections of Negroana," *Library Quarterly,* 14 (July 1944): 193; Battle, "Moorland-Spingarn Research Center, Howard University" 146.

[16]Minnie Finch, *The NAACP: Its Fight for Justice* (Metuchen, NJ: Scarecrow, 1981), 76, 103–104, 221; "Spingarn, Arthur B.," *Who Was Who in America with World Notables,* 1969–1973; "Spingarn's Work Hailed at Rites," *New York Times,* 6 Dec. 1971, late ed.: 42; "Heads Welfare Group; A. B. Spingarn Named by Association Aiding Negroes," *New York Times,* 3 Jan. 1940, late ed.: 19, *Who Was Who in America, 1897–1942,* Library ed., 1943; Logan 172. Finch gives October 30, 1939, as the date on which Arthur B. Spingarn received an appointment to succeed his brother Joel E. Spingarn, as president of the NAACP; the *New York Times* gives January 2, 1940, as the date of Spingarn's election to the presidency of the NAACP. Finch's reference to Joel E. Spingarn's death on September 11, 1939, does not agree with the July 26, 1939, date of death given in two other sources: *Who Was Who in America, 1897–1942,* and in Marshall Van Deusen's *J. E. Spingarn* (New York, Twayne Publishers, 1971) 73.

[17]Bontemps, 194–96; Battle, "Moorland-Spingarn Research Center, Howard University" 146–47; Culpepper 107–108; How-

ard University Acquires the Most Comprehensive Collection of Works by Negro Authors in the World," *Howard University Bulletin,* 28 (Dec. 1948; Jan.–Feb. 1949): 3–5.

[18]Battle, "Moorland-Spingarn Research Center, Howard University," 147–48.

[19]Richard Newman, comp., *Black Access: A Bibliography of Afro-American Bibliographies* (Westport, CT: Greenwood Press, 1984), xi-xii.

Selected Bibliography

Battle, Thomas C. "Moorland-Spingarn Research Center, Howard University." *Library Quarterly* 58 (Apr. 1988): 143–51.

Black Bibliophiles and Collectors: Preservers of Black History. Ed. Elinor Des Verney Sinnette, W. Paul Coates, and Thomas Battle. Washington, DC: Howard University Press, 1990.

Bontemps, Arna. "Special Collections of Negroana." *Library Quarterly* 14 (July 1944): 187–206.

Britton, Helen H. "Dorothy Porter Wesley: A Bibliographer, Curator, and Scholar." In *Women in the History of American Libraries and Librarianship.* Comp. and ed. Suzanne Hildenbrand. Forthcoming.

"Charles H. Wesley, Historian." *Negro Almanac: A Reference Work on the Afro-American.* 4th ed. Comp. and ed. Harry A. Ploski and James Williams. New York: Wiley, 1983. 1000–01.

Culpepper, Betty M. "Moorland-Spingarn Research Center: A Legacy of Bibliophiles." In *Black Bibliophiles and Collectors: Preservers of Black History.* Ed. Elinor Des Verney Sinnette, W. Paul Coates, and Thomas C. Battle. Washington, DC: Howard University Press, 1990.

"Curator at Howard University Is Visiting Scholar." *Harvard University Gazette* 14 Oct. 1988: 5.

Dictionary of American Biography. Vols. 9, 16, 18. New York: Scribner, 1928–58. 23 vols.

Dictionary of American Negro Biography. Ed. Rayford W. Logan and Michael Winston. New York: W. W. Norton, 1982.

Encyclopedia of Black America. Ed. W. Augustus Low and Virgil A. Clift. New York: McGraw-Hill, 1981.

Finch, Minnie. *The NAACP: Its Fight for Justice.* Metuchen, NJ: Scarecrow Press, 1981.

"Heads Welfare Group; A. B. Spingarn Named by Association Aiding Negroes." *New York Times* 3 Jan. 1940, late ed.: 19.

"Howard University Acquires the Most Comprehensive Collection of Works by Negro Authors in the World." *Howard University Bulletin* 28 (Dec. 1948–Feb. 1949): 3–5.

"James A. Porter; Art Historian, Painter." *Negro Almanac: A Reference Work on the Afro-American.* 4th ed. Comp and ed. Harry A. Ploski and James Williams. New York: Wiley, 1983. 1029.

Jefferson, Karen L. "Moorland-Spingarn Research Center. *American Visions* 4 (Aug. 1989): 46–47.

Josey, E. J., and Marva L. DeLoach, eds. *Ethnic Collections in Libraries.* New York: Neal-Schuman, 1983.

Logan, Rayford W. *Howard University: The First Hundred Years, 1867–1967.* New York: New York University Press, 1969.

Lubin, Maurice A. "An Important Figure in Black Studies: Dr. Dorothy B. Porter." *CLA Journal* 16 (June 1973): 514–18.

McCombs, Phil. "Touching History at Howard; University's Library of Black Culture Celebrates 75 Years of Growth." *Washington Post* 16 Dec. 1989, city ed.: Arts/Television/Leisure, D1 +.

Moorland Foundation, Howard University. Report, Oct. 1932. Washington, DC. Photocopy of typescript.

Moorland-Spingarn Research Center, Howard University. Annual Report, 1973–74. Washington, DC. Photocopy of typescript.

Negro Almanac: A Reference Work on the Afro-American. 4th ed.

Comp. and ed. Harry A. Ploski and James Williams. New York: Wiley, 1983.

Newman, Richard, comp. *Black Access: A Bibliography of Afro-American Bibliographies.* Westport, CT: Greenwood Press, 1984.

"Porter, Dorothy." *Black American Writers Past and Present: A Biographical and Bibliographical Survey.* By Theresa Gunnels Rush, Carol Fairbanks, and Esther Arata Spring. Vol 2. Metuchen, NJ: Scarecrow Press, 1975. 2 vols.

Porter, Dorothy B. Curriculum Vitae. Washington, DC, 1988.

———. "Fifty Years of Collecting." Introduction. *Black Access: A Bibliography of Afro-American Bibliographies.* Comp. Richard Newman. Westport, CT: Greenwood Press, 1984 [xvii]-xxviii.

———. "Phylon Profile, XIV: Edward Christopher Williams." *Phylon* 8 (Fourth Quarter 1947): 315–21.

"Porter, Dorothy Burnett; Librarian." *Living Black American Authors: A Bibliographical Directory.* By Ann Allen Schockley and Sue P. Chandler. New York: R. R. Bowker, 1973.

"Porter, Dr. James Amos." *In Black and White.* 3d ed. By Mary Mace Spradling. Vol. 2. Detroit: Gale Research Co., 1980. 2 vols.

Rhodes, Lelia G., comp. A Biographical Profile of Distinguished Black Pioneer Female Librarians (Selected). Jackson, MS: Jackson State University, 1963. Photocopy of typescript.

Roses, Lorraine Elena, and Ruth Elizabeth Randolph. *Harlem Renaissance and Beyond: Literary Biographies of 100 Black Women Writers, 1900–1945.* Boston: G. K. Hall, 1990.

Rush, Theressa Gunnels, Carol Fairbanks, and Esther Arata Spring. *Black American Writers Past and Present: A Biographical and Bibliographical Survey.* Vol. 2. Metuchen, NJ: Scarecrow Press, 1975. 2 vols.

Scarupa, Harriet Jackson. "The Energy-Charged Life of Dorothy Porter Wesley." *New Directions* 17 (Jan. 1990): 6–17.

Sims, Janet L., comp. *Progress of Afro-American Women: A Selected Bibliography and Resource Guide.* Westport, CT: Greenwood Press, 1980.

Spingarn, Arthur B. "Collecting a Library of Negro Literature." *Journal of Negro Education* 7 (Jan. 1938): 12–18.

"Spingarn, Arthur B." *Who Was Who in America with World Notables.* 1969–73.

"Spingarn's Work Hailed at Rites." *New York Times* 6 Dec. 1971, late ed.: 42.

"Spingarn, Joel Elias." *Who Was Who in America, 1897–1942.* Library ed., 1943.

Spradling, Mary Mace. *In Black and White.* 3rd ed. Vol. 2. Detroit: Gale Research Co., 1980. 2 vols.

Van Deusen, Marshall. *J.E. Spingarn.* New York: Twayne Publishers, 1971.

"Wesley, Charles H." *Who's Who Among Black Americans.* 4th ed. 1985.

"Wesley, Dr. Charles Harris." *In Black and White.* 3d ed. By Mary Mace Spradling. Vol. 2. Detroit: Gale Research Co., 1980. 2 vols.

Wesley, Dorothy Porter. Letters to the author. 1 Sept. 1989; 22 Nov. 1989.

———. Personal interview with author. Washington, DC, 10 July 1990.

———. Telephone interviews with author. 28 Mar. 1988; 26 Feb. 1989; 27 July 1989; Sept. 7, 1989; 13 Sept. 1989; 15 Sept. 1989; 22 Sept. 1989; 7 Aug. 1990.

Williams, Ora. *American Black Women in the Arts and Social Sciences: A Bibliographical Survey.* Rev. and expanded ed. Metuchen, NJ: Scarecrow Press, 1978.

BIBLIOGRAPHIES AND GUIDES TO COLLECTIONS

A. M. E. Book Concern. *Who's Who in Philadelphia*. Philadelphia: African Methodist Episcopal Book Concern, 1912.

"A Rare Collection of Negro Literary Works." *Negro History Bulletin* 17 (Apr. 1964): 162–163.

"A Selective Bibliography." *From the Dark Tower: Afro-American Writers 1900–1960*. Ed. Arthur P. Davis. Washington, DC: Howard University Press, 1981.

Abajian, James de T., comp. *Blacks in Selected Newspapers, Censuses and Other Sources: An Index to Names and Subjects*. Boston: G. K. Hall, 1977.

Amos, Preston E. *100 Years of Freedom: Bibliography of Books about the American Negro*. Washington, DC: Association for Study of Negro Life and History, 1963.

Arata, Esther Spring and Nicholas John Rotoli. *Black American Playwrights, 1800 to the Present: A Bibliography*. Metuchen, NJ: Scarecrow Press, 1976.

Arata, Esther Spring, et al. *Black American Writers Past and Present: A Biographical and Bibliographical Dictionary*. Metuchen, NJ: Scarecrow Press, 1975.

————. *More Black American Playwrights: A Bibliography*. Metuchen, NJ: Scarecrow Press, 1978.

Baker, Augusta. *Books about Negro Life for Children*. New York: New York Public Library, 1963.

————. *Stories: A List of Stories to Tell and to Read Aloud*. 5th ed. New York: New York Public Library, 1960.

Bell, Barbara. *Black Bibliographical Sources: An Annotated Bibliography.* New Haven: Yale University Press, 1970.

"Bibliographies: Selected African-American Women Writers." *Sturdy Black Bridges: Visions of Black Women in Literature.* Eds. Roseann P. Bell, Bettye J. Parker, and Beverly Guy-Sheftall. Garden City: Anchor Books, 1979.

Black History Calendar. Distribution Corporation, Box 8049, Los Angeles, CA 90008.

"Black Youth: A Bibliography." *Freedomways* 15 (Third Quarter 1975): 226–241.

Block, Adrienne Fried, and Carol Ann Neuls-Bates, comps. and eds. *Women in American Music.* Westport, CT: Greenwood Press, 1979.

Bontemps, Arna. "The James Weldon Johnson Memorial Collection of Negro Arts and Letters." *Yale University Library Gazette* 18 (Oct. 1943): 19–26.

Brigano, Russell Carl. *Black Americans in Autobiography: An Annotated Bibliography of Autobiographies and Autobiographical Books Written Since the Civil War.* Durham, NC: Duke University, 1974.

Bryant, Barbara. *Phoenix Films.* New York: Phoenix Films, 470 Park Avenue South. (Bibliography of audiovisual films for elementary, junior high, and high school)

Campbell, Dorothy W. *Index to Black American Writers in Collective Biographies.* Littleton, CO: Libraries Unlimited, 1983.

Carey, Dave, and Albert J. McCarthy. *Jazz Directory.* Fordingbridge, England, 1950.

Carr, Crystal. *Ebony Jewels: A Selected Bibliography of Books by and about Black Women.* Rev. ed. Inglewood, CA: Crenshaw-Imperial Branch Library, 1975.

Cedarholm, Theresa. *Afro-American Artists: A Bio-Bibliographical Directory.* Boston: Boston Public Library, 1973.

Chapman, Dorothy H. *Index to Black Poetry.* Foreword by Samuel W. Allen. Boston: G. K. Hall, 1974.

Clark, Edward. *Black Writers in New England.* Boston: National Park Service, 1985. (Bibliography and biographical notes)

Cole, Johnnetta B. "Black Women in America: An Annotated Bibliography." *Black Scholar* 3 (Dec. 1971): 42–53.

Corbin, Raymond M. *1999 Facts about Blacks: A Sourcebook of African-American Accomplishment.* Illustrations by Barbara Higgins Bond. n.p.: Beckham House Publishers, 1988.

Dandridge, Rita B. *Gathering Pieces: A Selected Bibliography of Ann Allen Shockley. Black American Literature Forum* 21 (Spring-Summer 1987).

———. "On Novels by Black American Women: A Bibliographical Essay." *Women's Studies Newsletter* 6 (Summer 1978): 28–30.

———. "On Novels Written by Selected Black Women: A Bibliographical Essay." *But Some of Us Are Brave.* Eds. Gloria Hull et al. Old Westbury, NY: The Feminist Press, 1982. 261–279.

Davis, Lenwood G. *A Bibliographical Guide to Black Studies.* Westport, CT: Greenwood Press, 1985.

———. *The Black Woman in American Society: A Selected Annotated Bibliography.* Boston: G. K. Hall, 1975.

Davis, Lenwood G., and Janet L. Sims. *Black Artists in the United States: An Annotated Bibliography of Books, Articles, and Dissertations on Black Artists, 1779–1979.* Foreword, James E. Newton. Westport, CT: Greenwood Press, 1980.

Davis, Marianna W., ed. *Contributions of Black Women to America.* Columbia, SC: Kenday Press, Inc., 1982.

DeLerma, Dominique, comp. *Bibliography of Black Music.* Foreword, Jessie Carnie Smith. Westport, CT: Greenwood Press, 1981.

Deodene, Frank, and William P. French. *Black American Fiction*

Since 1952: A Preliminary Check List. Chatham, NJ: Chatham Bookseller, 1970.

DjeDje, Jacqueline Cogdell. "Selective Discography of Afro-American Music." *Musics of the World: A Selective Discography, Part III.* Ed. Nora Yeh. Los Angeles: UCLA Ethnomusicology Archive: n.d., 4–11.

Duffy, Susan, comp. *Shirley Chisholm: A Bibliography of Writings by and about Her.* Metuchen, NJ: Scarecrow Press, 1988.

Einstein, Daniel. *Special Edition: A Guide to Network Television Documentary Series and Special News Reports, 1955–1979.* Metuchen, NJ: Scarecrow Press, 1987.

Enaboulele, Arlene B., and Dionne L. Jones. *A Resource Guide on Black Women in the United States.* Washington, DC: Mental Health Research Center, Institute for Urban Affairs and Research, Howard University, 1978.

Fabre, Genvieve E. *Afro-American Drama, 1850–1975.* Detroit: Gale Research, 1979.

Finkelman, Paul. *Slavery in the Courtroom: An Annotated Bibliography of American Cases.* Washington, DC: Library of Congress, 1985.

Fisher, Edith Maureen. *Focusing on Afro-American Research: A Guide on Annotated Bibliography.* Ethnic Studies Publication #1. San Diego: University of California, San Diego, 1973.

Fowler, Carolyn. *Black Arts and Black Aesthetics: A Bibliography.* Atlanta: First World Foundation, 1981.

Garcia, William Burres. "Church Music by Black Composers: A Bibliography of Choral Music." *Black Perspectives in Music* 2 (1974): 145–157.

George, Zelma. *A Guide to Negro Music: An Annotated Bibliography of Negro Folk and Art Music by Negro Composers or Based on Negro Thematic Material.* New York University, 1953; Ann Arbor, MI: University Microfilms.

———. *Bibliographical Index to Negro Music.* Master Catalogue of 9,592 titles. In Moorland Collection. Washington, DC: Howard University, 1944.

Gubert, Betty Kaplan. *Early Black Bibliographies, 1903–1918. Critical Studies on Black Life and Culture.* Vol. 25. New York: Garland Publishing, 1982.

Guide to Manuscripts and Archives in the Negro Collection of Trevor Arnett Library, Atlanta University. Atlanta: Atlanta University, 1971.

Guzman, Jessie P. "An Annotated List of Books by or Concerning Negroes in the United States, in Africa and in Latin America, 1938–1946." *Negro Yearbook.* Tuskegee Institute, AL: Department of Records and Research, 1947.

———. *Civil Rights and the Negro: A List of References Relative to Present Day Discussion.* Tuskegee Institute, AL: Department of Records and Research, 1950.

———. *Desegregation and the Southern States, 1957.* Legal Action and Voluntary Group Action. With Woodrow W. Hall. Tuskegee Institute, AL: Department of Records and Research, 1958.

———. *George Washington Carver, a Classified Bibliography.* Tuskegee Institute, AL: Department of Records and Research, 1953.

———. *George Washington Carver, a Classified Bibliography.* Tuskegee Institute, AL: Department of Records and Research, 1955.

———. "George Washington Carver: A Classified Bibliography." *Bulletin of Bibliography* 21.1 (May-Aug. 1953: 12–16; Part 2 in 21.2 (Sep.–Dec. 1953): 34–39.

Hart, Mary L, et al. *The Blues: A Bibliographic Guide.* Introd. William Ferris. New York: Garland Publishing, 1986.

Hill, George H., and Sylvia Saverson Hill. *Blacks on Television: A Selected Annotated Bibliography.* Metuchen, NJ: Scarecrow Press, 1985.

Hill, James Lee. "Bibliography of the Works of Chester Himes, Ann Petry and Frank Yerby." *Black Books Bulletin* 3 (Fall 1975): 60–72.

Holmes, Oakley N., comp. *The Complete Annotated Resource Guide to Black American Art.* Spring Valley, NY: Black Artists in America, c/o Macgowan Enterprises, 39 Wilshire Drive, 1978.

Hutson, Jean Blackwell. "African Materials in the Schomburg Collection of Negro Literature and History." *African Studies Bulletin* 3 (May 1960): 1–14.

Igoe, Lynn Moody, with James Igoe. *250 Years of Afro-American Art: An Annotated Bibliography.* New York: R. R. Bowker, 1981.

Index to Black Periodicals, 1984, 1985, 1986, 1987. Boston: G. K. Hall, 1988.

Index to Periodical Articles by and about Blacks. Boston: G. K. Hall, 1950.

Index to Periodical Articles by and about Negroes. Formerly entitled *Index to Periodical Articles by and about Blacks.* Boston: G. K. Hall, 1973ff.

Inge, Thomas, et al. *Black American Writers: Bibliographical Essays* (2 vols. Vol. 1: Women and Men.) New York: St. Martin's Press, 1978.

Jackson, Irene V., comp. *Afro-American Religious Music: A Bibliography and a Catalogue of Gospel Music.* Westport, CT: Greenwood Press, 1979.

Joyce, Donald. *Blacks in the Humanities: A Selected Bibliography.* Westport, CT: Greenwood Press, 1986.

Kallenbach, Jessamine S. *Index to Black American Literary Anthologies.* Boston: G. K. Hall, 1979.

Levi, Doris J., and Nerissa L. Milton. *Directory of Black Literary Magazines.* Washington, DC: Negro Bibliographic and Research Center, 1972.

Lewison, Paul. *A Guide to Documents in the National Archives for Negroes.* Washington, DC: American Council for Learned Societies, 1947.

List of Books by and about Negroes Available in the Libraries of the University of North Carolina and Duke University. Raleigh: University of North Carolina, n.d.

Livingston, Jane, and John Beardsley. *Black Folk Arts in America, 1930–1980.* Jackson, MS: Corcoran Gallery of Art/University of Mississippi Press, Center for the Study of Southern Culture, 1980.

McPherson, James M., et al. *Blacks in America: Bibliographical Essays.* New York: Anchor Books, 1972.

Marshall, A. P. *A Guide to Negro Periodical Literature.* Vols. 1–4. Winston-Salem, NC: A. P. Marshall, 1941. (Quarterly)

Matthews, Geraldine O., and the African-American Materials Project Staff. *Black American Writers, 1773–1949: A Bibliography and Union List.* Introd. George Shepperson. Boston: G. K. Hall, 1975.

Matthews, Miriam. "The Negro in California from 1781 to 1916: An Annotated Bibliography." A report submitted to the Graduate School of Library Science, University of Southern California, in partial fulfillment of the requirements for the research course in Library Science 290ab, Feb. 1944.

Maultsby, Portia K. "Selective Bibliography: U. S. Black Music." *Ethnomusicology* 3 (Sep. 1975): 421–449.

Middleton, David L. *Toni Morrison: An Annotated Bibliography.* New York: Garland Publishing, 1987.

Moseley, Vivian H. "Selected Bibliography on Guidance in Business Education." *Guidance Problems and Procedures in Business Education.* Somerville, NJ: Somerset Press, for the Eastern Business Teachers Association and the National Business Teachers Association, 1954.

Murphy, Beatrice. *Bibliographic Survey: The Negro in Print.* 117 R Street, NE, Washington, DC 20002 (no longer published).

Murray, Florence. *Negro Handbook.* New York: Malliet, 1942.

Page, James A., and Jae Min Roh, comps. *Selected Black American, African and Caribbean Authors: A Bio-Bibliography.* Littleton, CO: Libraries Unlimited, 1985.

Patterson, Lindsay. *Black Films and Film Makers.* New York: Dodd, Mead and Company, 1975.

Peabody Collection of Works by and about Negroes. Hampton, VA: Hampton Institute Press, 1945.

Peavy, Charles D. *Afro-American Literature and Culture Since World War II: A Guide to Informative Sources.* Detroit: Gale Research, 1979.

Perry, Margaret. *A Bio-Bibliography of Countee P. Cullen, 1903–1946.* Foreword by Don M. Wolfe. Westport, CT: Greenwood Press, 1971.

―――. *The Harlem Renaissance: An Annotated Bibliography and Commentary.* New York: Garland Publishing, 1982.

Peterson, Bernard L., Jr. *Contemporary Black American Playwrights and Their Plays.* Foreword by James V. Hatch. Westport, CT: Greenwood Press, 1985. (Index, bio-bibliography)

Porter, Dorothy B. *A Working Bibliography on the Negro in the United States.* Ann Arbor: University Microfilms, 1969.

―――. "Library Sources for the Study of Negro Life and History." *Journal of Negro Education* 5 (Apr. 1936): 232–244.

―――. *North American Negro Poets: A Bibliographical Check List of Their Writings (1760–1944).* Hattiesburg, MS: The Book Farm, 1945; New York: Burt Franklin, 1963.

―――. "The African Collection at Howard University." *African Studies Bulletin* 2 (Jan. 1959): 17–21.

―――. *The Negro in the United States.* Ann Arbor: University Microfilms, 1959.

Porter, Dorothy B., and Ethel M. Ellis. *Index to the Journal of Negro*

Education, Vols. 1–31. Washington, DC: Howard University, 1953.

Powers, Anne. *Blacks in American Movies: A Selected Bibliography.* Metuchen, NJ: Scarecrow Press, 1974.

Ramsly, Arnette M., ed. *Directory: National Black Periodicals and Journals.* Harlem: Afram Association, Inc., 1972.

Richardson, Marilyn. *Black Women and Religion: A Bibliography.* Boston: G. K. Hall, 1980.

Rollins, Charlemae Hill. *We Build Together: A Reader's Guide to Negro Life and Literature for Elementary and High School.* Chicago: National Council of Teachers of English, 1967.

Ruppli, Michael, comp. *Atlantic Records: A Discography.* Westport, CT: Greenwood Press, 1979.

Scally, Sister Mary Anthony. *Negro Catholic Writers 1900–1943: A Bio-Bibliography.* Detroit: Romig, 1945.

Sharp, Saundra, comp., ed. *Black History Film List: 150 Films and Where to Find Them.* Los Angeles: Saundra Sharp, 1989. (Poets Pay Rent Too, Box 75796 Sanford Station, Los Angeles, CA)

Shockley, Ann. *Afro-American Women Writers: An Anthology and Critical Guide.* Boston: G. K. Hall, 1988.

Shockley, Ann, and Sue Chandler. *Living Black American Authors: A Biographical Directory.* Foreword by Jessie Carney Smith. N.p.: R. R. Bowker Co., 1973.

Shortridge, Barbara Gimla. *Atlas of American Women.* New York: Macmillan, 1987.

Sims, Janet. *Marian Anderson: An Annotated Bibliography and Discography.* Westport, CT: Greenwood Press, 1981.

Sims, Janet L. *The Progress of Afro-American Women: A Selected Bibliography and Resource Guide.* Westport, CT: Greenwood Press, 1980.

Skowronski, JoAnn. *Black Music in America: A Bibliography.* Metuchen, NJ: Scarecrow Press, 1981.

————. *Women in American Music: A Bibliography.* Metuchen, NJ: Scarecrow Press, 1978.

Smith, Jessie Carney, ed. *Ethnic Genealogy: A Research Guide.* Foreword by Alex Haley. Westport, CT: Greenwood Press, 1983.

————, ed. *Images of Blacks in American Culture: A Reference Guide to Information Sources.* Foreword by Nikki Giovanni. Westport, CT: Greenwood Press, 1988.

————. "Special Collections of Black Literature in the Traditionally Black College." *College and Research Libraries* (July 1974): 322ff.

Southern, Eileen. "William Grant Still: List of Major Works." *Black Perspectives in Music* 2.3 (May 1971): 235–238.

Spradling, Mary. *In Black and White.* Kalamazoo, MI: Kalamazoo Public Library, 1971; Detroit: Gale Research, 1980.

Standifer, James, and Barbara Reeder. *Source Book of African and Afro-American Materials.* Vienna, VA: Music Educators National Conference, 1972, CMP7.

Stanford, Barbara Dodds, and Karima Amin. *Black Literature for High School Students.* Urbana, IL: National Council for Teachers of English, 1978.

Stetson, Erlene. "Bibliography of Female Slave Narratives." In the article: "Studying Slavery: Some Literary and Pedagogical Considerations on the Female Slave." *All the Women Are White, All the Blacks Are Men, BUT SOME OF US ARE BRAVE.* Eds. Gloria T. Hull, Patricia Bell Scott, and Barbara Smith. Old Westbury, CT: The Feminist Press, 1982.

Stewart-Green, Miriam. "Women Composers' Songs: An International Selective List." [1098–1980] *The Musical Woman: An International Perspective.* Westport, CT: Greenwood Press, 1983. 283–381.

Szwed, John, and Roger Abrahams. *Afro-American Folk Culture, Parts I and II.* Philadelphia: Institute for the Study of Human Issues, 1978. (Bibliography)

Taylor, Camille, and William A. Ballinger. *List of Black Derived Music and Black Related Music Materials Submitted by Music Companies and Individuals.* N.p.: The National Caucus of Music Educators National Conference, 1980.

Tignor, Eleanor Q. "A Bibliography of the Short Fiction of Rudolph Fisher." *The Langston Hughes Review* 1 (Spring 1982): 24.

Tolson, Ruth M. *Hampton Institute Press Publications, a Bibliography.* Hampton, VA: Hampton Institute, 1958.

Truesdell, Marilyn R. *Black Women and Religion: A Bibliography.* Copyright, Marilyn R. Truesdell, 1976.

Turner, Patricia. *Afro-American Singers, An Index and Preliminary Discography of Opera, Choral Music and Songs.* Minneapolis: Pat Turner, P. O. Box 14296, University Station, 1976.

White, Evelyn. *Selected Bibliography of Published Choral Music by Black Composers.* Metuchen, NJ: Scarecrow Press, 1972.

White, Evelyn D. *Choral Music by Afro-American Composers: A Selected Annotated Bibliography.* Metuchen, NJ: Scarecrow Press, 1981.

Whiteman, Maxwell. *A Century of Fiction by American Negroes, 1853–1952.* Philadelphia: Jacobs, 1955.

Williams, Ora. "A Bibliography of Works Written by American Black Women." *CLA Journal* 15.3 (Mar. 1972): 354–377.

———. "Works by and about Alice Ruth (Moore) Dunbar-Nelson: A Bibliography. *CLA Journal* 3.19 (Mar. 1976): 322–326.

Work, Monroe. *A Bibliography of the Negro in Africa and America.* New York: H. W. Wilson Co., 1926; New York: Argosy-Antiquarian, 1965; New York: Octagon, 1966.

Wright, Dorothy. "Comprehensive Thesaurus of Literature by and about the Negro." *School and Society* 62 (1946): 430–431.

Young, Carlene. "Black Scholar and the Social Sciences." *Black Scholar* 7 (Apr. 1976): 18–28.

Young, Pauline A. "The American Negro: A Bibliography for School Libraries." *Wilson Library Bulletin* 7 (May 1953): 563.

Databases

Bibliographical Retrieval Service [BRS]. 1200 Route 7, Lathan, NY 12110. Telephone: 800-833-4707; 518-783-1161.

Education Resources Information Center [ERIC]. Dialog Information Services, Inc. 3460 Hillville Avenue, Palo Alto, CA 94304.

Graham, Maryemma, project director. *Afro-American Novels*. Jackson, MS: The University of Mississippi, forthcoming.

OCLC. Databases, On-Line Union Catalogues. (More than 8,000,000 entries of books, periodicals, manuscripts, maps, recordings, music scores, audio-visuals held by member libraries.) Information Intelligence, Inc. Box 31098, Phoenix, AZ 85046. Telephone: 602-996-2283.

SDC/Orbit. 2500 Colorado Avenue, Santa Monica, CA 90606. Telephone: 800-421-6228; 213-820-4111. Telex: 652358.

CATALOGUES, ENCYCLOPEDIAS, HANDBOOKS, AND OTHER REFERENCE WORKS

A Classified Catalogue of the Negro Collection in the Collis P. Huntington Library. Hampton, VA: Hampton Institute Press, 1940.

A Directory of American Poets and Fiction Writers (1989–90 ed.). New York: Poets & Writers Inc. (72 Spring St.), 1989.

Afro-Americana, 1553–1906: Author Catalog of the Library Company of Philadelphia and the Historical Society of Pennsylvania. Boston: G. K. Hall, 1973.

Bell, Janet Cheatham. *Famous Black Quotations and Some Not So Famous*. Chicago: Sabay and Publications, 1986.

Black History Calendar. Distribution Corporation, P. O. Box 8048, Los Angeles, CA 90008.

Black Women: Achievements Against the Odds. A calendar for 1984–86. GMG Publishing, 25 West 43rd Street, New York, NY 10036.

Bontemps, Arna, and Jacqueline Fonville-Bontemps. *Forever Free: Art by African-American Women: 1862–1980*. Exhibit catalogue.

Brown, Rae Linda. *Music, Printed and Manuscript, in the James Weldon Johnson Memorial Collection of Negro Arts and Letters, Yale University An Annotated Catalog*. (Includes listings of 78-rpm records, photographs, ballet and opera scores, musical scores, lead sheets for "jazz musicians") New York: Garland Publishing, 1981. *Catalog of the E. Azalia Hackley Memorial Collection of Negro Music, Dance, and Drama*. Boston: G. K. Hall, 1979. (In the Detroit Public Library)

Catalogue, Heartman Collection. Houston, TX: Texas Southern University Press.

Chicago Public Library. *The Dictionary Catalog of the Vivian G. Harsh Collection of Afro-American History and Literature.* Boston: G. K. Hall, 1978.

Choral Music Guide for Church and School. Chicago: Carl Fisher Music Stores, 1988. (Publishers' catalog)

Clark, Chris, and Sheila Rush. *How to Get Along with Black People: A Handbook.* Foreword by Bill Cosby. New York: Joseph A. Opaku, Inc., 1971.

Cohen, Aaron I. *International Encyclopedia of Women Composers.* 2nd ed., rev. and enl. New York: Bowker, 1981.

Dannett, Sylvia G. L. *Profiles of Negro Womanhood. Vol. I, 1619–1900; Vol. II, 20th Century.* Yonkers, NY: Educational Heritage, 1964. (Negro Heritage Library)

Davis, John P., ed. *American Negro Reference Book.* Englewood Cliffs, NJ: Prentice-Hall, 1966.

Davis, Marianna W., ed. *Contributions of Black Women to America.* Columbia, SC: Kenday Press, Inc., 1982. (Box 3087, Columbia, SC 29230)

Dictionary Catalog of the Arthur B. Spingarn Collection of Negro Authors. Boston: G. K. Hall, 1970. 2 vols.

Dictionary Catalog of the Jesse E. Moorland Collection of Negro Life and History. Boston: G. K. Hall, 1972.

Dillard, Clarissa, and Uvelia Bowen, eds. *Virginia Union University Women Graduates: Resource Registry, 1976.* Richmond, VA: International Congress of Virginia Union University Graduates, 1976.

Eagon, Angelo. *Catalog of Published Concert Music by American Composers,* second edition. Metuchen, NJ: Scarecrow Press, 1969; supp., 1971; second supp., 1974.

Faust, Langdon Lynne. *American Women Writers.* Abr. New York: Ungar, 1988.

Feather, Leonard. *The Encyclopedia of Jazz in the Sixties.* New York: Horizon Press, 1966.

Fisk University Library, Nashville. *Dictionary Catalog of the Negro Collection of the Fisk University Library.* Boston: G. K. Hall, 1974.

Guzman, Jessie Parkhurst. *The Negro Yearbook. A Review of Events Affecting Negro Life, 1941–1946.* Tuskegee Institute, AL: Department of Records and Research, 1947.

———. *The Negro Yearbook. A Review of Events Affecting Negro Life, 1947–1951.* Tuskegee Institute, AL: Department of Records and Research, 1952.

Hancock, Sibyl. *Famous Firsts of Black Americans.* Illus., Shelton Miller. Gretna, LA: Pelican Publishing Co., 1987.

Murray, Florence. *The Negro Handbook, 1946–47.* New York: Wyn, 1947.

———. *The Negro Handbook, 1949.* New York: Macmillan, 1949.

New York Public Library, Schomburg Collection. *Dictionary Catalog of the Schomburg Collection of Negro Literature and History.* Boston: G. K. Hall, 1962.

1989 Calendar of Black Children. National Black Child Development Institute, 1463 Rhode Island Avenue, NW, Washington, DC 20005.

Old Slave Mart Museum and Library, Charleston, SC. *Catalog of the Old Slave Mart Museum and Library.* Boston: G. K. Hall, 1978.

Our Afro-American Heritage in Music. Chicago: Carl Fisher Music Stores, 1986. (Publishers' catalog)

Pack, Leaoneda Bailey, comp. and ed. *Broadside Authors and Artists: An Illustrated Bibliographical Dictionary.* Detroit: Broadside Press, 1974.

Ploski, Harry A., and Roscoe C. Brown. *The Negro Almanac.* New York: Bellwether, 1967.

Pool, Jeannie. *Women in Music History: A Research Guide.* New York: Pool, 1977.

Romero, P. J. *In Black America, 1968: The Year of Awakening.* Washington, DC: United Publishing Corporation, 1969.

Salk, Erwin A. *A Layman's Guide to Negro History.* Enl. ed. New York: McGraw-Hill, 1967.

Shockley, Ann Allen, and E. J. Josey, comps. and eds. *A Handbook of Black Librarianship.* Littleton, CO: Libraries Unlimited, 1977.

Shortridge, Barbara Gimla. *Atlas of American Women.* New York: Macmillan, 1987.

Sloan, Irvin J. *The American Negro: A Chronology and Fact Book.* Dobbs Ferry, NY: Oceana, 1965.

Southern, Eileen. *Biographical Dictionary of Afro-American and African Musicians.* Encyclopedia Black Music Series. Westport, CT: Greenwood Press, 1982.

The Chicago Afro-American Union Analytic Catalog: An Index to Materials on the Afro-American in the Principal Libraries of Chicago. Boston: G. K. Hall, 1982.

The Negro Almanac: A Reference Work on the Afro-American. Eds. and comps., Harry A. Ploski and James Williams. 4th ed. New York: Wiley, 1983.

The Negro Handbook. Compiled by editors of *Ebony.* Chicago: Johnson Publishing Co., 1966.

The Negro Handbook: An Annual Encyclopedia of the Negro. Tuskegee Institute, AL: Department of Records and Research, 1912–1967.

Wells, Ida B. *A Red Record: Lynchings in the United States, 1892–1893–1894.* Chicago, 1894; New York: Arno Press, 1971.

Who's Who Among Black Americans. Detroit: Gale Research, 1976ff.

Who's Who Among Black Women in California. Inglewood, CA: n.p., 1981.

Who's Who in Colored America. New York: Who's Who in Colored America Corporation, 1927; 7th and last ed., 1950.

PART II: COMPREHENSIVE LISTINGS

LITERARY ARTS

Anthologies and Collections Containing Works by and Edited by African-American Women

Alexander, Rae P., ed. *Young and Black in America.* New York: Random House, 1972.

Bambara, Toni Cade, ed. *The Black Woman.* New York: New American Library, 1970.

————, ed. *Tales and Stories for Black Folks.* New York: Doubleday, 1971.

Baraka, Amiri, and Amina Baraka, eds. *Confirmation: An Anthology of African-American Women.* New York: Quill, 1983.

Berry, Faith, ed. and introd. *Good Morning, Revolution: Writings of Social Protest by Langston Hughes.* Foreword by Saunders Redding. New York: L. Hill, 1973.

Booker, Sue. *Cry at Birth.* New York: McGraw-Hill, 1971.

Brooks, Gwendolyn, ed. *Jump Bad: A New Chicago Anthology.* Detroit: Broadside Press, 1971. (Fiction, poetry, reviews, criticism)

Brown, Patricia L., et al. *To Gwen with Love.* Chicago: Johnson Publishing Co., 1971.

Browning, Alice C. *Lionel Hampton's Swing Book.* Chicago: Negro Story Press, 1949.

Browning, Alice W., ed. *Black n' Blue.* Chicago: Browning, n.d.

Childress, Alice, ed. *Black Scenes.* New York: Doubleday, 1971.

Cooper, Anna Julia. *A Voice from the South.* Ed. Mary Helen Washington. *The Schomburg Library of Nineteenth-Century Black Women Writers* series. Gen. ed. Henry Louis Gates, Jr. New York: Oxford University Press, 1988.

Cromwell, Otelia, Lorenzo Turner, and Eva B. Dykes, eds. *Readings from Negro Authors.* New York: Harcourt Brace, 1931.

Danner, Margaret. *Impressions of African Art Forms.* Detroit: Broadside Press, 1968.

Davis, Ossie, and Ruby Dee. *A Collection of Books and Audio Cassette Tapes: My One Good Nerve,* Ruby Dee; *Two Ways to Count to Ten,* African Folktales read by Ruby Dee; *Dessa Rose,* author Sherley Williams, read by Ruby Dee, produced by Dove Books on tape; *Everybody Loves Oprah,* author Norman King, read by Ruby Dee, produced by Dove Books on tape; *The Poetry of Langston Hughes,* author Langston Hughes, narrated by Ossie Davis and Ruby Dee, produced by Caedmon Audio; *The Lost Zoo,* author Countee Cullen, read by Ruby Dee, produced by Caedmon Audio; *Why Mosquitos Buzz in People's Ears,* author Verna Aardema, narrated by Ossie Davis and Ruby Dee, produced by Caedmon Audio.

DeCosta-Willis, Mirriam, and Fannie Delk, eds. *Homespun Images: An Anthology of Black Memphis Writers and Artists.* Memphis: Lemoyne-Owen College, 1989.

Dee, Ruby, ed. *Glowchild and Other Poems.* New York: Third Press, 1972.

Detroit Public Schools. *Afro-America Sings.* Prepared by a Detroit Public Schools Workshop under the direction of Ollie McFarland. Editorial direction, John W. Pritchard. Detroit: The Board of Education of the School District of Detroit, 1971.

Dunbar-Nelson, Alice Ruth (Moore), ed. *Masterpieces of Negro Eloquence.* New York: The Bookery Publishing Co., 1914; Johnson Reprint Co., 1970.

————. *The Dunbar Speaker and Entertainer.* Naperville, IL: J. L. Nichols & Co., 1920.

Alice Dunbar–Nelson—poet, novelist, essayist, and critic.

Evans, Mari, ed. *Black Women Writers (1950–1980): A Critical Evaluation.* Introd. Stephen Henderson. New York: Anchor Books, 1984; Garden City: Doubleday, 1984. (Interviews, critical essays, bio/selected bibliographies)

Exum, Pat Crutchfield. *Keeping the Faith: Writings by Contemporary Black American Women.* Greenwich, CT: Fawcett, 1974.

Giovanni, Nikki. *Sacred Cows . . . . And Other Edibles.* New York: William Morrow, 1987. (Essays)

Guy, Rosa. *Children of Longing.* New York: Bantam, 1970. (Essays written by young Blacks in rural and urban USA)

Harper, Frances E. W. *Complete Poems of Frances E. W. Harper.* Ed. Maryemma Graham. *The Schomburg Library of Nineteenth-Century Black Women Writers* series. Gen. ed. Henry Louis Gates, Jr. New York: Oxford University Press, 1987.

Harper, Michael, and Robert B. Stepto, eds. *Chant of Saints: A Gathering of Afro-American Literature, Art, and Scholarship.* Urbana, IL: University of Illinois Press, 1979.

Harris, Trudier, and Thadious Davis, eds. *Afro-American Fiction Writers After 1955.* 6 vols. *Dictionary of Literary Biography.* Detroit: Gale Research, 1984.

Hull, Gloria T., ed. and introd. *The Works of Alice Dunbar-Nelson. The Schomburg Library of Nineteenth-Century Black Women Writers* series. Gen. ed. Henry Louis Gates, Jr. New York: Oxford University Press, 1988.

Jordan, June. *Civil Wars.* Boston: Beacon Press, 1981.

————. *On Call: Political Essays.* Boston: South End Press, 1985.

————, ed. *Soulscript: Afro-American Poetry.* New York: Zenith, 1970.

Kelly, Ernece, ed. *Points of Departure.* New York: John Wiley, 1972.

Pinkie Gordon Lane

Kunjufu, Johari M. [Johari Amini; Jewel C. Latimore]. *An African Frame of Reference*. Chicago: Institute of Positive Education, 1972. (Essays)

Lane, Pinkie Gordon, ed. *Discourses in Poetry*. 6th annual ed. Fort Smith, AK: South and West Publishers, 1972.

———. *Poems by Blacks*. Vol. 3. Fort Smith, AK: South and West Publishers, 1975.

Littleton, Arthur, and Mary W. Burger, eds. *Black Viewpoints*. New York: New American Library, 1971. (Essays)

Long, Richard A., and Eugenia W. Collier, eds. *Afro-American Writing: An Anthology of Prose and Poetry*. 2nd & enl. ed. New York: New York University Press, 1972; University Park, PA: Pennsylvania State University Press, 1985.

Lorde, Audre. *Sister Outsider*. The Crossing Press Feminist Series. Trumansburg, NY: The Crossing Press, 1984.

Love, Rose L., ed. *A Collection of Folklore for Children in Elementary School and at Home*. New York: Vantage Press, 1964.

Madgett, Naomi Long, ed. *A Milestone Sampler: 15th Anniversary Anthology*. Detroit: Lotus Press, Inc., 1988.

McFarlin, Annjennette Sophie. *Black Congressional Reconstruction Orators and Their Orations*. Metuchen, NJ: Scarecrow Press, 1976.

Miller, May. *Dust of Uncertain Journey*. Detroit: Lotus, 1975.

Miller, Ruth, ed. *Backgrounds to Blackamerican Literature*. Scranton, PA: Chandler Publishing Co., 1970.

———. *Blackamerican Literature: 1970-Present*. Foreword by John Hope Franklin. Beverly Hills, CA: Glencoe Press, 1971.

Murphy, Beatrice, ed. *An Anthology by Young Negro Poets*. New York: Messner, 1970.

————. *Ebony Rhythm.* New York: Exposition, 1948.

————. *Negro Voices: An Anthology of Contemporary Verse.* New York: Harrison, 1938.

————. *Today's Negro Voices: An Anthology by Young Negro Poets.* New York: Messner, 1970.

Murray, Alma, and Robert Thomas. *Black Perspectives.* New York: Scholastic Book Services, 1971.

Porter, Dorothy, ed. *Early Negro Writing, 1760–1840.* Boston: Beacon Press, 1970. (Collection of Black history, literature, music at Howard University, Washington, DC)

Pryse, Marjorie, and Hortense J. Spillers, eds. *Conjuring: Black Women, Fiction, and Literary Tradition.* Bloomington, IN: Indiana University Press, 1985.

Randall, Dudley, and Margaret C. Burroughs, eds. *For Malcolm: Poems on the Life and the Death of Malcolm X.* Preface and eulogy by Ossie Davis. Detroit: Broadside Press, 1967.

Randall, Dudley, and Margaret Danner. *Poem Counterpoem.* Detroit: Broadside Press, 1966.

Richardson, Willis, and May Miller, eds. *Negro History in Thirteen Plays.* Washington, DC: Associated Publishers, 1935.

Rollins, Charlemae Hill. *Christmas Gift: An Anthology of Christmas Poems, Songs, and Stories Written by and about Negroes.* Chicago: Follett, 1963.

Rush, Theressa Gunnels, Carol Fairbanks Myers, and Esther Spring Arata. *Black American Writers Past and Present: A Biographical and Bibliographical Dictionary,* 2 vols. Metuchen, NJ: Scarecrow Press, 1975.

Sanchez, Sonia. *We Be Word Sorcerers: 25 Stories by Black Americans.* New York: Bantam, 1973.

Sanchez, Sonia, ed. *Three Hundred and Sixty Degrees of Blackness*

Comin' at You: An Anthology of the Sonia Sanchez Writers Workshop at Countee Cullen Library in Harlem. New York: 5 X Publishing, 1971.

Sheffey, Ruthe T., and Eugenia Collier. *Impressions in the Asphalt Jungle of Urban America in Literature.* New York: Scribner's, 1972.

Shockley, Ann Allen. "The New Black Feminists." *Northwest Journal of African and Black American Studies* 2 (Winter, 1974): 1–5.

Sloan, Phyllis J., Angela Kinamore, and Beverly A. Russell. *Three Women Black.* Robbinsdale, MN: Guild Press, 1987.

Smith, Barbara. *Home Girls: A Black Feminist Anthology.* New York: Kitchen Table Press, 1983.

Strickland, Dorothy S., ed. *Listen Children.* Foreword by Coretta Scott King. Illust., Leo and Diane Dillon. New York: Bantam, 1982. (Anthology of Black Literature, ages 10 and up)

Walker, Alice. *Langston Hughes, American Poet.* New York: Harper-Collins, 1974.

Washington, Mary Helen, ed. *Black-Eyed Susans: Classic Stories by and about Black Women.* New York: Anchor Books, 1975.

———. *Invented Lives: Narratives of Black Women, 1860–1960.* Garden City, NY: Anchor Books, 1987; New York: Doubleday, 1987. (Introductory essays to individual authors, excerpts of works, bibliographic notes for individual authors)

———, Introd. *Midnight Birds: Stories of Contemporary Black Women.* Garden City, NY: Doubleday, 1975, 1980.

Wheatley, Phillis. *The Collected Works of Phillis Wheatley.* Ed. John C. Shields. *The Schomburg Library of Nineteenth-Century Black Women Writers* series. Gen. ed. Henry Louis Gates, Jr. New York: Oxford University Press, 1987.

Williams, Jayme Coleman, and McDonald Williams, eds. *The Negro Speaks: The Rhetoric of Contemporary Black Leaders.* New York: Noble and Noble, 1971.

Anthologies and Collections Edited by Non-African-American Women

Adams, William, comp. *Afro-American Literature: Drama.* Boston: Houghton Mifflin, 1970.

———. *Afro-American Literature: Essays.* Boston: Houghton Mifflin, 1970.

———. *Afro-American Literature: Fiction.* Boston: Houghton Mifflin, 1970.

———. *Afro-American Literature: Poetry.* Boston: Houghton Mifflin, 1970.

Adoff, Arnold, ed. *Black Out Loud: An Anthology of Modern Poems by Black Americans.* New York: Macmillan, 1970.

———. *Brothers and Sisters.* New York: Dell, 1970.

———. *I Am the Darker Brother: An Anthology of Modern Poems by Negro Americans.* New York: Macmillan, 1968.

———. *The Poetry of Black America Anthology of the 20th Century.* Introd. Gwendolyn Brooks. New York: Harper, 1973.

Alhamsi, Ahmed, and Harun Kofi Wangara, eds. *Black Arts: An Anthology of Black Creations.* Detroit: Black Art Publications, 1969.

Barbour, Floyd B., ed. *The Black Power Revolt.* Boston: Porter Sargent, 1968.

Barksdale, Richard, and Kenneth Kennamon, eds. *Black Writers of America.* New York: Macmillan, 1972.

Black Women's Oral History Project. Schlesinger Library, Radcliffe College, 1978ff.

Bontemps, Arna, ed. *American Negro Poetry.* New York: Hill and Wang, 1963.

Bontemps, Arna, and Langston Hughes, eds. *The Poetry of the Negro, 1746–1949.* New York: Doubleday, 1953.

Botkin, B. A., ed. *Lay My Burden Down: A Folk History of Slavery.* Chicago: University of Chicago Press, 1945.

Brasner, William, and Dominick Consolo, eds. *Black Drama, An Anthology.* Introd. Darwin T. Turner. Columbus, OH: Charles Merrill, 1970.

Brawley, Benjamin, ed. *Early Negro American Writers.* New York: Dover Publications, Inc., 1970.

Boulware, Marcus Manna, ed. *The Oratory of Negro Leaders: 1900–1968.* Westport, CT: Negro Universities Press, 1969.

Brown, Sterling, et al., eds. *The Negro Caravan.* Introd. Julius Lester. New York: Arno Press, 1970.

Chapman, Abraham, ed. *Black Voices.* New York: New American Library, 1968.

———. *New Black Voices.* New York: New American Library, 1972.

Clarke, John Henrik, ed. *Harlem, U.S.A.* Berlin: Seven Seas Publishers, 1964.

Cooke, Michael. *Afro-American Literature in the Twentieth Century.* New Haven: Yale University Press, 1984.

Coombs, Orde, ed. *What We Must See: Young Black Storytellers.* New York: Dodd, Mead and Company, 1971.

Couch, William, Jr., ed. *New Black Playwrights.* Baton Rouge, LA: Louisiana State University Press, 1968.

Cullen, Countee. *Caroling Dusk.* New York: Harper, 1927.

Culp, D. W., ed. *Twentieth Century Negro Literature.* Naperville, IL: n.p., 1902; New York: Arno Press, 1969.

Cunard, Nancy. *Negro Anthology.* London: Wishart, 1934.

Davis, Arthur, and Saunders Redding. *Cavalcade: Negro American Writing from 1760 to the Present.* Boston: Houghton Mifflin, 1971.

Davis, Arthur P., Ulysses Lee, and Sterling Brown, eds. *The Negro Caravan: Writing by American Negroes.* Introd. Julius Lester. New York: Dryden, 1941; New York: Arno, 1969.

Davis, Charles, and Daniel Walden. *On Being Black.* Greenwich, CT: Fawcett Publications, 1970.

Emanuel, James A., and Theodore Gross, eds. *Dark Symphony: Negro Literature in America.* New York: The Free Press, 1968.

Ford, Nick Aaron. *Black Insights.* Waltham, MA: Ginn and Co., 1971.

Ford, Nick Aaron, and H. L. Faggett, eds. *Best Short Stories by Afro-American Writers, 1925–1950.* Boston: Meador, 1950.

Gates, Henry Louis, ed. *Norton Anthology of Afro-American Literature.* Forthcoming.

———, gen. ed. *The Schomburg Library of Nineteenth-Century Black Women Writers.* New York: Oxford University Press, 1988.

Gayle, Addison, ed. *Black Expression: Essays by and about Black Americans in the Creative Arts.* New York: Weybright and Talley, 1969.

Hatch, James V., ed. Ted Shine, consultant. *Black Theater, U. S. A.: Forty-Five Plays by Black Americans, 1874–1974.* New York: The Free Press, 1974.

Hayden, Robert, et al., eds. *Afro-American Literature: An Introduction.* New York: Harcourt, 1971.

Henderson, Stephen. *Understanding the New Black Poetry.* New York: William Morrow & Co., 1973.

Hill, Herbert, ed. *Soon, One Morning: New Writing by American Negroes, 1940–1962.* New York: Knopf, 1968.

Hughes, Langston, ed. *The Best Short Stories by Negro Writers: An Anthology from 1899 to the Present.* Boston: Little, Brown, 1967.

Jones, LeRoi, and Larry Neal, eds. *Black Fire: An Anthology of Afro-American Writing.* New York: Morrow, 1968.

Kerlin, Robert, ed. *Negro Poets and Their Poems.* 3rd ed. Washington, DC: Associated Publishers, 1923.

King, Woodie. *Black Spirits: A Festival of New Black Poets in America.* Introd. Don L. Lee. Artistic cons. Imamu Amiri Baraka. Foreword Nikki Giovanni. New York: Vintage Books, 1972.

Lee, Don L., ed. *Dynamite Voices: Black Poets of the 1960s.* Detroit: Broadside Press, 1971.

Lerner, Gerda. *The Majority Finds Its Past: Placing Women in History.* New York: Oxford University Press, 1979.

Lerner, Gerda, ed. *Black Women in White America.* New York: Pantheon Books, 1972.

Levitt, Kendricks, ed. *Afro-American Voices: 1770s-1970s.* New York and Los Angeles: Oxford Book Co., 1970.

Lift Every Voice and Sing: A Collection of Afro-American Spirituals and Other Songs. New York: The Church Hymnal Corporation, 1981.

Locke, Alain, ed. *Plays of Negro Life: A Source Book of Native American Drama.* Illust. Aaron Douglass. Westport, CT: Negro Universities Press, 1970.

―――. *The New Negro: An Interpretation.* Introd. Allan H. Spear. New York and London: Johnson Reprint Corp., 1968.

Locke, Alain, and Montgomery Gregory, eds. *Plays of Negro Life.* New York: Harper, 1927.

Lomax, Alan, and Raoul Abdu, eds. *3000 Years of Black Poetry.* New York: Dodd, Mead and Company, 1970.

McMillan, Terry, ed. *Breaking Ice: An Anthology of Contemporary American Black Fiction.* Pref. by John Wideman. New York: Viking/Penguin, 1989.

Major, Clarence, ed. *New Black Poetry.* New York: International Publishers, 1969.

Miller, Adam David, ed. *Dices or Black Bones.* Boston: Houghton Mifflin, 1970.

Mirer, Martin, ed. *Modern Black Stories.* New York: Barron's Educational Series, 1971.

Mirikitoni, Janice, et al., eds. *Time to Greez! Incantations from the Third World.* Introd. Maya Angelou. San Francisco: Glide Publications, 1975.

Mitchell, Loften. *Black Drama.* New York: Hawthorn Books, Inc., 1967.

Morgan, Robin, ed. *Sisterhood Is Powerful: An Anthology of Writings from the Women's Liberation Movement.* New York: Random House, 1970.

Music Committee, Sunday School Publishing Board, ed. *Gospel Pearls.* Nashville, TN: Sunday School Publishing Board, National Baptist Convention, U.S.A., 1921.

Nemiroff, Robert, ed. *Les Blancs: The Collected Last Plays of Lorraine Hansberry.* Introd. Julius Lester. New York: Random House, 1972.

Patterson, Lindsay, comp. and introd. *Black Theater: A Twentieth Century Collection of the Work and Its Best Playwrights.* New York: Dodd, Mead and Company, 1971.

Randall, Dudley, ed. *The Black Poets.* New York: Bantam, 1971.

Richardson, Marilyn, ed. and introd. *Maria W. Stewart: America's First Black Woman Political Writer.* Bloomington, IN: Indiana University Press, 1987.

Richmond, M. A. *Bid the Vassal Soar: Interpretative Essays on the Life and Poetry of Phillis Wheatley and George Moses Horton.* Washington, DC: Howard University Press, 1974.

Robinson, William H. *Early Black American Poets.* Dubuque, IA: Wm. C. Brown Co., 1969.

Sherman, Joan, ed. *Collected Black Women's Poetry.* 4 vols. *The Schomburg Library of Nineteenth-Century Black Women Writers* series. Gen. ed. Henry Louis Gates, Jr. New York: Oxford University Press, 1987.

Sherman, Joan R. *Invisible Poets: Afro-Americans of the Nineteenth Century.* Urbana, IL: University of Illinois Press, 1974.

Shuman, R. Baird, ed. *Nine Black Poets.* Durham, NC: Moore Publishing Co., 1968.

Singh, Raman K., and Peter Fellowes. *Black Literature in America: A Casebook.* New York: Crowell, 1970.

Songs of Zion: Supplemental Worship Resources 12. Nashville, TN: Abingdon Press, 1981.

Staples, Robert, ed. *The Black Family: Essays and Studies.* Belmont, CA: Wadsworth Publishing Co., 1971.

Sternburg, Janet, ed. *The Writer on Her Work.* New York/London: W. W. Norton, 1980. (Essays by Toni C. Bambara, Alice Walker, Margaret Walker)

"The Bessie Smith Songbook." EMARCY 826 663–2. (Dinah Washington)

Turner, Darwin, ed. *Black American Literature: Essays.* Columbus, OH: Charles Merrill, 1969.

————. *Black American Literature: Fiction.* Columbus, OH: Charles Merrill, 1969.

————. *Black American Literature: Poetry.* Columbus, OH: Charles Merrill, 1969.

Vermont Square Writers Workshop. *Some Ground to Fall On, and Other Writings.* Los Angeles: Los Angeles Public Library, under the auspices of the Federal Library Services and Construction Act, 1971.

Wagner, Jean. *Black Poets of the United States from Paul Laurence Dunbar to Langston Hughes.* Trans. Kenneth Douglas. Urbana, IL: University of Illinois Press, 1973.

Watkins, Mel, and Jay David. *To Be a Black Woman: Portraits in Fact and Fiction.* New York: Morrow, 1970.

White, Newman Ivey, and Walter Clinton Jackson, eds. *An Anthology of Verse by American Negroes.* Durham, NC: Moore Publishing Co., 1970.

Wilentz, Ted, and Tom Weatherly, eds. *Natural Process: An Anthology of New Black Poetry.* New York: Hill and Wang, 1970.

Williams, John A., ed. *Beyond the Angry Black.* New York: New American Library, 1966.

Books for Young Readers

Afro-Americans: Then and Now. Item No. 56051. For primary grades. Westchester, IL: Benefic Press.

Baker, Augusta. *Best Loved Nursery Rhymes & Songs.* New York: Parents' Magazine Enterprises, 1973.

―――. *The Black Experience in Children's Books.* New York: New York Public Library, 1971; 1974.

―――. *The Golden Lynx and Other Tales.* Illust. Johannes Troyer. Philadelphia: Lippincott, 1960.

―――. *The Talking Tree.* Illust. Jo Lannes Troger. Philadelphia: Lippincott, 1955.

Baker, Augusta, and Eugenia Gerson. *Young Years: Best Loved Stories for Little Children.* New York: Home Library Press, 1960, 1963; New York: Parents' Magazine, 1963.

Bond, Jean Carey. *Brown Is a Beautiful Color*. Illust. Barbara Zuber. New York: Franklin Watts, 1972.

Boyd, Candy Dawson. *Breadsticks and Blessing Places*. New York: Macmillan, 1985.

Brooks, Gwendolyn. *The Tiger Who Wore White Gloves or What You Are You Are*. Chicago: Third World Press, 1974.

Brown, Margery W. *Animals Made by Me*. New York: Putnam, 1970. (Self-illustrated)

———. *No Jon, No Jon, No!* Boston: Houghton Mifflin, 1981.

———. *That Ruby*. Chicago: Reilly & Lee, 1989. (Self-illustrated)

———. *The Second Stone*. New York: Putnam, 1974.

———. *Yesterday I Climbed a Mountain*. New York: Putnam, 1976.

Burroughs, Margaret Taylor. *Jasper the Drummin' Boy*. Illust. Ted Lewin. Chicago: Follett, 1970.

———. *Whip Me Whop Me Pudding and Other Stories of Riley Rabbit and His Fabulous Friends*. Chicago: DuSable Museum of African American History, 1966.

Chambers, Lucille Arcola. *Negro Pioneers: Benjamin Banneker, Mathematician and Astronomer*. Art by John Neal. New York: C & S Ventures (P. O. Box 209), 1970.

Childress, Alice. *Gold Through the Trees*. (Dramatic revue, 8 scenes; historical play with music). Produced by the Committee for the Negro in the Arts, at Club Baron, Harlem, April 1952.

———. *Rainbow Jordan*. New York: Corvara, McCann and Geoghegan, 1981.

Clark, Margaret Goff. *Their Eyes on the Stars*. Champaign,IL: Garrard Publishers, 1973.

DeVeaux, Alexis. *An Enchanted Hair Tail*. New York: Harper, 1987. (Grades 1–3)

Dodds, Barbara. *Negro Literature for High School Students*. Urbana, IL: National Council of Teachers of English, 1968.

Douty, Esther M. *Charlotte Forten: Free Black Teacher*. Champaign, IL: Garrard Publishing Company, 1971.

DuBois, Shirley Graham [Shirley Graham]. *Booker T. Washington*. New York: Messner, 1955.

———. *George Washington Carver*. New York: Messner, 1944.

———. *His Day Is Marching On: A Memoir of W. E. B. DuBois*. Philadelphia: Lippincott, 1971.

———. *John Baptiste DuSable*. New York: Messner, 1953.

———. *Julius K. Nyerere: Teacher of Africa*. New York: Messner, 1975.

———. *The Story of Paul Robeson*. New York: Messner, 1967.

———. *The Story of Phillis Wheatley: Poetess of the American Revolution*. New York: Messner, 1949.

———. *There Once Was a Slave: The Heroic Story of Frederick Douglass*. New York: Messner, 1947.

———. *Your Most Humble Servant: The Story of Benjamin Banneker*. New York: Messner, 1949.

———. *Zulu Heart*. New York: The Third Press, 1974.

Feelings, Muriel L. *Jambo Means Hello*. New York: Dial Press, 1974.

———. *Moja Means One: The Swahilli Country Book*. Illust. Tom Feelings. New York: Dial, 1971, 1976.

———. *Zamani Goes to Market*. Illust. Tom Feelings. New York: Seabury, 1970.

Fitzhugh, Louise. *Nobody's Family Is Going to Change*. New York: Farrar, 1974. (Grades 6–9)

Giovanni, Nikki. *Ego Tripping and Other Poems for Young People.* Illust. George Ford. Westport, CT: Laurence Hill, 1974.

———. *Spin a Soft Black Song: Poems for Children.* New York: Hill and Wang, 1971.

———. *Vacation Time.* New York: William Morrow, 1979.

Graham, Ruth Morris. *Big Sister.* N.p.: *Cricket,* 1981.

———. *Penny Savings Bank. Cricket.* Chicago: Houghton Mifflin, 1979.

———. *The Happy Sound.* Chicago: Houghton Mifflin, 1970.

Greenfield, Eloise. *Bubbles.* Illust. Eric Marlow. Washington, DC: Drum and Spear, 1972.

———. *Daydreamers.* Illust. Tom Feelings. New York: Dial Press, 1981.

———. *Me and Nessie.* Illust. Moreta Barnett. New York: Crowell, 1975.

———. "Rosa Parks." *Ms.* 3 (August 1974): 71–74.

———. *She Come Bringing Me That Little Baby Girl.* Philadelphia: Lippincott, 1974.

———. *Sister.* New York: Crowell, 1974.

———. "Stories for Free Children: Rosa Parks." *Ms* 3.2 (August 1974): 71–74.

Guy, Rosa. *The Friends.* New York: Holt, Rinehart and Winston, 1973; Viking, 1976.

———., ed. *Children of Longing.* New York: Bantam, 1971.

Hamilton, Virginia. *A Little Love.* New York: Philomel/Putnam, 1984.

———. *Dustland.* New York: Greenwillow, 1980; London: MacRae, 1980.

―――. *Jahdu.* New York: Greenwillow, 1980.

―――. *Justice and Her Brother.* New York: Greenwillow, 1978.

―――. *M. C. Higgins, the Great.* New York: Macmillan, 1970.

―――. *Sweet Whispers, Brother Rush.* New York: Philomel, 1983.

―――. *The Gathering.* New York: Greenwillow, 1981.

―――. *The House of Dies Drear.* New York: Macmillan, 1968.

―――. *The Magical Adventures of Pretty Pearl.* New York: Harper, 1982.

―――. *The People Could Fly.* Narr. James Earl Jones. Illust. Dot Diane Dillon. New York: Knopf. (12 stories)

―――. *The People Could Fly: American Black Folktales.* New York: n.p., 1985. (4th grade up)

―――. *The Plant of Junior Brown.* New York: Macmillan, 1970.

―――. *The Time-Ago Tales of Jahdu.* New York: Macmillan, 1969.

―――. *W. E. B. DuBois: A Biography.* New York: Crowell, 1972.

―――. *Willie Bea and the Time the Martians Landed.* New York: Greenwillow, 1983.

―――. *Zeely.* New York: Macmillan, 1967.

Hansen, Joyce. *The Gift-Giver.* New York: Clarion Books, 1980.

Harnan, Terry. *African Rhythms—American Dance: Biography of Katherine Dunham.* New York: Knopf, 1974.

Hine, Darlene Clark. *When the Truth Is Told: A History of Black Women's Culture and Community in Indiana, 1875–1950.* Foreword by Shirley Herd. Indianapolis: National Council of Negro Women, Indianapolis Section, 1981.

Hunter, Kristin Eggleston. *Boss Cat.* New York: Scribner's, 1971; Avon, 1975.

————. *Guests in the Promised Land*. New York: Scribner's, 1973.

————. *Lou in the Limelight*. New York: Scribner's, 1981.

Jackson, Florence. *The Black Man in America, 1791–1861*. New York: Franklin Watts, 1971. (Grade 7 and up)

————. *The Black Man in America, 1861–1877*. New York: Franklin Watts, 1971. (Grades 4–6)

————. *The Black Man in America, 1877–1905*. New York: Franklin Watts, 1973. (Grade 5 and up)

————.*The Black Man in America, 1905–1932*. New York: Franklin Watts, 1971. (Grade 7 and up)

————. *The Black Man in America, 1932–1954*. New York: Franklin Watts, 1974. (Grades 4–6)

King, Helen H. *Willy*. Illust. Carole Byard. New York: Doubleday, 1971.

Landrum, Bessie. *Stories of Black Folk for Little Folk*. Atlanta: A. B. Caldwell Publishing Co., 1923.

Madgett, Naomi Long. *A Student's Guide to Creative Writing*. Detroit: Lotus Press, 1980.

Mathis, Sharon. *Ray Charles*. Ed. Susan Weber. New York: Crowell, 1973.

————. *Teacup Full of Roses*. New York: Viking, 1972.

————. *The Hundred Penny Box*. New York: Viking, 1975.

————. *The Sidewalk Story*. New York: Viking, 1971.

McKissack, Patricia E. *Flossie and the Fox*. Illust. Rachel Isadora. New York: Dial Press, 1986.

Meriwether, Louise. *Don't Take the Bus on Monday: The Rosa Parks Story*. Englewood Cliffs, NJ: Prentice-Hall, 1973.

————. *The Freedom Ship of Robert Smalls.* Illust. Lee Jack Morton. Englewood Cliffs, NJ: Prentice-Hall, 1971.

————. *The Heart Man: Dr. Daniel Hale Williams.* Englewood Cliffs, NJ: Prentice-Hall, 1971.

Moore, Emily. *Something to Count On.* New York: E. P. Dutton, 1980.

Petry, Ann. *Legends of the Saints.* New York: Crowell, 1970.

————. *Tituba of Salem Village.* New York: Crowell, 1964.

Robinson, Dorothy W. *The Legend of Africania.* Illust. Herbert Temple. Chicago: Johnson Publishing Co., 1974.

Rollins, Charlemae Hill. *Black Troubador: Langston Hughes.* New York: Rand McNally, 1949.

————. *Christmas Gift.* Line drawings by Tom O'Sullivan. Chicago: Follett Publishers, 1963.

Tarry, Ellen. *Janie Belle.* Illust. Myrtle Sheldon. New York: Garden City Publishing Co., 1940.

————. *Katherine Drexel, Friend of the Neglected.* Illust. Donald Bolognese. New York: Farrar Straus & Cudahy, 1950.

————. *The Runaway Elephant.* Illust. Oliver Harrington. New York: Viking, 1950.

————. *Young Jim The Early Years of James Weldon Johnson.* New York: Dodd, Mead and Company, 1967.

Taylor, Mildred. *Roll of Thunder, Hear My Cry.* New York: Dial Press, 1976.

————. *Song of the Trees.* New York: Dial Press, 1975.

————. *The Gold Cadillac.* Illust. Michael Hays. New York: Dial Press, 1987.

————. *Trouble's Child.* New York: Lothrop, Lee, & Shepard Books, 1985.

Taylor, Mildred D. *Let the Circle Be Unbroken.* New York: Dial Press, 1981.

Turner, Mae Caeser. *Uncle Ezra Holds Prayer Meeting in the White House.* New York: Exposition, 1970.

Vroman, Mary Elizabeth. *Harlem Summer.* Illust. John Martines. New York: Putnam, 1967.

Walter, Mildred. *Girl on the Outside.* New York: Lothrop, Lee, & Shepard Books, 1982. (Ages 12 and up)

Walter, Mildred Pitts. *Because We Are.* New York: Lothrop, Lee, & Shepard Books, 1983.

―――. *Justin and the Best Biscuits in the World.* Illust. Catherine Stock. New York: Lathrop, Lee, & Shepard Books, 1986.

―――. *Lillie of Watts Takes a Giant Step.* Illust. Bonnie Helene Johnson. Garden City, NY: Doubleday, 1971.

―――. *Ty's One-Man Band.* New York: Four Winds Press, 1980. (Kindergarten to Grade 3)

Watson, Willie Mae. *Martin Luther King.* Frontispiece by Persis Jennings. Syracuse, NY: New Readers Press, 1968.

Williams, Vera B. *Cherries and Cherry Pits.* New York: Mulberry Books 1986.

Yarbrough, Camille. *Cornrows.* Illust. Carole Byard. New York: Coward McCann, 1979.

Autobiographies and Biographies by and about African American Women

Adams, Elizabeth Laura. *Dark Symphony.* New York: Sheed and Ward, 1942.

Albert, Octavia V. Rogers. *The House of Bondage or Charlotte Brooks and Other Slaves.* Introd. Frances Smith Foster. *The Schomburg*

Library of Nineteenth-Century Black Women Writers. Gen. ed. Henry Louis Gates, Jr. New York: Oxford University Press, 1987.

Albertson, Chris. *Bessie Smith: Empress of the Blues.* New York: Schirmer Books, 1975.

Alexander, Sadie T. M. *Who's Who Among Negro Lawyers.* Biographical sketches of 219 of 1200 American Negro lawyers, and names and addresses of 136 others. Philadelphia: National Bar Association, n.d.

Anderson, Marian. "Hall Johnson." *New York Times* 24 May 1970.

――――. *My Lord, What a Morning.* New York: Viking, 1956.

Andrews, William L., introd. *Six Women's Slave Narratives. The Schomburg Library of Nineteenth-Century Black Women Writers.* Gen. ed. Henry Louis Gates, Jr. New York: Oxford University Press, 1987.

――――., ed. *Sisters of the Spirit: Three Black Women's Autobiographies of the Nineteenth Century.* Bloomington, IN: Indiana University Press, 1986. (Religious autobiographies)

Bailey, Pearl. *Talking to Myself.* New York: Harcourt, 1973. (paperback)

――――. *The Raw Pearl.* New York: Pocket Books, 1969.

Baker, Josephine, and Jo Boillon. *Josephine.* Trans. Mariana Fitzpatrick. New York: Paragon House, 1988.

Barlow, Leila Mae. *Across the Years: Memoirs.* Montgomery, AL: The Paragon Press, 1959.

Barthelemy, Anthony G., introd. *Collected Black Women's Narratives. The Schomburg Library of Nineteenth-Century Black Women Writers.* Gen. ed. Henry Louis Gates, Jr. New York: Oxford University Press, 1988.

Bates, Daisy. *The Long Shadow of Little Rock.* New York: David McKay Co., 1962; Fayetteville, AK: n.p., 1987.

Bearden, Jim, and Linda Butler. *The Life and Times of Mary Shadd Cary.* Toronto: NC Press, Ltd., 1977.

Bethune, Mary McLeod. "My Last Will and Testament." *Ebony* Mar. 1974: 44–50.

Billingsley, Ray A., ed. *The Journal of Charlotte E. Forten: A Free Negro in the Slave Era.* New York: Dryden Press, 1953.

Boone-Jones, Margaret. *Martin Luther King, Jr.: A Picture Story.* Illust. R. Scott. Chicago: Childrens Press, 1968.

———. *To Be Somebody: Portrait of Nineteen Beautiful Detroiters.* New York: Vantage Press, 1976.

Bradford, Sarah Elizabeth (Hopkins). *Scenes in the Life of Harriet Tubman.* Auburn, NY: W. J. Moss, printer, 1869.

Brown, Hallie Q. *Homespun Heroines and Other Women of Distinction.* Introd. Randall K. Burkett. *The Schomburg Library of Nineteenth-Century Black Women Writers.* Gen. ed. Henry Louis Gates, Jr. New York: Oxford University Press, 1987.

———. "Victoria Earle Matthews." *Homespun Heroines.* Zenia, OH: Aldine, 1926.

———, ed. *Homespun Heroines and Other Women of Distinction.* Foreword by Mrs. Josephine Turpin. Xenia, OH: Aldine, 1926.

Brown, Josephine. *Biography of an American Bondsman, by His Daughter.* Boston: R. F. Wallcut, 1855.

Browne, Rose Butler. *Love My Children.* New York: Meredith Press, 1969.

Brownmiller, Susan. *Shirley Chisholm: A Biography.* New York: Doubleday, 1971.

Buckley, Gail Lumet. *The Hornes: An American Family.* New York: Knopf, 1986.

Bundles, A'lelia Perry. "Black Foremothers: Our Creative Trail Blazers." *Spelman Messenger.* Reprint of speech given as Convocation address in Sisters Chapel, Oct. 20, 1983.

———. "Madam C. J. Walker—Cosmetics Tycoon." *Ms.* (July 1983).

Burroughs, Nannie H. *Making Their Mark.* Washington, DC: The National Training School for Women and Girls, n.d.

Burt, Olive W. *Mary McLeod Bethune: Girl Devoted to Her People.* Illust. James Cummins. New York: Bobbs-Merrill, 1970.

Campbell, Bebe Moore. *Sweet Summer: Growing Up With and Without My Dad.* New York: Putnam, 1989.

Cantarow, Ellen, with Susan G. O'Malley, and Sharon Hartman Strom. *Moving the Mountain: Women Working for Social Change.* Old Westbury, NY: The Feminist Press/McGraw-Hill, 1980.

Carnegie, Mary Elizabeth. *The Path We Tread: Blacks in Nursing, 1854–1984.* Philadelphia: Lippincott, 1946.

Carruth, Ella Kaiser. *She Wanted to Read: The Story of Mary McLeod Bethune.* Illust. Herbert McClure. Nashville: Abingdon Press, 1966; New York: Archway Paperback, 1969.

Carson, Josephine. *Silent Voices: The Southern Negro Woman Today.* New York: Dell, 1971.

Chapman, Abraham, comp. *Steal Away: Stories of the Slaves.* New York: Praeger, 1971. (Has bibliography)

Chase-Riboud, Barbara. *Sally Hemings.* New York: Avon, 1980.

Cherry, Gwendolyn, et al. *Portraits in Color: The Times of Colorful Negro Women.* New York: Pageant Press, 1962.

Chesnutt, Helen. *Charles Waddell Chesnutt: Pioneer of the Color Line.* Chapel Hill, NC: University of North Carolina Press, 1952.

Childress, Alice. "Tribute." *Freedomways* 11 (First Quarter 1971): 14–15. (Paul Robeson)

Chisholm, Shirley. *Unbought and Unbossed.* New York: Avon Publishers, 1952.

Clark, Septima. *Ready from Within Septima Clark and the Civil*

Rights Movement. Ed. Cynthia Stokes Brown. Navarro, CA: Wild Trees Press, 1986.

Clark, Septima (Poinsette), with LeGette Blythe. *Echo in My Soul.* Foreword by Harry Golden. New York: E. P. Dutton, 1962.

Collins, Marva. *Marva Collins' Way.* With Civia Tamarkin. Los Angeles: J. P. Tarcher; Boston: Distributed by Houghton Mifflin, 1982.

Conrad, Earl. *Harriet Tubman: Negro Soldier and Abolitionist.* New York: International Publishers, 1942; New York: Paul S. Eriksson, 1950.

Cooper, Anna Julia (Haywood). *A Voice from the South, by a Black Woman of the South.* Xenia, OH: Aldine, 1892.

Coppin, Fannie Jackson. *Reminiscenses of School Life, Hints on Teaching.* Philadelphia: AME Book Concern, 1913.

Crowley, Susan. "Spelman College Students Praise New President as 'an Inspiration.' " *AARP New Bulletin* 30.5 (May 1989): 16.

Daniels, Sadie Iola. *Women Builders.* Rev. and ed. by Charles H. Wesley and Thelma D. Perry. Washington, DC: Arno Press, 1970.

Davis, George. *Love, Black Love.* New York: Anchor Press/Doubleday, 1978.

Dawson, Osceola Aleese. *The Timberlake Store.* Carbondale, IL: Dunaway-Sinclair, 1959.

DeVeaux, Alexis. *Don't Explain: A Song of Billie Holiday.* New York: Harper, 1980; Writers and Readers, forthcoming.

Dillard, Clarissa, and Uvelia Bowen, eds. *Virginia Union University Women Graduates: Resource Registry, 1976.* Richmond, VA: International Congress of Virginia Union University Graduates, 1976.

Douty, Esther M. *Charlotte Forten: Free Black Teacher.* Champaign, IL: Garrard Publishing Co., 1971.

DuBois, Shirley Graham. "Tribute to Paul Robeson." *Freedomways* (First Quarter 1971): 6–7.

———. *Your Most Humble Servant: The Story of Benjamin Banneker.* New York: Messner, 1949. (Also see Graham, Shirley.)

Dunbar-Nelson, Alice Ruth Moore. "The Life of Social Service as Exemplified in David Livingstone." *Masterpieces of Negro Eloquence.* New York: The Bookery Publishing Co., 1914; Johnson Reprint Corp., 1970. (Speech delivered at Lincoln University, Pennsylvania, Mar. 7, 1913)

Dunham, Katherine. *Touch of Innocence.* New York & London: Cassell, 1960.

Edmonds, Helen G. *Black Faces in High Places.* New York: Harcourt, 1971.

Evers, Mrs. Medgar, with William Peters. *For Us the Living.* New York: Doubleday, 1967.

Faulkner, Audrey O., et al. *When I Was Comin' Up: An Oral History of Aged Blacks.* Hamden, CT: Archon Books, 1982.

Fauset, Arthur Huff. *Sojourner Truth.* New York: Russell and Russell, 1938.

Ferebee, Dorothy Boulding. Profile. *Black Women's Oral History Project.* Cambridge, MA: Radcliffe College, 1984.

Ferris, Luanne. *I'm Done Crying,* as told to Beth Day. New York: New American Library, 1970.

Fields, Mamie, with Karen Fields. *Lemon Swamp and Other Places: A Carolina Memoir.* New York: The Free Press, 1983.

Fiofiori, Tam. "Angela Davis: Portrait of a Revolutionary." *Black World* 6.21 (Apr. 1972): 82–84. (Review of a film)

Forten, Charlotte L. "Life on Sea Islands." *The Negro Caravan.* Ed. Sterling A. Brown et al. Introd. Julius Lester. New York: Arno Press, 1970.

————. *The Journal of Charlotte L. Forten*. Ed. Ray Allen Billington. New York: Collier Books, 1961.

Francis, Edith V. "Booker T. Washington, Temporizer and Compromiser." *Black Business Digest* January 1972.

Gayton, Virginia Clark. Profile. *Black Women's Oral History Project*. Cambridge, MA: Radcliffe College, 1980.

Gibson, Althea. *I Always Wanted to Be Somebody*. New York: Harper, 1958.

Giovanni, Nikki. *Gemini: An Extended Autobiographical Statement*. Indianapolis: Bobbs-Merrill, 1971.

Golden, Marita. *Migrations of the Heart: An Autobiography*. New York: Ballantine Books, 1983. *Black Pioneers*.

Goodwin, Ruby Berkley. *It's Good to Be Black*. Garden City, NY: Doubleday, 1951.

Greenfield, Eloise. *Paul Robeson*. New York: Crowell, 1975.

————. *Rosa Parks*. New York: Crowell, 1973.

Griffin, Judith Berry. *Nat Turner*. Illust. Leo Carty. New York: Coward, McCann and Geoghegan, 1970.

Griffiths, Mattie. *Autobiography of a Female Slave*. New York: New York Universities Press, 1857.

Grimke, Angelina W. *A Biographical Sketch of Archibald H. Grimke*. New York: Arno Press, 1970.

Grimke, Charlotte Forten. *The Journals of Charlotte Forten Grimke*. Ed. Brenda Stevenson. *The Schomburg Library of Nineteenth-Century Black Women Writers* series. Gen. ed. Henry Louis Gates, Jr. New York: Oxford University Press, 1987.

Guffy, Ossie. *Ossie: The Autobiography of a Black Woman*. As told to Caryl Ledner. New York: W. W. Norton and Co., 1971.

Guzman, Jessie Parkhurst. "Monroe Nathan Work and His Contributions." *Journal of Negro History* 34.5 (Oct. 1949): 428–461.

Lorraine Hansberry

———. "W. E. B. DuBois—The Historian." *Journal of Negro History* 30.4 (Fall 1961): 377–385.

Hamilton, Virginia. *Paul Robeson: The Life and Times of a Free Black Man.* New York: Harper, 1974.

Hansberry, Lorraine. "My Name Is Lorraine Hansberry, I Am a Writer." *Esquire* Nov. 1969: 140.

———. "The Legacy of W. E. B. DuBois." *Black Titan: W. E. B. DuBois.* Ed. John Henrik Clarke et al. Boston: Beacon Press, 1970.

———. *To Be Young, Gifted and Black: Lorraine Hansberry in Her Words.* Adapted by Robert Nemiroff. Englewood Cliffs, NJ: Prentice-Hall, 1969. (Also includes selections of her work)

Hare, Maud Cuney. *Norris Wright Cuney: A Tribute to Black People.* Introd. Robert C. Cotner. New York: The Crisis Publishing Co., 1913; Austin, TX: Steck-Vaughn, 1968.

Harnan, Terry. *African Rhythm—American Dance: A Biography of Katherine Dunham.* New York: Knopf, 1974.

Harper, Martha C. *Always Martha: An Autobiography.* Roanoke, Virginia: Martha C. Harper, 1990.

Haskins, James. *Barbara Jordan.* New York: Dial Press, 1977.

Hayden, Robert, and Jacqueline Harris. *Nine Black American Doctors.* Reading, MA: Addison-Wesley, 1976.

Hedgeman, Anna (Arnold). *The Trumpet Sounds.* New York: Holt, Rinehart and Winston, 1964.

Heidish, Marcy. *A Woman Called Moses.* Boston: Houghton Mifflin, 1976.

Height, Dorothy. Profile. *Black Women's Oral History Project.* Cambridge, MA: Radcliffe College, 1982.

Hicks, Nora Louise. *Slave Girl Reba and Her Descendants in America.* New York: Exposition Press, 1974.

Hine, Darlene Clark. "Co-Laborers in the Work of the Lord: Nineteenth-Century Black Women Physicians." *Send Us a Lady Physician: Women Doctors in America.* Ed. Ruth J. Abram. New York: W. W. Norton, 1985.

Holdredge, Helen. *Mammy Pleasant.* New York: Ballantine Books, 1972.

Holiday, Billie. *Lady Sings the Blues.* New York: Doubleday, 1956.

Holley, Miller Allie. "Alice Ruth Moore Dunbar-Nelson: The Individual." Biographical sketch written for Delta Sigma Theta Regional Conference, Sheraton Charles Hotel, June 2–5, 1968.

Holt, Rackman. *Mary McLeod Bethune.* New York: Doubleday, 1964.

Horne, Lena. *Lena.* New York: Doubleday, 1965.

Horne, Lena, as told to Helen Arustein and Carlton Moss. *In Person: Lena Horne.* New York: Greenberg, 1951.

Huggins, Nathan I., ed. *Madame C. J. Walker: Entrepreneur. Black Americans of Achievement* Series. New York: Chelsea House, 1989.

Hull, Gloria, ed. *Give Us Each Day: The Diary of Alice Dunbar-Nelson.* New York: Norton Press, 1986.

Hunter, Jane Edna. *A Nickel and a Prayer.* Nashville, TN: The Parthenon Press, 1940.

Hurst, Fannie. "Zora Hurston: A Personality Sketch." *Yale University Library Gazette* 35 (1961): 17–22.

Hurston, Zora N. *Dust Tracks on a Road.* Philadelphia: Lippincott, 1942; New foreword, Robert E. Hemenway. Champaign, IL: University of Illinois Press, 1984.

Ione, Carole. *Pride in Family: Four Generations of Americans of Color.* New York: Summit Books, 1991.

Jackson, Harrisene. *There's Nothing I Own That I Want.* Englewood Cliffs, NJ: Prentice-Hall, 1974.

Jackson, Mahalia. *Movin' Up.* New York: Avon Publishers, 1969.

Jacobs, Harriet. *Incidents in the Life of a Slave Girl.* Introd. Valerie Smith. *The Schomburg Library of Nineteenth-Century Black Women Writers* series. Gen. ed. Henry Louis Gates, Jr. New York: Oxford University Press, 1987.

Jones, Hettie. *Big Star Fallin Mama: Five Women in Black Music.* New York: Viking, 1974.

Jones, Martha. *If I Can Help Somebody: James E. Jones, In Memoriam.* Marshall, VA: Martha Jones, 1989.

Jordan, Barbara, and Shelby Jordan. *Barbara Jordan: A Self-Portrait.* New York: Doubleday, 1979.

Katz, Bernard, and Jonathan Katz. *Black Woman: A Fictionalized Biography of Lucy Terry Prince.* New York: Pantheon Books, 1973.

Keckley, Elizabeth. *Behind the Scenes: Or Thirty Years a Slave and Four Years in the White House.* Introd. James Olney. *The Schomburg Library of Nineteenth-Century Black Women Writers* series. Gen. ed. Henry Louis Gates, Jr. New York: Oxford University Press, 1987.

———. "The Death of Lincoln." *The Negro Caravan.* Ed. Sterling Brown et al. New York: Arno Press, 1970.

Kelley-Hawkins, Emma D. *Four Girls at Cottage City.* Boston: n.p., 1898; with Introd. Deborah E. McDowell in *The Schomburg Library of Nineteenth-Century Black Women Writers* series. Gen. ed. Henry Louis Gates, Jr. New York: Oxford University Press, 1987.

King, Coretta Scott. *My Life with Martin Luther King, Jr.* New York: Holt, Rinehart and Winston, 1969.

King, Mary. *Freedom Song: A Personal Story of the Civil Rights Movement.* New York: William Morrow, 1987.

Kitt, Eartha. *Thursday's Child*. New York: Duell, Sloan and Pearce, 1956.

Lanker, Brian. *I Dream a World*. Travelling photographic exhibit premiered February 1989 in Corcoran Gallery, Washington, DC.

Larison, Cornelius Wilson. *Silvia DuBois (Now 116 Years Old): A Biography of the Slav Who Whipt and Gand Her Freedom*. Ringer, NJ: n.p., 1883; ed. trans. introd. Jared C. Lobdell. *The Schomburg Library of Nineteenth-Century Black Women Writers* series. Gen. ed. Henry Louis Gates, Jr. New York: Oxford University Press, 1987.

Lewis, Alice A. "Angela Davis in Port Gibson, Mississippi." *Freedomways* 2.15 (Second Quarter 1975), 114–117.

Lightfoot, Sara Lawrence. *Balm in Gilead: Journey of a Healer*. Radcliff Biography Series. Reading, MA: Addison-Wesley Publishing Co., 1988.

Lockwood, Lewis C., and Charlotte Forten. *Two Black Teachers During the Civil War: Mary S. Peake: The Colored Teacher at Fortress Manor, and Life in the Sea Islands*. New York: Arno Press, and *The New York Times*, 1969.

Lorde, Audre. *Zami: A New Spelling of My Name*. Waterton, MA: Persephone Press, 1982.

Lovinggood, Penman. *Famous Modern Negro Musicians*. New introd. Eileen Southern. New York: DaCapo Press, 1978.

McCabe, Eliza C. *Black Women's Oral History Project*. Cambridge, MA: Radcliffe College, 1980.

McPheeters, Annie L. *Library Service in Black and White: Some Personal Recollections, 1921–1980*. Foreword by Jack Dalton. Metuchen, NJ: Scarecrow Press, 1988.

Marshall, Marguerite Mitchell. *An Account of Afro-Americans in Southeast Kansas, 1884–1984*. Manhattan, KS: Sunflower University Press, 1986.

———. *The Path to Peace*. New York: Vantage Press, 1982.

Masso, Clara Bodian. "On Mary McLeod Bethune and the National Council of Negro Women." *Freedomways* 1 (Fourth Quarter 1974): 51–53.

Mather, Frank Lincoln. *Who's Who of the Colored Race: A General Biographical Dictionary of Men and Women of African Descent.* Detroit: Gale Research, 1975 (Rpt. of edition published in Chicago, 1915).

Mebane, Mary Elizabeth. *Mary.* New York: Viking, 1981.

Meeks, Cathy. *I Want Somebody to Know My Name.* Nashville/New York: Thomas Nelson, Inc., 1978.

Meriwether, Louise. *Daddy Was a Number Runner.* New York: Pyramid Books, 1970/1971.

Moody, Anne. *Coming of Age in Mississippi.* New York: Dell, 1968.

Moore, Martha Edith Bannister. *Unmasked: The Story of My Life on Both Sides of the Race Barrier.* New York: Exposition Press, 1964.

Moore, Rebecca, ed. *The Jonestown Letters, Correspondence of the Moore Family—1970–1985.* Lewiston, NY: Mellen, 1986.

Morris, J. Kenneth. *Elizabeth Evelyn Wright, 1872–1906: Founder of Voorhees College.* Sewanee, TN: The University of the South, 1983.

Mossell, Mrs. Gertrude E. *The Work of the Afro-American Woman.* Philadelphia: C. S. Ferguson Co., 1980. (copyright 1894)

Mossell, Mrs. N. F. *The Work of the Afro-American Woman.* Ed. Joanne Braxton. *The Schomburg Library of Nineteenth-Century Black Women Writers* series. Gen. ed. Henry Louis Gates, Jr. New York: Oxford University Press, 1988.

Murray, Joan. *The News: An Autobiography.* New York: McGraw-Hill, 1968.

Murray, Pauli. *Proud Shoes: The Story of an American Family*. New York: Harper and Brothers, 1956.

———. *Song in a Weary Throat: An American Pilgrim*. New York: Harper, Row, 1987.

Njeri, Itabari. *Every Good-Bye Ain't Gone: Family Portraits and Personal Escapes*. New York: Random House, 1990.

Newman, Shirlee. *Marian Anderson: Lady from Philadelphia*. Philadelphia: Westminster Press, 1966.

Ortiz, Victoria. *Sojourner Truth: A Self-Made Woman*. Philadelphia: Lippincott, 1974.

Parker, J. A. *Angela Davis: The Making of a Revolutionary*. New York: Arlington House, 1973.

Pauli, Hertha. *Her Name Was Sojourner Truth*. New York: Appleton-Century-Crofts, Inc., 1962.

Peare, Catherine O. *Mary McLeod Bethune*. New York: Vanguard Press, 1951.

Peterson, Helen Stone. *Sojourner Truth: Fearless Crusader*. Illust. Victory Mays. Champaign, IL: Garrard Publishing Co., 1972.

Petry, Ann. *Harriet Tubman*. New York: Crowell, 1955.

———. *Tituba of Salem*. New York: Crowell, 1964.

Pittman, Evelyn LaRue. *Rich Heritage*. Oklahoma City: Harlow Publishing Corporation, 1944.

Pitts, Gertrude. *Tragedies of Life*. Newark, NJ: Author, 1939.

Professor, The. *Angela: A Revealing Close-up of the Woman*. North Hollywood, CA: Leisure Books, 1971.

Redford, Dorothy Spruill, with Michael D'Orso. *Somerset Homecoming: Recovering a Lost Heritage*. Introd. Alex Haley. New York: Doubleday, 1988.

Reid, Margaret. "Memorable Impressions of Two Great Teachers: Nick Aaron Ford and Waters E. Turpin." *Swords Upon This Hill: Preserving the Literary Tradition of Black Colleges and Universities.* Ed. Burney J. Hollis. Baltimore: Morgan State University Press, 1985.

Reynolds, Barbara. *And Still We Rise: Interviews with 50 Black Role Models.* Washington, DC: USA Today Books/Gannett New Media, 1988.

——. *Jesse Jackson: The Man, the Movement, the Myth.* Washington, DC: JFJ Associates; *Jesse Jackson: America's David,* 1985.

Robeson, Eslanda Goode. "Paul Robeson and the Provincetowners." *The Negro Caravan.* Ed. Sterling Brown et al. New York: Arno Press, 1970.

——. *Paul Robeson, Negro.* New York: Harper, 1930.

Robeson, Susan. *The Whole World in His Hands: A Biography of Paul Robeson.* Secaucus, NJ: Citadel Press, 1981.

Robinson, Wilhemena S. "Biographies in Black America, 1968." *Black America.* Ed. Pat Romero. Washington, DC: Associated Publishers, 1969.

Rollins, Charlemae Hill. *Black Troubadour: Langston Hughes.* New York: Rand McNally, 1949.

——. *Famous American Negro Poets.* New York: Dodd, Mead and Company, 1965.

——. *Famous Negro Entertainers of Stage, Screen, and TV.* New York: Dodd, Mead and Company, 1967.

——. *They Showed the Way: Forty American Negro Leaders.* New York: Crowell, 1964.

Rollock, Barbara. *Black Experience in Children's Books.* First published by Augusta Baker [in 1957] as *Books About Negro Life for Children.* New York: New York Public Library, 1984.

Rose, James M., and Barbara W. Brown. *Tapestry: A Living History of a Black Family in Southeastern Connecticut.* New London, CT: New London County Historical Society, 1979.

Rosenberg, Daniel. *Mary Brown: From Harpers Ferry to California.* New York: The American Institute for Marxist Studies, 1975.

Scarupa, Harriet Jackson. "Margaret Walker Alexander." *American Visions* 1.2 (Mar./Apr. 1986): 48–52.

Schuyler, Josephine. *Philippa, the Beautiful American: The Traveled History of a Troubadour.* New York: Philippa Schuyler Memorial Fund, 1969.

Schuyler, Philippa Duke. *Adventure in Black and White.* New York: R. Speller, 1960.

———. "Meet the George Schuylers." *Our World* 6 (Apr. 1951): 22–26.

———. "Why I Don't Marry." *Ebony* (July 1958): 78–80.

Seacole, Mary. *Wonderful Adventures of Mrs. Seacole in Many Lands.* Introd. William L. Andrews. *The Schomburg Library of Nineteenth-Century Black Women Writers* series. Gen. ed. Henry Louis Gates, Jr. New York: Oxford University Press, 1987.

Seider, Jean. *Voices of Another Time: Three Memories.* Philadelphia: Ishi Publications, 1985.

Seidman, Peter. "Eva Jessye." *Michigan Today* 21 (Apr. 1989): 1–4.

"Septima Poinsette Clark, Civil Rights Activist." "Portraits in Black Courage—A Woman's Story." *The Houston Post* Tuesday 28 Mar. 1989: D-2. (Materials based on interviews by Brian Lanker, photographer and compiler of *I Dream a World,* book and exhibit)

Shabazz, Betty. "The Legacy of My Husband, Malcolm X." *Ebony* (June 1969): 172 +.

Sheppard, Gladys. *Mary Church Terrell, Respectable Person.* Baltimore: Human Relations Press, 1951.

Shockley, Ann. "Pauline Hopkins: A Biographical Excursion into Obscurity." *Phylon* 33 (Spring 1972): 22–26.

Shockley, Ann, and Sue P. Chandler. *Living Black American Authors: A Biographical Directory.* Foreword by Jessie Carney Smith. New York: R. R. Bowker Co., 1973.

Smith, Amanda. *An Autobiography: The Story of the Lord's Dealings with the Colored Evangelist.* 1893; with introd. Jualynne E. Dodson in *The Schomburg Library of Nineteenth-Century Black Women Writers* series. Gen. ed. Henry Louis Gates, Jr. New York: Oxford University Press, 1988.

Smith, Jean. "I Learned to Feel Back." *The Black Power Revolt.* Ed. Floy Barbour. Boston: Porter Sargent, 1968.

Southern, Eileen. "Conversations with Fele Sowande, High Priest of Music." *Black Perspectives in Music* 1.4 (Spring 1976): 90–107.

Spady, James G. "Barbara Grant: TV Newscaster." *Black Women in Focus. The Philadelphia Observer* 21 Dec. 1988.

———. "Eloise Greenfield Writes for Black Children." *The Philadelphia New Observer* 21 Dec. 1988.

———. "Merze Tate: Educator, Political and Foreign Shaper and Armament Specialist." *Black Women in Focus. The Philadelphia Observer* 21 Dec. 1988.

———. "Muriel Feelings Exercises the Principle of Kazi in Community Development." *The Philadelphia New Observer* 22 February 1989.

———. "Yolanda King Finds Her Identity in the Theatre." Martin Luther King Supplement of *The Philadelphia New Observer* 11 January 1989.

Speare, Mrs. Chloe. *Memoir of Mrs. Chloe Speare, a Native of Africa Who Was Enslaved in Childhood and Died in Boston Jan. 3, 1815.* By a lady of Boston. Boston: J. Louny, 1832.

Sprague, Rosetta Douglass. *My Mother as I Recall Her.* N.p., n.p., 1900.

Sterling, Dorothy. *Black Foremothers: Three Lives.* 2nd ed. Foreword Margaret Walker. Introd. Barbara Christian. New York: City University of New York, The Feminist Press, 1988.

————. *We Are Your Sisters.* New York: W. W. Norton, 1984.

Sterling, Philip, and Rayford Logan. *Four Took Freedom: The Lives of Harriet Tubman, Frederick Douglass, Robert Smalls, and Blanche K. Bruce.* New York: Doubleday, 1967.

Stewart, Maria W. "Preface to the 1879 Edition of Meditations from the Pen of Mrs. Maria W. Stewart." *Maria Stewart, America's First Black Woman Political Writer.* Ed. and introd. Marilyn Richardson. Bloomington, IN: Indiana University Press, 1987.

Stewart, Ruth Ann. *Portia: The Biography of Portia Washington Pittman.* New York: Anchor Press/Doubleday, 1970.

Stokes-Brown, Cynthia. *Ready From Within.* Navarro, CA: Wild Trees Press, 1986.

Tarry, Ellen. *Katherine Drexel, Friend of the Neglected.* Illust. Donald Bolognese. New York: Farrar, Straus and Cudahy, 1950.

————. *The Third Door: The Autobiography of an American Negro Woman.* New York: McKay, 1955.

Taylor, Frank, with Gerald Cook. *Alberta Hunter: A Celebration.* New York: McGraw-Hill, 1987.

Taylor, Susie King. *Reminiscences of My Life in Camp with 33rd United States Colored Troops.* Boston: Author, 1902.

Terborg-Penn, Rosalyn. *The James Van Horn Kindred, 1800–1980.* Baltimore: Morgan State College, 1982.

Terrell, Mary Church. *A Colored Woman in a White World.* Washington, DC: Ransdell Inc., 1940.

Thomas, Debi. "The Word She Uses Is 'Invincible.'" *Time* 15 February 1988: 44–48, 57.

Thompson, Cecil Sr. *The Afro-American Quest for Freedom: Black America's Quest for Peace.* New York: Vantage Press, 1990.

Thompson, Era Bell. *American Daughter.* Chicago: University of Chicago Press, 1946.

————. "Love Comes to Mahalia." *Ebony* Nov. 1964: 50–61.

————. "The Vaughan Family: A Tale of Two Continents." *Ebony* February 1975: 53–58.

Titus, Frances W. *Narrative of Sojourner Truth: A Bondswoman of Olden Time.* New York: Arno Press, 1970.

Toppin, Edgar A. *A Biographical History of Blacks in America Since 1528.* New York: David McKay Company, 1971.

Trescott, Jacqueline. "The Hair Way to Success." *Washington Post* 22 February 1988.

Truth, Sojourner. *Sojourner Truth: Narrative and Book of Life.* Chicago: Johnson Pub. Co., 1970. (Biographies, essays, and brief commentary on Sojourner Truth)

Tucker, Susan. *Telling Memories Among Southern Women: Domestic Workers and Their Employees in the Segregated South.* New York: Schocken Books, 1989.

Turner, Lucy Mae. "The Family of Nat Turner, 1831–1954." *Negro History Bulletin* 18.6 (Mar. 1955): 129, 132, 145; 18.7 (Apr. 1955): 155–158.

Upsilon Omega Chapter, Alpha Kappa Alpha. *Black Women and Richmond: Sketches for Heritage I.* Richmond, VA: n.p., 1983.

Veney, Bethany. *The Narrative of Bethany Veney, A Slave Woman.* Introd. Reverend Bishop Mallalieu, commend. Reverend V. A. Cooper and Erastus Spaulding. Worcester, MA: n.p., 1889.

Vivan, Octavia B. *Coretta: The Story of Mrs. Martin Luther King, Jr.* New York: Fortress Press, 1970.

"Votes for Women: A Symposium by Leading Thinkers of Colored America." *Crisis* 4.10 (Aug. 1915): 178–192.

Vroman, Mary Elizabeth. *Shaped to Its Purpose: Delta Sigma Theta, The First Fifty Years.* New York: Random House, 1965.

Waldron, Robert. *Oprah!* New York: St. Martin's Press, 1987.

Waters, Ethel, with Charles Samuels. *His Eye Is on the Sparrow.* Garden City, NY: Doubleday, 1951.

Wells, Ida B. *Crusade for Justice: Autobiography of Ida B. Wells.* Ed. Alfreda Duster. Chicago: University of Chicago Press, 1970.

Wells, Sharon. *Forgotten Legacy: Blacks in Nineteenth Century Key West.* Key West, FL: Historic Key West Preservation Board, 1982.

Wheatley, Phillis. *Letters of Phillis Wheatley, the Negro Slave Poet of Boston.* Boston: n.p., 1864.

——. *Memoir and Poems of Phillis Wheatley, A Slave.* Boston: Isaac Knapp, 1838.

White, Barnetta McGhee. *In Search of Kith and Kin: The History of a Southern Black Family.* Baltimore: Gateway Press, 1986.

Williams, Minnie Simons. *A Colloquial History of a South Carolina Family Named Simons.* Copyright, Minnie Williams, 1990.

Williams, Patricia J. *The Alchemy of Race and Rights: Diary of a Law Professor.* Cambridge: Harvard University Press, 1991.

Williams, Rose Berthena Clay. *Black and White Orange.* New York: Vantage Press, 1961.

Wilson, Harriet E. *Our Nig: Sketches from the Life of a Free Black.* Introd. Henry Louis Gates, Jr. New York: Random House, 1783; n.p., 1808; Boston: G. C. Rand & Avery, 1859.

Pauline Young

Wilson, Mary, with Patricia Romanowski and Ahrgus Juilliard. *Dreamgirl: My Life as a Supreme.* New York: St.Martin's Press, 1987.

Winders, Gertrude Hecker. *Harriet Tubman: Freedom Girl.* Illust. William K. Plummer. New York: Bobbs-Merrill, 1969.

Young, Pauline. "Paul Laurence Dunbar: An Intimate Glance." *Freedomways* 12 (Fourth Quarter 1972): 319–329.

Novels

Ansa, Tina McElroy. *Baby of the Family*. San Diego: Harcourt Brace Jovanovich, 1989.

Bambara, Toni Cade. *The Salt Eaters*. New York: Random House, 1980.

Banks, Irma Louise. *Love in Black and White*. New York: Vantage Press, 1974.

Bellinger, Claudia. *Wolf Kitty*. New York: Vantage Press, 1959.

Brooks, Gwendolyn. *Maude Martha*. New York: Farrar, Straus, and Giroux, 1969.

Brown, Linda Beatrice. *Rainbow Roun' Mah Shoulder*. New York: Ballantine, 1989.

Campbell, Bebe Moore. *Your Blues Ain't Like Mine*. New York: Putnam, 1992.

Cary, Lorene. *Black Ice*. New York: Knopf, 1981.

Chase-Riboud, Barbara. *Echo of Lions*. New York: William Morrow, 1989.

Childress, Alice. *A Hero Ain't Nothin' But a Sandwich*. New York: Coward, McCann, and Geoghegan, 1973; Avon, 1974.

———. *A Short Walk*. New York: Coward, McCann & Geoghegan, 1979; New York: Bard, 1981.

———. *Like One of the Family*. New York: Independence Publishers, 1956.

———. *Rainbow Jordan*. New York: Coward, McCann, & Geoghegan, 1981.

DuBois, Shirley Graham. *Zulu Heart*. New York: Joseph Opaku Publishing Co., 1974.

Dunbar-Nelson, Alice Ruth (Moore). *A Modern Undine. The Works of Alice Dunbar-Nelson.* Vol. 3. Ed. Gloria Hull. *The Schomburg Library of Nineteenth-Century Black Women Writers* series. Gen. ed. Henry Louis Gates, Jr. New York: Oxford University Press, 1988. (Novelette)

————. "Confessions of a Lazy Woman." 1901. In the possession of Pauline Young, Wilmington, DE. (Typewritten).

————. "This Lofty Oak." CA, 1931. In the possession of Pauline Young, Wilmington, DE. (Typewritten)

Dunham, Katherine. *Kasamance: A Fantasy.* Illust. Bennie Arrington, after original designs of John Pratt. Photog. Patricia Commings. New York: Odarkai, 1974.

Edwards-Yearwood, Grace. *In the Shadow of the Peacock.* New York: McGraw-Hill, 1988.

Fauset, Jessie Redmond. *Comedy, American Style.* New York: Frederick A. Stokes, 1933. (1969)

————. *Plum Bun.* New York: Frederick A. Stokes, 1929.

————. *The Chinaberry Tree.* New York: Frederick A. Stokes, 1931.

————. *The Sleeper Wakes. The Crisis* 5 (September 1920): 224–226.

————. *There Is Confusion.* New York: Boni and Livewright, 1924.

Finch, Amanda. *Black Trail: A Novella of Love in the South.* New York: William-Frederick Press, 1951.

Fleming, Sarah Lee Brown. *Hope's Highway.* New York: Neale, 1917.

Garrett, Beatrice. *Welfare on Skid Row.* New York: Exposition Press, 1974.

Golden, Marita. *Migrations of the Heart.* New York: Ballantine Books, 1973.

———. *A Woman's Place.* New York: Doubleday, 1986.

———. *Long Distance Life.* New York: Doubleday, 1989.

———. *And Do Remember Me.* New York: Doubleday, 1992.

Greenfield, Eloise. *Sister.* New York: Crowell, 1974.

Guy, Rosa. *A Measure of Time.* New York: Holt, Rinehart and Winston, 1983.

———. *Bird at My Window.* Philadelphia: Lippincott, 1966.

———. *Mirror of Her Own.* New York: Delacort, 1981.

———. *My Love, My Love* Or, *The Peasant Girl.* New York: Holt, Rinehart and Winston, 1985.

———. *New Guys Around the Block.* New York: Delacorte, 1983; London: Gollancz, 1983.

———. *Ruby.* New York: Viking Press, 1976.

———. *The Disappearance.* New York: Delacorte, 1979; London: Gollancz, 1980.

———. *The Friends.* New York: Holt, Rinehart and Winston, 1973; New York: Viking Press, 1976.

Harper, Frances E. W. *Iola Leroy or Shadows Uplifted.* Ed. Frances Smith Foster. Philadelphia: Garriques Brothers, 1892; New York: AMS Press, 1969. In *The Schomburg Library of Nineteenth-Century Black Women Writers* series. Gen. ed. Henry Louis Gates, Jr. New York: Oxford University Press, 1988.

Hopkins, Pauline E. *Contending Forces: A Romance Illustrative of Negro Life North and South.* Introd. Richard Yarborough. 1900. In *The Schomburg Library of Nineteenth-Century Black Women Writers* series. Gen. ed. Henry Louis Gates, Jr. New York: Oxford University Press, 198?.

———. *Hagar's Daughters* and Others. *The Colored Magazine* March

1901–November 1903; Introd. Hazel V. Carby. In *The Schomburg Library of Nineteenth-Century Black Women Writers* series. Gen. ed. Henry Louis Gates, Jr. New York: Oxford University Press, 1988.

———. "Of One Blood" Or, "The Hidden Self." *Colored American Magazine.* (Began novel in 1902; it ran for 12 installments)

Hunter, Helen. *Magnificent White Men.* New York: Vantage Press, 1964. (science fiction)

Hunter, Kristin. *God Bless the Child.* New York: Scribner's, 1964.

———. *Guests in the Promised Land.* New York: Scribner's, 1973.

———. *The Lakestown Rebellion.* New York: Scribner's, 1978.

———. *The Soul Brothers and Sister Lou.* New York: Scribner's, 1968 (1969).

———. *The Survivors.* New York: Scribner's, 1975

Hurston, Zora Neale. *Jonah's Gourd Vine.* Philadelphia: Lippincott, 1934.

———. *Moses, Man of the Mountain.* Philadelphia: Lippincott, 1939.

———. *Moses, Man of the Mountain.* Introd. Blyden Jackson. Champaign, IL: University of Illinois Press, 1984.

———. *Seraph on the Suwanee.* New York: Scribner's, 1948.

———. *Tell My Horse.* Philadelphia: Lippincott, 1938.

———. *Their Eyes Were Watching God.* Philadelphia: Lippincott, 1937; (1969); Foreword by Sherley Anne Williams. Champaign, IL: University of Illinois Press, 1978.

Johnson, Mrs. A. E. *Clarence and Corinne.* 1890 Introd. Hortense J. Spillers in *The Schomburg Library of Nineteenth-Century Black Women Writers* series. Gen. ed Henry Louis Gates, Jr. New York: Oxford University Press, 1988.

————. *The Hazeley Family*. American Baptist Publication Society, 1894; with introd. by Barbara Christian in *The Schomburg Library of Nineteenth-Century Black Women Writers* series. Gen. ed. Henry Louis Gates, Jr. New York: Oxford University Press, 1988.

Jones, Gayl. *Corregidora*. New York: Random House, 1975.

————. *Eva's Man*. New York: Random House, 1976.

Jones, Nettie. *Mischief Makers*. New York: Weidenfeld, 1989.

Jordan, June. *His Own Where*. New York: Dell, 1971.

Jourdain, Rose. *Those the Sun Has Loved*. New York: Doubleday, 1978.

Larsen, Nella. *Passing*. New York and London: Knopf, 1929.

————. *Quicksand*. New York and London: Knopf, 1928; New York: Macmillan, 1971.

————. *Quicksand* and *Passing*. Ed. Deborah McDowell. New Brunswick: Rutgers University Press, 1988.

Lee, Andrea. *Sara Phillips*. New York: Penguin Books, 1984.

Lee, Audrey. *The Clarion People*. New York: McGraw-Hill, 1968.

————. *The Workers*. New York: McGraw-Hill, 1969.

McMillan, Terry. *Mama*. Boston: Houghton Mifflin, 1987.

————. *Waiting to Exhale*. New York: Viking, 1992.

Marshall, Paule. *Brown Girl, Brownstones*. New York: Random House, 1959.

————. *Daughters*. New York: Atheneum, forthcoming.

————. *Praisesong for the Widow*. New York: Putnam's, 1983.

————. *The Chosen Place, the Timeless People*. New York: Harcourt, 1969.

Mathis, Sharon Bell. *Listen for the Fig Tree.* New York: Avon, 1975.

Meriwether, Louise. *Daddy Was a Number Runner.* Introd. James Baldwin. Afterword Nellie McKay. New York: Pyramid Books, 1970; Old Westbury: Feminist Press, 1986.

Monroe, Mary. *The Upper Room.* New York: St. Martin's Press, 1985.

Morrison, Toni. *Beloved.* New York: Knopf, 1987.

————. *Song of Solomon.* New York: Knopf, 1977; New York: New American Library, 1978.

————. *Sula.* New York: Knopf, 1974.

————. *Tar Baby.* New York: Knopf, 1981; New York: New American Library, 1983.

————. *The Bluest Eye.* New York: Holt, Rinehart and Winston, 1970.

————. *Jazz.* New York: Knopf, 1992.

Murray, Michele. *Nellie Cameron.* Drawings by Leonora Prince. New York: The Seabury Press, 1971.

Naylor, Gloria. *Linden Hills.* New York: Ticknor & Fields, 1985.

————. *Mama Day.* New York: Ticknor & Fields, 1988.

————. *The Women of Brewster Place.* New York: Viking Press, 1982; Penguin Books, 1983.

————. *Bailey's Cafe.* New York: Harcourt, Brace Jovanovich, 1992.

Nelson, Annie Greene. *After the Storm.* Columbia, SC: Hampton Publishing Co., 1942.

————. *The Dawn Appears.* Columbia, SC: Hampton Publishing Co., 1944.

Nunez-Harrell, Elizabeth. *When Rocks Dance.* New York: Putnam, 1986; New York: Ballantine Books, 1988.

Overstreet, Cleo. *The Boar Hog Woman.* New York: Doubleday, 1972.

Petry, Ann. *Country Place.* Boston: Houghton Mifflin, 1947.

————. *The Narrows.* Boston: Houghton Mifflin, 1953.

————. *The Street.* New York: Pyramid Books, 1961.

Phillips, Jane. *Mojo Hand.* New York: Trident Press, 1966.

Polite, Carlene Hatcher. *Sister X and the Victim of Foul Play.* New York: Farrar, Straus, and Giroux, 1975.

————. *The Flagellants.* New York: Farrar, Straus, and Giroux, 1967.

Potter, Valaida. *Sunrise over Alabama.* New York: Comet Press, 1959.

Randall, Florence E. *The Almost Years.* New York: Atheneum, 1971.

Roberson, Sadie. *Killer of the Dream.* New York: Carlton Press, 1963.

Robinson, Dorothy W. *The Legend of Africans.* Illust. Herbert Temple. Chicago: Johnson, 1974.

Shaw, Letty M. *Angel Mink.* New York: Comet Press, 1957.

Shockley, Ann Allen. *Loving Her.* Indianapolis: Bobbs-Merrill, 1974.

————. *Say Jesus and Come to Me.* New York: Avon, 1982.

———. *The Black and White of It*. Weathersby Lake, MO: Naiad Press, 1980.

Southerland, Ellease. *Let the Lion Eat Straw*. New York: Scribner's, 1979; New York: New American Library, 1980.

Spencer, Mary Etta. *The Resentment.* Philadelphia: A. M. E. Book Concern, 1921.

Turner, Olive May. *Medga*. Boston: James H. Early, 1892.

Vaught, Estella U. *Vengeance Is Mine*. New York: Comet Press, 1959.

Vroman, Mary Elizabeth. *Esther*. New York: Bantam, 1963.

———. *Harlem Summer*. New York: Berkley, 1968.

Walker, Alice. *Possessing the Secret of Joy*. New York: Harcourt Brace Jovanovich, 1992.

Walker, Margaret. *Jubilee*. Boston: Houghton Mifflin, 1966.

Wallace, Elizabeth West. *Scandal at Daybreak*. New York: Pageant Press, 1954.

Washington, Doris V. *Yulan*. New York: Carlton Press, 1964.

West, Dorothy. *The Living in Easy*. Boston: Houghton Mifflin, 1948.

Wood, Lillian E. *Let My People Go*. Philadelphia: A. M. E. Book Concern, 1922.

Woods, Odella Phelps. *High Ground*. New York: Exposition Press, 1945.

Wright, Sarah E. *This Child's Gonna Live*. New York: Delacorte, 1969.

Wright, Zara. *Black and White Tangled Threads*. Chicago: Privately printed, 1920.

Short Stories

Alba, Nanina. "A Scary Story." *Negro Digest* 15 (July 1966): 65–68.

―――. "So Quaint." *Negro Digest* 13 (Feb. 1964): 76–79.

Bambara, Toni Cade. *Gorilla, My Love.* New York: Random House, 1960.

―――. "The Lesson." *Redbook's Famous Fiction.* N.p.: The Redbook Publishing Company, 1977.

Bambara, Toni Cade, ed. *Tales and Stories for Black Folks.* New York: Doubleday, 1971.

Banks, Brenda. "Like It Is." *Black World* 20 (June 1971): 53–57.

Bates, Arthenia. *Seeds Beneath the Snow: Vignettes from the South.* Washington, DC: Howard University Press, 1975.

Brooks, Gwendolyn. "Lincoln West." *New Writing by American Negroes, 1940–1962.* Sel., ed., introd., biographical notes by Herbert Hill. New York: Knopf, 1968.

Burroughs, Margaret. " 'Strawberry Blonde' That Is." *Black World* 19.9 (July 1970): 78–81.

Childress, Alice. "Mojo: A Black Love Story." *Black World* 20.6 (Apr. 1971): 54–82.

―――. "The Health Card" and "I Go To a Funeral." *Harlem, U.S.A.* Ed. and introd. John Henrik Clarke. Berlin: Seven Seas Publishers, 1964.

Clifton, Lucille. "The Magic Mama." *Redbook's Famous Fiction.* N.p.: The Redbook Publishing Company, 1977.

Collier, Eugenia. "Marigolds." *Black World* 19.9 (Nov. 1969): 54–62; *Brothers and Sisters.* Ed. Arnold Adoff. New York: Dell, 1970.

―――. "Sinbad the Cat." *Black World* 20.9 (July 1971): 53–55.

————. "Sweet Potato Pie." *Black World* 21.10 (Aug. 1972): 54–62.

Crayton, Pearl. "Cotton Alley." *Brothers and Sisters.* Ed. Arnold Adoff. New York: Dell, 1970.

Dove, Rita. *Fifth Sunday.* Callaloo Fiction Series. Lexington, KY: University of Kentucky, 1985.

Dunbar-Nelson, Alice (Moore). "His Great Career." *The Works of Alice Dunbar-Nelson.* Volume 3. Ed. Gloria T. Hull. *The Schomburg Library of Nineteenth-Century Black Women Writers* series. Gen. ed. Henry Louis Gates, Jr. New York: Oxford University Press, 1988.

————. "Hope Deferred." *Crisis* 8 (Sep. 1914): 238–242; *The Works of Alice Dunbar-Nelson.* Volume 3. Ed. Gloria T. Hull. *The Schomburg Library of Nineteenth-Century Black Women Writers* series. Gen. ed. Henry Louis Gates, Jr. New York: Oxford University Press, 1988.

————. "Mrs. Newly Wed and Her Servant." *The Works of Alice Dunbar-Nelson.* Volume 3. Ed. Gloria T. Hull. *The Schomburg Library of Nineteenth-Century Black Women Writers* series. Gen. ed. Henry Louis Gates, Jr. New York: Oxford University Press, 1988.

————. "No Sacrifice." *The Works of Alice Dunbar-Nelson.* Volume 3. Ed. Gloria T. Hull. *The Schomburg Library of Nineteenth-Century Black Women Writers* series. Gen. ed. Henry Louis Gates, Jr. New York: Oxford University Press, 1988.

————. "Science in Frenchtown—A Short Story." *The Saturday Evening Mail* Magazine Section (7 Dec. 1912): 8–9, 26, 27.

————. "The Ball Dress." *Leslie's Weekly* 93 (12 Dec. 1901); *The Works of Alice Dunbar-Nelson.* Volume 3. Ed. Gloria T. Hull. *The Schomburg Library of Nineteenth-Century Black Women Writers* series. Gen ed. Henry Louis Gates, Jr. New York: Oxford University Press, 1988.

————. *The Goodness of St. Rocque and Other Stories.* New York: Dodd, Mead and Company, 1899; Baltimore: McGrath Publishers, 1969; *The Works of Alice Dunbar-Nelson.* Volume 1. Ed. Gloria T. Hull. *The Schomburg Library of Nineteenth-Century*

Black Women Writers series. Gen. ed. Henry Louis Gates, Jr. New York: Oxford University Press, 1988.

————. "The Little Mother." Brooklyn, NY: *Standard Union* 7 Mar. 1900. Paul Laurence Dunbar Papers, Ohio Historical Society (Roll 5, frame 0046).

————. *Violets and Other Tales.* Boston: *The Monthly Review,* 1895; *The Works of Alice Dunbar-Nelson.* Volume 1. Ed. Gloria T. Hull. *The Schomburg Library of Nineteenth-Century Black Women Writers* series. Gen. ed. Henry Louis Gates, Jr. New York: Oxford University Press, 1988.

Dunham, Katherine. "Afternoon into the Night." *The Best Short Stories by Negro Writers: An Anthology from 1899 to the Present.* Ed. Langston Hughes. Boston: Little, Brown, 1967.

Evans, Mari. *JD.* New York: Doubleday, 1975.

Fauset, Jessie R. "The Meal." *Afro-American Voices, 1770s-1970s.* Ed. Ralph Kendricks and Claudette Levitt. Los Angeles: Oxford Book Co., 1970. (From *Chinaberry Tree*)

Franklin, J. E. "The Enemy." *Black Short Story Anthology.* Ed. Woodie King. New York: New American Library, 1972.

Greenfield, Eloise. "A Tooth for an Eye." *Black World* 9.19 (July 1970): 70, 77.

————. "Dream Panoply." *Black World* 3.19 (Jan. 1970): 54–58.

Hunter, Kristin. "Debut." *Black American Literature: Fiction.* Ed. Darwin T. Turner. Columbus, OH: Charles Merrill, 1969.

————. *Guests in the Promised Land.* New York: Scribner's, 1975.

Hurston, Zora Neale. "Drenched in Light." *Opportunity* 2 (Dec. 1924): 371–374.

————. "John Redding Goes to Sea." *Opportunity* 4 (Jan. 1926): 16–21.

————. *Spunk.* Berkeley: Turtle Island Foundation, 1985.

———. "Spunk." *Opportunity* 3 (May 1925): 171–173.

———. "Sweat." *Black American Literature: Essays, Poetry, Fiction, Drama.* Ed. Darwin T. Turner. Columbus, OH: Merrill, 1970.

———. "The Gilded Six-Bits." *Story in America.* Eds. Whit Burnett and Martha Foley. New York: Vanguard, 1934.

Jackson, Mae. "I Remember Omar." *Black World* 18:8 (June 1969): 83–85.

Jones, Gayl. "Spaces." *Black Scholar* 9.6 (June 1975): 53–55.

———. *White Rat.* New York: Random House, 1977.

Jones, Lois Amis. "Buddy: A Portrait in Black" and "Till Fen Comes Back." *Exploring the Black Experience in America.* New York: F. Peters, 1976.

Jones, Lola Amis. *Exploring the Black Experience in America: A Bicentennial Edition of Plays and Short Stories: 1976.* New York: F. Peters, 1976.

Jordan, June. "Stories for Free Children: 'New Life, New Room.' " *Ms.* 3.11 (May 1975): 55–58.

Lee, Audrey. "Alienation." *Black World* 21.1 (Nov. 1971): 64–66.

———. "I'm Going to Move Out of This Emotional Ghetto." *Black World* 2.19 (Dec. 1969): 63–68.

———. "Moma." *Black World* 4.18 (Feb. 1969): 64–65.

———. "The Black." *Black World* 12.19 (Oct. 1970): 64–72.

Marshall, Paule. "Reena." *Harper's Magazine* 335 (Oct. 1962): 154–164; also *The Black Woman.* Ed. Toni Cade. New York: New American Library, 1970; also *Black-Eyed Susans.* Ed. Mary Helen Washington. New York: Doubleday, 1975.

———. *Reena and Other Stories.* Old Westbury, NY: Feminist Press, 1983.

————. "Some Get Wasted." *Harlem, U. S. A.* Ed. and Introd. John Henrik Clarke. Berlin: Seven Seas Publishers, 1964.

Moody, Anne. *Mr. Death: Four Stories.* New York: Harper, 1975.

Oliver, Diane. "Neighbors." *Black Voices.* Ed. Abraham Chapman. New York: New American Library (Mentor), 1968.

Petry, Ann. "Harlem." *Holiday* (Apr. 1949).

————. "In Darkness and Confusion." *Black Voices.* Ed. Abraham Chapman. New York: New American Library (Mentor), 1968.

————. *Miss Muriel and Other Stories.* Boston: Houghton Mifflin, 1971.

Rodgers, Carolyn. "A Statistic Trying to Make It Home." *Black World* 18.8 (June 1969): 68–71.

————. " 'Walk Wid Jesus.' " *Essence* (Apr. 1972): 39, 71, 80.

Sanchez, Sonia, ed. *We Be Word Sorcerers: 25 Stories by Black Americans.* New York: Bantam, 1973.

Shockley, Ann Allen. "A Far Off Sound." *Umbra* 2 (Dec. 1963): 11–17.

————. "Is She Relevant?" *Black World* 15.3 (Jan. 1971): 58–65.

————. "To Be a Man." *Black World* 18.9 (July 1969): 54–65.

Smith, Jean. "Something-to-Eat." *Black World* 20.8 (June 1971): 70–76.

Vroman, Mary Elizabeth. "See How They Run." *The Best Short Stories by Negro Writers.* Ed. and Introd. Langston Hughes. Boston: Little, Brown, 1967.

Washington, Mary Helen, ed. *Black-Eyed Susans: Classic Stories by and About Black Women.* New York: Anchor Books, 1975.

West, Dorothy. "The Richer, the Poorer." *The Best Short Stories by Negro Writers.* Ed. and Introd. Langston Hughes. Boston: Little, Brown, 1967.

Young, Carrie Allen. "Adjoo Means Goodbye." *Beyond the Angry Black.* Ed. John A. Williams. New York: New American Library, 1966.

Plays

Amis, Lola Jones. *Helen. Three Plays,* by Lola Amis. New York: Exposition Press, 1965.

————. *The Other Side of the Wall. Three Plays,* by Lola Amis. New York: Exposition Press, 1965.

————. *The Places of Wrath. Three Plays,* by Lola Amis. New York: Exposition Press, 1965.

Bonner, Marita. *The Purple Flower. Black Theater, U. S. A.: Forty-Five Plays by Black Americans.* Ed. James V. Hatch, Cons. Ted Shine. New York: The Free Press, 1974.

Burrill, Mary. *They That Sit in Darkness. Black Theater, U. S. A.: Forty-Five Plays by Black Americans.* Ed. James V. Hatch, Cons. Ted Shine. New York: The Free Press, 1974.

Childress, Alice. *A Hero Ain't Nothin' but a Sandwich.* Produced by Radnitz & Mattel, 1977; Released by New World, 1978. (Television script, adapted from the novel)

————. *Florence: A One-Act Drama. Masses and Mainstream* 3 (Oct. 1950): 34–47.

————. "Gold Through the Trees." 1952. (Unpublished)

————. *Just a Little Simple.* Prod. Committee for the Negro in the Arts, at Club Baron in Harlem, September 1950.

————. *Let's Hear It for the Queen: A Play.* Illust. Loring Eutemey. New York: Coward, McCann, and Geoghegan, 1976.

————. "Mojo: A Black Love Story." *Black World* 20.6 (Apr. 1971): 54–82; New York: Dramatists Play Service, 1971.

————. *Mojo and String: Two Plays.* New York: Dramatists Play Service, 1971.

————. *The World on a Hill. Plays to Remember.* New York: Macmillan, 1968.

————. *Trouble in Mind. Black Theater.* Ed. Lindsay Patterson. New York: Dodd, Mead and Company, 1971. (comedy)

————. *Wedding Band: A Love/Hate Story in Black and White.* New York: French, 1973.

————. *When the Rattlesnake Sounds: A Play about Harriet Tubman.* New York: Coward, McCann, and Geoghegan, 1975.

————. *Wine in the Wilderness.* c. 1949. *Black Theater, U. S. A.: Forty-Five Plays by Black Americans.* Ed. James V. Hatch, Consultant Ted Shine. New York: The Free Press, 1974. 737–755.

Collins, Kathleen. (also Prettyman). *In the Midnight Hour.* Full-length drama produced at the Richard Allen Center for Culture and Art's International Black Festival, New York, 1982. Dir. Duane Jones.

————. *Only the Sky Is Free.* Richard Allen Center for Culture and Arts, 1986. (life of Bessie Coleman, first Black aviatrix)

————. *Portrait of Kathleen* (originally *Portrait of Katherine*) and *Almost Music* (musical fantasy in 5 acts), 1974.

————. *The Brothers.* 3 acts, produced at the Kuntu Repertory Theatre, Pittsburg, 1982. Dir. Dr. Vernell Lillie; produced at APT, Off-Broadway, 1982. Dir. Billie Allen; produced at the Richard Allen Center for Culture and Art's International Black Theatre Festival, New York, 1982. *Plays-in-Process* 1982–83; *The Woman's Project Anthology* (2nd), 1984; Wilkerson, Margaret. *9 Plays by Black Women,* 1986.

DeVeaux, Alexis. *The Tapestry.* 2 acts. 1976.

Dunbar-Nelson, Alice Ruth (Moore). "Gone White" and "Love's Disguise." *The Works of Alice Dunbar-Nelson.* Volume 3. Ed.

Gloria Hull. *The Schomburg Library of Nineteenth-Century Black Women Writers* series. Gen. ed. Henry Louis Gates, Jr. New York: Oxford University Press, 1988. (film scenario)

————. "Mine Eyes Have Seen." *The Crisis* 15 (Apr. 1918): 271–275; *The Dunbar Speaker and Entertainer*. Ed. Alice Dunbar-Nelson. Naperville, IL: J. L. Nichols, 1920; *Black Theater, U. S. A.: Forty-Five Plays by Black Americans*. Ed. James V. Hatch, Consultant Ted Shine. New York: The Free Press, 1974; *The Works of Alice Dunbar-Nelson*. Volume 3. Ed. Gloria Hull. *The Schomburg Library of Nineteenth-Century Black Women Writers* series. Gen. ed. Henry Louis Gates, Jr. New York: Oxford University Press, 1988.

————. "The Author's Evening at Home." *The Smart Set* (Sep. 1900): 105–106; *The Works of Alice Dunbar-Nelson*. Volume 3. Ed. Gloria Hull. *The Schomburg Library of Nineteenth-Century Black Women Writers* series. Gen. ed. Henry Louis Gates, Jr. New York: Oxford University Press, 1988.

Fields, Julia. *All Day Tomorrow*. Performed at Knoxville College, May 1966.

Gaines-Shelton, Ruth. *The Church Flight. Black Theater, U.S.A.: Forty-Five Plays by Black Americans*. Ed. James V. Hatch, Consultant Ted Shine. New York: The Free Press, 1974.

Goss, Clay. *Homecookin': Five Plays*. Washington, DC: Howard University Press, 1974.

Graham, Shirley. *Cool Dust*. Karamu Theatre. (Unpublished)

————. *Elijah's Ravens*. Karamu Theater. (Unpublished)

————. *It's Morning*. (Unpublished)

————. *Track Thirteen*. Boston: Expression Co., 1940.

Grimke, Angelina. *Rachel*. Boston: Corhill Co., 1920.

Hansberry, Lorraine. *A Raisin in the Sun*. New York: New American Library, 1959.

———. "Les Blancs," "The Drinking Gourd," and "What Use Are Flowers?" *Les Blancs: Collected Last Plays of Lorraine Hansberry.* Ed. Robert Nemiroff. New York: Random House, 1972.

———. *The Sign in Sidney Brustein's Window.* New York: New American Library, 1966.

———. *To Be Young, Gifted, and Black.* Adapt. Robert Nemiroff. Englewood Cliffs, NJ: Prentice-Hall, 1969.

Harrison, Paul Careter. *Totem Voices: Eight Plays from the Black World Repertory.* New York: Grove Press, 1989.

Hopkins, Pauline Elizabeth. *Slaves' Escape* Or, *The Underground Railroad.* Boston, Oakland Garden, 5 July 1880; ed. and rev. as *Peculiar Sam* or, *The Underground Railroad,* n.d. (musical)

Huntley, Elizabeth Maddox. *What Ye Sow.* New York: Court, 1955.

Hurston, Zora Neale. *Great Day.* N.p.: N.p., 1927.

———. "Mulebone: A Comedy of Negro Life in Three Acts," by Langston Hughes and Zora Neale Hurston. New York, 1931. (Unpublished)

———. "Polk County, A Comedy of Negro Life on a Sawmill Camp." (Unpublished)

———. "The First One: A Play." *Ebony and Topaz, A Collection.* Ed. Charles S. Johnson. New York: National Urban League, 1927.

Hurston, Zora Neale, Clinton Fletcher, and Tim Moore. "Fast and Furious." *The Best Plays of 1932–33 and The Year Book of the Drama in America.* New York: Dodd, Mead and Company, 1933.

Hurston, Zora Neale, and Dorothy Waring. *Polk County, a Comedy of Negro Life in a Sawmill Camp.* N.p.: n.p, 1927.

Jackson, Elaine. "Toe Jam." *Black Drama Anthology.* Eds. Woodie King and Ron Milner. New York: Columbia University Press, 1972.

Johnson, Georgia Douglas. *A Sunday Morning in the South. Black Theater, U. S. A.: Forty-Five Plays by Black Americans*. Ed. James V. Hatch, Consultant Ted Shine. New York: The Free Press, 1974.

————. *Blue Blood. Fifty More Contemporary One-Act Plays*. Ed. Frank Shay. New York: Appleton & Co., 1928.

————. *Frederick Douglass. Negro History in Thirteen Plays*. Eds. Willis Richardson and May Miller. Washington, DC: Associated Publishers, 1935.

————. "Plumes." *Plays of Negro Life*. Eds. Alain Locke and Montgomery Gregory. New York: Harper, 1927.

————. "William and Ellen Craft." *Negro History in Thirteen Plays*. Washington, DC: Associated Publishers, 1935.

Jones, Lola Amis. *Exploring the Black Experience in America: A Bicentennial Edition of Plays and Short Stories: 1976*. New York: F. Peters, 1976.

Kennedy, Adrienne. *A Beast's Story*. N.p, N.p., 1966.

————. *A Lesson in a Dead Language*. N.p, N.p., 1964.

————. "A Rat's Mass." *New Black Playwrights*. Ed. William Couch, Jr. Baton Rouge, LA: Louisiana State University Press, 1968.

————. "Funnyhouse of a Negro." *Black Drama: An Anthology*. Eds. William Brasmer and Dominick Consolo. Columbus, OH: Charles Merrill, 1970.

————. *One Act*. Minneapolis: The University of Minnesota Press, 1988. (Plays and autobiography)

————. *The Owl Answers*. N.p, N.p., 1963.

Livingston, Myrtle Smith. *For Unborn Children. Black Theater, U. S. A.: Forty-Five Plays by Black Americans*. Ed. James V. Hatch, Consultant Ted Shine. New York: The Free Press, 1974.

Mason, Judi. "A Star Ain't Nothin' But a Hole in Heaven." Produced at Grambling State University, Grambling, Louisiana, 1976.

———. *Livin' Fat.* Produced at Grambling State University, Grambling, Louisiana, n.d.; produced by the Negro Ensemble Company, New York, June 1–18, 1976.

McCray, Nettie (Salimu). "Growin' into Blackness." *New Plays from the Black Theatre.* Ed. Ed Bullins. New York: Bantam, 1969.

Miller, Laura Ann. *Git Away from Here, Irvine, Now Git.* N.p, N.p., 1969.

———. *The Cricket Cries.* N.p, N.p., 1967.

———. *The Echo of Sound.* N.p, N.p., 1967.

Miller, May. "Harriet Tubman." *Negro in Thirteen Plays.* Washington, DC: Associated Publishers, 1935.

———. "Riding the Goat." *Plays and Pageants from the Life of the Negro.* Ed. Willis Patterson. Washington, DC: Associated Publishers, 1930.

———. "Scratches." *Carolina Magazine* Apr. 1929.

Sanchez, Sonia. *I'm Black When I'm Singing, I'm Blue When I Ain't.* Atlanta: Jonathan Productions, 1982; performed for M. F. A. Thesis at Virginia Commonwealth University, 1985.

———. "Sister Son/Ji." *New Plays from the Black Theatre.* Ed. Ed Bullins. New York: Bantam, 1969.

———. *The Bronx Is Next. Drama Review.* Summer 1968.

Smith, Jean. "O. C.'s Heart." *Black World* 6.19 (Apr. 1970): 56–76.

Spence, Eulalie. *Fool's Errand.* New York: Samuel French, 1927.

————. *Foreign Mail.* New York: French, 1927.

————. "Help Wanted," *Saturday Evening Quill.* Boston: N.p., 1929.

————. *The Hunch. Opportunity Magazine* Apr. 1929.

————. "The Starter." *Plays of Negro Life.* Eds. Alain Locke and Montgomery Gregory. New York: Harper, 1927.

————. "Undertow." *Black Theatre, U. S. A.* Ed. James V. Hatch. New York: The Free Press, 1974.

Thomas, Veona. *Martin Luther King—A Personal Look.* Performed at Temple Emmanuel, Saddle Brook, NJ, January 1985.

————. *Nzinga's Children.* (2 acts) Prod. National Black Theatre, Flint, MI, February 1986.

Thompson, Eloise Bibb. *Africannus.* Los Angeles: n.p., 1922.

————. *Caught.* Chicago: n.p., 1925.

————. *Cooped Up.* New York: n.p., 1925.

Tillman, Katherine D. Thirty Years After Freedom. [N.p.]: [n.p., n.d.]

Townsend, Willa A. *Because He Lives: A Drama of Resurrection.* Nashville: Sunday School Publishers, Board of the National Baptist Convention, 1924.

Walker, Lucy. *Blood, Booze and Booty.* Prod. Eden Theatrical Workshop, Denver, at the Changing Scene Theater, 1975. (Bicentennial play)

————. *Social Action in One-Act Plays.* Denver: Lucy Walker, 1970.

Wilkerson, Margaret B., ed. and introd. *9 Plays by Black Women.* New York: New American Library (Mentor), 1986.

Wilson, Alice T. *How an American Poet Made Money.* New York: Pageant, 1968.

Poems

Amini, Johari (Jewel C. Latimore). "Folk Fable." *Black Arts.* Ed. Ahmed Alhamsi and Harun Kofi Wangaga. Introd. Keorapetse Kgoisitsile. Detroit: Black Arts Publications, 1969.

————. *Images in Black.* Chicago: Third World Press, 1969.

————. *Let's Go Somewhere.* Chicago: Third World Press, 1970.

Anderson, Mignon Holland. *Mostly Womenfolk and a Man or Two: A Collection.* Chicago: Third World Press, forthcoming.

Arthur, Barbara. *Common Sense Poetry.* Berkeley: Respect International Enterprises, 1969.

Avotoja. "A Soulful Sister." *Glide In/Out* 4 (Apr. 1972): 1.

Bennett, Gwendolyn B. "Hatred" and "Heritage." *American Negro Poetry.* Ed. Arna Bontemps. New York: Hill & Wang, 1963.

Bibb, Eloise. *Poems.* Boston: The Monthly Review Press, 1895.

Black Songs Series I: Four Poetry Broadsides by Black Women. Detroit: Lotus Press, 1977.

Bragg, Linda Brown. *A Love Song to Black Men.* Detroit: Broadside Press, 1974.

Brooks, Gwendolyn. *Annie Allen.* New York: Harper, 1949.

————. *A Street in Bronzeville.* New York: Harper, 1945.

————. *Bronzveville Boys and Girls.* New York: Harper, 1956.

————. *Family Pictures.* Detroit: Broadside Press, 1970.

————. "Medgar Evers." *Beyond the Angry Black.* Ed. John A. Williams. New York: New American Library, 1966.

————. *Reckonings.* Detroit: Broadside Press, 1975.

———. *Riot.* Detroit: Broadside Press, 1969.

———. *Selected Poems.* New York: Harper, 1960.

———. *The Bean Eaters.* New York: Harper, 1960.

———. "The Life of Lincoln West." *New Writing by American Negroes, 1940–1962.* Sel., ed., introd., biog. notes by Herbert Hill. New York: Knopf, 1968.

———. *The World of Gwendolyn Brooks: A Street in Bronzeville, Annie Allen, Maud Martha, The Bean Eaters, In the Mecca.* New York: Harper, 1971.

Brown, Mrs. Sarah Lee (Fleming). *Clouds and Sunshine.* Boston: The Cornhill Co., 1920.

Burrell, Evelyn Patterson. *Weep No More.* Philadelphia: The Burton Johns Publishing Co., 1973.

Butler, Anna L. *Touch Stone.* Wilmington, DE: Poetry Center, 1961.

Capdeville, Annetta Elam. *My Soul Sings: Lyrics.* Washington, DC: Author, 1978.

Chase-Riboud, Barbara. *From Memphis & Peking.* New York: Random House, 1974.

———. *Love Perfecting, Poems.* New York: Viking Press, 1979.

Clark, Cheryl. *Narratives: Poems in the Tradition of Black Women.* Latham, NY: Kitchen Table: Women of Color Press, 1983.

Clifford, Carrie. *The Widening Light.* Boston: Walter Reid Co., 1922.

Clinton, Gloria. *Trees Along the Highway.* New York: Comet Press, 1953.

Cobb, Pamela. *Inside the Devil's Mouth: First Poems.* Detroit: Lotus Press, 1974.

Collier, Eugenia. "Barbados." *Black World* 5.25 (Mar. 1976): 53.

Cumbo, Kattie M. "Africa Beauty Rose," "Washiri," "Age," "All Hung Up," "Domestics," "Another Time, Another Place," "Bahamas—I," "Bahamas—II," "Black Goddess," "Consumed (for Brother Leroi)," "Dark People," "A Song from Brooklyn," "Malcolm," "Black Sister," and others. *Nine Black Poets*. Ed. R. Baird Shuman. Durham, NC: Moore Publishing Co., 1968.

Curry, Linda. "Death Prosecuting" and "No Way Out." *Soulscript*. Ed. June Jordan. New York: Doubleday, 1970.

Danner, Margaret. *Impressions of African Art Forms*. Detroit: Broadside Press, 1960.

———. *Iron Lace*. Millbrook, NY: Kriya Press, 1968.

———. *To Flower*. Nashville: Hemphill Press, 1962.

Davis, Gloria. "To Egypt." *The New Black Poets*. Ed. Clarence Majors. New York: International Publishers, 1969.

Davis, Thulani. *Playing the Changes*. Middletown, CT: Wesleyan University Press, 1985.

Dee, Ruby, ed. *Glowchild and Other Poems*. Chicago: Third World Press, 1972.

Deep Rivers, A Portfolio: 20 Contemporary Black American Poets (with Teacher's Guide by Naomi Long Madgett). Detroit: Lotus Press, 1978.

Dunbar-Nelson, Alice. "April Is on the Way." *Ebony and Topaz*. New York: National Urban League, 1927; *The Works of Alice Dunbar-Nelson*. Volume 2. Ed. Gloria Hull. *The Schomburg Library of Nineteenth-Century Black Women Writers* series. Gen. ed. Henry Louis Gates, Jr. New York: Oxford University Press, 1988.

———. "Chalmette." *The Dunbar Speaker and Entertainer*. Naperville, IL: J. L. Nichols, 1929; *The Works of Alice Dunbar-Nelson*. Volume 1. Ed. Gloria Hull. *The Schomburg Library of Nineteenth-Century Black Women Writers* series. Gen. ed. Henry Louis Gates, Jr. New York: Oxford University Press, 1988.

————. "Communion." *Opportunity* 3 (July 1925): 216; *The Works of Alice Dunbar-Nelson.* Volume 2. Ed. Gloria Hull. *The Schomburg Library of Nineteenth-Century Black Women Writers* series. Gen. ed. Henry Louis Gates, Jr. New York: Oxford University Press, 1988.

————. "Delta Sigma Theta, National Hymn." *The Official Ritual of Delta Sigma Theta Grand Chapter.* Washington, DC: Delta Sigma Theta Sorority, 1950.

————. "Forest Fire." *Harlem: A Forum of Negro Life* 1 (Nov. 1928): 22; *The Works of Alice Dunbar-Nelson.* Volume 2. Ed. Gloria Hull. *The Schomburg Library of Nineteenth-Century Black Women Writers* series. Gen. ed. Henry Louis Gates, Jr. New York: Oxford University Press, 1988.

————. "I Sit and Sew." *Negro Poets and Their Poems.* Ed. Robert Kerlin. Washington, DC: Associated Publishers, 1898. Alice Dunbar Papers, Ohio Historical Society (Roll 6, frame 0871); *The Works of Alice Dunbar-Nelson.* Volume 2. Ed. Gloria Hull. *The Schomburg Library of Nineteenth-Century Black Women Writers* series. Gen. ed. Henry Louis Gates, Jr. New York: Oxford University Press, 1988.

————. "Sonnet" (also listed as "Violets"). *Crisis* Aug. 1917: 193.

————. "Summit and Vale." *Lippincott's Magazine* Dec. 1902: 715.

————. "The Lights at Carney's Point." *The Dunbar Speaker and Entertainer.* Ed. Alice Dunbar-Nelson. Naperville, IL: J. L. Nichols, 1920.

————. "To Madame Curie." *Public Ledger* (Philadelphia), 21 Aug. 1921.

————. "To the Negro Farmers of the United States." *The Dunbar Speaker and Entertainer.* Ed. Alice Dunbar-Nelson. Naperville, IL: J. L. Nichols, 1920.

Elliott, Emily. *Still Waters and Other Poems.* Cambridge: The Author, 1949.

Evans, Mari. "Coventry," "Black Jam for Dr. Negro," "My Man Let Me Pull Your Coat," "Status Symbol," "The Emancipation of

George-Hector (A Colored Turtle)." *Black Voices*. Ed. Abraham Chapman. New York: New American Library, 1968.

———. "I Am a Black Woman." New York: Morrow, 1970.

———. "I'm With You." *Negro Digest* 17 (May 1968): 31–36.

———. *Nightstar*. Illust. Nelson Stevens. Los Angeles: University of California, Los Angeles Center for Afro-American Studies, 1981.

———. *Where Is All the Music?* London: Paul Breman, Ltd., 1968.

Fauset, Jessie Redmond. "Christmas Eve in France," "Dead Firs," "Oriflamme," "Oblivion." *Book of American Negro Poetry*. Ed. James Weldon Johnson. New York: Harcourt, 1959.

Faust, Naomi. *Speaking in Verse*. Boston: Branden Press, 1975.

Fields, Julia. "A Poem for Heroes," "Boats in Winter," "If Love Dies," "And Beauty's All Around," "Chopin Deciphered," "The Generations," "Eulogy for Philosophers," and others. *Nine Black Poets*. Ed. R. Baird Shuman. Durham, NC: Moore Publishing Co., 1968.

———. "Alabama Suite." *Black World* 4 (Feb. 1975): 40–47.

———. *East of Moonlight*. Charlotte, NC: Red Clay Books, 1972.

———. *Poems*. Millbrook, NY: Krieger Press, 1968.

———. *Slow Coins*. Washington, DC: Three Continents Press, 1981.

Fordham, Mary Weston. *Magnolia Leaves: Poems*. Tuskegee Institute, AL: Department of Records and Research, 1897.

Giovanni, Nikki. *Black Feeling, Black Talk*. Detroit: Broadside Press, 1968.

———. *Black Feeling, Black Talk/Black Judgment*. New York: William Morrow, 1970.

———. *Black Judgment*. Detroit: Broadside Press, 1969.

————. *Cotton Candy on a Rainy Day*. New York: Quill, 1980.

————. *My House*. New York: Morrow, 1972.

————. *Night Comes Softly* [editor]. New York: Nik-Tom Publications, 1970.

————. *Poem of Angela Yvonne Davis*. Detroit: Niktom, Ltd. Broadside Poem, 1970.

————. *Re-Creation*. Detroit: Broadside Press, 1970.

————. "The Planet of Junior Brown." *Black World* 21.6 (Mar. 1972): 70–71.

————. *The Women and the Men*. New York: William Morrow, 1975.

————. *Those Who Ride the Night Winds*. New York: William Morrow, 1983.

Gregory, Carole. "David," "Migration," "NYC Love Poem," "Love Poem," "The Cosmic Attack on Poets," "Love from My Father," "Black Eurydice," "People," and others. *Nine Black Poets*. Ed. R. Baird Shuman. Durham, NC: Moore Publishing Co., 1968.

Grimke, Angelina W. "A Mona Lisa." *Black Writers of America*. Ed. Richard Barksdale and Kenneth Kinnamon. New York: Macmillan, 1972.

————. "Hushed by the Hands of Sleep," "Surrender," "When the Green Lies Over the Earth," "A Winter Twilight." *The Negro Caravan*. Eds. Sterling Brown et al. New York: Arno Press, 1970.

Grosvenor, Kali. *Poems by Kali*. Introd. William Melvin Kelley. Photog. Joan Nalifax and Robert Fletcher. New York: Doubleday, 1970.

Hansberry, Lorraine. "Flag from a Kitchenette Window." *Masses and Mainstream* 3 (Sep. 1950): 38–40.

————. "For a Young Negro I Have Met, A Love Song" and "Interim." *To Be Young, Gifted and Black: Lorraine Hansberry in*

Her Own Words. Adapted by Robert Nemiroff, with original drawings and art by Miss Hansberry. Introd. James Baldwin. Englewood Cliffs, NJ: Prentice-Hall, 1969. 80–81, 90.

———. "Lynchsong." *Masses and Mainstream* 4 (July 1951): 19–20.

Harper, Frances. *Atlanta Offering Poems.* Philadelphia: George S. Ferguson, 1895.

———. *Poems.* Philadelphia: Merryhew & Sons, 1871.

Harper, Frances E. "Bury Me in a Free Land," "Ethiopia," "President Lincoln's Proclamation of Freedom," "Fifteenth Amendment." *Early Negro American Writers.* Ed. Benjamin Brawley. New York: Dover Press, 1970.

———. "Eliza," "Bury Me in a Free Land," "Let the Light Enter," "The Slave Auction." *The Negro Caravan.* Eds. Sterling Brown et al. New York: Arno Press, 1970.

———. *Poems on Miscellaneous Subjects.* Boston: J. B. Yerringon and Son, 1854.

———. "The Colored People in America (1854)." *Afro-American Voices 1770's-1970's.* Eds. Ralph Kendricks and Claudette Levitt. Los Angeles: Oxford Book Co., 1970.

Harper, Frances E. W. *Moses, a Story of the Nile.* Philadelphia: printed by Merrihew, 1864; enl. Philadelphia: privately printed, 1889; enl. as *Idylls of the Bible,* Philadelphia: privately printed, 1901.

———. *Sketches of Southern Life.* Philadelphia: Merrihew & Sons, 1872.

Harrison, Hazel Clayton, ed. *Bearers of Blackness.* Robbinsdale, MN: Guild Press (Box 22583), 1987.

Hightower, Ruth. *From the Tower: Poetry and Reflections.* New York: Vantage, 1976.

House, Gloria. "Woman" and "Poem." *Black Arts.* Ed. Ahmed Alhamsi and Karun Kofi Wangara. Detroit: Black Arts Publications, 1969.

Howard, Vanessa. *A Screaming Whisper.* New York: Holt, Rinehart and Winston, 1972.

———. "Reflections" and "Monument in Black." *Afro-American Poetry.* Ed. June Jordan. New York: Doubleday, 1970.

[Humphrey], Myrtle Moss. *As Much As I Am.* Los Angeles: Capricorn House West, 1973.

———. "Be a Man . . . Boy," "On Love," "Shade of Difference," "Brother, Take My Hand," "Grits and Gravy." *Some Ground to Fall On.* Los Angeles: Vermont Square Writers Workshop sponsored by the Los Angeles Public Library under the auspices of the Federal Library Services and Construction Act Fund, 1971.

Hunt, Evelyn Tooley. *Toad-Song, A Collection of Haiku and Other Small Poems.* New York: Apple Press, 1966.

Ifetayo, Femi Fumni. *We the Black Woman.* Detroit: Black Arts Publications, 1970.

Jackson, Mae. *Can I Poet With You?* New York: Afro-Arts, 1969.

Jessye, Eva. *Selected Poems.* Pittsburg, KS: The Little Balkans Press, 1978.

———. "Spring with the Teacher," "The Singer," and "To a Rosebud." *Negro Poets and Their Poems.* Ed. Robert T. Kerlin. Washington, DC: Associated Publishers, 1923; 1927: 141–142.

Johnson, Alicia Loy. "Blue/Black Poems (or call them by their rightful names)," "On My Blk/ness," "A Black Poetry Day," "The Enemy of Man," "a day of PEACE, a day of peace," "The Long March." *Nine Black Poets.* Ed. R. Baird Shuman. Durham, NC: Moore Publishing Co., 1968.

Johnson, Georgia Douglas. *An Autumn Love Cycle.* New York: Neal, 1938.

———. "Black Woman," "Credo," "The Suppliant," "To William Stanley Braithwaite." *Black American Literature: Poetry.* Ed. Darwin T. Turner. Columbus, OH: Charles Merrill, 1969.

————. *Bronze: A Book of Verse.* Boston: Brimmer, 1922.

————. *The Heart of a Woman and Other Poems.* Boston: Cornhill, 1917; New York: AMS Press, 1975.

Johnson, Helene. "The Road," "Poem," "Invocation." *Negro Literature.* Ed. Arna Bontemps. New York: Hill & Wang, 1963.

Jones, Gayl. *Song for Anninho.* Ann Arbor: Lotus Press, 1981.

————. *The Hermit-Woman.* Detroit: Lotus Press, 1983.

————. "Tripart," "Many Die Here," "Satori." *Soulscript.* Ed. June Jordan. New York: Doubleday, 1970.

————. *Xarque and Other Poems.* Detroit: Lotus Press, 1985.

Jordan, June. *New Days: Poems of Exile and Return.* New York: Emerson Hall, 1976.

————. *Some Changes.* New York: E. P. Dutton, 1971.

————. *Who Look at Me?* Illust. with 27 paintings. New York: Crowell, 1969.

————, ed. *Soulscript: Afro-American Poetry.* New York: Doubleday, 1970.

Kendrick, Dolores. *Now Is the Thing to Praise.* Detroit: Lotus Press, 1984.

————. *The Women of Plums: Poems in the Voice of Slave Women.* New York: William Morrow & Co., 1988.

Lane, Pinkie Gordon. "A Quiet Poem." *Broadside Series.* No. 80. Detroit: Broadside Press, 1974.

————. "Children" and "For Bill." *Pembroke Magazine* 4 (1973): 26–28.

————. *Discourses in Poetry.* 5th ed. Ft. Smith, AK: South and West Publishers, 1972.

———. "Eulogy on the Death of Trees." *Poet: India* 5 (May 1973): 477.

———. "His Body Is an Eloquence." *To Gwen with Love.* Eds. Patricia L. Brown et al. Chicago: Johnson Publishing Co., 1971.

———. *I Never Scream: New and Selected Poems.* Detroit: Lotus Press, 1985.

———. "Mid-Summer Thoughts." *Poems by Poets.* Vol. 1. Ed. Sue Abbot Boyd. Ft. Smith, AK: South and West Publishers, 1973.

———. "On This Louisiana Day" and "Poems Extract." *Louisiana Review* 1 (Summer 1972): 105–106.

———. *The Mystic Female.* Ft. Smith, AK: South and West Publishers, 1978.

———. *Wind Thoughts.* Ft. Smith, AK: South and West Publishers, 1972.

Latimore, Jewel C. (Johari Amin). *Images in Black.* Rev. ed. Chicago: Third World Press, 1967.

Lorde, Audre. *Cables to Rage.* London: Paul Breman, 1973.

———. *From a Land Where Other People Live.* Detroit: Broadside Press, 1973.

———. "Naturally," "Fantasy and Conversation," "The Woman Thing," "And What about the Children." *Natural Process, An Anthology of New Black Poetry.* Eds. Ted Wilentz and Tom Weatherly. New York: Hill & Wang, 1970.

———. "Prologue." *Freedomways* 12 (First Quarter 1972): 31.

———. "Rites of Passage." *Freedomways* 10 (Third Quarter 1970): 246.

———. *The First Cities.* New York: Poets Press, 1967.

———. *The New York Head Shop and Museum.* Detroit: Broadside Press, 1971.

McBrown, Gertrude Parthenia. *The Picture-Poetry Book*. Illust. Lois Mailou Jones. Washington, DC: Associated Publishers, 1968.

McElroy, Colleen J. *Queen of the Ebony Isles*. Middletown, CT: Wesleyan University Press, 1984.

Madgett, Naomi. *Pink Ladies*. Detroit: Lotus Press, 1972.

————. *Exits and Entrances: New Poems*. Detroit: Lotus Press, 1978.

————. *Octavia and Other Poems*. Chicago: Third World Press, 1988.

————. *Soon I Will Be Done*. Detroit: Lotus Press, 1978.

————. (Naomi Cornelia Long). *Songs to a Phantom Nightingale*. New York: Fortuny's, 1941.

————. *Star by Star*. Detroit: Harlo Press, 1965.

————. *One and the Many*. New York: Exposition Press, 1956.

Mahone, Barbara. *Sugarfield Poems*. Introd. Hoyt W. Fuller. Detroit: Broadside Press, 1970.

Miller, May. *Dust of Uncertain Journey*. Detroit: Lotus Press, 1975.

————. *The Ransomed Wait*. Detroit: Lotus Press, 1983.

Moore, La Nese B. *Can I Be Right?* New York: Vantage Press, 1971.

Murphy, Beatrice M. *Love Is a Terrible Thing*. New York: Nolsen Book Press, 1945.

Murphy, Beatrice M. and Nancy L. Arnez. *The Rocks Cry Out*. Detroit: Broadside Press, 1969.

Murray, Pauli. *Dark Testament and Other Poems*. Norwalk, CT: Silvermine, 1970.

Nicholes, Marion. *Life Styles*. Detroit: Broadside Press, 1971.

Osbey, Brenda Marie. *Ceremony for Minneconjoux*. Callaloo Poetry Series. Louisville: University of Kentucky, 1983.

Parker, Patricia. "From Cavities of Bones," "I Followed a Path," "Assassination." *Dices or Black Bones.* Ed. Adam David Miller. Boston: Houghton Mifflin, 1970.

Parrish, Dorothy. "Ode to the Uncolored Man." *Black Art Writer's Literary Magazine* 1 (First Quarter 1971): 15.

Quigless, Helen. "Concert." *The New Black Poetry.* Ed. Clarence Major. New York: International Publishers, 1969.

Rashid, Niema. "Warriors Prancing, Women Dancing." *The New Black Poetry.* Ed. Clarence Major. New York: International Publishers, 1969.

Rawls, Isetta Crawford. *Flashbacks.* Detroit: Lotus Press, 1977.

Ray, Henrietta Cordella. "Dawn's Carol," "Our Task," "The Triple Benison." *An Anthology of Verse by American Negroes.* Eds. Newman Ivey White, Walter C. Jackson, and James Hardy Dillard. Durham, NC: Moore Publishing Co., 1924.

———. *Poems.* New York: Grafton Press, 1910.

Richards, Elizabeth Davis. *The Peddler of Dreams of Other Poems.* New York: W. A. Bodler, 1928.

Rodgers, Carolyn. *How i got ovah: New and Selected Poems.* New York: Anchor Books, 1976.

———. *Love Raps.* Chicago: Third World Press, 1969.

———. "My Lai as Related to No Vietnam Alabama." *Black World* 19 (Sep. 1970): 64–65.

———. *Now Ain't That Love.* Detroit: Broadside Press, 1970.

———. *Paper Soul.* Chicago: Third World Press, 1968.

———. *Songs of a Black Bird.* Chicago: Third World Press, 1969.

———. "The Children of Their Sin." *Black World* 20 (Oct. 1971): 78.

———. *The Heart as Ever Green.* New York: Doubleday, 1978; New York: Anchor Books, 1978.

Sanchez, Sonia. *A Blues Book for Blue Black Magical Women*. Detroit: Broadside Press, 1974.

———. "After Saturday Night Comes Sunday." *Black World* 20 (Mar. 1971): 53–59.

———. "For Our Lady." *Natural Process*. Eds. Ted Wilentz and Tom Weatherly. New York: Hill & Wang, 1970.

———. *Home Coming*. Detroit: Broadside Press, 1969.

———. *It's a New Day: Poems for Young Brothas and Sistuhs*. Detroit: Broadside Press, 1971.

———. *Liberation Poem*. Detroit: Broadside Press, 1971.

———. "Malcolm." *For Malcolm*. Eds. Dudley Randall and Margaret G. Burroughs. Detroit: Broadside Press, 1967.

———. "right-on: white America." *Soulscript: Afro-American Poetry*. Ed. June Jordan. New York: Doubleday, 1970.

———. *Under a Soprano Sky*. Trenton, NJ: Africa World Press, Inc. (Box 1892), 1987.

———. *We a BaddDD People*. Introd. Dudley Randall. Detroit: Broadside Press, 1970.

Shange, Ntozake. *Nappy Edges*. New York: St. Martin's Press, 1972, 1978.

Simcox, Helen Earle, ed. *Dear Dark Faces: Portraits of a People*. Detroit: Lotus Press, 1980.

Sims, Lillian. *Collections of Poems*. Chicago: Lillian Sims Publisher, 1971.

Sloan, Phyllis J., Angela Kinamore, and Beverly Russell. *Three Women Black*. Robbinsdale, MN: Guild Press, 1987.

Spencer, Anne. "Lady, Lady." *The New Negro*. Ed. Alain Locke. New York: Johnson Reprint Corp., 1968.

———. "Life-Long, Poor Browning," "At the Carnival," "Before

the Feast of Shushan," "Line to a Nasturtium." *The Negro Caravan.* Eds. Sterling Brown et al. New York: Arno Press, 1970.

————. "Lines to a Nasturtium" and "Letter to My Sister." *Black Writers of America.* Eds. Richard Barksdale and Kenneth Kinnamon. New York: Macmillan, 1972.

Stephany. *Moving Deep.* Detroit: Broadside Press, 1969.

Taylor, Gloria Lee. *Dreams for Sale.* New York: Exposition Press, 1953.

Terry, Lucy. "Bars of Flight." *The Black Poets.* Ed. Dudley Randall. New York: Bantam, 1971.

Thomas, Joyce Carol. *Blessing.* Berkeley: Jocato Press, 1975.

————. *Crystal Breezes.* Berkeley: Firesign Press, 1974.

Thompson, Carolyn. *Frank.* Detroit: Broadside Press, 1970.

Thompson, Clara Ann. *Songs from Wayside.* Rossmoyne, OH: Author, 1900.

Thompson, Dorothenia. *Three Slices of Black.* Chicago: Free Black Press, 1972.

Thompson, Priscilla Jane. *Ethiope Lays.* Rossmoyne, OH: Author, 1900.

Torres, Brenda. "Catechism." *Negro Digest* 18 (June 1969): 47.

Walker, Margaret. *For My People.* New Haven, CT: Yale University Press, 1942.

————. *October Journey.* Detroit: Broadside Press, 1973.

————. *Prophets for a New Day.* Detroit: Broadside Press, 1970.

Watkins, Violette Peaches. *My Dream World of Poetry, Poems of Imagination, Reality, and Dreams.* New York: Exposition Press, 1955.

Watson, Freida K. *Feelin's.* Introd. Jomo Don Shabazz. Los Angeles: A Krizna Publication, 1971.

Wheatley, Phillis. *Memoir and Poems of Phillis Wheatley: A Native African and a Slave.* Boston: Isaac Knapp, 1938.

————. *The Poems of Phillis Wheatley.* Ed. Julian D. Mason, Jr. Chapel Hill, NC: University of North Carolina Press, 1966.

————. "To the University of Cambridge in New England," "On the Death of the Rev. Mr. George Whitefield," "An Hymn to the Morning," "An Hymn to the Evening," "On Imagination," "To S. M., a Young American Painter on Seeing His Works," "His Excellency General Washington," "Liberty and Peace." *Early Negro American Writers.* Ed. Benjamin Brawley. New York: Dover Publications, 1970.

White, Paulette Childress. *Love Poem to a Black Junkie.* Detroit: Lotus Press, 1975.

————. *The Watermelon Dress: Portrait of a Woman.* Detroit: Lotus Press, 1984.

Articles/Essays/Books on Critical Issues: (A) By and about African-American Women on Cultural, Educational, Historical, Political, and Social Issues

Alston, Fannie, and R. Ora Williams. "Johnny Doesn't/Didn't Hear." *Journal of Negro Education,* Spring 1964: 197–200.

Amini, Johari. "Re-definition: Concept As Being." *Black World* (May 1972): 4–12.

Arnez, Nancy L. "A Study of Attitudes of Negro Teachers and Pupils Toward Their School." *Journal of Negro Education* (Summer 1963): 289–293.

Arnez, Nancy L., and Clara Anthony. "Working with Disadvantaged Negro Youth in Urban Schools." *School and Society* 20 (Mar. 1968): 202–204.

Austin, Elsie. "Casenotes." *University of Cincinnati Law Review,* 1928.

Ball, Jane Lee. "The Abandoned Culture of America's Black People." *The Humanist* (Sep./Oct. 1980).

Barnes, Annie S. *Black Women: Interpersonal Relationships in Profile.* Bristol, IN: Wyndham Hall Press (Box 877), n.d.

Bennett, Lerone, Jr. *Before the Mayflower: A History of Black America.* Rev. ed. 1962.

Berry, Mary Frances, and John Blassingame. *Long Memory: The Black Experience in America.* New York: Oxford University Press, 1982.

Bethune, Mary McLeod. "The Problems of the City Dweller." *Opportunity* (Feb. 1925): 54–55.

Bowen, Uvelia S. A. *Housekeeping Careers—A New Frontier.* Philadelphia: Heart, 1973.

––––––. *Rhyme, Reason and Responsibility.* Philadelphia: Heart, 1971. (Manual)

––––––. *Training Household Technicians.* Philadelphia: Heart, 1971.

––––––. *What Is a Day's Work?* Philadelphia: Personnel Resources, Inc., 1970.

Bowen, Uvelia S. A., Betty Henken, and Laura Lee. *Thursday's People on the Move!* Philadelphia: Heart, 1971.

Bradley, Gladyce N. "Teacher Education and Desegregation." *Journal of Negro Education* (Spring 1957): 200–203.

Brown, Charlotte Hawkins. *"Morning," An Appeal to the Heart of the South.* Boston: The Pilgrim Press, 1919.

Brown-Collins, Alice R., and Deborah Sussewell. "The Afro-American Woman's Emerging Selves." *Journal of Black Psychology,* 13.1 (August 1986): 1–11.

Butcher, Margaret Just. *The Negro in American Culture.* Rev. ed.

Based on materials of Alain Locke. New York: New American Library, 1956.

Carroll, Constance M. "Yet Another Slice of Pie." Paper read at the United States Office of Education Summer Institute, *Challenge: Women in Higher Education.* University of California, Irvine, June 25-July 1, 1972.

Clark, Cheryl. *Living as a Lesbian.* Ithaca, NY: Fregrand Books, 1986.

Collier, Eugenia, Joel Glasser, Edward Meyers, George Steele, and Thomas L. Wolf. *A Bridge to Saying It Well.* Springfield, VA: Norvec Publishing Co., 1970. (Freshman textbook)

Coner-Edwards, Alice F., and Jeanne Spurlock. *Black Families in Crisis: The Middle Class.* New York: Brunner/Mazel, 1988.

Crummell, Alexander. "The Black Woman of the South—Her Neglects and Her Needs." *African and America: Addresses and Discourses.* Washington, DC: B. S. Adams, 1883.

Curry, Gladys J. "Black Politics: A Brief Survey." *Viewpoints from Black America.* Ed. Gladys J. Curry. Englewood Cliffs, NJ: Prentice-Hall, 1970.

Daniels, Douglas Henry. *Pioneer Urbanites: A Social and Cultural History of Black San Francisco.* For. Nathan Irwin Huggins. Philadelphia: Temple University Press, 1980.

Dansby, Pearl Gore. "Black Pride in the Seventies: Fact or Fantasy?" *Black Psychology.* Ed. Reginald L. Jones. New York: Harper, 1972.

Davis, Elizabeth. *Lifting as They Climb: The National Association of Colored Women.* Washington, DC: The National Association of Colored Women, 1933.

DeCosta-Willis, Miriam. *1980 Holy Land and European Tour.* Memphis: COGIC Bookstore, 1980.

DeCosta[-Willis], Miriam. *The History of Beale Street: 1850–1950.* Washington, DC: Match Institution, 1973.

Miriam DeCosta–Willis

DuBois, Shirley Graham. "Egypt Is Africa." Part 1. *Black Scholar* (Sep. 1970): 20–22.

———. "Egypt Is Africa." Part 2. *Black Scholar* (Sep. 1970): 28–34.

———. "The Liberation of Africe." *Black Scholar* (Feb. 1971): 32–37.

———. "The Struggle in Lesotho." *Black Scholar* (Nov. 1970): 25–39.

Dunbar-Nelson, Alice Ruth (Moore). "Is It Time for the Negro Colleges in the South to Be Put in the Hands of Negro Teachers?" *The American Negro, His History and Literature.* Ed. D. W. Culp. New York: Arno Press, 1969.

———. "Negro Women in War Work." *Scott's Official History of the American Negro in the World War.* Ed. Emmett J. Scott. N.p.: n.p, 1919. 374–397.

———. "The Boys of Howard High." *The Dunbar Speaker and Entertainer.* Ed. Alice Dunbar-Nelson. Naperville, IL: J. L. Nichols, 1920.

———. "Training Teachers of English." *Education* (Oct. 1908): 97–103.

Dunbar-Nelson, Alice Ruth (Moore), et al. Untitled anti-lynching statement drafted in 1922 in support of the NAACP campaign. *Black Women in White America.* Ed. Gerda Lerner. New York: Random House (Vintage), 1973.

Dunham, Katherine. *Journey to Accompong.* Illust. Ted Cook. New York: Henry Holt, 1946.

———. *Island Possessed.* Garden City, NY: Doubleday, 1969.

Edelman, Marian Wright. *Families in Peril: An Agenda for Social Change.* Cambridge/London: Harvard University Press, 1987.

———. *The Measure of Our Success: a Letter to My Children and Yours.* Boston: Beacon Press, 1992.

Edmonds, Helen G. *The Negro and Fusion Politics in North Carolina,*

Dr. Edith V. Francis

1894–1901. Chapel Hill, NC: University of North Carolina Press, 1951.

Francis, Edith V. "Enter the Future with Confidence." *School Leader* (Jan./Feb. 1986).

Francis, Edith V., collaborator. *Educating Gifted Children.* New York: Harper Brothers, 1952.

Frazier, E. Franklin. *The Negro Family in the United States.* Rev./Abr. New York: The Dryden Press, 1951.

Fulani, Lenora. *The Psychopathology of Everyday.* New York/London: Harrington Park Press, 1988.

George, Yolanda Scott. "The Status of Black Women in Science." *The Black Collegian* (May/June 1979): 64.

George, Zelma Watson. "The Social Conditions of Slavery as Found in Slave Narratives." Unpublished manuscript, 1946.

Giddings, Paula. *Delta Sigma Theta and the Black Sorority Movement.* New York: William Morrow, 1988.

Goff, Regina Mary. *Problems and Emotional Difficulties of Negro Children as Studied in Selected Communities and Attributed by Parents and Children to the Fact That They Are Negro . . .* New York: Bureau of Publications, Columbia University, 1949.

Granger, Jean M. "Attitudes Toward National Personal Social Services Policy." *Child Welfare* 67 (1989): 301–315.

———. "Attitudes Toward Supportive Services for Families: Implications for a National Family Policy." *The Journal of Applied Social Sciences* 12 (1988): 222–249.

Granger, Jean M., and Doreen Portner. "Ethnic and Gender-Sensitive Social Work Practice." *Journal of Social Work Education* 21 (1988): 38–47.

Greenberger, Ellen, Wendy Goldberg, Tom Crawford, and Jean M. Granger. "Beliefs about the Consequences of Maternal Employment." *Psychology of Women Quarterly* 12 (1988): 35–59.

Guy-Sheftall, Beverly. "Black Women and Higher Education: Spelman and Bennett Colleges Revisited." *Journal of Negro Education* (Summer 1982): 275–287.

———. "Black Women's Studies at Spelman College." *Women's Studies Quarterly* (Summer 1986), forthcoming.

———. *Exhibit Catalog: Finding a Way: The Black Family's Struggle for an Education at the Atlanta University Center.* Atlanta: African-American Family History Association, 1982.

———. "Mothers and Daughters: A Black Perspective." *Spelman Messenger* 98 (1982): 4–5.

————. "Reflections on Forum '85 in Nairobi, Kenya: Voices from the International Women's Studies Community." *Signs* (Mar. 1986): 507–599.

————. "Women's Studies at Spelman College: Reminiscence from the Director." *Women's Studies International Forum* 9 (1986): 151–155.

Guzman, Jessie Parkhurst. *Desegregation and the Southern States, 1957.* Legal Action and Voluntary Group Action. With Woodrow W. Hall. Tuskegee Institute, AL: Department of Records and Research, 1958.

————. "Meeting the Social Needs of Students at Tuskegee Institute." *The Quarterly Review of Higher Education Among Negroes* 12 (Oct. 1944): 227–231.

————. *Some Achievements of the Negro Through Education.* Tuskegee Institute, AL: Department of Records and Research, 1954.

————. *The New South and Higher Education.* A symposium and ceremonies held in connection with the inauguration of Luther Hilton Foster, Fourth President of Tuskegee Institute. Tuskegee Institute, AL: Department of Records and Research, 1954.

————. "The Social Contributions of the Negro Woman Since 1940." *Negro History Bulletin* 11 (Jan. 1948): 86–94.

————. "The Southern Race Problem in Retrospect." *Vital Speeches* 25 (1 July 1959): 566–568.

————. *Tuskegee Institute Conference on the Disadvantaged.* Tuskegee Institute, AL: Tuskegee Institute Press, 1964. (Held in conjunction with the annual meeting of the Tuskegee Institute Board of Trustees, Oct. 25–26, 1964)

————. "Twenty Years of Court Decisions Affecting Higher Education in the South, 1938–1958." *Journal of Educational Sociology* 22 (Feb. 1958): 247–253.

Hackley, E. Azalia. *The Colored Girl Beautiful.* Kansas City, MO: Burton Publishing Co., 1916.

Hams, Middleton Harris, ed. *The Black Book*. New York: Random House, 1973. (Photo-history of Blacks)

Hansberry, Lorraine. "Congolese Patriot." Letter to the editor. *New York Times Magazine* (26 Mar. 1961): 4.

————. "Miss Hansberry on 'Backlash.'" *Village Voice* (23 July 1964): 10, 16.

————. "My Name Is Lorraine Hansberry, I Am a Writer." *Esquire* (Nov. 1969): 140.

————. "Negroes and Africa." Quoted extensively in this chapter in *The New World of Negro Americans*. Ed. Harold R. Isaacs. New York: John Day Co., 1965.

————. "The Black Revolution and the White Backlash" (transcript of a Town Hall forum with Ossie Davis, Ruby Dee, Lorraine Hansberry, Leroi Jones, John O. Killens, Paule Marshall, Charles E. Silberman, James Wechsler, and David Susskind, moderator) Almost complete transcript: *National Guardian* 26 (4 July 1964): 5–9. Partial excerpts: *Black Protest*, ed. with introd. and commentaries by Joanne Grant. New York: Fawcett World Library, 1968.

————. "The Nation Needs Your Gifts." *Negro Digest* (August 1946): 26–29.

————. "The Negro in American Culture" (symposium with James Baldwin, Emile Capouya, Lorraine Hansberry, Nat Hentoff, Langston Hughes, and Alfred Kazin); *The Black American Writer, Vol. I: Fiction*. Ed. C. W. E. Bigsby. Baltimore: Pelican Books, 1971.

Harper, Frances Ellen Watkins. "Colored Women of America." *The Englishwoman's Review* (Jan. 1878): 10–15.

Haskins, Jim. *The Cotton Club*. New York: Random House, 1977.

Haynes, Carrie Ayers. *Good News on Grape Street: The Transformation of a Ghetto School*. New York: Citation Press, 1975.

Hine, Darlene Clark. *When the Truth Is Told: A History of Black Women's Culture and Community in Indiana, 1875–1950*. Fore.

Shirley Herd. Indianapolis: National Council of Negro Women, Indianapolis Section, 1981.

Hobson, Sheila Smith. "Women and Television." *Sisterhood Is Powerful.* Ed. Robin Morgan. New York: Random House (Vintage), 1970.

Hooks, Rosie, Bernice Reagon, et al. *Black People and Their Culture: Selected Writings from the African Diaspora.* Washington, DC: Smithsonian Institution, 1976.

Hurston, Zora Neale. "A Negro Voter Sizes Up Taft." *The Saturday Evening Post* (8 Dec. 1951): 29, 150–152.

————. "I Saw Negro Votes Peddled." *American Legion Magazine* (Nov. 1959): 12, 13, 45–47, 59–60.

————. "What White Publications Won't Print." *Negro Digest* (Apr. 1947): 85–89.

Jackson, Jacqueline J. "A Black Sociologist Crystallizes Social and Psychological Needs to the Characteristics and Special Problems of Ghetto Youth." *Multimedia Materials for Afro-American Studies: A Curriculum Orientation and Annotated Bibliography of Resources.* Ed./comp. Dr. Harry A. Johnson. New York: R. R. Bowker, 1971.

————. "Aged Blacks: A Potpourri in the Direction of Reduction of Inequities." *Phylon* 32 (Third Quarter, Fall 1971): 260–280.

————. "Black Women in a Racist Society." *Racism and Mental Health.* Eds. B. Brown, B. Kramer, and C. Willie. Pittsburgh: Pittsburgh University Press, 1973.

"Joanne Little: America Goes on Trial." *Freedomways* (Second Quarter 1975): 87–88. (Editorial)

Johnson, Patricia Ann. "Intellectual Genocide." *Black World* (August 1974): 81–82.

Kirby, J. B. *Black Americans in the Roosevelt Era: Liberalism and Race.* Knoxville, TN: The University of Tennessee Press, 1980.

Lawrence, Margaret. *The Mental Health Team in the Schools.* New York: Behavioral Publications, 1971.

———. *Young Inner City Families: Development of Ego Strengths Under Stress.* New York: Behavioral Publications, 1975.

Lightfoot, Sara. *The Good High School: Portrait of Character and Culture.* New York: Basic Books, 1983.

———. *Worlds Apart: Relationships Between Families and Schools.* New York: Basic Books, 1978.

Lowenberg, Bert, and Roth Bogin, eds. *Black Women in Nineteenth-Century American Life.* University Park, PA: Pennsylvania State University Press, 1976.

Martin, Wyneta Willis. *Black Mormon Tells Her Story.* Salt Lake City, UT: Hawkes Publications, n.d.

Mosby, Doris P. "Toward a New Speciality of Black Psychology." *Black Psychology.* Ed. Reginald L. Jones. New York: Harper, 1972.

———. "Toward a Theory of the Unique Personality of Blacks—A Psychocultural Assessment." *Black Psychology.* Ed. Reginald L. Jones. New York: Harper, 1972.

Musgrave, Marian E. "Teaching English as a Foreign Language to Students with Sub-Standard Dialects." *Viewpoints from Black America.* Ed. Gladys J. Curry. Englewood Cliffs, NJ: Prentice-Hall, 1970.

Nash, Gary B. *Forging Freedom: The Formation of Philadelphia's Black Community, 1720–1840.* Cambridge: Harvard University Press, 1988.

Noble, Jeanne. "Negro Women Today and Their Education." *Journal of Negro Education* 26 (Winter 1957): 15–21.

———. *The Negro Woman's College Education.* New York: Columbia Teachers College, 1975.

Parks, A. G. *Black Elderly in Rural America.* Bristol, IN: Wyndham Hall Press, 1988.

Payne, Charles. "Ella Baker and Models of Social Change." *Signs* (Summer 1989): 885ff.

Pemberton, Gayle. *The Hottest Water in Chicago.* Boston: Faber and Faber, 1992.

Radcliffe, Florence J. *A Simple Matter of Justice: The Phillis Wheatley YWCA Story.* Pompano Beach, FL: Exposition Press of Florida, 1985.

Reynolds, Barbara. "Let's Open Our Hearts to Victims, Families." *USA Today* (21 February 1988): 9a.

Savage, W. Sherman. *Blacks in the West.* Westport, CT/London: Greenwood Press, 1976.

Schuyler, Philippa. *Who Killed the Congo?* New York: Devin-Adair Co., 1962.

Sims, Naomi. *All About Success for the Black Woman.* Garden City, NY: Doubleday, 1982.

Slaughter, Diana T., and Deborah J. Johnson, eds. *Visible Now: Blacks in Private Schools.* Westport, CT: Greenwood Press, 1988.

Smalley, Hazel C. "Quiet Experiment in Public Affairs." *Black Politician* (January 1971): 26, 27.

Smith, Jean. "I Learned to Feel Black." *The Black Power Revolt.* Ed. Floyd B. Barber. Boston: Porter, Sargent, 1968.

Spady, James G. "Black Women's Organizations in America: Some Historical Notes and Current Observations." *Black Women in Focus.* Philadelphia: *The Philadelphia New Observer* (21 December 1988).

————. "Christmas and Kwanza Celebrated at Bookstores Operated by Black Women." *Black Women in Focus.* Philadelphia: *The Philadelphia New Observer* (21 December 1988), n. pag.

Tate, Merze. *Diplomacy in the Pacific: The United States and the Hawaiian Kingdom: A Political History.* New Haven, CT: Yale University Press, 1965.

―――. *Hawaii: Reciprocity or Annexation*. East Lansing, MI: Michigan State University Press, 1968.

―――. *The United States and Armaments*. Cambridge, MA: Harvard University Press, 1948.

Van Ellison, Candice. "History of Harlem." *Harlem on My Mind: Cultural Capital of Black America 1900–1968*. Ed. Allon Schoener. New York: Random House, 1968.

Vroman, Mary Elizabeth. *Delta Sigma Theta, The First Fifty Years*. New York: Random House, 1968.

Walker (Alexander), Margaret. "Religion, Poetry, and History: Foundations for a New Educational System." *Viewpoints from Black America*. Ed. Gladys J. Curry. Englewood Cliffs, NJ: Prentice-Hall, 1970.

Washington, Mary Helen. "Teaching *Black-Eyed Susans:* An Approach to the Study of Black Women Writers." *Black American Literature Forum* (Spring 1977): 20–24.

Wells, Sharon. *Forgotten Legacy: Blacks in Nineteenth Century Key West*. Key West, FL: Historic Key West Preservation Board, 1982.

White-Katz, Maude. "End Racism in Education: A Concerned Parent Speaks." *The Black Woman: An Anthology*. Ed. Toni Cade. (See Bambara under "Anthologies")

Williams, Kenny J. *In the City of Men: Another Story of Chicago*. New York: Townsend Press, 1974.

Williams-Jones, Pearl. "Afro-American Gospel Music." *Development of Materials for a One-Year Course in African Music for the General Undergraduate Student*. Ed. Vada E. Butcher. Washington, DC: HEW Office of Education, 1970. 199–239.

Williams, Thelma O. "Bejing: Professional Exchange with Representatives of the Central Minority Nationality Institute, August 18, 1988." *Journal: People to People Music of the Minority Delegation to the People's Republic of China and Hong Kong, August 12–September 2, 1988*. Professor James A. Standifer, Delegation Leader. N.p.: Department of Citizen Ambassador

Program, People to People Citizen Ambassador Program, n.d.

Winch, Julie. *Philadelphia's Black Elite: Activism, Accommodation, and the Struggle for Autonomy, 1787–1848*. Philadelphia: Temple University Press, 1988.

Wolfe, Deborah Partridge. "A Faculty Member Responds." *The Campus and the Racial Crisis*. Eds. David Nichols and Olive Mills. Washington, DC: American Council on Education, 1970.

Woods, Gwendolyn Patton. "Pro-Black, Not Anti-White." *The Campus and the Racial Crisis*. Eds. David Nichols and Olive Mills. Washington, DC: American Council on Education, 1970.

Young, Margaret B. *How to Bring Up Your Child Without Prejudice*. Public Affairs Pamphlet No. 373. New York: n.p., n.d.

Young, Pauline A. "The Negro in Delaware, Past and Present." *Delaware, A History of the First State*. Vol. II. Ed. H. Clay Reed. New York: Lewis Publishing Co., 1947.

Yvonne. "The Importance of Cicely Tyson." *Ms.* (Aug. 1974): 45–47, 76–79.

Zinn, Maxine Baca. "Family, Race, and Poverty in the Eighties." *Signs* (Summer 1989): 856 + .

Articles/Essays/Books on Critical Issues: (B) By and about African-American Women on Racial and Sexual Issues

"Alabama's First Black Female Attorney Visits Law Center." *Law Report* (July 1989).

Beale, Frances M. "Double Jeopardy: To Be Black and Female." *Sisterhood Is Powerful*. Ed. Robin Morgan. New York: Random House (Vintage), 1970.

Black Women's Liberation Group. "State on Birth Control." *Sisterhood Is Powerful.* Ed. Robin Morgan. New York: Random House (Vintage), 1970.

Bond, Jean Carey, and Pat Perry. "The Changing Role of the Black Woman." *The Black Family: Essays and Studies.* Ed. Robert Staples. Belmont, CA: Wadsworth Publisher, 1971.

Brown-Collins, Alice R., and Deborah R. Sussewell. The Afro-American Woman: Emerging Selves." *Journal of Black Psychology* 13 (Aug. 1986): 1–11.

Burnham, Margaret. "Legacy of the 1960s: The Great Society Didn't Fail." *Scapegoating the Black Family: Black Women Speak.* Special issue of *The Nation* (24 July 1989): 122 +.

Campbell, Bebe Moore. *Successful Women, Angry Men: Backlash in the Two-Career Marriage.* New York: Random House, 1986.

Chisholm, Shirley. "Race, Revolution and Women." *Black Scholar* 3 (Dec. 1971): 17–21.

———. "Racism and Anti-Feminism," *Black Scholar* 1 (Jan.–Feb. 1970): 40–43.

———. *Unbought and Unbossed.* New York: Avon, 1970.

Clayton, Constance. "Children of Value: We Can Educate All Our Children." *Scapegoating the Black Family: Black Women Speak.* Special issue of *The Nation* (24 July 1989): 132 +.

"Concrete Ceiling Major Obstacle for Black Women." *Black Women in Focus. The Philadelphia New Observer* (21 Dec. 1988).

Conley, Madelyn. "Do Black Women Need the Women's Lib?" *Essence* 1 (Aug. 1970): 29–34.

Cummings, Gwenna. "Black Women Often Discussed But Never Understood." *The Black Power Revolt.* Ed. Floyd Barbour. Boston: Porter Sargent, 1968.

Davis, Ossie. "Challenge to the Nation for the Year 2000: Jobs, Peace, and Justice." Special issue of *The Nation* (24 July 1989).

Dunbar-Nelson, Alice Ruth (Moore). "Negro Women in War Work." *Scott's Official History of the American Negro in the World War.* Ed. Emmett J. Scott. N.p: n.p., 1919.

————. "Some of the Work of the National Association of Colored Women." *Long Island Review* 7 (Nov. 1899): 338–339.

Eckardt, A. Roy. *Black-Woman-Jew: Three Wars for Human Liberation.* Bloomington, IN: Indiana University Press, 1989.

Farley, Reynolds, and Walter R. Allen. *The Color Line and the Quality of Life in America.* New York: Russell Sage Foundation, 1987.

Giddings, Paula. *When and Where I Enter: The Impact of Black Women on Race and Sex in America.* New York: William Morrow, 1984.

Glasgow, Douglas G. *The Black Underclass: Poverty, Unemployment, and Entrapment of Ghetto Youth.* New York: Vintage Books, 1981.

Gresham, Jewell Handy. "The Rockefeller-Albert Snafu and the Honor of Ed Brooke." New York *Amsterdam News* (2 October 1976): 1.

————. "White Patriarchal Supremacy: The Politics of Family in America." *Scapegoating the Black Family: Black Women Speak.* Special issue of *The Nation* (24 July 1989): 116–122.

Gresham, Jewell Handy, and Margaret B. Wilkerson. "Introduction: The Burden of History." *Scapegoating the Black Family: Black Women Speak.* Special issue of *The Nation* (24 July 1989). 115–116.

Gutman, Herbert G. *The Black Family in Slavery and Freedom, 1750–1925.* New York: Vintage Books, 1976.

Guzman, Jessie Parkhurst. "The Role of the Black Mammy in the Plantation Household." *Journal of Negro History* 23 (July 1938): 349–369.

Jewell Gresham Nemiroff

————. "The Social Contributions of the Negro Woman Since 1940." *Negro History Bulletin* 11 (Jan. 1948): 86–94.

————. *Twenty Years of Court Decisions Affecting Higher Education in the South.* Tuskegee Institute, AL: Department of Records and Research, 1960.

Guzman, Jessie Parkhurst, ed. *Race Relations in the South.* Tuskegee Institute, AL: Department of Records and Research, 1956–64.

Hansberry, Lorraine. *The Movement: The Documentary of a Struggle for Equality.* New York: Simon and Schuster, 1964.

Harley, Sharon, and Rosalyn Terborg-Penn. *The Afro-American Woman: Struggles and Image.* Port Washington, NY/London: Kennikat Press, 1978.

Harris, Janet. *Students in Revolt.* New York: McGraw-Hill, 1970.

Height, Dorothy. *America's Promise.* New York: Woman's Press, 1946.

————. "Self-Help—A Black Tradition." *Scapegoating the Black Family: Black Women Speak.* Special issue of *The Nation* (24 July 1989). 136+.

————. *Step by Step with. . . .* Rev. ed. New York: National Board YWCA, Publishing Services, 1955.

————. *The Core of America's Race Problem.* New York: Woman's Press, 1945.

Hood, Elizabeth. "Black Women, White Women, Different Paths to Liberation." *Black Scholar* 9 (Apr. 1978): 45–46.

Hooks, Bell. *Ain't I a Woman: Black Women and Feminism.* Boston: South End Press, 1981.

————. *Feminist Theory: From Margin to Center.* Boston: South End Press, 1984.

————. *Talking Back, Thinking Feminist, Thinking Black.* Boston: South End Press, 1988.

Hunter, Charlayne. "Black Women and the Liberation Movement." *Black Politician* 2 (Jan. 1971): 15, 39.

Jackson, Jacqueline J. "Black Man/Black Woman—Creative Equals." *Essence* (Nov. 1973): 56, 57, 72 +.

————. "The Plight of Older Black Women in the United States." *Black Scholar* 7.7 (Apr. 1976): 47–55.

Jackson, Jacqueline Johnson. "Quadruple Jeopardy: Black and Female and Old and Poor: Historical and Contemporary Statuses of Black Females." *NCBA News* (National Caucus on the Black Aged) (Jan./Feb./Mar. 1974): 1, 5, 6, 7.

————. "Where Are the Black Men?" *Ebony* (Mar. 1972): 102, 104, 106.

Jackson, Yvonne. "The Black Female and the Women's Liberation Movement." *Black America* 2.1 (Mar.–Apr. 1971): 36–37, 63.

Johnson, Willa D., and Thomas L. Green, eds. *Perspectives on Afro-American Women.* Washington, DC: ECCA Publications, n.d.

Jones, Claudia. *An End to the Neglect of the Problems of the Negro Woman.* New York: National Women's Commission, 1949.

Jones, Viola Julia. "Women's Liberation as Seen from a Black Woman's Point of View." *Core* 1 (Nov. 1970): 16.

Jordan, June. "A Declaration of Independence I'd Just As Soon Not Have." *Civil Wars.* Boston: Beacon Press, 1981.

————. *Dry Victories.* San Francisco: Holt, Rinehart and Winston, 1972.

Joseph, Gloria I., and Jill Lewis. *Common Differences: Conflicts in Black and White Feminist Perspectives.* New York: Anchor Press, 1981.

Kennedy, Florynce. "Institutionalized Oppression Versus the Female." *Sisterhood Is Powerful.* Ed. Robin Morgan. New York: Random House (Vintage), 1970.

Koontz, Elizabeth. "Women of a Minority." *Voices of a Minority: The New Feminism*. Ed. Mary Lou Thompson. Boston: Beacon Press, 1971.

Ladner, Joyce. "Black Women Face the 21st Century: Major Issues and Problems." *Black Scholar* 17.5 (Sep./Oct. 1986): 12–19.

———. "Tanzanian Women and Nation Building." *Black Scholar* 3 (Dec. 1971): 22–28.

———. *Tomorrow's Tomorrow: The Black Woman*. New York: Doubleday, 1971.

Lewis, Diane. "A Response to Inequality: Black Women, Racism, and Sexism." *Signs* 3 (Winter 1977): 339–361.

McDougald, Elsie Johnson. "The Task of Negro Womanhood." *The New Negro*. Ed. Alain Locke. New York: Johnson Reprint Corp., 1968.

McGee, Lillian R. "One Not Hung Up on Woman's Liberation Movement." *Core* 1 (Nov. 1970): 13.

McKenzie, Marjorie. *Fifty Years of Progress for Negro Women*. Pittsburgh, PA: Pittsburgh Courier, 1960.

Malcolm, Shirley, Paula Quick Hall, and Janet Welsh Brown. *The Double Bind: The Price of Being a Minority in Science*. Washington, DC: American Association for the Advancement of Science, 1976.

Mossell, Mrs. Gertrude E. *The Work of the Afro-American Woman*. Philadelphia: C. S. Ferguson Co., 1980. (c. 1894)

"Mrs. Dunbar Made Strong Argument for Equal Suffrage." Untitled newspaper. AD papers, Ohio Historical Society. (Roll 7, frame 1187)

"Mrs. Dunbar on Woman's Suffrage." *Harrisburg Telegraph* (27 Oct. 1915). AD papers, Ohio Historical Society. (Roll 7, frame 1185)

"Mrs. Dunbar, Suffrage Lecturer." Untitled newspaper. AD papers, Ohio Historical Society. (Roll 7, frame 1185)

Newman, Pamela. "Take a Good Look at Your Problems." *Black Women's Liberation.* Eds. Maxine Williams et al. New York: Pathfinder Press, 1971.

Noble, Jeanne. *Beautiful, Also, Are the Souls of My Black Sisters.* Englewood Cliffs, NJ: Prentice-Hall, 1978.

Reid, Inez Smith. *"Together," Black Women.* New York: Emerson Hall, 1972.

Saunders, Doris E. *The Kennedy Years and the Negro.* Chicago: Johnson Publ. Co., 1954.

Sloan, Margaret. "Keeping the Black Woman in Her Place." Review of *Sweet Sweetback's Baadasss Song* by Melvin Van Peebles. *Ms.* Jan. 1974: 30–31.

Sterling, Dorothy, ed. *We Are Your Sisters: Black Women in the Nineteenth Century.* New York/London: W. W. Norton, 1984.

Stokes, Gail A. "Black Woman to Black Man." *The Black Family.* Ed. Robert Staples. N.p.: N.p., n.d.

Strong, Augusta. "Negro Women in Freedom's Battles." *Freedomways* 7 (Fall 1967): 302–315.

Taylor, Josephine. "Liberate Ourselves First." *Core* 1.9 (Nov. 1970): n.pag.

Terborg-Penn, Rosalyn, and Sharon Harley, eds. *The Afro-American Woman: Struggle and Images.* Port Washington, NY: Kennikat, 1978.

Thompson, Mary Lou, ed. *Voices of the New Feminism.* Boston: Beacon Press, 1971.

Wallace, Michele. *Black Macho and the Myth of the Superwoman.* New York: Dial Press, 1979.

Wattleton, Faye. "The Case for National Action." *Scapegoating the Black Family: Black Women Speak.* Special issue of *The Nation* (24 July 1989): 138 +

Williams, Maxine. "Why Women's Liberation Is Important to Black

Women." *Black Women's Liberation*. Eds. Maxine Williams et al. New York: Pathfinder Press, 1971.

Willingham, Sandra. "Our Latest Enemy: Women's Lib." *Core* 1.9 (Nov. 1970): n.pag.

In and about the Folk Tradition

Black Folk Art in America, 1930–1980. Jackson, MS: University of Mississippi, 1981. (Catalog for traveling exhibit)

Brooks, Gwendolyn. "At the Royal" and "Of DeWitt Williams on His Way to Lincoln Cemetery." *Book of Negro Folklore*. Eds. Langston Hughes and Arna Bontemps. New York: Dodd, Mead and Company, 1958.

Brown, Virginia Pounds. *Toting the Lead Row: Ruby Pickens Tartt, Alabama Folklorist*. N.p.: University of Alabama Press, 1981.

Cone, James. *The Spirituals and the Blues: An Interpretation*. New York: Seabury Press, 1972.

Courlander, Harold. *Negro Folk Music, U. S. A.* New York/London: Columbia University Press, 1963/1970.

Dance, Daryl Cumber. *Folklore from Contemporary Black Americans*. Bloomington: Indiana University Press, 1978.

———. *Folklore from Contemporary Jamaicans*. Knoxville: University of Tennessee Press, 1985.

———. *Long Gone: The Mecklenburg Six and the Theme of Escape in Black Folklore*. Knoxville: University of Tennessee Press, 1987.

———. *Shuckin' and Jivin': Folklore from Contemporary Black Americans*. Bloomington, IN: Indiana University Press, 1978.

Dark Madonna Symposium Tapes. UCLA Center for Comparative Study of Folklore and Mythology. Los Angeles, CA: n.p., n.d.

Dunham, Katherine. "The Negro Dance." *The Negro Caravan*. Eds. Sterling Brown et al. New York: Arno Press, 1970.

Faulkner, Audrey Olson, et al., eds. *When I Was Comin' Up: An Oral History of Aged Blacks*. Hamden, CT: Archon Books/The Shoe String Press, 1983.

Fisher, Miles Mark. *Negro Slave Songs in the United States*. New York: The Citadel Press, 1969.

Flournoy, Valerie. *The Patchwork Quilt*. Illust. Jerry Pinckney. New York: Dial Books for Young Readers, 1985.

Frankel, Barbara. *Childbirth in the Ghetto: Folk Beliefs of Negro Women in a North Philadelphia Hospital Ward*. San Francisco: R & E Research Associates, 1977.

Freeman, Roland L. *Something to Keep You Warm: The Roland Freeman Collection of Black American Quilts from the Mississippi Heartland; An Exhibition at the Mississippi State Historical Museum* (A division of the Department of Archives and History), June 14–August 9, 1981. Jackson, MS: n.p., 1981.

Frye, Gladys-Marie. *Night Riders in Black Folk History*. Knoxville, TN: University of Tennessee, 1975.

George, Zelma Watson. "An Analysis of the Use of Negro Folksong in Six Major Symphonic Works." Unpublished manuscript, 1933.

Goodwin, Ruby Berkley. *Six Stories Depicting Negro Life at the Time of "Twelve Negro Spirituals"*, by William Grant Still. Illust. Albert Barbelle. 2 vols. New York: Handy Brothers Music Co., 1937.

Haskett, Edythe Ranee. *Grains of Pepper: Folktales from Liberia*. N.p.: John Day, 1967.

Howorth, Lisa N. *Clementine Hunter: American Folk Art,* by James L. Wilson. Gretna, LA: Pelican Publishing Co., 1988; *The Southern Register* (Spring 1989).

Hurston, Zora Neale. "Conversions and Visions." *Negro Anthology*. Ed. Nancy Cunard. London: Wishart, 1934. 47–49.

————. *Jonah's Gourd Vine*. Philadelphia: Lippincott, 1934.

————. *Moses, Man of the Mountains*. Philadelphia: Lippincott, 1939.

————. *Mules and Men*. Philadelphia: Lippincott, 1935; New York: First Perennial Library Edition, Harper, 1970.

————. "Polk County, A Comedy of Negro Life on a Sawmill Camp." Unpublished manuscript, n.d.

————. "Spunk." *The New Negro*. Ed. Alain Locke. New York: Johnson Reprint Corp., 1968.

————. "Sweat." *Black American Literature: Fiction*. Ed. Darwin Turner. Columbus, OH: Charles Merrill, 1969.

————. *Tell My Horse*. Philadelphia: Lippincott, 1938.

Jessye, Eva. "Rock Mt. Sinai!" Ed. Julian Work. New York: Skidmore Music Company, 1965. (SATB)

Jessye, Eva, adapter. "He's Carried the Key and Gone Home." Ed. Julian Work. New York: Skidmore Music Company, 1965.

————. "Handcar Blues." Ed. Julian Work. New York: Skidmore Music Company, 1935. (SATB)

————. *My Spirituals*. Ed. Julian Work. New York: Robbins, Inc., 1927.

Kunjufu, Johari M. (Johari Amini; Jewel C. Latimore). *Folk Fable*. Chicago: Third World Press, 1969.

Lift Every Voice and Sing: A Collection of Afro-American Spirituals and Other Songs. New York: The Church Hymnal Corporation, 1981.

Livingston, Jane, and John Beardsley, eds. *Black Folk Art in America, 1930–1980*. Jackson, MS: University of Mississippi, 1981.

Scarborough, Dorothy. *On Trail of Negro Folk Songs*. Hatboro, PA: Folklore Associates, 1965.

Walker, Margaret. "Molly Means." *Book of Negro Folklore.* Eds. Langston Hughes and Arna Bontemps. New York: Dodd, Mead and Company, 1958.

Whiting, Helen Adele. *Negro Folk Tales for Pupils in the Primary Grades.* Illust. Lois Mailou Jones. Book I. Washington, DC: Associated Publishers, 1938.

Wilson, James L. *Clementine Hunter: American Folk Artist.* Gretna, LA: Pelican Publishers, 1988.

Work, John W., ed. *American Negro Songs and Spirituals.* New York: Bonanza Books, 1940.

Recordings

Sweet Honey in the Rock. *Believe I'll Run On* and *See What the End's Gonna Be.* Ukiah, CA (Box 996, 95482): Redwood Records, n.d.

————. *Feel Something Drawing Me On.* N.p.: Flying Fish Records, n.d.

————. *The Other Side.* N.p.: Flying Fish Records, n.d.

Literary History and Criticism

Abramson, Doris E. *Negro Playwrights in the American Theatre, 1925–1959.* New York: Columbia University Press, 1969.

Amini, Johari. "Big Time Buck White." *Black World* 20 (Oct. 1971): 72–74.

Arnez, Nancy L. "Racial Understanding Through Literature." *English Journal* 58 (Jan. 1969): 56–61.

Awkward, Michael. *Inspiriting Influences.* New York: Columbia University, 1989.

Baker, Houston A. *Singers of Daybreak: Studies in Black American Literature.* Washington, DC: Howard University Press, 1974.

Baker, Houston A., Jr. *Blues, Ideology, and Afro-American Literature: A Vernacular Theory.* Chicago: University of Chicago Press, 1984.

————. *The Journey Back: Issues in Black Literature and Criticism.* Chicago: University of Chicago Press, 1980.

Ball, Jane Lee. "Gordon Parks." *DLB,* Vol. 33. Eds. Trudier Harris and Thadious Davis. Detroit: Gale Research, 1984: 203–208.

Bambara, Toni Cade. "Voices from the Third World: Fragment from a Lost Diary and Other Stories: Women of Asia, Africa, and Latin America." Eds. Naomi Katz and Nancy Milton. *Ms* Aug. 1974; N.p.: Pantheon Books, n.d.

Barton, Rebecca C. *Race Consciousness and the American Negro . . . The Correlation between the Group Experience and the Fiction of 1900–1930.* Copenhagen: Busck, 1934.

————. *Witness for Freedom, Negro Americans in Autobiography.* New York: Harper, 1948.

Beard, Linda Susan. "The Black Woman Writer and the Diaspora." Conference at Michigan State University, East Lansing, Michigan, October 27–30, 1985. Report of proceedings in *Sage* 2 (Fall 1986): 70–71.

Bell, Bernard W. *The Afro-American Novel and Its Tradition.* Amherst: University of Massachusetts Press, 1987.

Bell, Roseann P., and Beverly Guy-Sheftall. "Images of Black Women, An Introduction to an Unpublished Manuscript." *Southern Exposure* 3 (1975): 62–63.

Bell, Roseann P., Betty J. Parker, and Beverly Guy-Sheftall, eds. *Sturdy Black Bridges: Visions of Black Women in Literature.* Illust. Leo Carty and Richard. New York: Anchor Books, 1979.

Berry, Faith. *Langston Hughes: Before and Beyond Harlem.* Westport, CT: Lawrence Hill and Company, 1983.

Bigsby, C. W. E. *The Black American Writer: Fiction.* Deland, FL: Everett/Edwards, 1969.

————. *The Black American Writer: Poetry.* Deland, FL: Everett/ Edwards, 1969.

Blake, E. L. "Zora Neale Hurston: Author and Folklorist." *Negro History Bull* 29 (Apr. 1966): 149–150.

Bogle, Donald. *Toms, Coons, Mulattos, Mammie, and Bucks.* New York: Viking Press, 1973.

Bond, Jean Carey. *Keeping the Faith: Writings by Contemporary Black American Women.* Ed. Pat Crutchfield Exum. Greenwich, CT: Fawcett Publications, n.d.; *Freedomways* 15 (Second Quarter 1975): 125.

Bone, Robert. *Down Home: A History of Afro-American Short Fiction from Its Beginnings to the Harlem Renaissance.* New York: Putnam, 1975.

Bone, Robert A. *The Negro Novel in America.* New Haven, CT: Yale University Press, 1958.

Brawley, Benjamin. *Early Negro American Writers: Biographical and Critical Introduction. Selections with Biographical and Critical Introductions.* Chapel Hill, NC: University of North Carolina Press, 1935.

————. *The Negro Genius.* Toronto: McClelland and Stewart, 1937.

————. *The Negro in Literature and Art.* New York: Dodd, Mead and Company, 1929.

Braxton, Joanne M. "Black American Women: A Tradition Within a Tradition." Dissertation, Yale University, 1984.

Brooks, Gwendolyn. *A Capsule Course in Black Poetry Writing.* Detroit: Broadside Press, 1975.

————. "Of Frank London Brown: A Tenant of the World." *Negro Digest* 18 (Sept. 1962): 44.

Brown, Sterling A. *Negro Poetry and Drama.* Washington, DC: Associates in Negro Folk Education, 1939; New York: Arno Press, 1969; combined with *The Negro in American Fiction.* New York: Atheneum, 1968.

Bruck, Peter, and Wolfgang Karrer, eds. *The Afro-American Novel Since 1960.* Amsterdam: B. P. Grunes, 1982.

Buncombe, Marie. "Androgyny as Metaphor in Alice Walker's Novels." *CLA Journal* 30.4 (June 1987): 419–427.

Butterfield, Stephen. *Black Autobiography in America.* Amherst, MA: University of Massachusetts Press, 1974.

Byrd, James W. "Zora Neale Hurston: A Novel Folklorist." *Tennessee Folklore Society Bulletin* 20 (1955): 37–41.

Carby, Hazel V. *Reconstructing Womanhood: The Emergence of the Afro-American Woman Novelist.* New York: Oxford University Press, 1987. (Also excellent bibliography)

Carter, Steven R. *Hansberry's Drama: Commitment Amid Complexity.* Urbana and Chicago: University of Illinois Press, 1991.

Childress, Alice. "A Woman Playwright Speaks Her Mind." *Freedomways* 6 (1966): 75–80.

Clarke, John Henrik. "The Neglected Dimensions of the Harlem Renaissance." *Black World* 20 (Nov. 1970): 124–125.

Clarke, Sebastian. "Sonia Sanchez and Her Work." *Black World* 20 (June 1971): 45–48, 96–98.

Collier, Eugenia. "A Pain in His Soul: Simple as Epic Hero." *Langston Hughes: Black Genius.* Ed. Therman O'Daniel. New York: William Morrow, 1971.

———. "Afro-American Writers." *Black World* 19 (Sep. 1970): 92–93.

———. "Ain't Supposed to Die a Natural Death." *Black World* 6 (Apr. 1972): 79–81.

———. "Black Phoenix." *Black World* 19 (Sep. 1970): 77.

———. "Heritage from Harlem." *Black World* 20 (Nov. 1970): 52–59.

————. "Some Black and Fettered Women." *Black World* 21 (Nov. 1971): 41.

————. "The Endless Journey of an Ex-Colored Man." *Phylon* 32 (Fourth Quarter, Winter 1971): 365–373.

————. "The Four-Way Dilemma of Claude McKay." *CLA Journal* 15 (Mar. 1972): 345–353.

————. "The Nightmare Truth of an Invisible Man." *Black World* 20 (Dec. 1970): 12–19.

————. "The Phrase Unbearably Repeated." *Phylon* 25 (1964): 288–296.

————. "Thematic Patterns in Baldwin's Essays." *Black World* 21 (June 1972): 28–34.

Collins, Patricia Hill. "A Comparison of Two Works on Black Family Life." *Signs* (Summer 1989): 875ff.

Crockett, J. "An Essay on Gwendolyn Brooks." *Negro History Bulletin* 19 (1955): 37–39.

Cunningham, Virginia. *Paul Laurence Dunbar and His Song.* New York: Biblo and Tannen, 1969.

Dance, Daryl. "James Baldwin." *Black American Writers: Bibliographical Essays, II: Richard Wright, Ralph Ellison, James Baldwin, and Amiri Baraka.* Eds. M. Thomas Inge, Maurice Duke, and Jackson R. Bryer. New York: St. Martin's Press, 1978.

Dandridge, Rita B. "In Adapting the Novel, Spielberg Left Out Too Much." Review of *The Color Purple,* by Steven Spielberg. *Black Film Review* 2.2 (Spring 1986): 16–18.

————. Rev. of *Black Women Novelists: The Development of a Tradition,* by Barbara Christian. *Melus* 9 (Winter 1982): 77–79.

————. "Louise Meriwether." *Dictionary of Literary Biography: Afro-American Fiction Writers after 1955.* Eds. Trudier Harris and Thadious M. Davis. Detroit: Gale Research, 1984. 182–186.

————. "Male Critics/Black Women's Novels." *CLA Journal* 23 (Sep. 1979): 1–11.

————. "On Novels Written by Black Women Authors: A Bibliographical Essay." *Women's Studies Newsletter* 6 (Summer 1978): 28–30.

Davis, Arthur P. "Gwendolyn Brooks: Poet of the Unheroic." *CLA Journal* 7 (Dec. 1963): 118.

————. "The Black-and-Tan Motif in the Poetry of Gwendolyn Brooks." *CLA Journal* 6 (Dec. 1962): 95–97.

Davis, Thadious M. *Faulkner's "Negro": Art and the Southern Context.* Baton Rouge: Louisiana State University Press, 1983.

DeCosta[-Willis], Miriam, ed. *Blacks in Hispanic Literature: A Collection of Critical Essays.* Port Washington, NY: Kennikat Press, 1977.

Dee, Ruby. "Exciting Novel by Talented Story Teller." Review of *The Autobiography of Miss Jane Pittman,* by Ernest J. Gaines. New York: Dial Press, n.d.; *Freedomways* 11 (Second Quarter 1971): 202–203.

————. "The Tattered Queens." *Negro Digest* 15 (Apr. 1966): 32–36.

Dempsey, David. "Uncle Tom's Ghost and the Literary Abolitionist." *Antioch Review* 6 (1946): 442–448.

Dreer, Herman. *American Literature by Negro Authors.* New York: Macmillan, 1950.

Dunbar-Nelson, Alice. "As in a Looking Glass." *The Washington Eagle* 1926–1930; *The Works of Alice Dunbar-Nelson.* Volume 2. Ed. Gloria Hull. *The Schomburg Library of Nineteenth-Century Black Women Writers* series. Gen. ed. Henry Louis Gates, Jr. New York: Oxford University Press, 1988.

————. "From a Woman's Point of View." *The Pittsburgh Courier* (2 Jan. 1926 to 18 Sep. 1926). (Title changed in Feb. 1926 to "Une Femme Dit."); *The Works of Alice Dunbar-Nelson.* Volume 3. Ed. Gloria Hull. *The Schomburg Library of Nineteenth-*

Century Black Women Writers series. Gen. ed. Henry Louis Gates, Jr. New York: Oxford University Press, 1988.

―――. "Paul Laurence Dunbar: Poet Laureate of the Negro Race." *The A. M. E. Church Review* 21 (Oct. 1914): 5–17.

―――. "An Artist in the Family," by Sarah Gertrude Millin. *Pittsburgh Courier* (27 Feb. 1930): 6.

―――. "Blind Spots," by Henry Smith Leiper. *Pittsburgh Courier* (1 Feb. 1930): 6.

―――. "*Bronze: A Book of Verse,* by Georgia Douglass Johnson." Review. Introd. W. E. B. DuBois. Boston: B. J. Brimmer Co. *The Messenger* 5 (May 1923): 698, 719.

―――. "Negro Literature for Negro Pupils." *The Southern Workman* 51 (Feb. 1922): 59–63.

―――. "Wordsworth's Use of Milton's Description of the Building of Pandemonium." Letter in *Modern Language Notes* 24.4 (Apr. 1909): 124–125.

Elder, Arlene A. *The "Hindered Hand," Cultural Implications of Early African-American Fiction.* Westport, CT/London: Greenwood Press, 1978.

Emmanuel, James A. "A Note on the Future of Negro Poetry." *Negro American Literature Forum* 1 (Fall 1967): 2–3.

Evans, Mari, ed. *Black Women Writers (1950–1980): A Critical Evaluation.* Garden City, NY: Anchor Books, 1984; New York: Doubleday, 1984.

Fields, Julia. "The Green of Langston's Ivy." *Negro Digest* 16 (Sep. 1967): 58–59.

Fisher, Dexter, ed. *The Third Woman: Minority Women Writers in the United States.* Boston: Houghton Mifflin, 1980.

Ford, Nick Aaron. "Alice Dunbar-Nelson." *Notable American Women, 1607–1950.* Eds. Edward T. James et al. Cambridge, MA: Harvard-Belknap University Press, 1971.

Fowler, Carolyn. *A Knot in the Thread: The Life and Work of Jacques Roumain.* Washington, DC: Howard University Press, 1981.

————. "Motif Symbolism in Jacques Roumain's 'Guiverneurs De La Rosee.' " *CLA Journal* 18 (Sept. 1974): 44–51.

Gant, Liz. "Les Blancs, by Lorraine Hansberry." *Black World* 6 (Apr. 1971): 46–47.

Garland, Phil. "The Prize Winners, Vastly Different New York Plays Bring Top Awards to Blacks." *Ebony* 25 (July 1970): 29–37.

Gayle, Addison. *The Way of the New World: The Black Novel in America.* Garden City, NY: Doubleday, 1973.

Giddings, Paula. "A Shoulder Hunched Against a Sharp Concern: Some Themes in the Poetry of Margaret Walker." *Black World* 21 (Dec. 1971): 20–25.

Giovanni, Nikki. *A Dialogue: James Baldwin and Nikki Giovanni.* Fore. Ida Lewis. Aft. Orde Coombs. Philadelphia: Lippincott, 1972.

————. "Black Poems, Poseurs and Power." *Negro Digest* 28 (June 1969): 30–34.

————. *"The Chosen Place, the Chosen People,* by Paule Marshall." *Black World* 19 (January 1970): 51–52, 84.

Giovanni, Nikki, and Margaret Walker. *A Poetic Equation: Conversations Between Nikki Giovanni and Margaret Walker.* Washington, DC: Howard University Press, 1974.

Gloster, Hugh. *Negro Voices in American Fiction.* Chapel Hill, NC: University of North Carolina Press, 1948.

Graham, Maryemma. "The Three Fold Chord: Blackness, Womanness, and Art, A Study of the Life and Work of Frances Ellen Watkins Harper." Master's Thesis, Cornell University, 1973.

Green, Marjorie. "Ann Petry Planned to Write." *Opportunity: A Journal of Negro Life* 24 (1946): 78–79.

Gresham, Jewell Handy. "America's Past, America's Ghosts." Rev. of *Beloved,* by Toni Morrison. *Christianity and Crisis* (4 Apr. 1988): 116–120.

Gresham, Jewell Handy, ed. "James Baldwin Comes Home." *Essence* 7 (June 1976): 54, 55, 80, 82, 85, 86.

Guy-Sheftall, Beverly. "A Conversation with Willa Player." *Sage: A Scholarly Journal on Black Women* 1 (Fall 1984): 16–19.

———. *"Ain't I a Woman, Black Women and Feminism,* by Bell Hooks." *Phylon* 44 (Mar. 1983): 84–85.

———. "Commitment: Toni Cade Bambara Speaks." *Sturdy Black Bridges.* Eds. Roseann P. Bell et al. Garden City, NY: Anchor Press/Doubleday, 1979: 230–249.

———. "Introduction, *No Crystal Stair: Visions of Race and Sex in Black Women's Fiction,* by Gloria Wade-Gayles." New York: Pilgrim Press, 1984.

———. *Migrations of the Heart: A Personal Odyssey,* by Marita Golden. New York: Anchor **Books,** 1983; *Black Southern Magazine* 1 (June 1984): 8.

———. "The Women of Bronzeville." *Sturdy Black Bridges.* Eds. Roseann P. Bell et al. Garden City, NY: Anchor Press/ Doubleday, 1979.

Gwin, Minrose C. *Black and White Women of the Old South: The Peculiar Sisterhood in American Literature.* Knoxville: University of Tennessee Press, 1985.

Hansberry, Lorraine. "A Letter from Lorraine Hansberry on *Porgy and Bess.*" *The Theater* (August 1959): 10.

———. "Genet, Mailer and the New Paternalism." *Village Voice* (1 June 1961): 10–15.

———. "Me Tink Me Hear Sounds in De Night." *American Playwrights on Drama.* Ed. Horst Frenz. New York: Hill & Wang, 1965.

————. "The Negro in the American Theatre." *American Playwright in Drama.* Ed. Horst Frenz. New York: Hill & Wang, 1965.

Harlem Renaissance: Art of Black America. New York: The Studio Museum in Harlem, 1987.

Harley, Sharon, and Rosalyn Terborg-Penn, eds. *The Afro-American Women: Struggles and Images.* New York: Kennikat Press, 1978.

Harris, Trudier. *Black Women in the Fiction of James Baldwin.* Knoxville: University of Tennessee Press, 1985.

————. "Ellison's 'Peter Wheatstraw': His Basis in Black Folk Tradition." *Mississippi Folklore Register* 9 (1975): 117–126.

————. *Exorcising Blackness: Historical and Literary Lynching and Burning Rituals.* Bloomington, IN: Indiana University Press, 1984.

————. *From Mammies to Militants: Domestics in Black American Literature.* Philadelphia: Temple University, 1982.

————. "The Eye as Weapon in *If Beal Street Could Talk.*" *Melus* 4 (Fall 1978): 54–66.

————. "The South as Woman: Climeric Images of Emasculation in *Just Above My Head.*" *Studies in Black American Literature.* Eds. Joe Weixlmann and Chester J. Fontenot. Greenwood, FL: Penkevill Publishing Co., 1983. 89–109.

————. "Violence in 'The Third Life of Grange Copeland.' " *CLA Journal* 2.19 (Dec. 1975): 238–247.

Hemenway, Robert, ed. *The Black Novelist.* Columbus, OH: Charles Merrill, 1970.

Hemenway, Robert E. *Zora Neale Hurston: A Literary Biography.* Fore. Alice Walker. Champaign, IL: University of Illinois Press, 1977.

Hernton, Calvin C. *The Sexual Mountain and Black Women Writers: Adventures in Sex, Literature, and Real Life.* New York: Anchor Books, 1987.

Hollis, Burney J. *Amid Visions and Revisions.* Baltimore: Morgan State University, 1985.

Hollis, Burney J., ed. *Sword upon This Hill.* Baltimore: Morgan State University, 1984.

Hooks, Bell. *Ain't I a Woman.* Boston: South End Press, 1981.

————. *Feminist Theory: From Margin to Center.* Boston: South End Press, 1984.

————. *Talking Back, Thinking Feminist, Thinking Black.* Boston: South End Press, 1988.

Huggins, Nathan. *Harlem Renaissance.* New York: Oxford University Press, 1971.

Hughes, Carl. *The Negro Novelist, 1940–1950.* New York: The Citadel Press, 1953.

Hughes, Langston. "Black Renaissance." *The Big Sea.* New York: Knopf, 1940.

Hull, Gloria. *Three Women Writers of the Harlem Renaissance. Everyman Studies in History, Literature and Culture.* Blacks in the Diaspora Series. Bloomington, IN: Indiana University Press, 1987.

————. "A Note on the Poetic Technique of Gwendolyn Brooks." *CLA Journal* 2 (Dec. 1975): 280–285.

————. " 'Under the Days': The Buried Life and Poetry of Angelina Weld Grimke." *Conditions Five* (Black Women's Issue). Ed. Lorraine Bethel and Barbara Smith (1979): 17–25.

Hull, Gloria T., Patricia Bell Scott, and Barbara Smith, eds. *But Some of Us Are Brave.* Old Westbury, NY: The Feminist Press, 1982.

Hutson, Jean S. Blackwell. "Choosing Books for Harlemites." *Opportunity* 17 (May 1939): 146–148.

Isaacs, Harold. "Five Writers and Their African Ancestors: Part I." *Phylon* 21 (1960): 66–70.

Jackson, Blyden. "Some Negroes in the Land of Goshen." *Tennessee Folklore Society Bulletin* 19 (1953): 103–107.

Jackson, Blyden, and Louis D. Rubin. *Black Poetry in America: Two Essays in Historical Interpretation.* Baton Rouge: Louisiana State University Press, 1974.

Jackson, Esther Merle. "The American Negro and the Image of the Absurd." *Phylon: The Atlanta University Review of Race and Culture* 23 (Winter 1962): 359–371.

Jaffee, Dan. "Gwendolyn Brooks: An Appreciation from the White Suburbs." *The Black American Writer, II: Poetry and Drama.* Ed. C. W. E. Bigsby. Baltimore: Penguin Books, 1969.

Johnson, Charles S. "Some Books of 1924." *Opportunity* 26 (Feb. 1925): 59. (Review J. Fauset)

Johnson, Helen Armstead. "Ododo," by Joseph A. Walker. *Black World* 6 (April 1971): 47–48.

Jones, Iva G. "Trollope, Carlyle, and Mill on the Negro: An Episode in the History of Ideas." *Journal of Negro History* 52 (1985): 185–189.

Jordan, June. "On Richard Wright and Zora Neale Hurston: Notes Toward a Balancing of Love and Hatred." *Black World* 13 (Aug. 1974): 4–8.

Joyce, Joyce Ann. *Richard Wright's Art of Tragedy.* Iowa City, IA: University of Iowa Press, 1986.

Julianelli, J. "Angelou: Interview." *Harper's Bazaar* (Nov. 1972): 124.

Kent, George E. "The Poetry of Gwendolyn Brooks, Part I." *Black World* 11 (Sep. 1971): 30–43.

———. "The Poetry of Gwendolyn Brooks, Part II." *Black World* 12 (Oct. 1971): 36–48, 68–71.

Killens, John O. "Broadway in Black and White." *A Forum* I.iii (1965): 66–70.

Krier, Beth Ann. "Maya Angelou: No Longer a 'Caged Bird.' " View Section, *Los Angeles Times* (24 Sep. 1976): 1, 8, 9.

Kuel, Linda. "Takes Two." Review of *Sula,* by Toni Morrison and *In Love and Trouble,* by Alice Walker. *Viva* 1.6 (Mar. 1974): 35.

Lee, Donald L. "The Poets and Their Poetry." *Dynamite Voices I: Black Poets of the 1960's.* Ed. Don L. Lee. Detroit: Broadside Press, 1971.

"Les Blancs." *Nation* 211 (30 Nov. 1970): 573.

Lewis, Theophilus. "Social Protest in *A Raisin in the Sun.*" *Catholic World* 190 (1959): 31–35.

Littlejohn, David. *Black on White: A Critical Survey of Writings by American Negroes.* New York: Grossman Publishers, 1966.

McDowell, Deborah. "New Directions for Black Feminist Criticism." *The New Feminist Criticism.* Ed. Elaine Showalter. New York: Pantheon Books, 1985.

———. "The Self in Bloom: Alice Walker's *Meridian.*" *CLA Journal* 24.3 (Mar. 1981): 262–275.

McDowell, Deborah E., and Arnold Rampersad, eds. *Slavery and the Literary Imagination.* Baltimore/London: The Johns Hopkins University Press, 1989.

McFarlin, Annjennette Sophie. *Black Congressional Reconstruction Orators and Their Orations, 1869–1879.* Metuchen, NJ: Scarecrow Press, 1976.

McKay, Nellie Y. *Critical Essays on Toni Morrison.* Boston: G. K. Hall, 1988.

Miller, Adam David. "Brown Girl, Brownstones." *Black Scholar* 9 (May 1972): 56–58.

———. "Some Observations on the World of Toni Morrison." *Good News: A Publication of the Laney College Faculty* 2.2 (Spring–Summer 1978): 26–29.

Mitchell, Loften. *Black Drama.* New York: Hawthorn Books, 1967.

Morrison, Toni. *Playing in the Dark: Whiteness and the Literary Imagination.* Cambridge: Harvard University Press, 1992.

Nicholas, Denise. "Blacks in Television." *Black World* 6 (Apr. 1976): 36–42.

Njeri, Itabari. "Black Not Like Me." *Two Trips Through 'The Colored Museum.'* " Calendar Section, *Los Angeles Times* (12 June 1988): 46, 47.

Parks, Carole A. "J. E. Franklin, Playwright." *Black World* 6 (Apr. 1972): 49–50.

Payne, Ladell. *Black Novelists and the Southern Literary Tradition.* Athens, GA: University of Georgia Press, 1981.

Perry, Margaret. *Silence to the Drums: A Survey of the Literature of the Harlem Renaissance.* Westport, CT: Greenwood Press, 1976.

Perry, Ruth, and Martine Watson Brownley. *Mothering the Mind: Twelve Studies of Writers and Their Silent Partners.* New York: Holmes & Meier, 1984.

Petry, Ann (Lane). "The Novel in Social Criticism." *The Writer's Book.* Ed. Helen Rose. Presented by the Author's Guild. New York: Harper, 1950.

Pool, Rosey E. "Robert Hayden: Poet Laureate." *Negro Digest* 15 (June 1966): 164–175.

Pryse, Marjorie, and Hortense J. Spillers, eds. *Conjuring: Black Women, Fiction, and Literary Tradition.* Bloomington, IN: Indiana University Press, 1985.

Redding, Saunders. *The Lonesome Road: A Narrative History of Blacks in America.* New York: Anchor/Doubleday, 1973.

Redmond, Eugene B. *Drumvoices: The Mission of Afro-American Poetry.* Garden City: Anchor/Doubleday, 1976.

Reid, Margaret A. "A Rhetorical Analysis of Black Protest Poetry

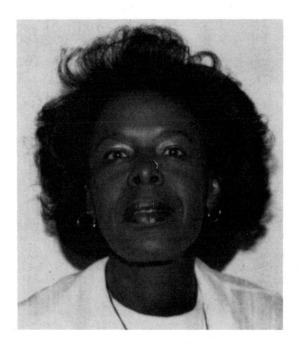

Margaret Reid

of the Sixties." *MAWA Review* 1.2, 1.3 (Summer–Fall 1982): 50–55.

———. "Langston Hughes: Rhetoric and Protest." *Langston Hughes Review* 3 (Spring 1984): 13–20.

———. "The Image of the Child in Contemporary Black Literature." *The Leaflet* 85 (Spring 1986): 29–36.

Robinson, William H. *Critical Essays on Phillis Wheatley.* Boston: G. K. Hall, 1982.

Rogers, Norma. "Struggle for Humanity." Review of *Meridian,* by

Alice Walker. New York: Harcourt Brace Jovanovich, 1976; *Freedomways* 16 (Second Quarter 1976): 120–122.

―――. "To Destroy Life." Review of *A Hero Ain't Nothing But a Sandwich,* by Alice Childress. New York: Coward, McCann, and Geoghegan, n.d.; *Freedomways* 1 (First Quarter 1974): 72–75.

Rushing, Andrea Benton. "The Changing Same: Images of Black Women in Afro-American Poetry." *Black World* 11 (Sep. 1975): 18–30.

Russell, Mariann B. "Elements of the City in Williams' Arthurian Poetry." *Mythlore* (Fall 1979): 10–19.

―――. "Ghetto Laughter: A Note on Tolson's Style." *Obsidian* 5 (Spring 1979): 7–16.

―――. *Melvin B. Tolson's* Harlem Gallery: *A Literary Analysis.* Columbia, MO: University of Missouri Press, 1980.

Sheffey, Ruth T. *The Literary Reputation of Aphra Behn.* Microfilm, 1981.

―――. *A Rainbow Round Her Shoulder: The Zora Neale Hurston Symposium Papers.* Baltimore: Morgan State University Press, 1982.

Sherman, Joan R. *Invisible Poets: Afro-Americans of Nineteenth Century.* Urbana/Chicago/London: The University of Illinois Press, 1974.

Shockley, Ann Allen. "Oral History: A Research Tool for Black History." *Negro History Bulletin* 41 (Jan.–Feb. 1978): 187–189.

Sloan, Margaret Edmondson. "Keeping the Black Woman in Her Place." (film) *Ms.* (Jan. 1974): 30–31.

Smith, Barbara. "Beautiful, Needed, Mysterious." Review of *Sula,* by Toni Morrison. New York: Knopf, 1974; *Freedomways* 14 (First Quarter 1974): 72–75.

Smith, Valerie. *Self Discovery and Authority in Afro-American Narrative.* Cambridge: Harvard University Press, 1987.

Smitherman, Geneva. "Ron Milner, People's Playwright." *Black World* 6 (Apr. 1976): 4–19.

Southerland, Ellease. "Zora Neale Hurston: The Novelist-Anthropologist's Life/Works." *Black World* 23 (Aug. 1974): 20–30.

Starling, Marion Wilson. *The Slave Narrative: Its Place in American History*. Dissert. New York University, 1946; Washington, DC: Howard University Press, 1988.

Tate, Claudia. "All the Preacher's Women." *Review of Almost Midnight*, by Don Belton. New York: Beech Tree Books; The *New York Times Book Review* Section (17 Aug. 1986).

———. *Black Women Writers at Work*. New York: Continuum, 1983.

Teer, Barbara Ann. "Needed: A New Image." *The Black Power Revolt*. Ed. Floyd Barbour. Boston: Porter Sargent, 1968.

The American Negro Writer and His Roots. (Selected Papers from the First Conference of Negro Writers, Mar. 1959) New York: American Society of African Culture, 1960.

"The Sign in Sidney Brustein's Window." *National Review* 17 (Mar. 23, 1965): 250.

Tignor, Eleanor Q. "Rudolph Fisher: Harlem Novelist." *The Langston Hughes Review* 1 (Fall 1982): 13–22.

———. "The College Language Association: 1983–1984 and Beyond." *CLA Journal* 286 (June 1983): 367–383.

———. "The Short Fiction of Rudolph Fisher." *The Langston Hughes Review* 1 (Spring 1982): 18–23.

———. "Toni Morrison's Pecola: A Portrait of Pathos." *MAWA Review* 1 (Spring 1982): 24–26. (Middle Atlantic Writers Association)

Turner, Darwin T. "The Negro Novelist and the South." *Southern Humanities Review* 1 (1967): 21–29.

————. "Zora Neale Hurston: The Wandering Minstrel." *In a Minor Chord: Three Afro-American Writers and Their Search for Identity.* Carbondale, IL: Southern Illinois University Press, 1971.

Wade-Gayles, Gloria. *No Crystal Stair: Visions of Race and Sex in Black Women's Fiction.* New York: The Pilgrim Press, 1984.

Walker, Margaret. *Demoniac Genius: A Portrait of the Man, A Critical Look at His Work.* New York: Warner, Inc., 1988.

————. *How I Wrote "Jubilee."* Chicago: Third World Press, 1972.

Washington, Mary Helen. "Black Women Image Makers." *Black World* 10 (Aug. 1974): 10–18.

————. *Invented Lives: Narrative of Black Women 1860–1960.* New York: Anchor Books, 1987.

Watson, Carol McAlpine. *Prologues: The Novels of Black American Women 1891–1965.* Westport, CT: Greenwood Press, 1985.

Whitlow, Roger. *Black American Literature: A Critical History.* Totowa, NJ: Rowan & Allanheld, 1984.

Williams, Kenny Jackson. *They Also Spoke.* Nashville, TN: Townsend Press, 1970.

Yellen, Jean Fagan. *The Intricate Knot: The Negro in American Literature, 1776–1863.* New York: New York University, 1971.

AUDIO-VISUAL MATERIALS BY AND ABOUT AFRICAN-AMERICAN WOMEN AND THEIR WORKS

A Woman Called Moses. TV movie about Harriet Tubman, 12–13 Feb. 1988 (Channel 11, KTTV Fox). Starring Cicely Tyson, with Will Geer, Robert Hooks, James Wainwright, and Jason Bernard.

Almos' a Man. (A Richard Wright story starring LeVar Burton and Madge Sinclair) Merit Audio Visual, Box 392, New York 10024 ($59.95).

Amini, Johari M. *Spectrum in Black.* Scott, Foresman, 1971. (Includes poetry of Amini)

Anthology of Negro Poets. Includes Gwendolyn Brooks and Margaret Walker. Folkways Records FL 9791.

Autobiography of Miss Jane Pittman. Extension Media Center (2223 Shattuck Ave., Berkeley, CA 94720), 1974.

Bambara, Toni Cade. Interview: origins, work, philosophy. 58 mins. Columbia, MO: The American Audio Prose Library, Inc. Order No. 2022, $10.95.

————. Reading ("The Organizer's Wife") and interview as a set. Columbia, MO: The American Audio Prose Library, Inc. Order No. 2023, $20.00.

————. Reads short story: "The Organizer's Wife." 52 mins. Columbia, MO: The American Audio Prose Library, Inc. Order No. 2021, $10.95.

————. *Tony Cade Bambara Interview.* Columbia, MO: The American Audio Prose Library, Inc., n.d. (58 min.)

Black America Speaks. Vinnie Burrows, James Earl Jones, Josephine

161

Premice, Josh White, Jr., Langston Hughes. Columbia, MO: The American Audio Prose Library, Inc. Six casettes in a binder: Order No. PCC 23, $49.00. Teachers Guide: Order No. PCC 23 TG, $2.00.

Black Authors (Wright, Hansberry, James Weldon Johnson, Langston Hughes, Gwendolyn Brooks, James Baldwin). (Jr. and Sr. High School level) Merit Audio Visual (Box 392, New York 10024), n.d.

Black on Black. Individual films on Shirley Chisholm, Coretta King, and others. Produced and distributed by Timelli, 1971. 60 min. Rental $7.50; purchase $50.

Black Writer Mini-Package. (James Baldwin, Ernest Gaines, Paule Marshall, Toni Morrison, Alice Walker) Interview with Kay Bonetti, separate or with Reading Series. Columbia, MO: The American Audio Prose Library, Inc. Reading Series, includes 5 author readings: Order SS-21, $54.75 (reg.), $43.75 (sp.). Interview Series, includes 5 authors: Order SS-22, $54.75 (reg.), $43.75 (sp.). Complete Series, including 5 readings and 5 interviews: Order SS-23, $109.50 (reg.), $81.95 (sp.).

Black Writer Series. (Chinua Achebe, James Baldwin, Toni Cade Bambara, Ernest Gaines, Paule Marshall, Toni Morrison, Gloria Naylor, Michael Thelwell, Alice Walker, John Edgar Wideman, Al Young). Interviews with Kay Bonetti, available separately or with Reading Series. Columbia, MO: The American Audio Prose Library, Inc. Reading Series, includes 11 authors: Order SS-11, $132.45 (reg.), $105.95 (sp.). Interview Series, includes 11 authors: Order SS-12, $132.45 (reg.), $105.95 (sp.). Complete series, includes 11 readings and 11 interviews: Order SS-13, $264.90 (reg.), $195.95 (sp.).

Black Writer Series. (Naylor, Achebe, Baldwin, Bambara, Gaines, Marshall, Morrison, Thelwell, Walker, Wideman, Al Young). Interviews with Kay Bonetti are available separately or with Reading Series. Columbia, MO: The American Audio Prose Library, Inc. Reading Series, all 11 authors reading: Order No. SS-11, $105.95. Interview Series, all 11 authors interviewed: Order No. SS-12, $105.95. Complete series combined: Order No. SS-13, $197.96.

Bontemps, Arna, ed. *Anthology of Negro Poets.* Includes readings by

Gwendolyn Brooks, Margaret Walker, Langston Hughes, Sterling Brown, Claude McKay, Countee Cullen. Folkways Records FL 9791.

Brannon, Jean M., comp. and ed. Reader, Dorothy Washington. *The Negro Woman.* Excerpts from works by Phillis Wheatley and Harriet Tubman. Folkways Records FH 5523.

Brooks, Gwendolyn. *Gwendolyn Brooks Reading Her Poems with Comment.* 19 January 1961. Library of Congress 109 LW 3237.

———. "Kitchenette," "Song of the Yard," "The Preacher Ruminates," "The Children of the Poor," "Old Laughter," and "Beverly Hills, Chicago." *Anthology of Negro Poets,* Folkways Records FL 9791.

Brooks, Gwendolyn, and Peter Viereck. A joint reading by the two poets at the YMHA Poetry Center, New York. Library of Congress 110 LWO 2863. Reel 2.

Burroughs, Margaret G. *What Shall I Tell My Children Who Are Black?* Sound-A-Rama SOR 11 2S 12.

Burrows, Vinnie. *Vinnie Burrows.* Production Listening Library, Inc., 1 Park Ave., Greenwich, CT 06870.

Dark Madonna Symposium: Women, Culture & Community Rituals. Visual Media Archive, UCLA Center for the Comparative Study of Folklore and Mythology, University of California, Los Angeles 90024–1530.

Delta Sigma Theta. *Roses and Revolutions.* Delta Sigma Theta Telecommunications, Inc. Production, 1836 New Hampshire Avenue, Washington, DC 20009.

Delta Sigma Theta Sorority. *Count Down at Kusini.* Dist. Columbia Pictures, 1976.

Evans, Mari. *Singing Black.* Indianapolis: Reed Visuals, 1976.

"Eyes on the Prize" (TV Movie) (Civil Rights Years, Washington). PBS, 1 Feb. 1988.

Fannie Lou Hamer: Portrait in Black. (film) New York: Sterling Educational Films (241 East 34 St. 10016), 1972.

Featherston, Elena. *Visions of Spirit*. (Portrait of Alice Walker and examination of *The Color Purple*) Premier showing, Palace of Fine Arts (3301 Lyon Street) San Francisco, Apr. 1988.

First Steps: An Education Album for All Ages. Thinkers World (TW 1001), 1977. Box 77846, Los Angeles, CA 90007.

Fundi: The Story of Ella Baker. (film) (Documentary of the life of a little-known major Civil Rights figure) Franklin Lakes, NJ: Fundi Productions, n.d.

Giovanni, Nikki. *Cotton Candy on a Rainy Day*. Folkways.

―――. *Legacies*. Folkways.

―――. *Like a Ripple on a Pond*. Nik Tom.

―――. *Nikki Giovanni Reads Re: Creation*. Detroit: Broadside, n.d. $5.00.

―――. *The Reason I Like Chocolate*. Folkways.

―――. *The Way I Feel*. Atlantic Records.

―――. *Truth Is on Its Way*. Right-on Records 15001.

"Great Black Women: Achievers against the Odds." (TV Movie) (Whoopie Goldberg, Shirley Chisholm, Billie Holliday, Bessie Smith, The Pointer Sisters, Eula McClaney, Oprah Winfrey) Narr. Tanya Hart. Los Angeles Channel 9, 3 Feb. 1988.

Gwendolyn Brooks Reading Her Poetry. Introd. Poem by Don L. Lee. Caedmon TC 1244.

Hallelujah. (musical film) Prod. King Vidor; Mus. Dir. Eva Jessye. MGM, 1929.

Hansberry, Lorraine. *A Raisin in the Sun* (the complete play, 3 records, with Ossie Davis, Ruby Dee, Claudia McNeil, Diana Sands, Leonard Jackson, Zakes Mokae, Sam Schacht, Harold Scott. Dir. Lloyd Richards. New York: Caedmon Records, 1972.

―――. *A Raisin in the Sun*. Audio-Film Center, 2138 E. 75th St., Mt. Vernon, NY 10550. 127 min. Rental $25.00.

————. *Lorraine Hansberry on Her Art and the Black Experience* (discussing her work and philosophy, the theater, the Black experience, and the challenge of the artist in mid-century America). New York: Caedmon Records TC 1352. 12 in. LP $6.50; CDL 51352 cassette $7.95.

————. *Lorraine Hansberry Speaks Out: Art and the Black Revolution.* Sel. and ed. Robert Nemiroff. New York: Caedmon Records, 1971.

Harriet Tubman and the Underground Railroad. Extension Media Center (2223 Shattuck Avenue, Berkeley, CA 94720), 1964.

Historical Interpretation of Negro Spirituals and "Lift Every Voice and Sing." Dorothy Conley Elam, researcher and narrator. Lavinia A. Franklin, organist. Camden, NJ: Recorded Publications Co. Write Mrs. Dorothy Elam, Rt. 2 Box 371C, Berlin, NJ 08009.

Hughes, Langston, and Margaret Danner. "Writers of the Revolution." *Black Forum* H-1725, Motown Record Corp.

Hunter, Kristin. *Minority of One.* (TV documentary) CBS, 1955.

————. *The Landlord.* United Artists, New York, n.d.

I Am Somebody. Extension Media Center, 1970.

I Know Why the Caged Bird Sings. (based on Maya Angelou's autobiography the same title) Merit Audio Visual, Box 392, New York 10024 ($89.95).

Jordan, June. *For Somebody to Start Singing.* Black Box 1, Watershed Foundation, 1980.

————. *Things That I Do in the Dark.* N.p.: Spoken Arts, 1978.

Jordan, June, and Bernice Reagon. *For Somebody to Start Singing.* Audio-Forum 23462. 59 min. 1980. Audio-Forum, 96 Broad St., Guilford, CT 06437.

King. (story of M. L. King, starring Paul Winfield and Cicely Tyson) Merit Audio Visual (Box 392, New York 10024), n.d. ($99.95)

King, Coretta Scott. *Coretta Scott King Reads from "My Life With Martin Luther King."* New York: Caedmon Records TC 2060. Two 12-in. LPs, $13.00.

————. *Free at Last! Free at Last!* New York: Caedmon Records TC 1407.

————. *My Life with Martin Luther King, Jr.* New York: Caedmon TC 9300.

————. *The Freedom Movement.* New York: Caedmon Records TC 1406.

Kitt, Eartha, and Moses Gunn. *Black Pioneers in American History* (19th Century), Vol. 1. (Reading the autobiographies of Charlotte Forten, Frederick Douglass, Susie King Taylor, and Nat Love) New York: Caedmon Records TC 1252. 12-in. LP, $6.50; CDL 51252 cassette, $7.25.

Lightfoot, Sara Lawrence. Interview with Bill Moyers. *Bill Moyers' World of Ideas.* Prod. Catherine Taige. PBS, 12 Oct. 1988. Moyers' Videotapes, c/o Journal Graphics, 267 Broadway, New York 10007.

Like It Is. (Award-winning program, WABC-TV) Secaucus, NJ: Citadel Press (120 Enterprise Avenue), n.d.

Lorraine Hansberry: The Black Experience in the Creation of Drama. (film, 35 min.; also VHS or Beta) Films for the Humanities (128D, Box 2053, Princeton NJ 08543), 1975.

Madgett, Naomi. *Naomi Madgett, Donald Hall, and Dan Gerber Reading Their Poems and Talking to Students.* Michigan Council for the Arts, 10215 E. Jefferson Avenue, Detroit MI 48214. (Video)

Margaret Sloan on Black Sisterhood. (Video cassette) Public Television Library (475 L'Enfant Plaza SW, Washington, DC 20024), 1974.

Marshall, Paule. Interview and discussion about the "creative process as it applies to her work" and other personal insights about her background and *Brown Girl, Brownstones.* 82 mins. Columbia, MO: The American Audio Prose Library, Inc. Order No. 4132, $10.95.

————. Reading and interview as a set. Columbia, MO: The American Audio Prose Library, Inc. Order No. 4133, $20.00.

————. Reads *Brown Girl, Brownstones* and *Praisesong for the Widow.* 55 mins. Columbia, MO: The American Audio Prose Library, Inc. Order No. 4131, $10.95.

Morrison, Toni. Interview. 79 mins. Columbia, MO: The American Audio Prose Library, Inc. Order No. 3112, $10.95.

————. Reading excerpts of *Tar Baby.* 57 min. Columbia, MO: The American Audio Prose Library, Inc. Order No. 3111, $10.95.

————. Reading from *Song of Solomon.* 178 mins. Columbia, MO: The American Audio Prose Library, Inc. Order No. 55038–2, $14.95.

————. Reading and interview as a set. Columbia, MO: The American Audio Prose Library, Inc. Order No. 3113, $20.00.

Naomi Madgett, Donald Hall, and Dan Gerber Reading Their Poems and Talking to Students. Detroit, MI: Michigan Council for the Arts (10125 E. Jefferson Ave. 48214), n.d.

Naylor, Gloria. Interview. 60 mins. Columbia, MO: The American Audio Prose Library, Inc. Order No. 8082, $12.95.

————. Readings from *The Women of Brewster Place* and *Mama Day.* 60 mins. audio. Columbia, MO: The American Audio Prose Library, Inc. Order No. 8081, $12.95.

————. Readings from *The Women of Brewster Place* and *Mama Day* and Interview, combined as a set. Columbia, MO: The American Audio Prose Library, Inc. Order No. 8083, $23.00.

Parker, Patricia. *The Poetry of Pat Parker and Judy Grahn: Where Would I Be Without You.* Olivia Records, 1975.

Poets Reading Their Poetry for OCC-TV. Robert Hayden, Naomi Madgett, and Dudley Randall Read the Six Poems They Want To Be Remembered By. 8mm., black and white, 50 min. Rental: Oakland Community College, Orchard Lake, MI 48030.

Sanchez, Sonia. *Homecoming.* Broadside Voices. 5-inch reel, $5.00.

————. *We a BadddDDD People.* Broadside Voices. 5-inch reel, $5.00.

Sands, Diana, and Moses Gunn. *Black Pioneers in American History* (19th-20th Century), Vol. 2. (Reading the autobiographies of Mary Church Terrell, W. E. B. DuBois, Josiah Henson, and William Parker) New York: Caedmon Records TC 1229. 12-in LP, $6.50; CDL 51244 cassette, $7,95.

School Daze. Prod. Spike Lee. Columbia Pictures.

She's Gotta Have It. Starring Tracy Camilla Jones, Tommy Redmond Hicks. Prod. Spike Lee. Columbia Pictures.

Smith, Joe, ed. *Off the Record: An Oral History of Popular Music.* (Includes stories of Ella Fitzgerald, Tina Turner) New York: Warner Books, 1988.

————. *The Bessie Smith Story.* Columbia CL 855–858, 1956.

Sounder. (Video of Black sharecropper family's struggle for economic and psychological survival during the Depression, starring Paul Winfield and Cicely Tyson) Merit Audio Visual (Box 392, New York 10024), n.d. ($79.95)

Stephany. *Stephany Reads "Moving Deep."* Detroit: Broadside. $5.00.

The Afro-American's Quest for Education: A Black Odyssey (Adventures in Negro History), Vol. III. Commentary, Elsie M. Lewis. Prod. Pepsi-Cola. (HRP-103)

The American Woman: Portraits of Courage. Narr., host, Patricia Neal. Prod. Concepts Unlimited. (includes portraits of Black women, including Ida B. Wells, Rosa Parks, Gwendolyn Brooks, and others) Shown on Los Angeles Channel 9, 19 Sep. 1988.

The Autobiography of Miss Jane Pittman. (Cicely Tyson) Merit Audio Visual (Box 392, New York 10024), n.d. ($59.95)

The Black Woman. 16 mm, 52 min. Bloomington, IN: Bloomington Audio-Visual Center, 1970. (Nikki Giovanni, Lena Horne, Bibi Amina Baraka, and other Black women "discuss their role in contemporary society"; also performance by Roberta Flack, Loretta Abbott, and Nikki Giovanni)

The Negro Woman. Prod. Listening Library Inc., 1 Park Ave., New York 10036. $5.79.

The Negro Woman. Jean Brannon, comp. and ed. Reader, Dorothy Washington. Excerpts from works by or about Phillis Wheatley, Harriet Tubman, Frances Harper, Sojourner Truth, Ida B. Wells Barnett, Mary Church Terrell, Mary McLeod Bethune. Folkways Records FC 77552A.

The Negro Writer in America (James Baldwin, Lorraine Hansberry, Langston Hughes, Alfred Kazin, and Emile Capouya in a discussion on Black writing in America) 1961. 45 min. Pacifica WBAI 23062. Audio-Forum, 96 Broad St., Guilford, CT 06437.

The Role of the Black Woman in America. Discussion by four Black women: Peachie Brooks, Verta S. Grosvenor, Flo Kennedy, Elinor Norton. 50 min. Pacifica Tape Library, 2217 Shattuck St., Berkeley, CA 94704. $10.50.

The Women of Brewster Place. (Oprah Winfrey, Olivia Cole, Robin Givens, Jackee, Paula Kelly, Lonette McKette, Phyllis Yvonne Stickney, Lynn Whitfield, Cicely Tyson, Moses Gunn, Paul Winfield) (Film for ABC, in production for television)

Tubman, Harriet. *Harriet Tubman.* Chicago: Society for Visual Education, Inc. (1345 Diversey Parkway 60614), n.d.

Vroman, Mary Elizabeth. *A Bright Road.* M-G-M.

When You This See, Remember Me. (Section of *Four Saints in Three Acts,* which features Black artists and provides some background on the first American opera in which Black classical musicians sang and acted) 89 min. Del Mar, CA (110 15th St 92014): McGraw Hill/CRM, n.d.

Women of Color Series. (Toni Cade Bambara, Louise Erdrich, Maxine Hong Kingston, Paule Marshall, Toni Morrison, Gloria Naylor, Alice Walker) Interviews with Kay Bonetti available separately or with Reading series. Columbia, MO: The American Audio Prose Library, Inc. Reading Series (7 authors): Order No. SS-31, $78.65 (reg.), $62.95 (sp.). Interview Series: (7 authors): Order No. SS-32, $78.65 (reg.), $62.95 (sp.). Complete Series: Order No. SS-33, $157.50 (reg.), $117.95 (sp.).

Dr. Eva Jessye. (Photo courtesy of University of Michigan Information Services)

PERFORMING ARTS
MUSIC: ARRANGERS, COMPOSERS, LYRICISTS, PERFORMERS

Dr. Eva Jessye Is Our History[1]

Singer and educator William Warfield made a profound statement when he wrote, "Dr. Eva Jessye is a part of our history."[2] Jessye, who died February 21, 1992, at 97, was a part of our history which exceeded her longevity. Jeannie Pool, Music Consultant for KPFK, Los Angeles, called Jessye "our link with the 19th century."[3] Jessye (also an actress, educator, journalist, lecturer, and poet) was an important part of our history because she was "the first Black woman to earn international distinction as a choral director."[4] She was widely recognized as having pioneered in the movement that established professional choirs.

Her achievements during her 97 years were countless. In 1929, King Vidor called her to Hollywood to be choral director for the movie *Hallelujah,* generally known as the first all-Black motion picture. She was chosen by two American composers to train the choruses for their operas. In 1934, Virgil Thomson selected her to train her choir for his and Gertrude Stein's *Four Saints in Three Acts.*[5] In 1935, George Gershwin chose Jessye to train the choir for the premiere performance of *Porgy and Bess.*[6] She stayed on as choral conductor for that opera for thirty years. As indicated below, Jessye's musical career did not begin or end with her association with Vidor, Thomson, or the Gershwins. For she organized choirs, composed, arranged, and conducted during most of her adult years. In 1951, her choir appeared with the Chicago Symphony. In 1972, she directed her folk oratorio *Paradise Lost and Regained* in the Washington

Cathedral. So outstanding was her continuing work that Governor John Carlin made her Kansas Ambassador of the Arts in 1981. Kansas and a number of cities have proclaimed "Eva Jessye Days."[7]

Although she worked in all musical genres, it was Negro spirituals that attracted much of her energy. For she was one of a small band of musicians who chose to preserve the spiritual. This last act made her our link with the 17th and 18th centuries and a guardian of documents of Black spirituality, Black militancy, and unparalleled Black cooperation and creativity.

Just as Jessye was a link with our remote past, by preserving North American music and collecting and teaching rare Negro spirituals, she was a link with our present and our future. Her connections were through these songs.

In 1929, Dr. Jester Hairston, actor, choral director and lecturer, joined the Eva Jessye Choir immediately after he was graduated from Tufts University. He graciously credits Jessye and Hall Johnson with teaching him all he knows about the spiritual.[8] At his 20th anniversary concert held February 10, 1985, at the Dorothy Chandler Pavilion in Los Angeles, Dr. Albert McNeil, an educator and the director-founder of the Albert McNeil Singers, paid homage to Hairston, with whom McNeil began to work when McNeil was about seventeen.

Each of these choral directors was or is an accomplished musician known throughout the world. Each would have been a musician without the other. The links, however, are important to music history.

Jessye made her first conscious commitment to preserve the spiritual when she was about thirteen. When she was a student at the joint state and A.M.E.-supported and all-Black Western University in Quindaro, Kansas, Professor R. G. Jackson, the choirmaster, asked one choir member after another to sing the verse, "I can hear the trumpet sound / to wake the nations underground. . . ." from the spiritual "My Lord, What a Morning." No one could or would sing the passage. When Jackson got to Jessye, however, she sang the verse as she had heard Blacks sing spirituals in her native Coffeyville, Kansas. As she sang, the other choir members began to laugh derisively. Jessye's reaction was to vow, "Someday, I will make you have respect for the spiritual."[9]

According to Jessye, shortly after this incident, the famous educator Booker T. Washington visited the school, which had a state-supported industrial-education program similar to that at Tuskegee. Before Washington spoke, the choir sang two selections, "O Divine Redeemer" and Washington's favorite spiritual, "Every Time I Feel the Spirit." He praised the choir for its excellent singing and made a plea that these young people "never forget the songs of our mothers and fathers."

Jessye responded, "I will never forget the songs of my ancestors!"[10]

If Jessye were to keep her vows about the spirituals, she had to have a viable medium, a choir. From 1914 to 1919, while she attended Langston University and taught in the public schools of Taft and Muscogee, Oklahoma, she formed choirs. No matter where the choir was, a basic part of the repertoire was the spiritual.

In 1919, Jessye was invited to become Chairperson of the Department of Music at Morgan State College in Baltimore. During her brief term at Morgan, she developed a first-rate choir which sang spirituals, anthems, and folksongs throughout the city.[11] In 1925, she became the director of the popular Dixie Jubilee Singers in Baltimore.

The Dixie Jubilee Singers created quite a sensation in Baltimore when they acquired a "new spiritual." "Dixie Singers Get Spiritual" blazoned the headlines of this article excerpted from the *Afro-American*:

> Enclosed I am sending you a sketch of the melody only. I don't think it has ever been written, if so we haven't been able to find it. The first verse runs:
>
> > I've been 'buked and I've been scorned,
> > I've been 'buked and I've been scorned,
> >   Been scorned, chil-len,
> > I've been 'buked and I've been scorned,
> > I've had a hard time sho's yo' born.[12]

The letter writer, Dean D. D. Mitchell of Tuggle University in Birmingham, Ala. and Jessye were among those musicians aware of the importance of recording for posterity our oral history in the form of the spiritual. The song is anthologized in Jessye's *My Spirituals.*

When Jessye and the Dixie Jubilee Singers relocated in New York, they accepted engagements everywhere—in churches, schools, and theaters. The Dixie Jubilees were heard at the Rivoli Theatre before movies were shown and at the Capitol Theatre as part of the *Major Bowes Family Hour.*[13]

In spite of Jessye's determination and industry, work could be scarce. During one of the "no-work" periods, Jessye, in desperate need of money for food and rent, seized the opportunity (three weeks), to set down and arrange some spirituals she had heard in the "free-state" of Kansas, a state to which slaves and freed Blacks migrated.

In a shabby one-room New York apartment that had a cot, a table, and a chair, she compiled the anthology *My Spirituals.* This volume, which consists of lovely illustrations, poems, regional anecdotes, and sixteen spirituals received praises from Percy Goetschius,[14] music theoretician, Paul Robeson,[15] singer and thespian, and Gwendolyn Bennett,[16] author. *My Spirituals* is another way in which Jessye fulfilled her promise about keeping the spiritual alive.

But there were still other ways through which she could keep her vows. Legend has it that Jessye found a tattered copy of John Milton's epic *Paradise Lost* in a trash can. According to another account, she found the work in an old book store.[17] Where she found the work is not important. What is important is that it inspired her to create her folk oratorio *Paradise Lost and Regained,* placing Milton's classical religious poems written in blank verse within a framework of such Negro spirituals as "When Moses Smote the Waters," "Joshua Fought the Battle of Jericho," "O What a Beautiful City," and "Ride On, King Jesus."

Paradise Lost and Regained premiered on NBC Radio in 1931.[18] It received an enthusiastic standing ovation when presented in the Washington Cathedral in 1972.[19] Black United Methodist ministers of Philadelphia and vicinity sponsored the oratorio at the historic Tindley Temple in Philadelphia in 1974.[20] The work was performed at Pittsburg State University, Pittsburg, Kansas, in 1978.[21]

Jessye has also immortalized the spiritual in "Christ in

Negro Spirituals," 1981, and in "The Chronicle of Job," 1936, both dramatic musical works.

Her commitment to elevating and preserving the spiritual encompasses establishing collections, giving lectures, and conducting workshops on the spiritual. The Eva Jessye Collections at Clark College, Atlanta, the University of Michigan, Ann Arbor, and Pittsburg State University, Pittsburg, Kansas, are said to be virtual treasure troves of authentic and rare spirituals.[22]

For more than eighty years now, Jessye was about the business of preserving "our" history; but Eva Jessye was more than a preserver of our history. For almost 100 years, she was a vital part of our history.

by Ora Williams

Notes

[1]This article is a revision of one which appeared in *The Women's Studies Newsletter,* California State University, Long Beach, Spring 1984.

[2]Written interview with William Warfield, 20 October 1984.

[3]Jeannie Pool, introductory comments, KPFK, Los Angeles radio program, 15 February 1985.

[4]"Eva Jessye," *Ebony,* May 1974.

[5]John Houseman, *Run-Through: A Memoir* (New York: Simon & Schuster, 1972), 102–108.

[6]Personal interview with Eva Jessye, 10 January 1983.

[7]"Eva Jessye Fills Halls with Sounds of Triumph," *Collegio,* 2 October 1978.

[8]Personal interview with Jester Hairston, 28 September 1984.

[9,10]Personal interview Jessye, 10 January 1983.

[11]"Dixie Singers are Kept Busy." *The Afro-American,* 3 January 1925.

[12]"Dixie Singers Get 'New Spiritual.' " *The Afro-American,* 17 February 1925.

[13]"Dixie Jubilee Singers in 'Uncle Tom's Cabin.' " *The New York Age,* 2 November 1927.

[14]Percy Goetschius, letter to Jessye, 16 April 1927.

[15]Paul Robeson, letter to Jessye, 21 September 1927.

[16]Gwendolyn Bennett, "Review of *My Spirituals,* arranged and edited by Eva Jessye (New York: Robbins-Engel, 1927), $2.50; in *Opportunity* (November 1974):18.

[17,18]Jessye, interview 24 October 1984.

[19]Joan Reinthaler, "Folk Oratorio." The Washington Post, 12 July 1972.

[20]"Paradise Lost & Regained," Tindley Temple Program, 5 October 1974.

[21]Joan Perkins, "Dr. Eva Jessye Re-Creates 'Paradise'," Glassboro, NJ *State College Whit,* 9 May 1974.

[22]"At 87, Music Dynamo Dr. Jessye Has 'So Much More to Do'." *The Atlanta Constitution,* 15 January 1982.

Selected Bibliography

Primary Sources

Jessye, Eva A. *My Spirituals.* Illus. Millar of Roland Co. Eds. Gordon Whyte and Hugo Frey. New York: Robbins-Engel, Inc., 1927. (16 spirituals, poems, and ancedotes).

———. "The Life of Christ in Negro Spirituals." Cop., 1931.

———. "Paradise Lost and Regained." Based on text of John Milton's *Paradise Lost.* Broadcast NBC Radio, 1931; premiered Washington Cathedral, 1972.

———. "Chronicle of Job." Cop., 1932.

———. "By Heck." New York: Marks, 1925. SATB and piano.

———. "Congo Love Song." The Eva Jessye Choral Series. New York: Marks, 1956. SSTB and piano.

———. "E.I.O." Ed. Julian Work. Texas Panhandle folk dance caper. New York: Skidmore Music Co., 1965. SATB/TTBB.

———, adaptor. "Hand Car Blues." Ed. Julian Work. New York: Skidmore Music Co., 1965. SATB/TTBB.

———. "He's Carried the Key and Gone Home." Ed. Julian Work. New York: Skidmore Music Co., 1965. SATB.

———. "I Belong to That Band." Spiritual shout. New York: Skidmore, 1965. SATB/Soprano and Piano/ Bass and piano.

———. "Move! Let Me Shine." Spiritual. New York: Skidmore, 1965. SATB and piano.

———. "Nobody." Adaptation of Bert Williams' work. Eva Jessye Choral Series. New York: Marks, 1926. SATB and piano.

———. "Rock Mt. Sinai." Ed. Julian Work. Spiritual. New York: Skidmore, 1965. SATB.

———. "Simon the Fisherman." Evanston: Summy-Birchard, 1947. Secular folk song set in Georgia. SATB and narrators.

———. "Sold to Georgia." Used for 1927 film of *Uncle Tom's Cabin*. New York: Robbins-Engel, 1927.

———. "The Breeze and I." Eva Jessye Choral Series. New York: Edward B. Marks, 1928. SATB and piano.

———. "When the Saints Go Marching In." Eva Jessye Choral Series. New York: Edward B. Marks, 1966. SATB and piano.

———. "Who Is That Yonder?" Spiritual. New York: Skidmore, 1965. SATB and piano.

Secondary Sources

Abdul, Raoul. *Blacks in Classical Music: A Personal History.* New York: Dodd, Mead and Co., 1977.

Anderson, E. Ruth, comp. *A Biographical Dictionary.* Second ed. Boston: G. K. Hall and Co., 1982.

Armitage, Merle, ed. and designer. *George Gershwin.* New York: Longmans, Green, 1938.

ASCAP Biographical Dictionary, 4th ed. New York: Jacques Cattell Press, 1980.

Black, Donald Fisher. "The Life and Work of Eva Jessye and Her Contributions to American Music." Ann Arbor: U.M.I. Dissertation Service, 1987.

Cleghorn, Charles Eugene. *Biographical Dictionary of American Music.* West Nyack, NY: Parking Publishing Co., 1973.

Clift, Virgil A. and W. Augustine Low. *Encyclopedia of Black America.* New York: McGraw-Hill, 1981.

Congressional Record, 26 September 1985.

Cooper, Dawn. "Eva Jessye, Afro-American Woman: Her Contribution to American Music and Theatre." In partial fulfillment for a Master's Degree, Hunter College, 1979.

Cuney-Hare, Maud. *Negro Musicians and Their Work.* Washington, DC: Associated Press, 1939; New York: DeCapo Press, 1974.

Ewen, David. *George Gershwin: His Journey to Greatness.* Englewood Cliffs, NJ: Prentice-Hall, Inc., 1970.

"Famed Choral Director Dr. Eva Jessye, 97, Dies." *Jet,* 16 March 1992, p. 8.

Jablonski, Edward. *The Encyclopedia of American Music.* New York: Doubleday, 1981.

"Jubilee Singers at Morgan College." *The Afro-American,* (8 August 1925).

Kerlin, Robert Thomas. *Negro Poets and Their Poems.* 3rd ed. Washington, DC: Associated Press, 1923.

Lanker, Brian. Photographs and interviews. *I Dream a World.* New York: Stewart, Tabori, & Chang, 1989.

Locke, Alain. "Toward a Critique of Negro Music." *Opportunity* (November–December, 1934): 328–331; 367–387.

Roach, Hildred. *Black American Music: Past and Present.* Boston: Crescendo Publishing, 1973.

Southern, Eileen. *The Music of Black Americans: A History.* New York: W. W. Norton, 1971; 1983.

Spradling, Mary Mace. *In Black and White: A Guide to Magazine Articles, Newspaper Articles, and Books Concerning More than 15,000 Black Individuals and Groups.* 3rd ed. Detroit: Gale Research, 1980.

"The Etude Historical Musical Portrait Series." *The Etude Magazine* 52 (December 1934):598.

White, Evelyn Davidson, comp. *Choral Music by Afro-American Composers.* Metuchen NJ: The Scarecrow Press, 1981.

MUSIC: ARRANGERS, COMPOSERS, LYRICISTS, PERFORMERS

Akers, Doris. *Doris Akers' Favorite Gospel Songs.* Hollywood, CA: Mama Music (1328 N. Highland Avenue), n.d.

Armstead, Josie, Valerie Simpson, and Nicholas Ashford. *I Don't Need No Doctor.* Hollywood, CA: Baby Monica Music Inc., n.d.; New York: Renleigh Music Corp., n.d.

Ashby, Dorothy. "A-Wandering." *Afro-America Sings.* Eds. Ollie McFarland et al. Detroit: Board of Education, 1971.

Ashford, Nick, and Valerie Simpson. "Reach Out and Touch Somebody's Hand." *Lift Every Voice and Sing: A Collection of Afro-American Spirituals and Other Songs.* New York: The Church Hymnal Corporation, 1981.

Austin, Lovie. *I've Got the Blues for Rampart Street.* New York: Mills Music Corp., 1923.

Bradbury, William B. "Even Me." Arr. Roberta Martin. *Songs of Zion.* Nashville, TN: Abingdon Press, 1981.

Campbell, Lucie E. "Footprints of Jesus." *Songs of Zion.* Nashville, TN: Abingdon Press, 1981.

———. *He Understands, He'll Say "Well Done."* Memphis: Campbell & Williams, 1950.

———. *He'll Understand and Say "Well Done."* Memphis, TN: Campbell & Williams, 1950; *Lift Every Voice and Sing: A Collection of Afro-American Spirituals and Other Songs.* New York: The Church Hymnal Corporation, 1981.

———. *Something Within.* Memphis: Campbell & Williams, 1919; 1950.

———. "The Lord Is My Shepherd." *Gospel Pearls.* Nashville, TN: Sunday School Publishing Board of the National Baptist Convention, 1921.

———. *Tramping.* Memphis: Campbell & Williams, n.d.

Carlisle, Una Mae. *Walkin' by the River.* N.p.: Gower Music Company, n.d.

Cox, Ida. *Bone Orchard Blues.* Northern Music Corp., 1928.

———. *'Fore Day Creep.* Northern Music Corp., 1928.

———. "Graveyard Dream Blues." Northern Music Corp., 1923.

———. *Midnight Hour Blues.* Northern Music Corp., 1928.

———. *Western Union Blues.* Northern Music Corp., 1928.

Cox, Ida, and Jesse Crump. *Death Letter Blues.* Northern Music Corp., 1924.

Cox, Ida, and Lovie Austin. *Weary Way Blues.* Northern Music Corp., 1924.

DuBois, Shirley Graham. *Tom-Tom.* Three-act opera, premiered in concert form by NBC Radio, 26 June 1932; stage performance, Cleveland Stadium, 1932.

Evanti, Lillian. *Dedication.* Words by Georgia Douglas Johnson. New York: Handy Brothers, 1948.

———. *Forward March to Victory.* 1943. (Inspired during the Battle of the Coral Sea—completed after victory in Africa and capitulation of Pantelleria and Pampedusa) Translated into Chinese, Dutch, Spanish, Czech, French, and in Yugoslavia.

———. *Hail to Fair Washington.* Words by Georgia D. Johnson. 1953.

————. *High Flight.* Words by John Gillespie Magee, Jr. New York: Handy Brothers, 1948.

————. *Himno Panamericano.* Arr. Felix Guenther (for 3-part treble, 1st soprano, 2nd soprano, alto) New York: Edward B. Marks Music Corp., RCA Building, 1941.

————. *I'm Yours for Tonight.* New York: Columbia Music Co., n.d.

————. *My Little Prayer.* Words by Mrs. Bruce Evans. New York: Handy Brothers, 1948.

————. *Speak to Him Thou.* Words by Alfred Lord Tennyson. New York: Handy Brothers, 1948.

————. *Thank You Again and Again.* New York: Handy Brothers, 1948.

————. *The Mighty Rapture.* Words by Edwin Markham. New York: Handy Brothers, 1948.

————. *Tomorrow's World.* Words by Georgia Douglas Johnson, 1948. (Chorus, SATB)

————. *Twenty-Third Psalm.* New York: Handy Brothers, 1947.

————. *United Nations.* 1953. (mixed voices)

Franklin, Aretha. *All the King's Horses.* Cop. A. Franklin, 1972. c/o Feinman and Krasilovsky.

Graham, Shirley. *Little Black Sambo.* 1938. (Unpublished)

————. *Tom-Tom.* 1932. Three-act opera, premiered in concert form by NBC Radio, 26 June 1932; stage performance, Cleveland Stadium, 1932.

Grant, Micki (Minnie McCutcheon). "All I Need," "Billie Holiday," "Children's Rhymes," "Do a Little Living for Peace," "Don't Bother Me, I Can't Cope," "Good Vibrations," "Harlem Streets," "Help," "I Gotta Keep Movin'," "It Takes a Whole Lot of Human Feeling," "Lock Up the Doors," "My

Love's So Good," "Name Name Is Man," "They Keep Coming," "Time Brings About a Change," "You Think I Got Rhythm," and others. *Don't Bother Me, I Can't Cope.* Performed at the Edison Theatre, New York, and at the Mark Taper Forum, Los Angeles, 1972. Pub. Tommy Valando.

————. *Behind a Moonbeam.* Hastings Music Corp., n.d.

————. *Come Back, Baby.* Copyright Micki Grant.

————. *Perfect If.* Copyright Micki Grant.

Green, Lil. *In the Dark,* or, *Romance in the Dark.* Duchen Music Corp., n.d.

Hackley, Emma Azalea (Smith). *Carola.* New York: Handy Brothers, 1953.

Hagan, Helen. *Concerto in C Minor.* Unpublished. Played by Ms. Hagan at her graduation from the Yale University School of Music, 1911, with New Haven Symphony Orchestra. (for piano and orchestra)

Handy, D. Antoinette. *Contemporary Black Images in Music for Flute.* The Trio Pro Viva and Gladys P. Norris, piano; Ronald Lipscomb, cello. Music of 10 contemporary Black composers represented through 11 compositions for solo flute; solo alto flute; flute, cello, and piano; flute and cello; and flute, violin, and piano.

————. *Hommage a Haute Savoie.* Ettrick, VA: BM & M, Box 103.

————. Trio Pro Viva. *Contemporary Black Images in Music for Flute.* Joseph Kennedy, violin; Ronald Lipscomb, cello; Gladys Norris, piano; William Terry, piano. Eastern ERS-513.

Harris, Margaret R. "Collage One." 1970. 17pp.

————. *Dear Love.* 1970.

————. *Grievin'.* 1970. 4 pp.

————. *Tonite's Goodbye.* 1970.

Hegamin, Lucille. *Mississippi Blues*. MCA.

Hill, Bertha. "Pratt's City Blues." *Chippie*. MCA, 1926.

Hunter, Alberta. *Down Hearted Blues*. Music by Lovie Austin. New York: Mills Music Corp., 1923.

———. *I Got a Mind to Ramble*. New York: Leeds, n.d.

———. *I Want to Thank You, Lord*. New York: Leeds, n.d.

———. *Streets Paved with Gold*. New York: Fred Fischer, Co., Inc., n.d.

———. *The Love I Have for You*. N.p.: Peer International, n.d.

———. *Will the Day Ever Come When I Can Rest*. New York: Fred Fischer, n.d.

———. *You Better Change*. New York: Handy Brothers, n.d.

Hunter, Alberta, Ethel Waters, and Fletcher Henderson. *Down South Blues*. New York: Mills Music Corp., n.d.

Jackson, Mahalia. "Lord, Don't Move This Mountain. *Songs of Zion*. Nashville, TN: Abingdon Press, 1981.

Jenkins, Ella. *The Ella Jenkins Song Book for Children*. Illust. Peggy Lipschitz. New York: Oak Publications, 1973.

Jessye, Eva. (See introductory essay.)

Johnson, Doris Alene. *He's Always There*. Newark, NJ: Sagos, n.d.

———. *He's Worthy to Be Praised*. Kansas City, MO: Doris Johnson, 1977.

———. *Touch Christ*. Kansas City, MO: Doris Johnson, 1975.

Johnson, Edith. *Nickel's Worth of Liver*. N.p.: Northern Music Corp., 1929.

King, Betty Jackson. "A Lover's Plea." Poem by Wm. Shakespeare. (for voice)

———. "Dawn." Poem by Paul Laurence Dunbar. (for voice)

———. "Fantastic Mirror." (for piano)

———. Four Season Sketches: "Spring Intermezzo," "Summer Interlude," "Autumn Dance," "Winter Holiday." (for piano)

———. "God Shall Wipe Away All Tears." (requiem for voice)

———. "Mother Goose Parade." (for piano)

———. *Nuptial Suite:* "Processional," "Nuptial Song," "Recessional." (for organ)

———. "Rejoice in the Lord Always." (voice and piano) Composer.

———. *Saul of Tarsus* (Biblical opera). Excerpts of this and the other works listed above were performed by The Imperial Opera Company, Chicago, at the Riverside Church, New York, 12 August 1972. *Saul of Tarsus* was premiered at DuSable High School, Chicago, 1952. The Biblical libretto was compiled by the late Reverend Fred D. Jackson.

———. *This Little Light of Mine.* Carol Stream, IL: Hope Publishing Company, 1978. (SATB and piano)

Liston, Melba Doretta. "Blues Melba," "You Don't Say." *Melba Liston and Her 'Bones.'* MGM Stereo Se 1013.

McCanns, Shirley Graham (DuBois). *I Promise.* Words by Lorenz Graham. New York: Handy Brothers, 1934.

McFarland, Ollie. "Alphabet Travelogue." *Afro-America Sings.* Eds. Ollie McFarland et al. Detroit: Board of Education, 1971.

———. "Balloons" (Lullaby). *Afro-America Sings.* Eds. Ollie McFarland et al. Detroit: Board of Education, 1971.

———. "Fireworks." *Afro-America Sings.* Eds. Ollie McFarland et al. Detroit: Board of Education, 1971.

————. "O Mary." *Afro-America Sings.* Eds. Ollie McFarland et al. Detroit: Board of Education, 1971.

————. "Rise Up Shepherd and Follow." *Afro-America Sings.* Eds. Ollie McFarland et al. Detroit: Board of Education, 1971.

McGowan, Mildred Thornhill. "Street Sounds." n.p.

————. "Street Sounds of Delaware." n.p.

————. "The Children Speak." n.p. (musical)

————. "You and Your Neighborhood." n.p.

McLin, Lena. *All the Earth Sing Unto the Lord.* Text based on Psalm 96. Park Ridge, IL: Neil A. Kjos, 1967. (SATB a cappella. Ed. 5459)

————. *Challenge.* Park Ridge, IL: General Words and Music Co. (SATB chorus, piano, optional trumpet, tenor sax, bass guitar, drums)

————. *Done Made My Vow to the Lord.* Park Ridge, IL: Neil A. Kjos, 1971. (SATB chorus and baritone solo)

————. *Eucharist of the Soul: A Liturgical Mass.* Park Ridge, IL: General Words and Music Co., 1972. (SATB accompanied. Ed. GC 41)

————. *For Jesus Christ Is Born.* Park Ridge, IL: Neil A. Kjos, 1971. (SATB chorus a cappella)

————. *For the Air That's Pure.* Park Ridge, IL: General Words and Music Co., 1970.

————. *Free at Last! A Portrait of Martin Luther King, Jr.* Park Ridge, IL: Neil A. Kjos, 1973. (SATB chorus, soprano, and baritone [or mezzo-soprano] solo)

————. *Friendship.* Park Ridge, IL: General Words and Music Co., 1972. (SATB accompanied. Ed. GC 39)

————. *Give Me That Old Time Religion.* Park Ridge, IL: General Words and Music Co., 1978. (SATB chorus a cappella)

———. *Glory, Glory Hallelujah.* Park Ridge, IL: Neil A. Kjos, n.d. (SATB chorus, soprano solo, and piano)

———. *Gwendolyn Brooks.* Park Ridge, IL: General Words and Music Co., 1972. (SATB accompanied. Ed. GC 21)

———. *I Am Somebody.* New York: Edward B. Marks Music Corp., 1971. (SATB chorus, narrator, and piano)

———. *I Want Jesus to Walk With Me.* Westbury, NY: Pro Art Publications, 1969. (SATB chorus and piano)

———. *If They Ask You Why He Came.* Park Ridge, IL: General Words and Music Co., 1971. Ed. GC 35.

———. *If We Could Exchange Places.* New York: Marks Music Corp., 1971. (words by composer) (SATB chorus, flute, electric piano, and electric bass guitar)

———. *I'm Moving Up.* New York: Sildet Music Co., 1971. (words by composer) (SATB chorus and piano)

———. *I'm So Glad Trouble Don't Last Always.* Park Ridge, IL: Neil A. Kjos, 1974. (SATB chorus and piano)

———. *In This World.* Park Ridge, IL: General Words and Music Co., and Neil A. Kjos, n.d. (SATB) (Except "I Love No One But You," all in collection)

———. *Is There Anybody Here.* New York: Pro Arts Publications, 1969. (SATB chorus and piano)

———. *Let the People Sing Praise Unto the Lord.* Park Ridge, IL: General Words and Music Co., 1973. (SATB chorus, piano or organ, and Bb trumpet)

———. *Lit'le Lamb, Lit'le Lamb.* Park Ridge, IL: Neil A. Kjos, 1969. (SATB chorus and soprano solo a cappella)

———. "Memory." Poem by Paul L. Dunbar. Park Ridge, IL: General Words and Music Co., 1976. (SATB with optional accomp. Ed. GC 79)

———. *New Born King.* Park Ridge, IL: General Words and Music

Co., 1972. (SATB a cappella; piano for rehearsal only. Ed. GC 23)

———. *Now That We're Leaving.* Park Ridge, IL: General Words and Music Co., 1978. (SATB chorus and piano)

———. "Praise God from Whom All Blessings Flow." *Songs of Zion: Supplemental Worship Resources 12.* Nashville, TN: Abingdon Press, 1981.

———. *Psalm 100.* Westbury, NY: Pro Arte, 1971. (mixed chorus)

———. *Psalm 117.* Westbury, NY: Pro Arte, 1971.

———. *Sanctus and Benedictus.* Park Ridge, IL: General Words and Music Co., 1971. (SATB accompanied)

———. *Since He Came Into My Life.* Park Ridge, IL: General Words and Music Co., 1976. (SATB accompanied. Ed. GC 80)

———. *Te Deum Laudamus.* Park Ridge, IL: General Words and Music Co., 1976. (SATB accompanied. Ed. GC 56)

———. *The Colors of the Rainbow.* New York: Pro Arte, 1971. (mixed chorus)

———. *The Earth Is the Lord's.* Westbury, NY: Pro Art Publications, 1969. (SATB chorus)

———. *The Little Baby.* Park Ridge, IL: Neil A. Kjos, 1971. (SATB accompanied with optional solo. Ed. 5855)

———. *The Torch Has Been Passed.* Park Ridge, IL: General Words and Music Co., 1974. (SATB a cappella. Ed. GC 20)

———. *Two Introits.* Park Ridge, IL: General Words and Music Co., 1978. (SATB chorus and piano)

———. *We've Just Got to Have Peace All Over This World* (words by composer). New York: Sildet Music Co., 1971. (SATB chorus and piano)

———. *What Will You Put Under Your Christmas Tree?* Park Ridge,

IL: General Words and Music Co., 1971. (SATB accompanied. Ed. GC 22)

——. *Winter, Spring, Summer, Autumn.* Park Ridge, IL: Neil A. Kjos, 1974. (SATB. Ed. 5899)

——. *You and I Together.* Park Ridge, IL: General Words and Music Co., 1978. (SATB chorus and piano)

McLin, Lena J., arr. *Cert'nly Lord, Cert'nly Lord.* Park Ridge, IL: Neil A. Kjos, 1967. (Ed. 5458)

——. *Down by the River.* Park Ridge, IL: Neil A. Kjos, n.d. (SATB a cappella. ED 5915)

——. *My God Is So High.* Park Ridge, IL: Neil A. Kjos, 1972. (SATB a cappella. Ed. 5881)

——. *Writ'en Down My Name.* Park Ridge, IL: Neil A. Kjos, 1967. (SATB a cappella with baritone solo. Ed. 5460)

Martin, Roberta. "God's Amazing Grace." *Songs of Zion.* Nashville, TN: Abingdon Press, 1981.

Martin, Roberta Evelyne. *Search My Heart.* Chicago: Bowles Publishing Co., 1935.

Matthews, Lucy. *Didn't It Rain.* Arr. Roberta Martin. Chicago: Martin Morris Music, Inc., 1965.

Moore, Dorothy Rudd. *Baroque Suite for Unaccompanied Cello.* Three movements. New York: Rudmor, n.d.

——. *Dirge and Deliverance.* Two movements. New York: Rudmor, n.d. (for cello and piano)

——. *Dream and Variations.* New York: Rudmor Publishers (33 Riverside Drive). 18 min. Commissioned by Ludwig Olshansky. (piano)

——. *From the Dark Tower.* New York: Rudmor, n.d. (Orchestration of four songs from the song cycle of the same name) (mezzo-soprano and orchestra)

————. *From the Dark Tower: A Song Cycle for Mezzo-Soprano, Cello, and Piano.* New York: Rudmor, n.d. (A setting of eight poems by Black American poets)

————. *Lament for Nine Instruments.* One movement. New York: Rudmor, n.d.

————. *Modes for String Quartet.* Three movements. New York: Rudmor, n.d.

————. *Moods for Viola and Cello.* Duo, three movements. New York: Rudmor, n.d.

————. *Reflections.* One movement. New York: Rudmor, n.d. (symphonic wind ensemble)

————. *Songs.* New York: Rudmor, n.d. (A song cycle, setting of 12 quatrains from "The Rubaiyat" of Omar Khayyam, for mezzo-soprano and oboe)

————. *Symphony No. 1.* One movement. New York: Rudmor, n.d.

————. *Three Pieces for Violin and Piano.* Three movements. New York: Rudmor, n.d.

————. *Trio No. 1.* Three movements. New York: Rudmor, n.d. (violin, cello, and piano)

Moore, Undine Smith. *Bound for Canaan's Land.* New York: Witmark Music Publishers, 1960. (mixed chorus)

————. *Daniel, Daniel Servant of the Lord.* New York: Witmark, 1953. (mixed chorus)

————. *Fare Ye Well.* New York: Witmark, 1951. (mixed chorus)

————. *Hail, Warrior.* New York: Witmark, 1958. (mixed chorus)

————. *Let Us Make Man in Our Own Image.* New York: Witmark, 1960. (mixed chorus)

————. *Mother to Son.* New York: Witmark, 1955. (mixed chorus)

Consuela Lee Moorehead

————. *Striving After God.* New York: Witmark, 1958. (mixed chorus)

Moorehead, Consuela Lee. "Kick It Out, Tigers." *School Daze.* Dir. Spike Lee. Columbia Pictures, 1988.

Nickerson, Camille. "Dance, Baby, Dance." *Five Creole Folk Songs.* Boston: Boston Music Co., 1947.

———. "Dear I Love You So." *Five Creole Folk Songs*. Boston: Boston Music Co., 1947.

———. "Go to Sleep." *Five Creole Folk Songs*. Boston: Boston Music Co., 1947.

———. *Gue-Gue solingaie* (Lemoine). New York: Leeds, 1948. (4-part chorus and piano)

———. "Lizette, My Dearest One." *Five Creole Folk Songs*. Boston: Boston Music Co., 1947.

———. "Mister Banjo." *Five Creole Folk Songs*. Boston: Boston Music Co., 1947.

———. *You Don' Know When*. New York: Handy Brothers, 1939.

Perry, Julia. *Be Merciful Unto Me, O God*. Words from Psalm 57:1,2. New York: Galaxy Music Corp. (chorus of mixed voices, with soprano and bass solos; organ acc. available)

———. *By the Sea*. New York: Galaxy, n.d.

———. *Carillon Heigh Ho*. Ed. John Finley Williamson. New York: Carl Fischer. (SATB divided a cappella)

———. *Frammenti dalle Lettere de Santa Caterina*. New York: Southern Music Co. (soprano, mixed chorus, and orchestra)

——— (arr.). *Free at Last*. New York: Galaxy, 1951.

———. *Homunculus*. New York: Carl Fischer, 1966. (soprano and percussionists)

———. *Homunculus*. New York: Carl Fischer, 1966. (percussion and harp)

———. *Homunculus C. F.* New York: Southern Music Publishing Co., 1966. (10 percussionists, harp, and piano)

———. *How Beautiful Are the Feet*. New York: Galaxy, 1953. (medium voice and piano)

————. *I'm a Poor Li'l Orphan in the Worl'.* New York: Galaxy Music Corp., 1952. (voice and piano)

————. *Lord, What Shall I Do?* Boston: McLaughlin and Reilly Co., 1949. (voice and piano)

————. *Our Thanks to Thee.* New York: Galaxy, 1951. (Anthem for Thanksgiving or general use; chorus or mixed voices with contralto solo; piano acc. available)

————. *Pastoral.* New York: Southern Music Co., 1962. (flute and strings sextet)

————. *Second Piano Concerto.* New York: Peer-Southern Organization, 1965. (piano and orchestra)

————. *Short Piece.* 8 min. New York: Peer-Southern Music Co., 1952. (orchestra)

————. *Songs of Our Savior.* New York: Galaxy, 1953. (chorus of mixed voices, unacc.)

————. *Stabat Mater.* New York: Southern Music Co. (Latin poem by Jacophone da Todi, XIII Century. Trans. by composer. Score in Latin and English words. For contralto and string quartet or string orchestra)

————. *Symphony No. 6.* New York: Carl Fischer, 1966. (band)

————. *The Cask of Amontillado.* One-act opera. New York: Southern Music Co., n.d.

————. *Violin Concerto.* New York: Carl Fischer, 1966. (violin and orchestra)

————. *Ye, Who Seek the Truth.* New York: Galaxy, 1952. (chorus of mixed voices with tenor solo; organ acc. also available)

Pittman, Evelyn. *Anyhow.* New York: Carl Fischer, 1952. (SATB chorus a cappella)

————. *Joshua.* New York: Carl Fischer, 1955. (SATB chorus, soli, piano)

————. *Nobody Know de Trouble I See.* New York: Carl Fischer, 1954. (SATB chorus and unspecified solo a cappella)

Pittman, Evelyn La Rue. *Rich Heritage: Songs, Stories, Pictures.* Vol. 1. New White Plains, NY: Rich Heritage Co., 1968.

————. *Rock-a-My-Soul.* New York: Carl Fischer, 1952. (baritone and 5-part chorus)

————. *Sit Down Servant.* New York: Carl Fischer, 1949. (SATB chorus, alto and baritone solos, a cappella)

————. *Trampin'.* Stamford, CT: Jack Spratt Music Co., 1961. (SATB chorus a cappella)

————. *We Love America.* Oklahoma City: Evelyn Pittman, 1951. (SATB chorus)

Price, Florence B. *A Sachem's Pipe.* New York: Carl Fischer, 1935. (piano, grade 3)

————. *Adoration.* Dayton, OH: Lorenz, n.d. (organ)

————. *An April Day.* Words by Joseph F. Colte. New York: Handy Brothers, 1949.

————. *Anticipation (La anticipación).* Chicago: McKinley Music Co., 1928. (piano) (Publ. pl. no. 2241)

————. *At the Cotton Gin.* New York: Schirmer, n.d.

————. *Bright Eyes.* Bryn Mawr, PA: Theodore Presser, 1937.

————. *By Candlelight.* Chicago: McKinley Publishing, n.d. (violin and piano)

————. *Cabin Song.* Bryn Mawr, PA: Theodore Presser, 1937.

————. *Clover Blossoms.* Chicago: McKinley, 1947. (piano)

————. "Cobbler." Words by David Morton. (Unpublished) (voice and piano)

————. "Concert Overture No. 1." (Based on Negro spirituals) 10 min. (Unpublished)

————. "Concert Overture No. 2." (Based on three Negro spirituals) 12 min. (Unpublished)

————. "Concerto for Piano and Orchestra." 16 min. (Unpublished)

————. "Concerto in D Major." 16 min. (violin and orchestra) (Unpublished)

————. "Concerto in F Minor." (piano and orchestra) (Unpublished)

————. *Cotton Dance.* New York: Carl Fischer, n.d.; *Oxford Piano Course,* Fifth Book. New York: Oxford University Press, 1942.

————. *Criss Cross.* Chicago: McKinley, 1947.

————. *Dances in the Canebrakes.* Los Angeles: Affiliated Musicians, Inc., 1953.

————. *Doll Waltz (Vals de la musica).* Chicago: McKinley, 1928. (piano)

————. *The Engine (La maquine de vapor).* Chicago: McKinley, 1928.

————. *Heav'n Bound Soldier.* Arr. Florence B. Price. New York: Handy Brothers, 1949. (Negro spiritual for women's voices)

————. *Here and There.* Chicago: McKinley, n.d. (piano)

————. "Hoe Cake." *Three Little Negro Dances.* Bryn Mawr, PA: Theodore Presser, n.d. (two scores for two pianos)

————. "I Am Bound for the Kingdom." *Two Traditional Negro Spirituals.* New York: Handy Brothers, n.d.

————. "I'm Workin' on My Building." *Two Traditional Negro Spirituals.* New York: Handy Brothers, n.d.

———. "In Quiet Mood." Chicago: Summy, n.d.; New York: Galaxy, n.d. (organ)

———. *Levee Dance.* Bryn Mawr, PA: Theodore Presser, 1937. (piano)

———. *Little Negro Dances.* Bryn Mawr, PA: Theodore Presser, 1939. (band)

———. *March of the Beetles.* Chicago: McKinley, 1947. (piano)

———. *Mellow Twilight.* Chicago: McKinley, n.d. (violin and piano)

———. "Mississippi River Symphony." 10 min. (orchestra) (Unpublished)

———. *Morning Sunbeam.* Bryn Mawr, PA: Theodore Presser, 1937.

———. *My Soul's Been Anchored in de Lord.* New York: Carl Fischer, 1937. (voice and piano)

———. *Nature's Magic.* Words by Mary Rolofson Gamble. Chicago: Summy, 1953. (secular choral music for treble voices)

———. *New Moon.* Chicago: Gamble Hinged Music Co., n.d. (women's chorus with optional soprano obligato and 4-hand acc.)

———. *Night.* Words by Louise C. Wallace. New York: Edward Marks, 1945. (voice and piano)

———. *Nobody Knows the Trouble I See.* Bryn Mawr, PA: Theodore Presser, 1937. (piano)

———. *Out of the South Blew a Wind.* New York: Edward B. Marks, 1946. (voice and piano)

———. *Rock-a-bye.* Chicago: McKinley, 1947.

———. "Sonata in E Minor." 1959. (piano) (Unpublished)

————. *Song for Snow.* New York: Carl Fischer, 1957. (SATB chorus and piano)

————. *Songs to a Dark Virgin.* Lyrics by Langston Hughes. New York: G. Schirmer, 1941.

————. *Sympathy.* (Paul Laurence Dunbar). Manuscript in the Sibley Library, Eastman School of Music, Rochester, NY.

————. "Symphony in C Minor." Four movements. 22 min. (Unpublished)

————. "Symphony in D Minor." Four movements. 20 min. (Unpublished)

————. "Symphony in E Minor." Four movements. 20 min. (Unpublished)

————. "Symphony in G Minor." Four movements. 25 min. (Unpublished)

————. "Symphony No. 3 in E Minor." (orchestra) (Unpublished)

————. "The Butterfly." *Pieces We Like to Play.* Eds. Gail Martin Haake, Charles J. Haake, and Osborne McConathy. New York: Carl Fischer, 1936.

————. "The Gnat and the Bee." *Pieces We Like to Play.* New York: Carl Fischer, n.d.

————. *The Goblin and the Mosquito.* Chicago: Summy, 1951. (piano)

————. *The Moon Bridge.* Words by Mary Rolofson Gamble. Chicago: Gamble, Hinged Music Co., 1939.

————. *The Rose.* New York: Carl Fischer, 1936. (piano, grade 3)

————. *The Sea Swallow.* Chicago: Summy, n.d. (piano)

————. *The Waltzing Fairy (El duende valsante).* Chicago: McKinley, 1928. (piano) (Publ. pl. no. 2244)

————. *The Waterfall (La cascada)*. Chicago: McKinley, 1928. (piano, grade 2)

————. *The Zephyr (El cafiro)*. Chicago: McKinley, 1938. (Mexican folk song, transcribed for piano, grade 3) (Publ. pl. no. 2279)

————. *Three Little Negro Dances*. Bryn Mawr, PA: Theodore Presser, 1949. (two pianos)

————. "Ticklin' Toes." *Three Little Negro Dances*. Bryn Mawr, PA: Theodore Presser, n.d. (two scores for two pianos)

————. *To My Little Son*. Words by Julia Davis. Manuscript in the Sibley Library, Eastman School of Music, Rochester, NY.

————. *Two Traditional Spirituals*. New York: Handy Brothers, 1948.

————. *Were You There When They Crucified My Lord?* New York: Carl Fischer, n.d.; New York: Oxford University Press, n.d. (piano)

————. *Witch of the Meadow*. Words by Mary R. Gamble. Chicago: Gamble, Hinged Music Co. (SSA)

Rainey, Gertrude ("Ma"). *Boweavil Blues*. New York: Northern Music Corp., 1924.

————. *Broken Hearted Blues*. New York: Northern Music Corp., 1929.

————. *Counting the Blues*. New York: Northern Music Corp., 1929.

————. *Deep Moaning Blues*. New York: Northern Music Corp., 1928.

————. *Hear Me Talkin' to You*. New York: Northern Music Corp., 1928.

————. *See See Rider*. New York: Leeds Music Corporation, 1934; 1944.

Rainey, Gertrude ("Ma"), and J. Mayo Williams. *Titanic Man Blues*. New York: Northern Music Corp., 1926.

Reagon, Bernice. "Matriarch Blues." *The Sound of Thunder*. Atlanta, GA: Kin Tell Corporation, 1200 Spring St., NW 30309, n.d.

Richardson, Esther, and J. Rosamond Johnson. *A Voice Said Cry*. New York: Handy Brothers, 1945.

Robinson, Gertrude Rivers. "Moods for Soprano Saxophone and Piano." Performed by Reginald Jackson (soprano saxophone) and Constance Hobson (piano) at the 4th annual program on the "Music of the Black American Composer," Smithsonian Institution 15 May 1988; and at the Fifth International Congress on Women in Music, Germany, 1988.

Schuyler, Philippa Duke. *African Rhapsody*. 1965.

―――. *Around the World Suite*. 1960.

―――. *Chisamharu the Nogomo* (Mozambique). Premiered the New York Town Hall, 13 Sep. 1964.

―――. "Country Boy." Arr. Juan Hines. 1957.

―――. "Cynthia." With Juan Hines. 1957.

―――. *Eight Little Pieces*. (piano)

―――. *Manhattan Nocturne*. Scored for 100-piece symphony, 1943. Premiered by the New York Philharmonic Orchestra, Carnegie Hall. First-prize composition in Grinnell Foundation Contest, Detroit, MI. Also performed by the Chicago and San Francisco Symphonies.

―――. *Old Father William, Arabian Love Song, Hymn to Proserpina,* and *Maelstrom*. Ca. 1948.

―――. *Rococo*. Words by Charles A. Swinburne. Words and music, Philippa Duke Schuyler. New words changed and added, Philippa Duke Schuyler, 1961.

————. *Rumpelstiltskin.* Scherzo from her *Fairytale Symphony.* Orch. by composer. Premiered by the New York Philharmonic Orchestra, 1944. Also played by the Boston Pops and Cincinnati Symphony.

————. *Rumpelstiltskin.* Para piano. Buenos Aires: Ricordi Americana. (12 pp.)

————. *Sleepy Hollow Sketches.* 1946. The piano transcription premiered at United Nations celebration, Tarrytown on the Hudson, birthplace of Washington Irving. Later, played by the New York Junior Symphony Orchestra and at the Fisk Musical Festival. Also an award-winning composition.

————. *The Legend of Mahdi.* 1965.

————. *The Legend of the Mahdi.* Based on themes from Omdurman, Sudan. Music copyright by Philippa Duke Schuyler, 1965.

————. *The Nile Fantasy.* 1. "Inshallah, or Fate . . . Contemplation and Submission"; 2. "Violence and Terror"; 3. "The Long Road to Peace." (piano and orchestra) Premiered in Cairo, Egypt, by the Cairo Symphony Orchestra with Miss Schuyler as soloist, 10 Dec. 1965. Premiered in America at a memorial recital for Miss Schuyler, 24 Sep. 1967, Leonard de Paur, cond. Arr. Margaret Bonds.

————. *The Rhapsody of Youth.* Premiered in Port au Prince, Haiti, 1948. Miss Schuyler received the Medal of Merit and Honor from President Magloire for this composition.

————. *The White Nile Suite.* 1954. Musical sage depicting Arab history in Egypt and the Sudan. (piano)

————. *The White Nile Suite.* 1965. Musical sage depicting Arab history in Egypt and the Sudan. (piano)

————. "The Wolf," "Autumn Rain," "The Jolly Pig." *Three Little Pieces.* 1938. (piano)

————. *Three Little Pieces.* Copyright Mrs. George Schuyler, 10 Nov. 1938.

———. *Three Songs*. Sung as part of the Philippa Schuyler Memorial Concert, by Camilla Williams, 24 Sep. 1967, New York Town Hall. Leonard de Paur, conductor.

Schuyler, Philippa Duke, arr. *No Bed of Roses,* by Juan Hines. 1957.

Schuyler, Philippa, and John Kelly, arr. *New Moon.* Copyright 1960.

Schuyler, Philippa, and Juan Hines, arr. *Country Boy.* Copyright 1957.

———. *Cynthia.* Copyright 1957.

———. "New Moon." 1950.

Simone, Nina. *Compensation.* Words by Paul L. Dunbar. New York: Rolls Royce Music, n.d.

———. *Nobody.* New York: Sam Fox, 1964.

———. *Real-Real.* New York: Rolls Royce Co., n.d.

———. *Revolution.* With Weldon Irvin, Jr. Mt. Vernon, NY: Ninandy Music Co., n.d.

———. *To Be Young, Gifted and Black.* Arr. H. Smith. Mt. Vernon, NY: Ninandy Music Co., n.d. (SATB)

Simpson, Valerie, and Nicholas Ashford. "Reach Out and Touch Somebody's Hand." Arr. Richard Smallwood. *Lift Every Voice and Sing: A Collection of Afro-American Spirituals and Other Songs.* New York: The Church Hymnal Corporation, 1981.

———. *Tear It on Down.* N.p.: Erva Music Publishing Co.,n.d.

Sisson, Eleanor Handy. "A Prayer for Peace." New York: Handy Brothers, 1946.

Smith, Bessie. *Baby Doll.* N.p.: Gus Kahn Music Co., 1927.

———. *Dixie Flyer Blues.* N.p.: Empress Music Inc., 1925.

———. *Don't Fish in My Sea.* New York: Northern Music Corp., 1928.

————. *Reckless Blues.* N.p.: C. R. Publishing Co., 1925.

Smith, Bessie, and Gertrude "Ma" Rainey. *Weeping Woman Blues.* New York: Northern Music Corp., n.d.

Smith, Bessie, and Clarence Williams. *Jail House Blues.* New York: MCA, Inc., and Empress Music, Inc., 1924.

Smith, Clara. *Black Woman's Blues.* N.p.: Mayfair Music Corp., 1927.

Smith, Clara, and Stanley S. Miller. *Every Woman's Blues.* N.p.: Mills, n.d.

Smith, Mamie, and Porter Grainger. *Plain Old Blues.* N.p.: Mills, 1923.

Smith, Undine (Moore). *Undine Smith Moore Song Book.* Virginia State College Concert Choir, Dr. Carl Harris, Jr., cond. Rich-sound Records 4112N10 (Afro-American Heritage Series, vol. 3). Available through Virginia State College, Box 352, Petersburg, VA.

Spivey, Victoria. *Black Snake.* N.p: n.p, n.d.

————. *Brown Skin.* N.p: n.p., n.d.

————. *Murder in the First Degree.* N.p: n.p., n.d.

————. *T. B. Blues.* N.p.: Mayfair Music Corp., 1927.

Stallworth, Dottie C. "All People Can Live Together." Composer.

————. "Christmas Time Bossonova." Composer.

————. "Get It Together." Composer.

————. "Guide Me, Jesus." *Religious Education Series.* Morristown, NJ: Silver-Burdett, 1976.

————. "His Spirit of Love." *Religious Education Series.* Morristown, NJ: Silver-Burdett, 1976.

————. "I Hear Sounds." Morristown, NJ: Silver-Burdett, 1977.

Dottie Stallworth

———. "Let's Keep What We Have for Tomorrow." Composer.

———. "Love Everybody Wherever You Go." Composer.

———. "Make the World a Better Place." Morristown, NJ: Silver-Burdett, 1976.

———. "Spread It All Around." Composer.

———. " 'Tis spring." Composer.

———. "Trust in God." Morristown, NJ: Silver-Burdett, 1977.

———. "Turn Back Your Thermostat." Composer.

———. " 'Twill Be a Rocking Christmas." Composer.

———. *Up Above My Head, I Hear Music in the Air.* New York: Montauk Music Inc., n.d.

———. "We Ought to Live Like Grandma Lived: She Didn't Have Pollution." Composer.

———. "What's Keeping Us from Being Me and You?" Composer.

Ward, Clara. "Until I Found the Lord." Arr. Dorothy Pearson. *Songs of Zion.* Nashville, TN: Abingdon Press, 1981.

Waters, Ethel, Fletcher Henderson, and Lewis Mitchell. *Kind Lovin' Blues.* Mills.

Waters, Ethel, and Sidney Easton. *Maybe Not at All.* N.p.: C. R. Publishing Co., 1925.

Wilburn, LaVilla Tullos. "Dear Miss Minnie," and "Green, Green, Rocky Road." *Afro-America Sings.* Eds. Ollie McFarland et al. Detroit: Board of Education, 1971.

———. "Goodnight, Donna Jean, Goodnight." *Afro-America Sings.* Eds. Ollie McFarland et al. Detroit: Board of Education, 1971.

———. "There Was a Babe." *Afro-America Sings.* Eds. Ollie McFarland et al. Detroit: Board of Education, 1971.

————. "There You Are." *Afro-America Sings.* Eds. Ollie McFarland et al. Detroit: Board of Education, 1971.

————. "This Is My Land." Words, Langston Hughes. *Afro-America Sings.* Eds. Ollie McFarland et al. Detroit: Board of Education, 1971.

————. "This Is the Christmas Time." *Afro-America Sings.* Eds. Ollie McFarland et al. Detroit: Board of Education, 1971.

————. "Who Has Seen America?" Words by Ollie McFarland. *Afro-America Sings.* Eds. Ollie McFarland et al. Detroit: Board of Education, 1971.

Williams, Mary Lou. *Camel Hop.* New York: Robbins Music Co., n.d.

————. *In the Land of OO-ble-dee.* New York: Capital Songs. Copyright Criterion Music Corp.

————. *Just an Idea.* N.p.: Jewell Music Publ. Co., n.d.

————. *Lonely Moments.* Arr. Mary Lou Williams and Milton Orent. Piano conductor scores (orchestra and parts). New York: Harman Music Co., n.d.

————. *Mass of the Lenten Season.*

————. *Mary Lou's Mass.* Performed at City Center Theater, New York, Mar. 1972, by Alvin Ailey American Dance Theater, Mary Lou Williams, conductor.

————. *New American Music.* New York Section Composers of the 1970s. Vols. 1–3. Folkways FTS 33901–3.

————. "Nursery Rhymes No. 2."

Williams, Mary Lou, William Johnston, and Leo Mosley. *Pretty-Eyed Baby.* N.p.: Pickwick Music Corp., 1951.

Williams, Mary Lou, Jack Lawrence, and Paul Webster. *What's Your Story, Morning Glory.* N.p.: Advanced Music Corp., n.d.

Thelma O. Williams

Williams, Thelma O. (Iola Bolles). "The Alphabet," "Circle Around," "Columbus," "Let's Build a Tower," "The Little Fish," "Move Like This," "The Old Man," "Our Little Piano," "To the Center." Children's songs in *The Growing With Music Series, K-6*. Englewood Cliffs, NJ: Prentice-Hall, 1966.

Music History and Criticism

Abdul, Raoul. *Blacks in Classical Music*. New York: Dodd, Mead and Company, 1974.

Anderson, E. Ruth. *Contemporary American Composers: A Biographical Dictionary*. Boston: G. K. Hall, 1976.

Bailey, Peter A. "Spotlight on the Black Theater Alliance." *First World* (Jan.–Feb. 1977): 50–52.

Bego, Mark. *Aretha Franklin: The Queen of Soul*. New York: St. Martin's Press, Inc., 1989.

Butcher, Vada. *Annual Report from the Center for Ethnic Music*. Washington, DC: Howard University Press, 1970–71.

———. *Development of Materials for a One-Year Course in African Music for the General Undergraduate Student*. Washington, DC: Howard University Press, 1970.

Cornell, Jean Gay. *Mahalia Jackson, Queen of Gospel Song*. Champaign, IL: Garrard Publishing Co., 1974.

Cundey-Hare, Maud. *Negro Musicians and Their Music*. Washington, DC: Associated Publishers, 1936; DaCapo Press, 1974.

DeLerma, Dominique R. *Black Music in Our Culture*. Kent, OH: Kent State, 1970.

———. *Reflections on Afro-American Music*. Kent, OH: Kent State, 1973.

————. *Afro-American Opportunity Resource Papers: Monographs I and II*. Minneapolis: AAMOA, 1974–75.

Dominy, Jeannine. *Leontyne Price*. New York: Chelsea House Publishers, 1992.

Floyd, Samuel A., Jr. *The Music of Black American Composers: An Anthology*. Carbondale, IL: Southern Illinois University Press, n.d.

George, Zelma Watson. "An Analysis of the Use of Negro Folksong in Six Major Symphonic Works." (Unpublished manuscript, 1933)

————. "Making Use of Negro Thematic Material, Symphonic Works Played by Major Orchestras, 1920–1945." (Unpublished manuscript, 1946)

————. "Negro Music in American Life." *American Negro Reference Book*. Ed. John P. Davis. Englewood Cliffs, NJ: Prentice-Hall, 1966.

Glass, Paul. *Songs and Stories of Afro-Americans*. N.p.: Grosset & Dunlap, 1971. (for children)

Gray, John. *Blacks in Classical Music*. Westport, CT: Greenwood Press, 1988.

————, ed. *Blacks in Classical Music: A Bibliographical Guide to Composers, Performers, & Ensembles*. Westport, Ct., 1988.

Green, Mildred Denby. *Black Women Composers: A Genesis*. Boston: Twayne Publishers, 1983.

Handy, Antoinette. *Black Music: Opinions and Reviews*. Introd. Edgar A. Toppin. Ettrick, VA: BM & M (Box 103), n.d.

————. *Black Women in American Bands and Orchestras*. Metuchen, NJ: Scarecrow Press, 1981.

————. *The International Sweethearts of Rhythm*. Metuchen, NJ: Scarecrow Press, 1983.

Hanson, Howard, ed. *The Scribner Music Library.* Vol. II. New York: Scribner's, 1973.

Harrison, Daphne Duval. *Black Pearls: Blues Queens of the 1920s.* New Brunswick, NJ/London: Rutgers University Press, 1988.

Hart, Mary L. *Folk Music and Modern Sound.* Jackson, MS: University Press of Mississippi, 1982.

Jackson, Irene V. "Black Women and the Afro-American Song Traditions." *Sing-Out!* 2 (July–Aug. 1976): 10–13.

———. "Music Among Blacks in the Episcopal Church: Some Preliminary Considerations." *Lift Every Voice and Sing: A Collection of Afro-American Spirituals and Other Songs.* New York: The Church Hymnal Corporation, 1981.

Jackson-Brown, Irene V. "Afro-American Song in the Nineteenth Century: A Neglected Source." *Black Perspectives in Music* 1.4 (Spring 1976): 23–28.

Jalon, Allan. "Leontyne Price as 'Masterclasser.' " Calendar Section, *Los Angeles Times* 18 Aug. 1986: 14.

McDearmon, Kay. *Mahalia.* New York: Dodd, Mead and Company, 1976.

McFarland, Ollie, et al. *Afro-America Sings.* Detroit: Board of Education, 1971. (182 pages of songs; also historical and biographical information, pictures, and illustrations)

McGinty, Doris. *Ethnomusicology: U. S. Black Music Issue* 19 (Sep. 1975). Eds. Portia K. Maultsby (guest) and Gerard Behague. *Black Perspectives in Music* 1.4 (Spring 1976): 117–118.

McLin, Lena. "Black Music in Church and School." *Black Music in Our Culture.* Ed. Dominique-Rene DeLerma. Kent, OH: Kent State University Press, 1970, pp. 35–41.

McMillan, Lewick. "Mary Lou Williams: First Lady of Jazz." *Downbeat* 38 (27 May 1971): 16–17.

Marsh, J. B. T. *The Story of the Jubilee Singers.* New York: Negro University Press, 1969.

Maultsby, Portia. *Afro-American Religious Music: A Study in Musical Diversity.* Springfield, OH: Hymn Society of America, 1981.

————. "Influences and Retention of West African Musical Concepts in U.S. Black Music. *The Western Journal of Black Studies* III (Fall 1979): 201.

————. "Music of Northern Independent Churches During the Ante-Bellum Period." *Ethnomusicology* 3.19 (Sep. 1975): 401–402.

Oakley, Giles. *The Devil's Music: A History of the Blues.* London: British Broadcasting Co., 1979.

O'Meally, Robert. *Lady Day: The Many Faces of Billie Holiday.* New York: Arcade Publishing, 1991.

Patterson, Lindsay, comp. and ed. *The Negro in Music and Art.* (International Library of Negro Life and History) New York: Publisher Co., Inc. Association for Study of Negro Life and History, n.d.

Roach, Hildred. *Black American Music: Past and Present.* Boston: Crescendo Publishing Co., 1973.

————. *Black American Music: Past and Present.* Vol. II. Malabar, FL: Robert E. Krieger Publishing Co., 1985.

————. *Black American Music: Past and Present.* 2nd ed. Melbourne, FL: Krieger Publishing Co., 1992.

Schuyler, Philippa Duke. "Music of Modern Africa." *Music Journal* 18 (Oct. 1960): 60–63.

Smith, Jessie Carney. "Developing Collections of Black Literature." *Black World* 20.8 (June 1971): 18–29.

Southall, Geneva. *Blind Tom: The Post-Civil War Enslavement of a*

Hildred Roach—Music Historian.

Black Musical Genius. Minneapolis: Challenge Productions, Inc. (Box 9624, 55440), 1980.

————. "White Antebellum and Past Emancipation Attitudes, as Revealed in the 1865 Court Case of Blind Tom, Musical Genius." Paper presented at the Association for Negro Life and History, 18 Oct. 1973.

Southern, Eileen. "America's Black Composers of Classical Music." *Music Educator's Journal* 62 (Nov. 1975): 46, 59.

————. *Biographical Dictionary of Afro-American and African Musicians.* Encyclopedia of Black Music series. Westport, CT: Greenwood Press, 1982.

————. *The Buxheim Organ Book.* N.p.: Institute in Medieval Music, 1963.

————. *The Music of Black Americans.* New York: Norton, 1971; 1983.

Spady, James G. "Black Women Pioneers in Music." *Black Women in Focus. The Philadelphia New Observer* 21 Dec. 1988.

Spelman, A. B. *Black Music.* New York: Schocken Books, 1966. (Includes C. Taylor, O. Coleman, et al.)

Walker, Wyatt T. *Somebody's Calling My Name.* Valley Forge, PA: Judson Press, 1975.

Williams-Jones, Pearl. "Afro-American Gospel Music: A Brief Historical and Analytical Survey (1930–1970)." *Development of Materials for a One Year Course in African Music for the General Undergraduate Student.* Washington, DC: Howard University Press, 1970.

————. "Afro-American Gospel: A Crystalization of Black Aesthetics." *Journal for the Society of Ethnomusicology,* 1975.

————. "Performance Style in Black Gospel Music." *Black People and Their Culture.* Ed. Linn Shapiro. Washington, DC: Smithsonian Institution, 1976, 26–41.

Wilson, Warren George. "Black Classical Musicians: Their Struggle to the Top." *Essence* (Sep. 1974): 59, 91, 94, 97.

Young, Pauline. "Negro Folk Music and Dancing." *Candid* 1.6 (Nov. 1938): 14.

———. "Negro Popular Music." *Candid* 1.8 (Jan. 1939): 14–15.

Yuhasz, Sister Marie Joy. "Black Composers and Their Piano Music." *The American Music Teacher* 19 (Apr./May 1970): 28.

Zaimont, Judith Lang, Ed.-in-Chief. Assoc. eds. Catherine Overhauser and Jane Gottliebe. *The Musical Woman: An International Perspective.* Westport, CT: Greenwood Press, 1980.

Recordings

Addison, Adele. *Twelve Poems of Emily Dickinson,* Aaron Copland. (Three choruses) CBS Masterworks. 32 110017, 1967. 2 s, 12 in., 33–1/3.

Andrews, Inez. *A Letter to Jesus.* Songbird LP 201.

Armstrong, Lillian Hardin (Lillian Hardin). *Dropping Schucks.* Music Corporation of America (MCA), 1926.

———. *Flat Foot.* MCA, 1926.

———. *I'm Gonna Get Cha.* MCA, 1926.

———. *Jazz Lips.* MCA, 1926.

———. *King of the Zulus.* MCA, 1926.

———. *Louis Armstrong Story,* Vol. 1, Hot Five. Columbia CL 351.

———. *Louis Armstrong Story,* Vol. 2, Hot Seven. Columbia CL 852.

———. *Papa Dip*. MCA, 1926.

———. *Perdido Street Blues*. MCA, 1926.

———. *Skit-Dat-De Dat*. MCA, 1926.

———. *The Immortal King Oliver*. Milestone MLP 2006.

———. *Tight Blues*. MCA, 1926.

———. *You're Next*. MCA, 1926.

Armstrong, Lillian Hardin, and Walter Melrose. *My Sweet Lovin' Man*. New York: Melrose Music Corp., 1923.

Arroyo, Martina. *Adromache's Farewell*, Samuel Barber. New York Philharmonic. Columbia ML 5912. 1963.

———. *Judas Maccabaeus*, George Friedrich Handel. Also with Grace Bumbry. Westminster XWL 3310. 1959.

———. *Momente*, Karlheing Stockhousen. Nonesuch Records H 71157. 1967.

———. *Requiem*, Op. 48, Gabriel Urban Faure. Decca DL 710169. 1970.

———. *Stabat Mater*, Gioacchino Antonis Rosina. Columbia ML 6142. 1965.

———. *Symphony No. 9, Op. 125, D Minor*, Ludwig Van Beethoven. Columbia M2S 795 (MS 7211–7212). 1969.

Arroyo, Martina, and others. *La Juive*, Halevy. New Philharmonia Orchestra, Antonion de Almeida, conductor. Ambrosian Opera Chorus, John McCarthy, Director. RCA ARL-1–0447 Stereo, Red Seal.

Arroyo, Martina, with Anna Moffo, Richard Tucker, Bonaldo Giaiotti. *La Juive*, Halevy (highlights). RCA ARL—0447 Stereo, Red Seal. 1974.

Austin, Lovie. *The Immortal Ma Rainey.* Milestone MLP 2001.

Baker, Anita. *Giving You the Best That I Got.* Electra 374058.

Baker, Josephine, and Spencer Williams. *Black Bottom Fall.* MCA, 1927.

———. *Lonesome Lovesick Blues.* MCA, 1926.

Brighten the Corner Where You Are: Black and White Urban Hymnody. (Roberta Martin Singers, Sister Rosetta Tharpe, Willie Mae Ford Smith, Marion Williams) New World Records NW224, 1978.

Brown, Elaine. "And All Stood By," "The End of Silence," "The Panther," "Very Black Man." *Seize the Time.* Vault, Stereo 131.

Buddy Tates Invites You "To Dig" a Basket of Blues. (Victoria Spivey, Lucille Hegamin, Hannah Sylvester) High Blues Fidelity LP-1001-B, original recordings, Spivey Productions.

Bumbry, Grace. *Don Carlo,* Giuseppe Verdi. Libretti by Mey and DuLocles. Seraphim IC 6004. 1964. 6S, 12 in. 33–1/3 rpm, microgroove.

———. *Judas Maccabaeus,* Georg Friedrich Handel. (English Phonodisc.) (Also, Martina Arroyo) Westminster WXL3310. 6S, 12 in., 33–1/3 rpm, microgroove.

———. *Messiah,* Georg Friedrich Handel. (complete version, original instrumentation) (Also, Joan Sutherland) Ed. Herbage. London A 4357 (X. 5665–5667) 1966.

Caesar, Shirley. "I'll Go." *Shirley Caesar and the Institutional Choir of Brooklyn.* HOB 266.

———. "Stranger on the Road." *Shirley Caesar and the Caesar Singers.* HOB 299.

Chapman, Tracy. *Tracy Chapman.* Elektra 36982.

————. "Fast Car, Fast Talkin' Bout a Revolution, etc." Elektra 153582.

Davis, Osceola. *Negro Spirituals.* (Osceola Davis, soprano; Jorma Hynninen, baritone; Ilmo Ranta, piano) Compact disc digital audio. Ondine Ode 715–2.

Devore, Jessye, and Harold L. Oram, with Gustav Heningburg. *The Believers: The Black Experience in Song.* Written and performed by Voices, Inc., Musical Director and Vocal dimensions Brooks Alexander. Based on book by Jo Jackson and Joseph A. Walker. Directed by Barbara Ann Teer. RCA Victor Dynagroove Recording LSO-1151.

Elam, Dorothy Conley, and Lavinia A. Franklin. *Historical Interpretation of Negro Spirituals and Lift Every Voice and Sing.* Camden, NJ: Recorded Publications, n.d.

Flack, Roberta. *First Take.* Atlantic SD 8230.

Franklin, Aretha. *Aretha Franklin, Soul Singer.* McGraw-Hill Films, 330 W. 42nd St., New York 10036. 25 min. Rental $25. Purchase $3325. In color.

————. *Aretha Now.* Atlantic Stereo, SD 8788.

————. "Call Me." *Aretha's Greatest Hits.* Atlantic SD 8295.

————. *Once in a Lifetime.* Harmony Records HS 11349.

Franklin, Aretha (with James Cleveland and the Southern California Community Choir). *Amazing Grace.* Atlantic Stereo SD 2–906.

Handy, D. Antoinette (assisted by Trio Pro Viva). *Contemporary Black Images in Music for the Flute.* Eastern ERS-513. Available from T & T Associates, Box 292, Raleigh, NC 27602.

Hinderas, Natalie. *Natalie Hinderas Plays Music by Black Composers.* Desto Records, Lake Record Sales Corp., Franklin Lakes, NJ. 12-inch LP.

Holiday, Billie. *All or Nothing at All.* Verve 68329.

———. *Billie Holiday: God Bless the Child.* 2 records. Columbia G30782.

———. *Billie Holiday: The Golden Years.* Vol. 1. Columbia C3L-21.

———. *Billie Holiday: The Golden Years.* Vol. 2. Columbia C3L-40.

———. *Billie Holiday's Greatest Hits.* Columbia (monaural) CL2666.

———. *Billie Holiday's Greatest Hits.* Phonodisc. (Microgroove and stereophonic) Decca DL 75040.

———. *Billie's Blues,* Or, "I Love My Man." New York: Edward Marks, 1962. (Voice and piano, pl. no. 14603)

———. *Ella Fitzgerald and Billie Holiday at Newport.* American Record Society, 1937.

———. *Essential Billie Holiday.* Verve (stereo) 68410; 8-track cartridge 8140; monaural 8410.

———. *Fine and Mellow.* New York: Edward Marks, 1940.

———. *Gallant Lady.* Monmouth-Evergreen Records MES 7046.

———. *Lady Day: A Collection of Classic Jazz Interpretations by Billie Holiday.* (All-star accompaniments) Columbia CL 637.

———. *Lady in Satin, Billie Holiday.* Columbia CL 1157; Stereo CS 8040.

———. *Lady Love.* United Artists 15014; stereo 5636; solid state stereo 18040.

———. "Lover Man." *The Birth of Soul!* Decca Records DL 7925. (Louis Armstrong, Ella Fitzgerald, Billie Holiday, Sister Rosetta Tharpe, Louis Jordan, Buddy Johnson, Lionel Hampton, Ray-O-Vacs, The Flamingos, Jay McShann, Lucky Millinder) Stereo.

————. *Solitude.* Verve: stereo 68074; 8-track cartridge 8140; monaural 8074.

————. *The Best of Billie Holiday.* Verve V68808.

————. *The Lady Sings,* Vol. 1. Ace of Hearts (monaural) 151.

————. *The Quintessential Billie Holiday.* Vol. I, 1933–1935. Columbia CK 40646.

Holiday, Billie, and Arthur Herzog. *Don't Explain.* New York: Northern Music Corp., n.d.; Matrix No. 73006A.

————. *God Bless the Child.* New York: Edward Marks, 1969. (vocal duet with piano, pl. no. 15408)

Horne, Lena, and Harry Belafonte. *Harry and Lena.* From the television special *Harry and Lena.* RCA Stereo PRS-295.

Houston, Whitney. *Whitney.* Arista 356154.

International Favorites. Philippa Schuyler, pianist. Mono Vol. I. Middle Tone Records, Emmanual A. Middleton Music Publishers, 1576 Broadway, New York 10036.

Jackson, Mahalia. *In the Upper Room.* Kenwood 474.

————. *Just As I Am.* Kenwood 479.

————. *Mahalia.* Kenwood 486.

Jailhouse Blues. Jacket Notes, Bernice Johnson Reagon, Leon F. Litwack, and Rosetta Reitz. Rosetta Records. (Field recordings of Black women inmates in Mississippi's Parchman Prison in 1936, 1939) Available from American Folklife Center, Library of Congress, Washington, DC.

Jenkins, Ella. *"And One and Two" and Other Songs.* Folkway Records FC 7544 (701 Seventh Ave., New York).

————. *Early Childhood Songs.* Scholastic Records FC 7630.

————. *"My Street Begins at My House," and Other Songs and Rhythms from the "Me Too Show."* Folkways Records FC 7543.

Johnson, Doris Alene. *Gospel Music Workshop Live in New York.* Savoy SGL 7006.

————. *The Doris Johnson Singers.* Savoy 14439.

Joy to the World. Placido Domingo, Leona Mitchell, Placido Domingo Jr., London Symphony Orchestra, London Voices. Hallmark Cards, 1988.

Knight, Gladys, and the Pips. *Greatest Hits.* Soul 723; S81723; S75723.

Liston, Melba. *Uhuru Afrika.* (with Andy Weston and Langston Hughes) Roulette R65001.

Moore, Undine Smith. *Bound for Canaan's Land.* Richsound 4112N10.

————. *Children Don't You Get Weary.* Richsound 4112N10.

————. *Daniel, Daniel, Servant of the Lord.* Richsound 4112N10.

————. *Hail Warrior.* Richsound 4112N10.

————. *I Just Come from the Fountain.* Richsound 4112N10.

Norman, Jessye. *Die Gatnerin Aus Liebe,* Wolfgang Mozart. Philips.

Patterson, Willis. *Art Songs by Black American Composers.* University of Michigan Records.

Perry, Julia. *A Short Piece for Orchestra.* Performed by the Imperial Philharmonic Orchestra of Tokyo, cond. William Strickland. Composers Recordings, Inc. CRI-145.

————. *Homunculus C. F.* Percussion Ensemble, cond. Paul Price. Composers Recordings, Inc. CRI-S252. (percussion, harp, and piano)

———. *Stabat Mater.* Performed by Makiko Asakura, mezzosoprano; the Japan Philharmonic Symphony Orchestra, cond. William Strickland. (contralto, string quartet, or string orchestra) Composers Recordings, Inc. CRI-133.

Porgy and Bess. Lyrics, DuBose Heyward and Ira Gershwin. Libretto, DuBose Heyward. Eva Jessye Choir. Program notes, Louis Untemeyer. Decca DL 9024.

Price, Florence. "My Soul's Been Anchored in de Lord." Performed by Marian Anderson. Victor 1799 (out of print).

———. "My Soul's Been Anchored in de Lord." Performed by Ellabell Davis. London LPS-182 (out of print).

———. *My Soul's Been Anchored in de Lord.* Performed by Leontyne Price. Orchestra conducted by Leonard de Paur on *Swing Low Sweet Chariot* (Fourteen spirituals). RCA LSC 2600.

———. *Our House.* Light Records LS 5608.

Price, Leontyne. *Aida,* Giuseppi Verdi. Libretto, Antonia Chislonzoni. RCA Victor LM 6158. 1962. 6 s, 12–1/2, 33–1/3 rpm, microgroove. Also Rita Gorr, Jon Vickers, Robert Merrill, Giorgio Tozzi. Rome Opera House and Chorus. George Solti, conductor.

———. *Hermit Songs,* Samuel Barber. Columbia ML 4988. 1955. 1 s, 12 in, 33–1/3 rpm, microgroove. American Music Series.

———. *Prima Donna, Volume 3.* Great Soprano Arias from Gluck to Poulenc. London Symphony Orchestra, Edward Downes, conductor. RCA LBC-3163, Stereo.

Price, Leontyne, with Rev. Ernest T. Campbell, Dr. Benjamin Mays, Dr. Howard Thurman, and Dr. Peter H. Samson. *In Memoriam: Whitney Moore Young, Jr. (1921–1971).* RCA LM-3219, Red Seal Mono, 16 Mar. 1971.

Rainey, Gertrude ("Ma"). *Blame It on the Blues.* Milestone 2008.

———. *Blues the World Forgot.* Biograph 12001.

————. *Bo Weavil Blues*. Riverside RL 8007.

————. *Cellbound Blues*. Milestone MLP 2001.

————. *Counting the Blues*. Riverside RPP 12–101, microgroove.

————. *Immortal Ma Rainey*. Milestone 2001.

————. *Ma and Pa's Poorhouse Blues*. Audubon AAM.

————. *On My Babe Blues*. Biograph 12011.

————. *Queen of the Blues*. Biograph 12032.

————. *See See Rider*. Riverside RLP 1001.

Reagon, Bernice. *The Sound of Thunder*. Atlanta: Kin-Tel Recording Studios.

Simone, Nina. *Black Gold* (featuring "To Be Young, Gifted and Black"). RCA LSP-4248.

————. *Nina Simone at Carnegie Hall*. Colpia CP-455.

Sister Thea: Songs of My People. Krystal Records, Boston.

Smith, Bessie. *Any Woman's Blues*. Columbia G30126.

————. *Empress*. Columbia G39818.

————. *Empty Bed Blues*. Columbia G30450.

————. *The Bessie Smith Story*. Columbia CL 88578.

————. *World's Greatest Blues Singer*. Columbia Gp33.

Smith, Muriel. *The Glory of Christmas*. Peter Knight Orchestra and Chorus. Philips Stereo PHS 600–111; Mono PHM 200–111.

Smith, Muriel, with Ann Buckles. *The Crowning Experience*. Mus.

Dir. Paul Dunlop. Capital. Copyright Moral Rearmament, 640 Fifth Avenue, New York.

Spivey, Victoria. *Kings and the Queen.* High Blues Fidelity LP 1014A, original recordings, Spivey Productions.

Spivey's Blues Showcase. Victoria Spivey, Lefty Dizz, Sparky Rucker, Otis Spann, Ralph Russ, Danny Russo, Harris Rosenfeld, Charlie Colatta, Dane Mygine, Louis Vitale. High Blues Fidelity LP-1017A.

Stallworth, Dottie C. (and Trio). *I Wish I Knew How it Feels to Be Free* and *Wave.* Art Records, 685 15th Avenue, Irvington, NJ.

Sweet Honey in the Rock. *Believe I'll Run On* and *See What the End's Gonna Be.* Redwood Records, Box 996, Ukiah, CA 95482.

————. *Feel Something Drawing Me On.* Flying Fish Records.

————. *The Other Side.* Flying Fish Records.

Taylor, Maude Cummings. *The Day Is Nearly Done.* (Spiritual) New York: Handy Brothers, n.d. (voice and piano)

Tharpe, Sister Rosetta. *Precious Memories.* Savoy MG 14214.

————. *Singing in My Soul.* Savoy MG 14224.

————. *Strange Things Are Happening Every Day.* Decca, 1958.

The Birth of Soul! Louis Armstrong, Billie Holiday, Ella Fitzgerald, Sister Rosetta Tharpe, Marie Knight, et al. Prod. Milt Gabler. Decca Jazz and Heritage Series DL 79245.

The Divine Sarah Vaughan: The Columbia Years, 1949–1953. Columbia Mono C2–4165.

The Queen and Her Knights: Victoria Spivey. Victoria Spivey, Sir Alonzo ("Lonnie") Johnson, Sir Eurreal ("Little Brother") Montgomery, Sir Peter ("Memphis Slim") Chatman, and Sir William ("Sonny") Greer. Spivey LP 1006.

The Victoria Spivey Recorded Legacy of the Blues. High Blues Fidelity LP-2001-A, Spivey Vintage Recordings.

The Voice of Freedom House (Recording with the Eva Jessye Choir, Alexander Smallens, Director) Columbia Recording Corporation Freedom House, formerly at 32 E. 51st Street, New York.

Thomas, Carla. *Gee Whiz!* East Publications, 1960. Atlantic Records.

Three Kings and the Queen. Victoria Spivey, Roosevelt Sykes, Big Joe Williams, and Lonnie Johnson. Spivey LP 1004.

Victoria and Her Blues. High Blues Fidelity Spivey Lp 1002.

Ward, Clara. *Clara Ward "Soul and Inspiration".* Pickwick 33 SPC-3251-B.

Williams, Mary Lou. *A Keyboard History.* Jazzione 1206.

―――. *Kansas City Jazz.* Decca (A)DL 8044.

―――. *Ladies of Jazz.* Atlantic 1271.

―――. *Music for Peace.* Mary Records.

―――. *Storyville* 906 ("Messin' Round in Montmartre").

―――. *The Women in Jazz.* Storeyville LP916.

Williams, Mary Lou, et al. *An Evening with Scott Joplin.* New York Public Library, 1972. John Motley, Director. (A gift of Nonesuch Records; soloist and chorus, with piano acc.)

CHOREOGRAPHY/DANCE

Choreographers

Dunham, Katherine. *Bal Negre*. Revue, 1947.

———. *Carib Song*. Music play, Boston Schubert Theatre, 2 Sep. 1945.

———. *L'Ag'Ya*.

———. *Le Jazz Hot*. Presented at Windsor Theater, 18 Feb. 1940.

———. "Rara Tonga," "Florida Swamps Shinny," "Woman with a Cigar," "Rites de Passages," "L'Ag'Ya," "Shango." *Tropical Review*, Martin Beck Theater, New York, 1943.

———. *Rites of Passage*, Baltimore Theatre, Los Angeles, 1939.

———. *Rites of Passage*, in *Tropical Revue*, Martin Beck Theatre, Sep. 1943.

———. "Shango," "L'Ag'Ya," "Haitian Roadside," "Rhumba," "Sin," "Naningo," "The Choro," "La Comparsa." *Bal Negre*, Belasco Theatre, New York, 1946.

———. *Star Spangled Rhythm*. Paramount, 1942. (Dick Powell, Eddie Anderson, Betty Hutton, Mary Martin, Katherine Dunham)

———. *Tropical Revue*, Boston Opera House, 4 Dec. 1944.

Primus, Pearl. "A Lesson in Jazz," "African Ceremonial," "Hard Time Blues," "Rock Daniel," "Strange Fruit." YMHA, 92nd Street, New York, 14 Feb. 1943.

Dance History and Criticism

Aschenbrenner, Joyce. *Katherine Dunham: Reflections in the Social and Political Context of Afro-American Dance.* Notion of the Dunham Method and Technique. With Lavinia Williams. New York: Cord, 1981.

Barber, Beverly Anne Hillsman. "Pearl Primus in Search of Her Roots, 1943–1970." Dissert. Florida State University, 1984.

Beckford, Ruth. *Katherine Dunham: A Biography.* Foreword Arthur Mitchell. New York: M. Dekker, 1979.

Biemiller, Ruth. *Dance: The Story of Katherine Dunham.* Garden City/New York: Doubleday, 1969.

Buckle, Richard. *Katherine Dunham, Her Dancers, Singers, Musicians.* London: Ballet Press, 1949.

Creaque-Harris, Leah. "Katherine Dunham's Multicultural Influence." *Tiger Lily,* 1.2 (n.d.): 26–29.

"Dancers and Dancing." *Black Magic: A Pictorial History of the Negro in American Entertainment.* Langston Hughes and Milton Meltzer. Englewood Cliffs, NJ: Prentice-Hall, 1967. 264–267.

"De Lavallade, Carmen." *Current Biography* (Dec. 1967): 8–12.

DjeDje, Jacqueline Cogdell. *Katherine Dunham: Reflections on the Social and Political Contexts of Afro-American Dance,* by Joyce Aschenbrenner, with Lavinia Williams. *Ethnomusicology: Journal of the Society of Ethnomusicology* 26.3 (1982): 473–474.

Dunham, Katherine. *Dances of Haiti.* Photographer, Patricia Cummings. Los Angeles: UCLA Center for Afro-American Studies, 1983.

⸻. "The Negro Dance." *The Negro Caravan.* Eds. Sterling Brown et al. New York: Arno Press, 1970.

Elias, Albert. "Conversation with Katherine Dunham." *Dance Magazine* (Feb. 1956): 16.

Dr. Jacqueline Cogdell DjeDje

Emery, Lynn Fauley. *Black Dance from 1619 to Today.* New chapter
by Dr. Brenda Dixon Stowell. Foreword Katherine Dunham.
Palo Alto, CA: National Press Books, 1972; Princeton, NJ:
Princeton Book Company Publishers, 1988.

Gresham, Joi. "The Dance and Cultural Series: A Curriculum
Review Model for the Teaching of African American Dance in
Academe." Monograph submitted for the DuBois Department

of Afro-American Studies, New African House, University of Massachusetts, Amherst, MA, 1989.

Gwyn, Eleanor W. Faucette. "A Key Determinant of Dance Style: The Structural Use of the Dance Instrument as Illustrated by the Choreography of Katherine Dunham's Rites of Passage." Thesis, University of Wisconsin, 1978.

Hering, Doris. "Carmen de Lavallade and Her Theatre of Dance." *Dance Magazine* XLII (May 1968): 31.

―――. "Katherine Dunham in 'Bambouche.'" *Dance Magazine* (Dec. 1962): 66–67.

Kisselgoff, Anna. "Black Choreographers Go on Display." *The New York Times,* 17 March 1979.

Lloyd, Margaret. *The Borzoi Book of Modern Dance.* A republication. New York: Dance Horizons, 1947; 1974.

Long, Richard. *The Black Tradition in American Dance.* New York: Rizzoli, 1989.

Martin, John. *Book of the Dance.* New York: Tudor Publishing Company, 1963.

―――. "Negro Dance Art Show in Recital." *The New York Times,* 19 Feb. 1940.

―――. "The Dance: Dunham." *The New York Times,* 17 Nov. 1986.

Mishnunm, Virginia. "Dance: Dunham 'Tropical Review.'" *The Nation* 9 (Oct. 1943): 416.

Orme, Frederick. "The Negro in the Dance as Katherine Dunham Sees Him." *The American Dancer* (Mar. 1938): 46.

"Primus, Pearl (Eileen)." *Current Biography* (Apr. 1944): 34–37.

Spady, James G. "The Vitality of Dance as Practiced by Pearl Primus." *Black Women in Focus. The Philadelphia New Observer,* 21 Dec. 1988.

Audio-Visual Materials about Dancers and Their Work

Dunham, Katherine, choreographer. *Cabin in the Sky.* Broadway
    musical.

————. *Carnival of Rhythm.* Short film of Dunham dances, Warner
    Bros., 1944.

————. *Casbah.* Film, Universal.

————. *Green Mansions.*

————. *Pardon My Sarong.* Dir. Earle C. Kenton. Universal, 1943.

————. *Stormy Weather.* Twentieth Century Fox, 1943.

VISUAL ARTS

Ceramicists, Cinematographers, Film Makers, Painters, Photographers, and Sculptors

Bennett, Gwendolyn. "Winter Landscape." 1936. *The Negro in Art.* Ed. Alain Locke. Arlington Heights, IL: Metro Books, 1969. (Rpt. of 1940 ed.)

Bolton, Shirley. "Opus I." "Black Man." *Black Artists on Art.* Eds. Samella Lewis and Ruth C. Waddy. Vol. 2: 44–45. Pasadena, CA: Ward Ritchie, n.d.

Brown, Vivian. "Seven Deadly Sins," "Peopled Mountains," "Getting Out." *Black Artists on Art.* Eds. Samella Lewis and Ruth C. Waddy. Pasadena, CA: Ward Ritchie, n.d.

Burke, Selma. "Lafayette," *Modern Negro Art.* Ed. James Amos Porter. New York: Arno Press, 1969.

Burroughs, Margaret. "Sojourner Truth." *American Negro Art.* Ed. Cedric Dove. Boston: New York Graphic Society, 1965.

Butler, Sheryle. "Composition." *Black Artists on Art.* Eds. Samella Lewis and Ruth C. Waddy. Vol. 2: 31. Pasadena, CA: Ward Ritchie, n.d.

Catlett, Elizabeth. "Black Is Beautiful III." Lithograph (13 x 13.5). Elizabeth Catlett catalog, Studio Museum, Harlem, 1957.

———. "Black Maternity." Lithograph (16 x 21.5), 1959.

———. *Black Unity.* Cedar (20.5 x 24 in.), 1968. The Brockman Gallery, Los Angeles.

———. "El Baile," and "Which Way?" *An Exhibition of Black Women Artists.* Catalog, University of California, Santa Barbara, n.d.

———. *Figura.* Sol Lieber Collection, New York.

———. "Habla la Mujer Negro [The Black Woman Speaks]." Lithograph (27.5 x 18.75), 1960.

———. *Homage to My Young Black Sisters.* Cedar (7.5 in.), 1969. The Artist.

———. "Indian Woman." Lithograph (13.5 x 16.25). Elizabeth Catlett catalog, Studio Museum, Harlem, 1958.

———. "Latin America Dice 'No'!" Linocut (22 x 23.5), 1968.

———. *Magic Mask.* Mahogany (10–5/8 in.), 1971. The Artist.

———. "Malcolm X Speaks for Us." Linocut (37.5 x 27.75), 1969.

———. *Mother and Child.* Cedar (26 in.), 1971. Brockman Gallery, Los Angeles.

———. "Mujeres de America [Women of America]." Woodcut (13.75 x 18.75), 1963.

———. "Negro es Bello I [Black is Beautiful]." Lithograph (13 x 20), 1968.

———. *Negro Girl.* Marble, 1939. *The Negro in Art.* Ed. Alain Locke. Arlington Heights, IL: Metro Books, 1969. (p. 115)

———. *Negro Mother and Child.* Bronze, 1940. Alonzo K. Aden.

———. *Negro Woman.* Wood. Atlanta University.

———. "Newsboy." Lithograph (10 x 12–5/8). Elizabeth Catlett catalog, Studio Museum, Harlem, 1958.

———. *Nude Torso.* Bronze (13.75 in.), 1969. The Artist.

———. *Olmec Bather.* Bronze (22 in.), 1967. The Artist.

————. "Pan [Bread]." Linocut (17.5 x 23). Elizabeth Catlett catalogue, Studio Museum, Harlem, n.d.

————. *Pensive Figure.* Bronze (22 in.), 1967. Mr. and Mrs. Harvey Rambach, New York City.

————. *Political Prisoner.* Cedar (71.25 in.), 1971. The Artist.

————. *Pregnancy.* Walnut (33 in.), 1970. Brockman Galley, Los Angeles.

————. "Rafaela." Seriograph (9.25 x 13.75), 1959.

————. *Rebozo II.* Cast Stone (13–3/16 in.), 1967. The Artist.

————. *Rebozo IV.* Bronze (11 in.), 1965. Dr. and Mrs. J. P. Jones, New York City.

————. "Rebozos." Lithograph (20 x 13), 1968.

————. *Recognition.* Black onyx (16.5 in.), 1970. The Artist.

————. "Sirvienta [Servant]." Linocut (13 x 10), 1962.

————. "Shoeshine Boy." Lithograph (23 x 17.75), 1958.

————. "Skipping Boy." Lithograph (17–5/8 x 23), 1958.

————. *Sister.* Green marble (13 in.), 1971. The Artist.

————. *Target Practice.* Bronze (13.5 in.), 1970. The Artist.

————. *The Black Woman Speaks.* Tropical wood (16–1/8 in.), 1970. Brockman Gallery, Los Angeles.

————. "The Torture of Mothers." Lithograph (13 x 20), 1970.

————. "Vendedora de Periodicus [Newspaper seller]." Lithograph (17.75 x 23). Elizabeth Catlett catalogue, Studio Museum, Harlem, 1958.

————. "Watts/Detroit/Washington/Harlem/Newark." Linocut (27.75 x 37.5), 1970.

Chase, Barbara. *Adam and Eve.* Bronze, 1958; "Bulls," 1958. Galleria L'Oblisco, Rome.

———. *Victorious Bullfighter.* Bronze, 1958. Dr. Perry Oteenburg, PA.

Collins, Kathleen (see also Prettyman). *The Cruz Brothers and Miss Malloy.* Color film, 16 mm, 54 min., 1980. (based on Henry Roth's novel *The Cruz Chronicle*)

———. *Gouldtown: A Mulatto Settlement.* N.p: n.p., n.d.

———. *Losing Ground.* Color film, 16 mm, 90 min., 1981. Winner of individual media grant from NEA 1981; AFT Screenwriting Grant 1981; prize for "First Feature" at Portugal's Figuroa da Foz International Film Festival.

Conwill, Kinshasha. "Untitled." Mixed media. Brockman Gallery, 4334 Degnan Blvd., Los Angeles, CA.

Dash, Julie, writer and director. *Daughters of the Dust.* An American Playhouse and WMG Production, 114 min, C. 1991. Released by Kino International.

Fuller, Meta Warick. *Ethiopia Awakening.* Schomburg Library, New York.

———. *Water Boy.* Harmon Foundation.

Gafford, Alice, with oil painting titled "Champagne Break." In the permanent collection at Howard University Art Gallery.

———. "Still Life with Antiques." Oil painting in the permanent collection of The Bowers Museum, Santa Ana, CA.

———. "The Tea Party." Oil painting, in the permanent collection of the Long Beach, California, Art Museum.

Jeffries, Rosalind. "Maska," "Masks." *An Exhibition of Black Women Artists.* Catalogue, University of California, Santa Barbara.

Johnson, Karen, Illust. *Poems Around Struggle and Love,* by Mshariri S. Weusi. San Francisco: Julian Richardson Associates, 1976.

————. Untitled poster of African boys. Available, San Francisco: Marcus Bookstore.

Jones, Lois Mailou. "Dance Mask." Mixed media (22.25 x 35.5), 1972; "Moon Masque." Acrylic-collage (41 x 29). *Black Artists on Art.* Eds. Samella Lewis and Ruth C. Waddy. Pasadena, CA: Ward Ritchie, n.d. Vol. 1, Rev. ed. 97–98.

Lewis, Edmonia. *Abraham Lincoln,* marble; *Asleep. Modern Negro Art.* Ed. James Amos Porter. New York: Arno Press, 1969.

————. *Hagar.* Marble. Frederick Douglass Institute.

————. *James Peck Thomas.* Marble, 1880. Mrs. James Blair.

————. *Old Indian Arrow Maker and His Daughter.* Marble, 1872. James H. Ricau, Piermont, NY.

McClinton, Diane T. "Lost in the City." Acrylic on canvas. Brockman Gallery, 4334 Degnan Blvd., Los Angeles, CA.

Marshall, Enrica. "Energy Out." Collage. Brockman Gallery, 4334 Degnan Blvd., Los Angeles, CA.

Matabane, Paula W. "Extra Change—The Little Film with a Big Heart." *Sisters* (Spring 1989): 29.

Montgomery, E[vangeline] J. "Statement: Sargent Claude Johnson." *Black Reflections, I: The Paintings and Sculpture of Sargent Johnson/Charles Dawkins.* San Francisco: Sanderson Museum of the San Francisco African-American Historical and Cultural Society, 1976.

Okwumabua, Constance. "Epilogwu Dancers." Acrylic (5 x 6). *Black Artists on Art.* Eds. Samella Lewis and Ruth C. Waddy. Pasadena, CA: Ward Ritchie, n.d. Vol. 1., rev. ed., p. 115.

Rogers, Brenda. "Flower Pot." (16 x 20) *Black Artists on Art.* Eds. Samella Lewis and Ruth C. Waddy. Pasadena, CA: Ward Ritchie, n.d. Vol. 1, rev. ed., p. 63.

Simon, Jewel W. "Walk Together Children." Mono-print (16 x 21), 1964. *Black Artists on Art.* Eds. Samella Lewis and Ruth C. Waddy. Pasadena, CA: Ward Ritchie, n.d. Vol. 1, rev. ed., p. 108.

Waring, Laura. "Alonso Aden" and "Frankie." *Modern Negro Art.* Ed. James Amos Porter. New York: Arno Press, 1969.

Wayner, Carole J. "The Children." *An Exhibition of Black Women Artists.* Santa Barbara, CA: University of California, Santa Barbara.

Art History and Criticism

Bearden, Romare, and Harry Henderson. *6 Black Masters of American Art.* Garden City/New York: Doubleday, 1972.

Biggers, John, and Carroll Simms, with John Edward Weems. *Black Art in Houston.* College Station and London: Texas Southern A & M University Press, 1978.

Bogle, Donald. *Black Arts Annual, 1987/88.* New York: Garland, 1989.

Coar, Valencia Hollins. *A Century of Black Photographers: 1840– 1960.* Providence, RI: Rhode Island School of Design, Museum of Art, 1983.

Cripps, Thomas. *Black Film as Genre.* Bloomington: Indiana University Press, 1978.

Dover, Cedric. *American Negro Art.* New York: Studio, Longacre Books, 1960; New York Graphic Society; Chatham, Eng.: W. & J. Mackey, 1962.

Driskell, David C. *Two Centuries of Black American Art.* Catalog notes Leonard Simon. New York: Los Angeles County Museum/Alfred A. Knopf, 1976.

Fax, Elton C. *Black Artists of the New Generation.* Foreword, Romare Bearden. New York: Dodd & Mead Co., 1977.

Fine, Elsa Honig. *The Afro-American Artist*. New York: Hacker Art Books, 1982.

Livingston, Jane, and John Beardsley. *Black Folk Art in America, 1930–1980*. Published for Corcoran Gallery of Art. Jackson, MS: The Center for the Study of Southern Culture/The University Press of Mississippi, 1982.

Locke, Alain Le Roy. *The New Negro: An Interpretation*. Introd. Allan H. Spear. New York: Johnson Reprint, 1968.

Moutoussamy-Ashe, Jeanne. *Viewfinders: Black Women Photographers*. Kali Diana Grosvenor, Research Assistant; Deborah Willis-Ryan, Consultant. New York: Dodd, Mead and Company, 1986.

Porter, James Amos. *Modern Negro Art*. New preface by author. New York: Arno Press and *The New York Times*, 1969.

———. *Ten Afro-American Artists of the Nineteenth Century: An Exhibition Commemorating the Centennial of Howard University*. Washington, DC: Howard University, 1967.

Whiting, Helen Adele. *Negro Art and Rhymes*. Washington, DC: Associated Publishers, 1963.

———. *Negro Art, Music and Rhyme for Young Folks*. Illust. Lois Mailou Jones. 2 vols. Washington, DC: Associated Publishers, 1938.

———. *Negro Art, Music and Rhyme*. Illust. Lois Mailou Jones. Book II. Washington, DC: Associated Publishers, 1967.

CULINARY AND OTHER ARTS

African News Cookbook: African Cooking for Western Kitchens. Africa News Service, Box 3851, Durham NC 27702.

Ashley, Eliza. *Thirty Years at the Mansion.* Ed. Hillary Clinton. Little Rock, AR: August House, 1985.

Blivens, S. Thomas. *The Southern Cookbook.* Hampton, VA: Press of the Hampton Institute, 1912.

Bowser, Pearl, and Joan Eckstein. *A Pinch of Soul.* New York: Avon Books, 1970.

Butler, Cleora. *Cleora's Kitchen* Or, *Eight Decades of Cooking.* Tulsa, OK: Council Oaks Books, Ltd., 1985.

Clark, Libby. "Food for Thought." *The Philadelphia New Observer* 15 July 1989.

"Cuisine: Kingfish Trinidadian Style." *Sisters* (Spring 1989): 35.

"Cuisine: Traditional Variations." *Sisters* (Winter 1988): 35.

Curtia, James. "A Century of Black Cookery." *Essence* 116.1 (May 1985): 164.

Darden, Norma Jean, and Carole Darden. *Spoonbread and Strawberry Wine: Recipes and Reminiscences of a Family.* Line drawing, Doug Jamieson. New York: Fawcett Crest, 1978.

DeKnight, Freda. *A Date with a Dish.* Chicago: Johnson Publishing Co., 1962; New York: Hermitage Publishing Co., 1970.

Dickerson, Helen. *I Just Quit Stirrin' When the Tastin's Good.* Comp., tested, ed. Cissy Finley Grant. Illust. Lyne Cherry. Cape May: Chalfonte Hotel, 1986.

Dixon, Ethel. *Big Mama's Old Black Pot: Recipes.* Ed. Charlene Johnson. Phot. Wayne Turner. Alexandria, VA: Gabriel Press, 1982.

Female members of the Atlanta Chapter of Tuskegee Airmen, Inc. *Flying High with Creative Cookery.* Marymal Dryden and Lillie Oslin, chairs. Lenexa, KS: Cookbook Publishers, Inc., 1980.

Ferguson, Sheila. *Soul Food: Classic Cuisine from the Deep South.* New York: Weidenfeld & Nicholson, 1989.

Gaskins, Ruth L. *A Good Heart and a Light Hand.* New York: Simon and Schuster, 1968; 1969.

Griffin, Hattie Rinehart. *Soul-food Cookbook.* New York: Carlton Press, 1969.

Griggs, Ed. D., and Mildred B. Griggs. "Make Ahead Salads." *Sisters* (Fall 1988): 41.

Hampton Institute Cookbook. Karla Longree, 1945.

Hunter, Flora M. *Cookbook.* Springhill Plantation, Thomas County, GA: n.p, n.d.

Jackson, Mahalia. *Mahalia Jackson Cooks Soul.* Nashville: Aurora Publishers, 1970.

Jackson, Mary, and Lelia Wishart. *The Integrated Cookbook: The Soul of Good Cooking.* Chicago: Johnson Publishing Co., 1972.

Jackson, Peggy. "The Art of Drying Flower." *Essence* 2 (Mar. 1972): 42–43, 65.

Jefferson, Louise E. *The Decorative Arts of Africa.* New York: Viking Press, 1973.

Ladies of Trinity A. M. E. Church. *From Our Kitchen to Your Kitchen.* Pastor Alvin Stokes, Bridgeton, NJ. Pleasonton, KS: Fundcraft Publishing, n.d.

Lyle, Jan, comp. "Hoppin' John" and "African Finger Foods." *Black Folk: Journal of Afro-American Folklore* 1 (Spring 1972): 4.

Lyons, Charlotte. "Date with a Dish." *Ebony*. (each issue)

———. "Date with a Dish: Tropical Coolers." *Ebony* 44 (July 1989): 96–98, 100.

Mahammitt, Mrs. Sarah Helen (Tolliver). *Recipes and Domestic Service: The Mahammitt School of Cookery*. Omaha, NE: Mrs. T. P. Mahammitt, 1939.

Mendes, Helen. *The African Heritage Cookbook*. New York: Macmillan, 1971.

Nash, Jonell. "Delectable Dips." *Essence* 20.1 (May 1989): 102.

———. "Food: Bountiful Brunch." *Essence* 20.1 (May 1989): 95.

———. "Recipes: Easy Elegance." *Essence* 20.1 (May 1989): 98.

National Council of Negro Women. *The Black Family Reunion Cookbook: Recipes & Food Memories*. Introd., Dorothy Height. Food editor, Libby Clark; Cover artist, Varnette Honeywood; Writer, Janet Cheatham Bell; Food consultant, Jessica B. Harris; Text/Design, Acuff/Pollary. Memphis: Wimmer Companies, 1991.

Newborn, Venezuela Richardson. "Weekend Brunch." *Essence* (Apr. 1972): 49, 64.

Paige, H. *Aspects of Afro-American Cookery*. Southfield, MI: Aspect Publishing Co. (Box 0384, Lathrup Village, MI 48076–39X), 1987.

Perry, Trudy. "Down Home Cuisine with Health in Mind." *Sisters* (Fall 1988): 15.

Porter, M. E. "New Southern Cookery Book." *The Negro in the United States*. Washington, DC: Library of Congress, 1969.

Princess Pamela. *Soul Food Cookbook*. New York: New American Library, 1969.

Sandler, Joan. "The Black Presence—A Theatre of Creative Alternatives," *Black Art* (An International Quarterly) 1.1 (Fall 1976): 40–47.

Sanford, Maggie. *New Afro-American Cuisine.* Houston, TX: Pride & Co., 1987.

Scott, Natalie. *Mandy's Favorite Recipes.* Gretna, LA: Pelican, 1987.

Sims, Naomi. *All about Success for the Black Woman.* Garden City, NY: Doubleday, 1982.

"Tasty Foods for a Healthy Heart." *Ebony* 44 (July 1989): 110+.

The Master's Ladies Rainbow Club of Christ Second Baptist Church, Long Beach, CA., comps. *A Book of Favorite Recipes.* Shawnee Mission, KS: Circulation Service, 1968–1982.

The Women of St. George's Episcopal Church (Washington, DC). *Golden Jubilee Cookbook of Favorite Recipes.* Shawnee Mission, KS: Circulation Service (Box 7306), 1968–1979.

Tuskegee Institute Cookbook. 1st bulletin, #2, 1898–1936.

Verta Mae (Grosvenor). *Vibration Cooking or Travel of a Geechee Girl.* New York: Doubleday, 1970.

PART III: WEST COAST BLACK WOMEN IN THE ARTS AND SOCIAL SCIENCES

CHRONOLOGICAL HISTORY OF WEST COAST BLACK WOMEN

1864   Mary Ellen Pleasant, civil rights advocate and abolitionist, sued the San Francisco Street Car Company for rude treatment given her and two other Black women.

1867   Amanda and Emma Hyers, great vocal artists, received critical acclaim for their first public recital at the Metropolitan Theatre, Sacramento, CA.

1872   Biddy Mason, Pioneer, laundry woman, philanthropist, was one of the founders of the first Black church in Los Angeles, the First A.M.E. Church.

1912   Charlotta (Spears) Bass, civil rights fighter and politician, became the owner, editor, and publisher of *The Eagle (The California Eagle,* the first black newspaper in Los Angeles.

1918   Dr. Vada Somerville, noted clubwoman and community leader in Southern California, was the first African-American woman to graduate from the University of Southern California, Los Angeles, School of Dentistry.

Dr. Ruth Temple, the first woman graduate from the Loma Linda Medical College, was the first African-American woman to practice medicine in the state of California

1926   Lorenza Jordan Cole, concert pianist and public school teacher, won Juilliard Musical Foundation Scholarships.

1927   Miriam Matthews, collector of Black Art, books, documents, photographs and was the first Black professional librarian hired by the Los Angeles Public Library.

Fay M. Jackson, former managing editor of the California News and co-founder of *Flash,* a weekly news magazine, covered the coronation of King George VI and made a special presentation before the French Parliament for the Associated Negro Press.

Dr. Vada J. Somerville. (Photo courtesy the Collection of Miriam Matthews)

Lorenza Jordan Cole in piano recital.

1930   Lorenza Jordan Cole, Internationally known concert pianist, studied in London, England, with "eminent pedagogue," Tobian Matthay.

1939   Bernice Bruington became the first Black high school principal in Los Angeles.

        Hattie McDaniel won the Academy Award for her role in "Gone With the Wind."

1941   Choreographer Ruth Beckford founded the African Haitian Dance Company.

1943   Dr. Ruth Temple organized and founded the Community Health Association, Inc., a health study club, in Los Angeles.

1945   Dr. Ruth Temple developed the concept of Community Health Week, now proclaimed a permanent institution in California by the California Legislature.

1948   Charlotta Bass, editor of the California *Eagle,* and a founding member of he Progressive Party, became the National Co-Chairman of Women for Henry Wallace.

1952   Charlotta Bass became the first Black woman to run for the second highest office in the land, as Vice Presidential candidate on the Progressive Party ticket.

1962   The California Legislature resolved that Community Health Week, a concept designed by Dr. Ruth Temple, be held the third week in March.

          Ruth Waddy founded the West Arts Associates, Inc.

1965   Ailen C. Hernandez was appointed to the Equal Employment Commission (EEOC).

1966   Yvonne Brathwaite Burke won a seat in the California State Assembly.

1967   Zelma Lipscomb, Long Beach, California, became the first woman, and to date, the only woman to serve as president of the Long Beach NAACP.

1969   Margaret Douroux, composer, choral director, counselor, teacher, received the best song award from the James Cleveland Academy of Gospel Music for her composition "Give Me a Clean Heart," and she received the A.C.C. Pauline Musician Achievement Award.

1972   Yvonne Brathwaite Burke became the first Black woman to serve as Vice Chairman of the Democratic National Convention; and she was the first Black woman from California to be elected to Congress.

1973   Yvonne Brathwaite Burke gave birth to a daughter, becoming the first member of Congress to have a child while in office.

          In 1973, Cicely Tyson, actress, won the Emmy Award for her role in *The Autobiography of Miss Jane Pittman.*

1974   Betty Gadling, Director of the Voices of Evergreen Radio Choir, the Director of Music at the Evergreen Baptist Church, and a member of the San Francisco School of Music and Drama, choreographed and wrote a musical sketch called "Reflection," which was presented at the Oakland Auditorium Theatre.

1975   Shirley Verrett opened the Metropolitan Opera Season with her perfomance in Rossini's *The Siege of Corinth.*

1976   Celestine Shambray, founder and director of the Shambray Chorale, was awarded the Bicentennial Woman of the Year by the Los Angeles Human Reflections Commission.

1977   Miriam Matthews, librarian, African-American historian, consultant, and recipient of numerous awards, was appointed to the California Heritage Preservation Commission by Governor Edmund G. Brown.

1978   Ella Fitzgerald received an honorary doctorate from Boston University.

1981   Poet, playwright, educator, novelist, Ntozake Shange won *The Los Angeles Times* poetry prize.

1984   Lula Washington, choreographer and founder of Los Angeles Contemporary Dance Theater, produced the Black Dance Festival at the Olympic Arts Festival.

1985   California State University, Long Beach, hosted the Eva Jessye Symposium in which twelve institutions participated, September 14–October 4, 1985.

     The City of Long Beach, California, declared September 15, 1985 Eva Jessye Day.

1987   The California State University, Long Beach women's basketball team, largely composed of Black women, was the only college team to defeat the U.S.S.R. National Women's Olympic Basketball Team.

     Civil rights activists, Marnesba Tillmon Tackett, was honored at the Equal Justice Awards Dinner by One Hundred Black Men of Los Angeles. Mrs. Tackett was a former member of the Board of Commissioners of the Housing Authority, Los Angeles, former director of Greater Los Angeles, and one of the founders of the Committee for Representative Government.

1988   January 31: Black American Cinema Society honored Billy Dee Williams when it promoted "HELD BLACK TALKIES ON PARADE" film festivals: Goal: to raise

Marnesba Tackett—civil rights activist.

funds for the Mayme A. Clayton Collection, the largest and most substantial compilation of rare books, documents, music, films and memorabilia on Black American culture in the Western United States, second largest of its kind in the world—second to the Schomburg Collection.

California State University, Dominguez Hills, established the Miriam Matthews Award in honor of the distinguished librarian, historian, and collector Miriam Matthews. The award will be presented annually to individuals who have made significant contributions to the field of African-American history and culture.

Miriam Matthews, retired librarian, historian, and consultant was one of four persons in 1988 to become a Fellow of the Historical Society of Southern California.

The California Afro-American Museum dedicated the exhibit *Black Angelenos: The Afro-American in Los Angeles, 1850–1950* to Miriam Matthews, Librarian, Historian, Consultant, and Community Activist, for her Assistance in constructing the exhibition.

The California Afro-American Museum featured the works of Sandra Rowe in an exhibit titled "S/ relationships." Ms. Rowe was the artist-in-residence at the museum.

May 1988, Ntozake Shange received an honorary doctorate from Haverford College, Haverford, PA.

February 26, Debi Thomas, who competed against Katerina Witt at Calgary in the Short program, figure skating, won first place for the Short program.

Angela Miles-Davis became the first female police helicopter pilot in Compton, CA.

Florence Griffith Joyner and Jackie Joyner-Kersee, sisters-in-law, set world records at the Olympics held in Seoul, Korea. Jackie Joyner-Kersee won the gold medal in the Olympic heptathlon competition for her jump of 23 feet and 10–¼ inches. Florence Griffith Joyner won the Olympic women's 100 meter race in 10.54.

Joyner won gold medals in the 100 and 200 meter races, setting a world record; a gold in the 100 meter relay, and a silver in the 400 meter relay.

Keba Phipps was also among the Black American women who participated in the Olympic sports, Seoul, Korea.

1989   Dr. Hansonia Caldwell, Dean of Humanities and Fine Arts, California State University, Dominguez Hills, was elected 5th Vice President of International Mu Phi Epsilon. Dr. Caldwell is the first African-American elected to the board of this 10,000 member organization, founded in 1903.

1990   Claudia Mitchell-Kernan became Vice Chancellor for U.C.L.A. graduate programs and Dean of its graduate divisions.

1991   Former Congresswoman Yvonne Brathwaite Burke and State Senator Diane Watson declared their candidacy for the Los Angeles Supervisor's seat being vacated by Kenneth Hahn.

1992   Professor Gertrude Rivers Robinson, Loyola Marymount, had her *Bayangang for Western Septet Balinese Octet Dances with Visuals* performed by the Afro-American Chamber Society, under the direction of Denise White-McCrae,at the Afro-American Museum, Los Angeles.

REFERENCE WORKS

Black History Calendar. Distribution Corporation, Box 8049 Los Angeles, CA. 90008.

Carr, Crystal. *Ebony Jewels: A Selected Bibliography of Books by and about Black Women.* Rev. ed. Inglewood, CA: Crenshaw-Imperial Branch Library, 1975.

DjeDje, Jacqueline Cogdell. *Black American Religious Music from Southeast Georgia.* Folkways Records FS 34010.

———. "Selected Discography of Afro-American Music." *Musics of the World: A Selected Discography, Part III.* Ed. Nora Yeh. Los Angeles: UCLA Ethnomusicology Archive: n.d., 4–11.

———. Tape Composite. *Composite of one String Fiddle Music from the Hausa of Northern Nigeria and Dagomba of Northern Ghana.* Los Angeles: UCLA Ethnomusicology Archive: n.d. (four 7" reel tapes)

———. Tape Composite. *Composite of Black American Religious Songs.* Los Angeles: UCLA Ethnomusicology Archive (14 7" reel tapes)

Fisher, Edith Maureen. *Focusing on Afro-American research: A Guide on Annotated Bibliography.* Ethnic Studies Publication #1. San Diego: University of California. San Diego, 1973.

Fisher, Sethard and other. *Black Elected Officials in California.* Introd. by Mervyn M. Dymally. San Francisco: n.p., 1978.

Goode, Kenneth G. *California's Black Pioneers: A Brief Historical Survey.* Foreword by Wilson Riles. Santa Barbara: McNally and Loftin, 1974.

Crystal Carr

Lapp, Rudolph. *Afro-Americans in California.* San Francisco: Boyd and Fraser Co., 1979.

Matthews, Miriam. "The Negro in California from 1781 to 1916: An Annotated Bibliography." A report submitted to the Graduate School of Library Science, University of Southern California, in partial fulfillment of the requirements for the research course in Library Science 290ab, Feb. 1944.

Moseley, Vivian H. "Selected Bibliography on Guidance in Business Education." *Guidance Problems and Procedures in Business Education.* Somerville, NJ: Somerset Press, for the Eastern Business Teachers Association, 1954.

Pool, Jeannie G. *Women in Music History: A Research Guide.* Ansonia Station Box 436, New York, NY.

Sharp, Saundra, comp., ed. *Black History Film List: 150 Films and Where to Find Them.* Los Angeles: Saundra Sharp, 1989. (Poets Pay Rent Too, Box 75796 Sanford Station, Los Angeles, CA)

Who's Who Among Black Women in California. Inglewood, CA: n.p., 1981.

Who's Who in the West. Chicago: Marquis, 1949.

Williams, Ora. "A Bibliography of Works Written by American Black Women." *CLA Journal* 15.3 (Mar. 1972): 354–377.

———. "Works by and about Alice Ruth (Moore) Dunbar-Nelson: A Bibliography." *CLA Journal* 3.19 (Mar. 1976): 322–326.

LITERARY ARTS

Books for Young Readers

Christian, Barbara. *Creative Essays: Adventures in Writing for Grades 7–12.* Belmont, CA: Fearson Teachers' Aides, 1980.

Clifton, Lucille. *Amifika.* New York: Dutton, 1977.

———. *An Ordinary Woman.* New York: Random House, 1974.

———. *Don't You Remember?* New York: Dutton, 1973.

———. *El Nino Que No Creia en la Primavera.* Trans. of *The Boy Who Didn't Believe in Spring.* New York: Dutton, 1976.

———. *Everett Anderson's 1–2-3.* New York: Holt, Rinehart and Winston, 1977.

———. *Everett Anderson's Christmas Coming.* New York: Holt, Rinehart and Winston, 1971.

———. *Everett Anderson's Christmas Coming.* New York: Holt, Rinehart and Winston, 1972.

———. *Everett Anderson's Friend.* Illust. Ann Grifalconi. New York: Holt, Rinehart and Winston, 1976.

———. *Everett Anderson's Goodbye.* Illust. Ann Grifackoni. New York: Holt, Rinehart and Winston, 1983.

———. *Everett Anderson's Nine Month Long.* New York: Holt, Rinehart and Winston, 1978.

———. *Everett Anderson's Year.* New York: Holt, Rinehart and Winston, 1974.

————. *Good News About the Earth.* New York: Random House, 1972.

————. *Good Times.* New York: Random House, 1970.

————. *Good, Says Jerome.* New York: Dutton, 1973.

————. *My Brother Fine With Me.* New York: Holt, Rinehart and Winston, 1975.

————. *Some of the Days of Everett Anderson.* Illust. Evaline Ness. New York: Holt, Rinehart and Winston, 1970.

————. *The Black BC's.* Illust. Don Miller. New York: Dutton, 1970.

————. *The Boy Who Didn't Believe in Spring.* New York: Dutton, 1973.

————. *The Lucky Stone.* New York: Delacorte Press, 1979.

————. *The Times They Use to Be.* New York: Holt, Rinehart and Winston, 1974.

————. *The Two-Headed Woman.* Amherst: University of Massachusetts, 1980.

Diop, Birago. *Mother Crocodile.* Trans. adopt. Rosa Guy. Illust. John Steptoe. New York: Delacorte Press, 1981.

Graham, Ruth Morris. *Big Sister.* Illust. Julie Downy. Boston: Houghton Mifflin, 1981.

————. *The Happy Sound.* Chicago: Follett, 1970.

————. *Penny Savings Bank. Cricket,* 1976. Boston: Houghton Mifflin, 1979; *Burning Bright.* Ed. Zena Sutherland. Open Court, LaSalle, IL: Reading and Language Arts Curriculum Center, 1985; *Over the Moon.* Comps. and eds. Zena Sutherland and Marilyn F. Cunningham. Open Court, LaSalle, IL: Reading and Language Arts Curriculum Center, 1989; *Weavers.* Eds. William Diur et al. Atlanta: Houghton Mifflin, 1989.

Holt, Delores L. *The ABC's of Black History.* Illust. Samuel Bhang. Los Angeles: The Ward Ritchie Press, 1971; 1973.

Ruth Morris Graham

Johnson, Nelle. *The Wisdom of an Owl.* Los Angeles: Atlantic-Richfield and others, 1975. Available from Vernon Branch, Los Angeles Public Library. (Author was aunt of Ralph Bunche.)

Thomas, Joyce Carol. *Bright Shadow.* New York: Avon, 1983.

——. *Journey.* New York: Scholastic, 1988.

——. *The Golden Pasture.* New York: Scholastic, 1986.

——. *Water Girl.* New York: Avon, 1986.

Walker, Alice. *You Can't Keep a Good Woman Down.* New York: Harcourt Brace Jovanovich, 1971.

Wilson, Beth. *I Like Nighttime.* San Francisco: Anthelion, 1977.

——. *Martin Luther King, Jr.* New York: Putnam, 1971.

——. *Martin Luther King, Jr.* New York: Putnam, 1973.

——. *Muhammad Ali.* New York: G. P. Putnam's Sons, 1974.

——. *The Great Minu.* Chicago: Follett, 1974.

Autobiographies and Biographies by and about African-American Women

Angelou, Maya. *All God's Children Need Travelling Shoes.* New York: Random House, 1986.

——. *Gather Together in My Name.* New York: Random House, 1974.

——. *I Know Why the Caged Bird Sings.* New York: Random House, 1969.

——. *The Heart of a Woman.* New York: Random House, 1981.

——. *Singin' and Swingin' and Gettin' Merry Like Christmas.* New York: Random House, 1976.

Bass, Charlotta A. *Forty Years: Memoirs from the Pages of a Newspaper*. Los Angeles: Charlotta A. Bass, 1969; 1970.

Beasley, Delilah L. *The Negro Trail Blazers of California*. A compilation of records from the California Archives at Bancroft Library, University of California at Berkeley; also from diaries, old papers, conversations of old pioneers in California. Los Angeles, 1919; New York: Negro Universities Press, 1919.

Brown, R. Donald. "An Interview with William Grant Still." Ed. Judith Anne Still. 13 Nov., 4 Dec. 1967. Fullerton, CA: Oral History Program, California State University, Fullerton, CA.

Cawthron, Janie. *The Legacy of Janie M. Cawthron*. N.p.: Cawthron Enterprise, 1985.

Chall, Malca. *Odessa Cox: The Twenty-Seven Year Campaign for Southwest Junior College*, 1977. Introd. Sandra Cox and Agnes Moreland Jackson. *Women in Politics Oral History Project*. Bancroft Library, University of California, Berkeley. Berkeley, CA: The Regents of California, 1978.

Clifton, Lucille. *Generations: A Memoir*. New York: Random House, 1976.

Cole, Maria Ellington, and Louie Robinson. *Nat King Cole: An Intimate Biography*. New York: William Morrow, 1972.

Davis, Angela. *Angela Davis: An Autobiography*. New York: Random House, 1974.

Douroux, Margaret Pleasant. *About My Father's Business: The Ministry of Reverend Earl Amos Pleasant*. N.p: n.p., 1977.

Evers, Mrs. Medgar with William Peters. *For Us the Living*. New York: Doubleday, 1967.

Graham, Ruth Morris. *The Saga of the Morris Family*. Columbus, GA: The Brentwood Christian Communications, 1984.

Headlee, Judith Anne Still. "Carrie Still Shepperson: The Hollows of Her Footsteps." *Forum* (University of Texas) 15 (Spring 1977): 60–65.

————. "Let Grieving Go." *The Single Parent* 18 (Oct. 1975): 12–13, 16.

————. "One Equal to None." *Living Single* (Aug. 1984).

Headlee, Judith Anne Still, ed. "An Interview with William Grant Still," by R. Donald Brown.

Hull, Gloria, ed. *Give Us Each Day: The Diary of Alice Dunbar-Nelson.* New York: W. W. Norton, 1984.

Jackson, Agnes Moreland. "Introduction to *Odessa Cox.*" (Los Angeles' example of the spirit of Fannie Lou Hamer), Bancroft Oral History Project on Significant Black California Women, University of California, Berkeley, Spring 1978.

Matthews, Miriam. "Alice Taylor Gafford." *Family Savings Community New Letter* 1.1 (Oct. 1967): 1, 3.

————. "Beulah Ecton Woodard." Part of Beulah Woodard Scrapbook sent to Surmondt Museum in Aachen, Germany, 1954.

————. "Phylon Profile, XXIII: William Grant Still—Composer." *Phylon* 12.2 (Second Quarter 1951): 106–112.

————. "Profile." *Black Women's Oral History Project,* Schlesinger Library, Radcliff College, 1981.

————. "Ruth Janetta Temple." *Black Women's Oral History Project,* Schlesinger Library, Radcliff College, 1981.

"Maya Angelou, Author." "I Dream a World, Part III." *The Houston Post* 28 Mar. 1989: D-3; Material taken from *I Dream a Dream,* book and exhibit, by Brian Lanker.

Mills, Earl. *Dorothy Dandridge.* Los Angeles: Holloway House, 1970.

Mumford, Esther. *Seattle's Black Victorians, 1852–1901.* Seattle: Ananse Press, 1980.

Mungen, Donna. *The Life and Times of Biddy Mason.* N.p.: MC Printing Company, 1976.

Robinson, Beverly J. *Aunt {ant} Phyllis*. Los Angeles: Women's
Graphic Center, 1982.

Thurman, Sue Bailey. *Pioneers of Negro Origin in California*. San
Francisco: Acme Publishing Co., 1949.

Turner, Tina. *I, Tina*. New York: Avon, n.d.

Novels

Austin, Doris Jean. *After the Garden*. New York/Scarborough, ON:
New American Library, 1987.

Blaylock, Enid V. *Librespouse*. Port Washington, NY: Ashly,
1981.

Butler, Octavia. *Clay's Ark*. New York: St. Martin's Press, 1984.

———. *Dawn*. New York: Warner, 1987.

———. *Kindred*. New York: Doubleday, 1970; Pocket Books,
1980.

———. *Mind of My Mind*. New York: Doubleday, 1977; New
York: Avon, 1978.

———. *Patternmaster*. New York: Doubleday, 1976; New York:
Avon, 1979.

———. *Survivor*. New York: Doubleday, 1978; New York: New
American Library, 1979.

———. *Wild Weed*. New York: Doubleday, 1980; New York:
Anchor Books, 1981.

Cartier, Xam Wilson. *Be-Bop, Re-Bop*. New York: Ballantine
Books, 1987.

Clifton, Lucille. *All Us Come Across the Water*. New York: Holt,
Rinehart and Winston, 1973.

Enid Blaylock

Monroe, Mary. *The Upper Room.* New York: St. Martin's Press, 1985.

Shange, Ntozake. *Sassafras, Cypress, & Indigo.* New York: St. Martin's Press, 1982.

———. *Betsey Brown.* New York: St. Martin's Press, 1985.

Thomas, Joyce Carol. *Bittersweet.* (poetry) San Jose, CA: Firesign Press, 1973.

———. *Blessing.* (poetry) Berkeley: Jacato Press, 1975.

————. *Crystal Breezes.* (poetry) Berkeley: Firesign Press, 1974.

————. *Golden Pasture.* New York: Scholastic Inc., 1986.

————. *Inside the Rainbow.* (poetry) Palo Alto, CA: Zikawina Press, 1982.

————. *Marked by Fire.* New York: Avon, 1982.

————. *Water Girl.* New York: Avon, 1986.

Walker, Alice. *Meridian.* New York: Harcourt Brace Jovanovich, 1970.

————. *Meridian.* New York: Harcourt, 1975; also excerpted in *Essence* (July 1976): 36–40, 73–78.

————. *The Color Purple.* New York: Harcourt Brace, 1982.

————. *The Temple of My Familiar.* San Diego/New York: Harcourt Brace Jovanovich, 1989.

————. *The Third Life of Grange Copeland.* New York: Harcourt, 1970.

Williams, Sherley. *Dessa Rose.* New York: William Morrow, 1986.

Short Stories

Angelou, Maya. *Now Sheba Sings the Song.* (Text, Angelou; drawings, Tom Feelings) New York: Dial/Dutton, 1987.

Coleman, Wanda. *A War of Eyes and Other Stories.* Santa Rosa, CA: Black Sparrow Press, 1988.

————. *Imagoes.* Santa Rosa, CA: Black Sparrow Press, 1983.

————. "Watching the Sunset." *Black World* 4.19 (Feb. 1970): 53–54.

Cooper, J. California. *A Piece of Mine.* Foreword, Alice Walker. Navarro, CA: Wild Trees Press (Box 378), 1984.

Sherley Anne Williams—novelist, critic, and poet (Photo courtesy of Thomas Victor and Sherley Anne Williams. © Thomas Victor. Reprinted with permission of Sherley A. Williams.)

————. *Homemade Love.* New York: St. Martin's Press, 1986.

————. *Some Soul to Keep.* New York: St. Martin's Press, 1987.

Walker, Alice. "Diary of an African Nun." *The Black Women.* Ed. Toni Cade. New York: N.p., 1970.

————. "Roselly." *Ms.* 1 (Aug. 1972): 44–47.

————. "The Welcome Table." *Freedomways* 10 (Third Quarter 1970): 242–246.

————. "To Hell with Dying." *Best Short Stories by Negro Writers.* Ed. Langston Hughes. Boston: Little, Brown and Co., 1967.

————. *You Can't Keep a Good Woman Down.* San Diego/New York/London: Harcourt Brace Jovanovich, 1971–1981.

Williams, Sherley. "Tell Martha Not to Moan." *The Black Woman: An Anthology.* Ed. Toni Cade. New York: New American Library, 1970.

Plays

Angelou, Maya. *The Best of These,* 1966.

————. *The Clawing Within,* 1966–67.

Booker, Sue. *The Flags.* One act drama. *Cry at Birth.* N.p.: Booker and others, 1971.

Cooper, J. California. *Center Stage.* Berkeley: Sea Urchin Press, 1980.

————. *How Now?* Prod. Black Repertory Group, Berkeley, 1973.

————. *Loners.* Prod. Black Repertory Group, Berkeley, 1970s; Mills College, Oakland, CA.

————. *Strangers.* (also *Ahhh, Strangers*) Performed at San Francisco Palace of Fine Arts, 1978.

———. *The Unintended.* Prod. Black Repertory Group, Berkeley, June 1983.

McKee, Sharon. *Unfinished Business.* Prod. Inner City Cultural Center, Los Angeles, 2 Nov. 1987.

Meyers, Paulene. "Mama." Performed at Los Angeles Studio Theatre Playhouse, 8–30 May 1975.

Moore, Elvie. "Angela Is Happening." Performed in Los Angeles, 1971.

Richards, Beah. *A Black Woman Speaks.* Los Angeles: Inner City Press, 1974.

———. *One Is A Crowd.* Musicalized version of the play by the same name. Presented at the Inner City Cultural Center, Feb.–Apr. 1988.

Shange, Ntozake. *Three Pieces.* New York: St. Martin's Press, 1981; New York: Penguin, 1982.

———. *Three Pieces: Spell #7; A Photograph: Lovers in Motion; Boogie Woogie Landscape.* New York: St. Martin's Press, 198?; N.p.: Penguin, 1982.

———. *Three Views of Mt. Fuji.* Prod. in Lorraine Hansberry Theatre, San Francisco, 1987.

Sharp, Saundra. *The Sistuhs.* Prod. Shaw Players, Raleigh, NC, 1977; also in Los Angeles and Oakland.

———. *We Write the Songs.* One hr. script written for Quincy Jones Music Workshop, Los Angeles.

Thomas, Joyce Carol. *A Song in the Sky.* San Francisco: Montgomery Theater, Summer 1976.

———. *Ambrosia.* San Francisco, Little Fox Theater, Summer 1978.

———. *Look! What a Wonder!* Berkeley: Berkeley Community Theater, Sep. 1976.

———. *Magnolia.* Old San Francisco Opera House, Summer 1977.

Saundra Sharp—poet and playwright.

Walton, Sibyl Renee. *Club House Agenda.* Presented 1 Nov. 1987 at Inner City Cultural Center (1803 New Hampshire Avenue, Los Angeles, CA).

Wilkerson, Margaret B. *The Funeral.* Performed by Kumoja Players, Richmond, CA at Sojourner Truth Presbyterian Church, weekends 28 Sep.–18 Oct. 1975.

Wilkerson, Margaret B., ed. and introd. *Nine Plays by Black Women.* New York: Mentor/New American Library, 1986.

Poems

Ai. *Cruelty.* Boston: Houghton Mifflin, 1973.

———. *Killing Floor.* Boston: Houghton Mifflin, 1979.

———. *Sin.* Boston: Houghton Mifflin, 1986.

Alba, Namina. *The Parchments: A Book of Verse.* N.p.: Merchants Press, 1962.

———. *The Parchments II: A Book of Verse.* N.p.: privately printed, 1967.

Angelou, Maya. *And Still I Rise,* New York: Random House, 1978.

———. *O Pray My Wings Are Gonna Fit Me Well.* New York: Random House, 1975.

———. *Shaker, Why Don't You Sing?* New York: Random House, 1983.

Atungaye, Monifa. *Provisions.* Detroit: Lotus Press, Inc., 1989.

Ayo, Zera. "Investigation." Los Angeles: Author (Box 77130), 1963.

Bilbrew, Mrs. A. C. H. "The Black Boys in Khaki." Beasely, Delilah L. *The Negro Trail Blazers of California.* New York: Negro Universities Press, 1919.

Bogus, Diane. "Dippity-Did/Done or Can You Do." (To Black Women) *Night Comes Softly*. Ed. Nikki Giovanni. New York: Nik-Tom Publications, 1970.

―――. *Her Poem: An Anniversary Chronology*. Inglewood, CA: W. I. M., 1979.

―――. *I'm Off to See the Goddam Wizard, Alright!* Chicago: Author, 1971.

―――. *Sapphires' Sampler*. College Corner, OH: W. I. M., 1982.

―――. *Woman in the Morn*. Stratford, CT: Soap Box, 1977; Ingelwood, CA: N.p., 1979.

Brown, Beth. *Satin Tunnels*. Detroit: Lotus Press, Inc., 1989.

Chaney, Regina. *Brown Sugar: Anthology*. Long Beach, CA: Hwong Publishing Co., 1974.

―――. *My Favorite Things*. Long Beach, CA: Brown Sugar Enterprises, 1976.

Clifton, Lucille. *An Ordinary Woman*. New York: Random House, 1974.

―――. *Good News About the Earth*. New York: Random House, 1973.

―――. *Good Times: Poems*. New York: Random House, 1969.

―――. *Two-Headed Woman*. Amherst: University of Massachusetts Press, 1980.

Clifton, Michelle T. *An Ordinary Woman* (poem). New York: Random House, 1974.

―――. *High Blood Pressure*. Los Angeles: West End Press (Box 291499), 1986.

Coleman, Beverly. "The Self-Determination of a Mammy." *Night Comes Softly*. Ed. Nikki Giovanni. New York: Nik-Tom Publications, 1970.

Coleman, Wanda. *Heavy Daughter Blues: Poems and Stories, 1968–1986*. Santa Rosa, CA: Black Sparrow Press, 1987.

———. *African Sleeping Sickness: Stories & Poems.* Santa Rosa: Black Sparrow Press, 1990.

Cortez, Jayne. *Coagulations: New and Selected Poems.* New York: Thunder's Mouth Press, 1984.

———. *Firespitter.* New York: Bola Press, 1982.

———. *Just Give Me a Cool Drink of Water 'fore I Die.* New York: Random House, 1971.

Fabio, Sarah Webster. *A Mirror: A Soul.* San Francisco: J. Richardson, 1967.

———. *Black Is a Panther Caged.* N.p.: N.p., 1972.

———. *Jujus and Jubilees, Critical Essays in Rhyme about Poets/Musicians/Black Heroes with Introductory Notes.* Oberlin, OH: N.p., 1973.

———. *Saga of the Black Man.* Oakland, CA: Turnover Bookstore, 1968.

Ford, Annie L. *My Soul Bone Aches.* Port Hueneme, CA: Christian Press, 1973.

Headlee, Judith Anne Still. "A Nation Blessed." *The Newport Ensign,* 10 Sep. 1980: 4.

———. "Cadence." *Phi Delta Gamma Journal* xxxix (Aug. 1977): 77.

———. "Challenge." *Phi Delta Gamma Journal* XLIII (May 1981): 58.

———. "In Praise of Prisms." *Phi Delta Gamma Journal* LXI (June 1979): 62.

———. "Not Wisely But Well." *Phi Delta Gamma Journal* (May 1984): 4.

———. "The Citadel." *Phi Delta Gamma Journal* XLII (May 1980): 10.

———. "Time Lapse." *The Single Parent* XXII (Apr. 1980): 17.

————. "Toward Distant Shores." *ABC Choral Art Series.* New York: American Book Company, 1974: 26–30.

————. "We, the Women." *Phi Delta Gamma Journal* XL (June 1978): 5.

Johnson, Dorothy Vena. "Ants," "Escape," "His Smile," "Jewels," "Leashed," "Milk," "The Bride," and "To a Courageous Mother." *Poems for Radio.* New York: Poetry House, 1945.

————. "Bread for Sale" and "One World." *National Poetry Anthology of Verse.* Written by teachers in schools and colleges. Los Angeles: National Poetry Association, 1949.

————. "Epitaph for a Bigot," "Post War Ballad," "Road to Anywhere," and "Success." *Ebony Rhythm.* Ed. Beatrice M. Murphy. New York: Exposition Press, 1948.

Miller, May. *Collected Poems.* Detroit: Lotus Press, Inc., 1989.

Moses, Louise Jane. *Shadow Castings.* Los Angeles: Brockman Gallery, 1983.

Richardson, Nola. *Even in a Maze.* Los Angeles: Crescent Publications, 1975.

————. *When One Loves.* Los Angeles: Celestial Arts, 1974.

————. *When One Loves: The Black Experience in America.* Photos by John H. Thompson, Ronald Phillips, Roger Lubin. Millbrae, CA: Celestial Arts, 1974.

Russell, Beverly A. Contributor to *Three Women Black.* Robbinsdale, MN: Guild Press, 1987.

Shange, Ntozake. "amsterdam avenue / arsenio / y tu," "toussaint," "cross oceans into my heart." *Invisible City* 19–20 (Oct. 1976): 22–23.

————. *For Colored Girls Who Have Considered Suicide When the Rainbow Is Enuf!.* San Lorenzo, CA: Shameless Hussy Press, 1975.

————. *Nappy Edges: Love's a Lil Rough/Sometimes.* New York: St. Martin's Press, 1978; New York: Bantam, 1980.

————. "on becomin successful," "memory," and "like the fog & the sun teasin the rapids." *Mademoiselle* (Sept. 1976): 28.

————. *Ridin' the Moon in Texas: Word Paintings.* New York: St. Martin's Press, 1987.

————. (also Paulette Williams). "Three" (for International Women's Day). *Black Scholar* 9.6 (June 1975): 56–61.

Sharp, Saundra. *From the Windows of My Mind.* New York: Togetherness Productions, 1970.

————. *In the Midst of Change.* Photo. Chester Higgins, Jr., Cornell Norris, and Ronalt St. Clair. Los Angeles: Togetherness Productions, 1972.

————. *New Blues from a Brown Baby. Rock Against the Wind: Black Love Poems.* Ed. Lindsay Patterson. New York: Dodd, Mead and Company, 1973.

Smith, Sandria. *Dria.* Long Beach, CA: The Author, 1974.

Thomas, Joyce Carol. *Bittersweet.* San Jose, CA: Firesign Press, 1973.

————. *Black Child.* New York: Zamani Productions, 1988.

————. *Inside the Rainbow.* Palo Alto, CA: Zikawina Press, 1982.

Walker, Alice. "Facing the Way" and "Forgiveness." *Freedomways* 15 (Fourth Quarter 1975): 265–267.

————. "Facing the Way," "The Abduction of Saints," and "Forgiveness." *Freedomways* 15 (Fourth Quarter 1975): 265–267.

————. *Good Night Willie Lee, I'll See You in the Morning.* New York: Dial Press, 1979.

————. *Horses Make a Landscape Look More Beautiful.* New York: Harcourt Brace Jovanovich, 1986.

———. "Hymn." *Afro-American Literature: An Introduction.* Eds. Robert Hayden, David J. Burrows, and Frederick R. Lapides. New York: Harcourt, 1971.

———. *Once: Poem.* New York: Harcourt, 1976.

———. "Rock Eagle" and "South." *Freedomways* 11 (Fourth Quarter 1971): 367–368.

———. "Talking to My Grandmother Who Died Poor Some Years Ago (While Listening to Richard Nixon Declare, 'I Am Not a Crook')" *Black Scholar* 9.6 (June 1975): 62.

———. *The Revolutionary Petunias.* New York: Harcourt, Brace n.d.

Walker, Alice, ed. *I Love Myself When I Am Laughing: A Zora Neale Hurston Reader.* Introd. Mary Helen Washington. New York: The Feminist Press, 1979.

Watson, Freida K. *Feelin's.* Introd. Jomo Don Shambazz. Los Angeles: A Krizna Publication, 1971.

Webster, Censa Faye. *Echoes in My Quiet Corner.* Illust. Martha Hernandez and Rita Adams. N.p.: Castle Printers, 1977.

Welch, Leona Nicholas. *Black Gibraltar.* Illust. Doug Noble. San Francisco: Leswing Press, 1971.

Williams, Cecilia. "The Glory of the Coming Man." Delilah L. Beaseley. *The Negro Trail Blazers of California.* New York: Negro Universities Press, 1919: 264.

Williams, Sherley. *The Peacock Poems.* Middletown, CT: Wesleyan University Press, 1975.

Articles/Essays/Books by West Coast
African-American Women on Critical Issues

Angelou, Maya. *Now Sheba Sings the Song.* Art, Tom Feelings. New York: Dial/Dutton, 1987.

Bass, Charlotta A. *Forty Years: Memoirs from the Pages of a Newspaper.* Los Angeles: Charlotta A. Bass, 1960.

Bilbrew, A. C. "Report on the Status of the American Negro Women of Yesterday, Today, and Tomorrow." For a women's meeting held in Copenhagen, Denmark, 21–24 Apr. 1960. Los Angeles: The Sojourner Truth Industrial Club, Inc., n.d.

Blaylock, Enid V. "Article 3.3: California's Answer to Cultural Diversity in the Classroom." *Phi Delta Kappan* (Nov. 1975), n. pg.

———. "Careers: How to Make the Right Choice." *Trinidad Guardian* (4 July 1989).

———. "Caribbean Union College: Campus of Study, Worship and Work." *Trinidad Guardian* (9 Nov. 1987): 12.

———. "Education Master Plan for TT." *Trinidad Guardian* (23 Sep. 1988): 10.

———. "Feminist Movement Viewed by Black." *Los Angeles Sentinel* (25 Mar. 1976).

———. "How to Train Your Parents and Teachers." *Trinidad Guardian* (15 Nov. 1988): 12.

———, ed. *I Am a Black Woman Who . . . .* Lomita, CA: Continuity Transcript & Features Publishers, 1977.

———. "If You Must Disagree, Please Do." *Trinidad Guardian* (12 June 1989).

———. "International Fair at Caribbean Union College." *Trinidad Guardian* (28 Apr. 1988): 19.

————. "Lawyers: A Public Image Problem." *Trinidad Guardian* (1 Mar. 1989).

————. "Nation-Building: Developmental View." *Trinidad Guardian* (Sep. 1987).

————. "Preservation of Cultural Heritage." *Trinidad Guardian* (20 Jan. 1988): 10.

————. "Test Makers Don't Give the Schools Credit." *Los Angeles Times* (9 Nov. 1977).

————. "What Is Your Social Inheritance?" *Trinidad Guardian* (21 June 1989).

Bruce, Beverlee. "Afro-Americans and Language." *Ufahamu: Journal of the African Activities Association* 1 (Fall 1970): 63–67.

Burke, Yvonne Brathwaite. "The Kind of World I Want for My Child." *Ebony* 29.5 (Mar. 1974): 149–153.

Butts, Trudi, Betty S. Williams, and Kathy Hedicke, eds. *Care of the Geriatric Patient*. A Manual for the Nurse Aide. Washington, DC: Department of Health, Education, and Welfare, Health Resources Administration, n.d.

Campbell, Bebe Moore. *Successful Women, Angry Men*. New York: Random House, 1986.

Cleaver, Kathleen. "Black Scholar Interview." *Black Scholar* 3 (Dec. 1971): 54–59.

Cooper, June M. "Training of Teachers of Speech for the Economically Disadvantaged Black American Student." *Western Speech* (Spring 1970): 139–143.

Creel, Margaret Washington. *A Peculiar People: Slave Religion and Community-Culture Among the Gullahs*. New York: New York University Press, 1988.

Davis, Angela. "Political Prisoners, Prisons, and Black Liberation." *If They Come in the Morning*. Eds. Angela Davis and Bettina Apthecker. New York: Joseph A. Opaku, Inc., 1971.

————. "Rape, Racism, and the Capitalist Setting." *Black Scholar* 9 (Apr. 1978): 24–30.

————. "Reflections on the Black Woman's Role in the Community of Slaves." *Black Scholar* 3 (Dec. 1971): 3–15.

————. *Soul and Soledad.* Flying Dutchman Productions. ATCO Records (1841 Broadway, New York 10023). Stereo FD 10141.

Davis, Angela Y. *Women, Culture & Politics.* New York: Random House, 1989.

Davis, Angela, and other political prisoners. *If They Come in the Morning.* Foreword Julian Bon. New York: Joseph A. Opaku, Inc., 1971.

George, Barbara, and Mary Jane Dundar. *Ramifications of the Vast Regulatory Powers of the Consumer Product Safety Commission.* Long Beach, CA: California State University, Long Beach, 1977.

Goode, Kenneth G. *California's Black Pioneers: A Brief Historical Survey.* Foreword. Wilson Riles. Santa Barbara, CA: McNally and Loftin, 1973.

Granger, Jean M. *Field Instruction Model for Baccalaureate Social Work* (Monograph). Foreword Gerald M. Gross. Syracuse, NY: School of Social Work, Syracuse University, 1982.

Granger, Jean M., and Signe Staenes. *Field Instruction Model for Baccalaureate Social Work.* Foreword Gerald M. Gross. Syracuse, NY: School of Social Work, Syracuse University, 1982.

Headlee, Judith Anne Still. "An Educational Approach to Negro Individualism." *English Journal* 59 (Jan. 1970): 34–39.

————. "An Employer's Guide for the Unemployed Woman." *Dawn Magazine* 10 (Feb. 1984): 30–33, 81–85.

————. "Dawn Dines Out." *Dawn Magazine for the Orange County Woman* 5 (July 1978): 31–33.

————. "From Weasels to Whales." *The Phi Kappa Phi Journal* 54 (Summer 1974): 31–33.

————. "I Survived an Alaskan Break-up." *The Link* (Armed Services Magazine) 32 (Feb. 1974): 22–25.

————. "Inside the Fan Mail Factory." *California Today Magazine* (2 Apr. 1978): 30–38.

————. "Learning to Talk with Our Children." *The Single Parent* 17 (Dec. 1974): 11–14, 24.

————. "Negro Free Enterprise: A March Forward Single." *The Freeman* 35 (Jan. 1985): 40–48.

————. "Patriotism: To Be or Not to Be." *Freeman* 10 (July 1970): 414–420. (This article was awarded a plaque by the Freedoms Foundation in 1971 and was read into *The Congressional Record*.)

————. "Sex and the Professional Woman." *Phi Delta Gamma Journal* 40 (June 1978): 47–49. (A correction of the previous printing in Aug. 1977)

————. "The Friendly Center: Where Home Is a Caring Person." *Orange City News* 10 (30 Aug. 1978/6 Sep. 1978): 11, 14, 17.

————. "Violence as 'Free Expression.'" *The Phil Kappa Phi Journal* 54 (Winter 1974): 63ff.

Hernandez, Aileen. "Money: Small Change for Black Women." *Ms.* (August 1974): 16–18.

Houchins, Susan, Introd. *Spiritual Narratives. The Schomburg Library of Nineteenth-Century Black Women Writers* series. Gen. ed. Henry Louis Gates, Jr. New York: Oxford University Press, 1988.

Jackson, Agnes Moreland. "God's People Require Liberation." *Christianity and Crisis* 34.20 (25 Nov. 1974): 269–272.

————. "Respect for Personhood: The Foundation of Teacher Preparation." *Teacher Preparation Newsletter* v (Summer 1987): 103. California State Polytechnic University, Pomona.

―――. "To See the 'ME' in 'THEE': Challenge to ALL White Americans, or White Ethnicity from a Black Perspective and a Sometimes Response to Michael Novak." *Soundings* (An Interdisciplinary Journal) 56.1 (Spring 1973): 21–44.

Joseph, Gloria I., and Jill Lewis. *Common Differences: Conflicts in Black and White and Black and White Feminist Perspectives.* Boston: Anchor Press, 1981.

Maddox, Marion. "Breaking the Poverty Cycle: The Inner-City Community College Prepares to Educate Disadvantaged Re-entry Women for Self-Sufficiency." Dissertation, Claremont Graduate School, Claremont, CA, 1988.

Majors, Gerri, with Doris Saunders. *Black Society.* Chicago: Johnson Publishing Company, 1977.

Matthews, Miriam, and Mary Murdoch. "Weeding and Replacement." Paper presented at the University of Southern California workshop on "Improving the Book Collection," Mar. 1959.

Mitchell, Ella Pearson. *Those Preachin' Women.* Valley Forge, PA: Judson Press, 1985.

Mitchell, Gwendolyn. "Attention and Address: The Dual Responsibility of Blacks in Higher Education." *Religion and Intellectual Life* 5.4 (Summer 1988): 26–33.

Moseley, Vivian H., and Dolores B. Ashley. *Unique Bulletin Board Ideas.* Illust. S. L. Mindingall, Jr. Los Angeles: Precision Printers, 1964.

Moses, Yolanda T. "Black American Women and Work: Historical Contemporary Strategies for Empowerment—II." *Women's Studies International Forum* 8.4 (1985): 351–359.

―――. "Black and American Indian Relations: Lost, Stolen or Strayed." Special edition of *Western Journal of Black Studies* on Black Pioneers in Anthropology (Spring 1983).

―――. "Female Status, the Family and Male Dominance in a West Indian Community." *Black Woman Cross-Culturally.* Filomina Chioma Study. Cambridge: Schenkman Publishing Co., 1980.

―――. "Female Status, the Family and Male Dominance in a West Indian Community." *Signs: Journal of Women in Culture and Society* 3.4. Chicago: University of Chicago Press, 1977.

―――. "Language, Culture and the Workplace." *Golden West Purchasor,* May 1983.

―――. "Migrant Societies: Women Who Wait: A West Indian Case." *Women and National Development.* Wellesley: Wellesley College Press, 1977.

―――. "Racism and Anti-Semitism in the Women's Movement." *Comment* 14.2 (Oct. 1983): 3, 7.

―――. "Woman Talk: Man Talk. What are the Differences: Sexism and Language." *The New Golden West Purchasor* 63.3 (July 1983): 32–54.

Moses, Yolanda T., and Lillian H. Jones. "Doing the Job: Ethnic & Women's Studies in a Polytechnic University." *Women's Studies International Forum* 8.2 (1986).

Moses, Yolanda T., and Patricia Higgins, eds. *Multicultural Education: Classroom Applications.* Athens, GA: University of Georgia, 1983.

Rhodes, Barbara. "The Changing Role of the Black Woman." *The Black Family.* Ed. Robert Staples. Belmont, CA: Wadsworth Press, 1971.

Shange, Ntozake. *See No Evil: Prefaces, Reviews, & Essays.* San Francisco: Momo's Press, 1984.

Solomon, Barbara B. *A Training Program for Senior Citizen Project Staff.* Proceedings of the Experimental Training Program for Senior Citizen Project Staff, Rossmoor Cortest Institute for the Study of Aging and the California Commission on Aging, 1968.

―――. "Alternative Social Services and the Black Woman." *Alternative Social Services for Women.* Ed. Naomi Gotlieb. New York: Columbia University Press, 1980: 333–340.

―――. *Analysis of Data on Program Initiation and Trainee Selection:*

Research Report #1. Kedren Community Mental Health Center, Los Angeles, Jan. 1975.

———. "Assessment, Service & Black Families." *Empowering the Black Family.* Eds. Sylvia Sims Gray et al. Ann Arbor, MI: National Child Welfare Training Center, University of Michigan School of Social Work, 1985.

———. "Better Planning Through Research." *Proceedings of the Institute on Minority Aging.* 4th ed. Ed. Percil Stanford. San Diego: Center on Aging, California State University, San Diego, 1976.

———. "Big Sister, Little Sister: A Final Report." With Thelma Eaton. A final report to Pasadena-Foothill Valley YWCA and California Council on Criminal Justice, June 1975.

———. *Black Empowerment: Social Work in Oppressed Communities.* New York: Columbia University Press, 1976.

———. "Black Families: A Social Welfare Perspective." With Helen Mendes. *Changing American Families.* Eds. Virginia Tufte and Barbara Myerhoff. New Haven, CT: Yale University Press, 1979.

———. "Computer Applications in Field Research." *Final Report on Demonstration Research Related to Alternative Methods of Delivering Public Assistance Services* 2. Frances Feldman, Project Director. Submitted to California State Department of Social Welfare, 1968.

———. "Conceptualizations of Identity in Social Work Practice." *Social Work Review* (Mar. 1967): 1–9.

———. "Education for Delivery of Effective Mental Health Services in Black Communities." *Manpower Considerations in Providing Mental Health Services to Ethnic Minority Groups.* A report of the Mental Health Man Power Planning and Development Project, Western Interstate Commission for Higher Education, Nov. 1980.

———. "Empowering Women: A Matter of Values." *Women Power and Change.* Eds. Ann Wieck and Susan P. Vandiver. New York: National Association of Social Workers, 1981.

————. "Ethnicity, Mental Health and the Older Black Aged." *Ethnicity, Mental Health, and Aging.* Summary of Proceedings of workshop, 13–14 Apr. 1970. University of Southern California, Andrus Gerontology Center, 1970.

————. "Ethnicity, Social Policy, and Aging." *Prospects and Issues.* Eds. Richard H. Davis and Margaret Neiswander. University of Southern California Gerontology Center, 1973.

————. "Growing Old in the Ethnosystem." With Thelma Eaton. *Proceedings of Institute on Minority Aging.* Ed. Percil Stanford. San Diego: Center for Aging, Big Sister Project of the Pasadena-Foothill Valley YWCA: *A Progress Report on the Evaluative Research Component,* 15 June 1974.

————. "Human Development: Sociocultural Basis." *Encyclopedia of Social Work.* Forthcoming.

————. "Is It Sex, Class or Race." *Social Work.* Nov. 1976: 420.

————. *Mental Health Services in Inner Churches.* Final Report to National Institute of Mental Health, Grant #MH 6129–01AL. Jan. 1984.

————. "Minority Group Issues and Benefit Programs for the Elderly." Human Resources Corporation Report to Federal Council on Aging, Report on Impact of Federal Policies on Minority Elderly. Under Contract HEW-105-77-3004. Mar. 1978.

————. "Power: The Troublesome Factor in Cross-Cultural Supervision." *Smith Journal of Social Work* (Spring 1983).

————. "Revolutions of the Powerless: A Social Work Response to the Status Revolutions of the Seventies." Washington, DC: National Association of Social Workers, 1980.

————. "Social and Protective Services." *Community Services and the Black Elderly* (monograph). Ed. Richard H. Davis. Los Angeles: University of Southern California, Gerontology Center, 1970.

————. "Social Functioning of Economically Dependent Aged." *The Gerontologist* 7 (Sep. 1967): 213–217.

————. "Social Group Work in the Adult Out-Patient Psychiatric Clinic." *Social Work* 13 (Oct. 1968).

————. "Social Work with Afro-Americans." *Social Work: A Profession of Many Faces.* Eds. Armando Morales and Bradford W. Sheaford. Boston: Allyn and Bacon, 1983.

————. "The Black Aged: A Status Report." Human Resources Corporation Report to Federal Council on Aging, Mar. 1978.

————. "The Delivery of Mental Health Services to Afro-Americans and Their Families: Translating Theory into Practice." *The Assessment and Treatment of Afro-American Families.* Eds. Gloria Powell, Gail Wyatt, and Barbara Bass. New York: Grune and Stratton, 1981.

————. "The Ethnic Factor in the Delivery of Services to the Elderly: The Leon and Josephine Winkelman Lecture" (monograph). School of Social Work, the University of Michigan, 11 Nov. 1980.

————. "The Future of Social Work Skill." *Social Work in Practice.* Eds. Bernard Ross and S. H. Khinduka. Washington, DC: National Association of Social Workers, 1976.

————. "Value Issues in Working with Minority Clients." *Handbook of Clinical Social Work.* Eds. Aaron Rosenblatt and Diana Woldfogel. San Francisco: Jossey-Bass, 1983.

Walker, Alice. *In Search of Our Mothers' Gardens.* San Diego: Harcourt, 1983.

————. *Living by the Word.* San Diego/New York/London: Harcourt, 1988.

————. "What Can the White Man . . . Say to the Black Woman?" *The Nation* (22 May 1989).

Waters, Maxine. "Government Must Respond: Drugs, Democrats, and Priorities." *Scapegoating the Black Family: Black Women Speak.* Special issue of *The Nation* (24 July 1989). 141 + .

Wilkerson, Margaret B., and Jewell Handy Gresham. "Sexual Politics of Welfare: The Radicalization of Poverty." *Scapegoat-*

ing the Black Family: Black Women Speak. Special issue of *The Nation* (24 July 1989). 126+.

Williams, Ruby Ora. "In '68 Human Rights Come First." *The Camp Fire Girl* 47 (May 1968): 3, 4.

———. "Universal Kinship." *The Camp Fire Girl* 46 (Feb. 1967): 3.

Literary Criticism/History

Christian, Barbara. *An Ordinary Woman.* Poems by Lucille Clifton. New York: Random House, 1974; *Black Scholar* 1.7 (Sep. 1975): 52–54.

———. *Black Feminist Criticism: Perspectives on Black Women Writers.* Maxwell House, Fairview Park, Elmsford, New York: Pergamon Press, Inc., 1985.

———. *Black Women Novelists: The Development of a Tradition, 1892–1976.* Westport, CT: Greenwood Press, 1980.

———. "Ralph Ellison: A Critical Study." *Black Experience.* Ed. Addison Gayle, Jr. New York: Weybright & Tally, 1969: 353–365.

Davis, Angela. "Racism and Contemporary Literature on Rape." (Specific review of Susan Brownmiller's *Against Our Will*) *Freedomways* 16 (First Quarter 1976): 25–33.

DjeDje, Jacqueline Cogdell. *Katherine Dunham: Reflections on the Social and Political Contexts of Afro-American Dance,* by Joyce Aschenbrenner, with Lavinia Williams. *Ethnomusicology: Journal of the Society of Ethnomusicology* 26.3 (1982): 473–474.

Fabio, Sarah. "A Black Paper: An Essay on Literature." *Negro Digest* 18.9 (July 1969): 26–29.

———. "Tripping with Black Writing." *The Black Aesthetic.* Ed. Addison Gayle. Garden City, NY: Doubleday, 1971.

Foster, Frances Smith. "A Review of *No Crystal Stair,* by Gloria

Wade-Gayles. *Black American Literature Forum* 19 (1985): 93–94.

————. "Adding Color and Contour to Early American Self-Portraitures: Autobiographical Writings of Afro-American Women." *Conjuring: Black Women, Fiction, and Literary Tradition.* Ed. Marjorie Pryse and Hortense Spillers. Bloomington, IN: Indiana University Press, 1985: 25–38.

————. "American Indian Women: Telling Their Lives," by Gretchen M. Bataille and Kathleen Mullen Sands. *Journal of San Diego History* 31 (1985): 324–326.

————. "Britton Hammon's Narrative: Some Insights into Beginnings." *CLA Journal* 21 (1977): 44–53.

————. "Changing Concepts of the Black Woman." *Journal of Black Studies* 3 (June 1973): 433–454.

————. "Charles Wright: Black Humorist." *CLA Journal* 15 (1971): 44–53.

————. "Frances Ellen Watkins Harper and the Aesthetics of Popular Theory." Selected for consideration by *Pacific Coast Philology.*

————. "In Respect to Females: Contradictions in the Depiction of Slave Women by Male and Female Narrators." *Black American Literature Forum* 15 (1981): 66–70.

————. "Neither Auction Block nor Pedestal: The Life and Religious Experiences of Jarena Lee, A Coloured Lady." *The Female Autograph.* Ed. Domna C. Stanton. New York: The New York Literary Forum, 1984.

————. "Octavia Butler: Black Female Future Fiction." *Extrapolation* 25 (1982): 37–49.

————. "Progress Report Autobiographies." *New American Library History.* Ed. LaVonne Ruoff. New York: Modern Language Association, forthcoming.

————. "Sharon Bell Mathis." *Afro-American Fiction Writers After 1950: Dictionary of Literary Biography* 33. Eds. Trudier

Harris and Thadious Davis. Detroit: Gale Research, 1984: 170–173.

———. "Slave Testimony." *Dictionary of American Slavery*. Ed. Randall M. Miller and John David Smith. Westport, CT: Greenwood Press (accepted for publication).

———. "The Black and White Masks of Franz Fanon and Ralph Ellison." *Black Academy Review* 1 (1970): 46–58.

———. "The Line Converges Here: Review of S. A. Williams' *The Peacock Poems*." *Callaloo* 1 (1979): 151–152.

———. "*The Slave's Narrative*, by Charles T. Davis and Henry Louis Gates, Jr." *The New York Times Book Review* 7 July 1985.

———. "The Struggle Continues: A Review of *This Bridge Called My Back*, by Cherrie Moraga and Gloria Anzaldua." *Callaloo* 18 (1983): 132–134.

———. *The Works of Frances Ellen Watkins Harper*. Proposal solicited and under consideration by Feminist Press.

———. "Ultimate Victims: Black Women in Slave Narratives." *Journal of American Culture* (1978): 845–854.

———. "Voices Unheard, Stories Untold: Teaching Women's Literature from a Regional Perspective in California." *The Radical Teacher* 14 (1979): 19–22.

———. *Witnessing Slavery: The Development of Ante-bellum Slave Narratives*. Westport, CT: Greenwood Press, 1979.

———. "*Women, Ethnics, and Exotics: Images of Power in Mid-Nineteenth Century American Fiction*, by Kristin Herzog." *Melus*, forthcoming.

———. "*You May Plow Here*, by Thordis Simonsen." *The New York Times Book Review* (9 Mar. 1986).

Foster, Frances Smith, with Charles P. Henry. "Black Women's Studies: Threat or Challenge." *Western Journal of Black Studies* 6 (1982): 15–22.

Fowler, Carolyn. "Solid at the Core." A review of *In Love and Trouble: Stories of Black Women,* by Alice Walker. New York: Harcourt, 1973; *Freedomways* 14 (First Quarter 1974): 59–62.

Guy-Sheftall, Beverly. "Literary Profile," "Alice Walker, You Can Go Home Again." *Black Southern Magazine* 1 (June 1984): 9.

Harris, Jessica. "An Interview with Alice Walker." *Essence* (July 1976): 33.

Harris, Trudier. "Folklore in the Fiction of Alice Walker: A Perpetuation of Historical and Literary Traditions." *Black American Literature Forum* 2 (Spring 1977): 3–8.

————. "Tiptoeing Through Taboo: Incest in Alice Walker's 'The Child Who Favored Daughter.'" *Modern Fiction Studies* 28 (Autumn 1982): 495–505.

Headlee, Judith Anne Still. "Roxana: The Focus of Mark Twain's Racial Understanding." *Phil Delta Gamma Journal* XXV (June 1974): 21–23.

————. Story line and three chapters provided for Molli Aghadjian's book *The Fourteenth Duchess.* New York: Manor Books, Inc., 1978.

Hull, Gloria T. *Color, Sex, and Poetry: Three Women Writers of the Harlem Renaissance.* Bloomington, IN: Indiana University Press, 1987.

Hull, Gloria, ed. and introd. *The Works of Alice Dunbar-Nelson.* 3 vols. *The Schomburg Library of Nineteenth-Century Black Women Writers* series. Gen. ed. Henry Louis Gates, Jr. New York: Oxford University Press, 1988.

Jackson, Agnes Moreland. "Critical Explorations: Poems of Alice Dunbar-Nelson." *An Alice Dunbar-Nelson Reader.* Ed. Ora Williams. Washington, DC: University Press, 1979.

————. "Stephen Crane's Imagery George's Mother." *Arizona Quarterly* 24.4 (Winter 1969): 313–318.

Marsh, Vivian Osborne. "Origin and Distribution of Negro Folk-

Dr. Carolyn Mitchell

lore in America." Master's thesis, University of California, Berkeley, 1921.

Mitchell, Gwendolyn. "A Laying on of Hands: Transcending the City in Ntozake Shange's *for colored girls who have considered suicide when the rainbow is enuf.*" *Women Writers and the City: Essays in Feminist Literary Criticism.* Ed. Susan Merrill Squier. Knoxville: The University of Tennessee Press, 1984: 230–248.

————. "Cross-Gender Significance of the Journey Motif in Selected Afro-American Fiction." *Colby Library Quarterly* (special issue on Women and Literature) 18.1 (Mar. 1982): 26–38.

————. "Henry Dumas." *Afro-American Poets Since 1955.* Eds. Trudier Harris and Thadious Davis. Vol. 41. Detroit: Gale Research, n.d.: 89–99.

————. "Henry Dumas and Jean Toomer: One Voice." *Black American Literature Forum* 22.2 (Summer 1988): 297–309.

Pryse, Marjorie, and Hortense Spillers, eds. *Conjuring Black Women, Fiction and Literary Tradition.* Bloomington, IN: Indiana University Press, 1985.

Russell, Sandi. *Render Me My Song: African American Women Writers from Slavery to the Present.* New York: St. Martin's. 1991.

Smith, Sidonie Ann. "The Song of a Caged Bird: Maya Angelou's Quest for Self-Acceptance." *Southern Humanities Review* 7 (Fall 1973): 365–374.

Trescott, Jacqueline. "The Friction of Paradoxes Sparkles with Alice Walker." *Washington Post* 19 Sep. 1976: 26.

"Viva Interview: Maya Angelou: Author, Civil Rights Leader, Film Director." *Viva* 1.6 (Mar. 1974): 62–63, 96, 99, 102.

Walker, Alice. "A Daring Subject Boldly Shared." Review of *Loving Her,* by Ann Shockley. Indianapolis: Bobbs-Merrill, 1976; *Ms.* 3 (Apr. 1976): 120–124.

————. "A Writer Because of, Not in Spite of, Her Children." *Second Class Citizen,* by Buchi Emecheta. New York: George Braziller, n.d.; *Ms.* 2 (Jan. 1976): 40, 106.

————. "In Search of Our Mothers' Gardens." *Ms.* May 1974: 60–64, 105; *Southern Exposure: Generations of Women in the South* (Winter 1977): 60–64.

————. "In Search of Zora Neale Hurston." *Ms.* 3 (Mar. 1975): 74–75.

————. *Langston Hughes, American Poet.* New York: Harper and Row, 1974.

————. Untitled review of *Good Morning Revolution: Uncollected Writings of Social Protest by Langston Hughes.* Ed. Faith Berry. Foreword Saunders Redding. New York: Hill and Co., n.d.; *Black Scholar* 7 (July–Aug. 1976): 53–55.

Weller, Sheila. "Work in Progress: Maya Angelou." *Intellectual Digest* 3 (June 1973): 1.

Williams, Frances E. "More Apologies for Racism." "Two Trips Through 'The Colored Museum.' " Calendar Section, *Los Angeles Times* 12 June 1988: 46, 47.

Williams, Ora. "Alice Moore Dunbar Nelson." *Dictionary of Literary Biography,* 50. Eds. Trudier Harris and Thadious Davis. Detroit: Gale Publishing Company, 1986.

————. "Alice Ruth (Moore) Dunbar-Nelson: Another Harlem Renaissance Poet." *Zora Neale Hurston Forum* (special issue) 1.2 (Spring 1987): 12–18.

Williams, [Ruby] Ora. "An In-Depth Portrait of Alice Dunbar-Nelson." Diss., microfilm or xerographic copies. Ann Arbor, MI: University Microfilms, 1974.

Williams, Sherley. *Give Birth to Brightness.* New York: Dial, 1972.

————. *Someone Sweet Angel Chile.* New York: William Morrow, 1982.

"Women, Playwrights: Themes and Variations." *The New York Times, Arts & Leisure* (7 May 1989): 1, 42.

AUDIO-VISUAL MATERIALS

Angelou, Maya. *A Portrait of Maya Angelou.* Bill Moyers. Washington, DC: Corporation for the Entertainment and Learning, in association with WNET/Thirteen/PBS Video, 1982. (58 min.)

——. Excerpts from *I Know Why the Caged Bird Sings.* Two cassettes, 179 mins. Columbia, MO: The American Audio Prose Library, Inc., n.d. Order No. 55369 ($14.95).

——. *Georgia, Georgia.* St. Louis, MO: Cinema Releasing, n.d.

——. *The Poetry of Maya Angelou.* GWP Records ST 20001.

Clara's Heart. (Movie) (Whoopie Goldberg, Michael Ontkean, Kathleen Quinlan). Dir. Robert Mulligan. Warner Brothers, 1986.

Clifton, Lucille. *The Place for Keeping.* Audio-Forum 23615. Two readings. 45 min. Recorded 1974, 1979. Audio-Forum, 96 Broad St., Guilford, CT 06437.

DjeDje, Jacqueline Cogdell. *Black American Religious Music from Southeast Georgia.* Folkways Records FS 34010.

——. Record Notes. *Traditional Women's Music from Ghana.* Recorded by Verna Gillis. Ethnic Folkways Records FE 4257.

——. Tape Composite. *Composite of One String Fiddle Music from the Hausa of Northern Nigeria and Dagomba of Northern Ghana.* Los Angeles: UCLA Ethnomusicology Archive: n.d. (four 7" reel tapes)

——. Tape Composite. *Composite of Black American Religious Songs.* Los Angeles: UCLA Ethnomusicology Archive: n.d. (14 7" reel tapes)

Shange, Ntozake. *For Colored Girls Who Have Considered Suicide/ When the Rainbow is Enuf!* Original Cast Recordings, Shakespeare Festival Productions. Prod. Oz Scott, Herbert Harris, Frank Kulaga. Buddah Records, 1969.

The Color Purple. (Whoopie Goldberg, Oprah Winfrey, and others) Merit Audio Visual (Box 392, New York 10024), 1985 ($99.95)

Walker, Alice. Interview about themes in short story "1955" and about "her views on variety of subjects: Art and America, art and politics, art and feminist writers." Columbia, MO: The American Audio Prose Library, Inc., n.d. Order No. 1162 ($10.95).

————. Reading "1955" (short story). 36 mins. Columbia, MO: The American Audio Prose Library, n.d. Order No. 1161 ($10.95).

————. Reading and interview as a set. Columbia, MO: The American Audio Prose Library, Inc., n.d. Order No. 1163 ($20.00).

————. *Visions of the Spirit* (portrait of Alice Walker). Prod., Dir. Elena Featherston. Premiere performance, Palace of Fine Arts, San Francisco, 29 Apr. 1988.

PERFORMING ARTS

Music: Arrangers, Composers, Lyricists, Performers

Akers, Doris. "Ask What You Will," "He Knows and He Cares," "I Cannot Fail the Lord," "Lord Keep My Mind on Thee," "My Song of Assurance," "Prayer Is the Answer," "Sweet, Sweet Spirit," "Trouble," "You Can't Beat God Giving." *Doris Akers' Favorite Gospel Songs,* Vol. I. Hollywood, CA: Manna Music, Inc. (1328 N. Highland), n.d.

————. "Deeper in the Lord". Los Angeles: Manna Music, 1958.

————. "Don't Stop Using Me". Los Angeles: Manna Music, 1958.

————. "God Is So Good". Los Angeles: Thurston Frazier, 1956.

————. "God Will If You Will". Los Angeles: Thurston Frazier, 1958.

————. "Grow Closer". Los Angeles: Thurston Frazier, 1952.

————. "You Can't Beat God Giving". Los Angeles: Manna Music, 1957.

Ayo, Zera. "Bring Peace to the World." (vocal) Hollywood: Zayo Publications, 1960.

————. "Save Me." Hollywood: Zayo Publications, 1962.

Bonds, Margaret. "Bright Star." (vocal) Beverly Hills, CA: Pasca, 1970.

————. "Children's Sleep." Words by Vernon Glasser. New York: Carl Fischer, 1946.

———. "Didn't It Rain." (for medium voice) New York: Beekman Music, 1967; Bryn Mawr, PA: Theodore Presser, 1900.

———. "Dry Bones," "I'll Reach Heaven," "Lord, I Just Can't Keep from Crying," "Sit Down Servant," "You Can Tell the World." *Five Spirituals*. New York: Mutual Music Society, 1946.

———. "Empty Interlude". (popular song for voice and piano) New York: Robbins Music, n.d.

———. "Ezek'l Saw the Wheel." New York: Beckman Music Co., 1959.

———. *Five Spirituals* ("Dry Bones," "Sit Down Servant," "Lord I Just Can't Keep From Crying," "You Can Tell the World," also for voice and orchestra; "I'll Reach to Heaven" for voice and piano). New York: Mutual Music Society, 1946.

———. "Georgia." With Andy Razaff and Joe Davis. New York: Dorsey Brothers, 1939.

———. "Go Tell It on the Mountain." New York: Beekman Music Co., 1962.

———. *He's Got the Whole World in His Hands.* (songs with piano) New York: Beekman Music Co., n.d.

———. "He's Got the Whole World in His Hands" and "Sit Down Servant." Performed by Leontyne Price. Dir. Leonard de Paur. *Swing Low Sweet Chariot* (14 spirituals). RCA-LSC 2600.

———. *Hold On.* (voice with piano) New York: Beekman, 1962; New York: G. Schirmer, n.d.

———. "I Got a Home in-a That Rock." New York: Beekman, 1959. (Arr.)

———. "I Shall Pass Through This World." London: Bourne Co., 1966.

———. "I Too." Words by Langston Hughes. New York: Ricordi, 1959.

———. "I Wish I Knew How It Would Feel to be Free"; "Sinner

Please Don't Let This Harvest Pass"; "Standin' in the Need of Prayer". Performed by Leontyne Price and the Rust College Choir, dir. Lassaye Van Buren Holmes. RCA-LSC 3183.

———. "Joshua Fit Da Battle of Jericho." New York: Beekman Music Co., 1967.

———. "Mary Had a Little Baby" (From *The Ballad of the Brown King*). (piano) New York: Sam Fox Publishing Co., 1962.

———. "Mary Had a Little Baby." *The Ballad of the Brown King*. (women's chorus) New York: Sam Fox Publishing Co., 1963.

———. "Minstrel Man." Words by Langston Hughes. New York: Ricordi, 1959.

———. "Peach Tree Street." With Andy Razaff and Joe Davis. New York: Dorsey Brothers, 1939.

———. "Rainbow Gold." Words by Roger Chaney. New York: Chappell and Co., 1956.

———. "Sing A-Ho That I Had the Wings of a Dove." New York: Chappell, 1960.

———. "Sinner, Please Don't Let This Harvest Pass." 1960.

———. "Spring Will Be So Sad." New York: Mutual Music Society, 1941.

———. *The Ballad of the Brown King.* Text by Langston Hughes. (A Christmas cantata for chorus of mixed voices (SATB) with piano accompaniment; score, 56 pp) New York: Sam Fox, 1961.

———. "The Negro Speaks of Rivers." Lyrics by Langston Hughes. New York: Handy Brothers, 1946.

———. *Three Dream Portraits.* (voice and piano) Words by Langston Hughes. Poems from *The Dream Keeper.* New York: Ricordi, 1959.

———. "Three Sheep in a Pasture." New York: Clarence Williams, 1940.

———. "To a Brown Girl Dead." Words by Countee Cullen. Boston: R. D. Row Music Co., n.d.; New York: G. Schirmer, n.d.

———. "Troubled Water." New York: Sam Fox, 1967.

———. "When the Dove Enters In." With Langston Hughes. 1963.

———. "You Can Tell the World." (SATB, score 8 pp.) Arr. Charles N. Smith. New York: Mutual Music Society. (MCS 123)

Cleaver, Esther A. "Can You See God?" Los Angeles: Dex-es Publishing House, n.d.; Newark, NJ: Savoy Music Co., 1974.

Cole, Olivia, words and melody. "Precious to Me" and "Oh, How Wonderful." Walter M. Walker, harmony. Bakersfield, CA: Olivia Cole, 1976.

Coltrane, Alice. "Atomic Peace," "Gospel Trane," "I Want to See You," "Lovely Sky Boat," "Ohnedruth," "Organic Beloved." *A Monastic Trio*. ABC Records, AS 9156.

———. "The Anka of Amen-ka," "Battle at Armageddon," "Hare Krishna," "Oh Allah," "Sit a Ram." *Universal Consciousness.* Impulse AS 9210.

———. "Isis and Osiris," "Journey in Satchidnanda," "Shiva-Loka," "Something about John Coltrane," "Stop Over Bombay." *Journey in Satchidnanda.* Impulse Stereo AS 9203.

Crouch, Sandra. "He's Worthy." Newbury Park, CA: Lexicon Music, 1983; *New Inspirational Soul.* Newbury Park, CA (Box 2222, 91320): Lexicon Music, 1984.

———. *Sandra Couch Choral Arrangements.* (SATB) Newbury Park, CA: Lexicon Music, 1986.

———. *Sandra Couch Choral Arrangements.* Light Records: Album LS-5855; cassette LC-5855.

———. *We Sing Praises.* (choral) Newbury Park, CA: Lexicon Music, Inc., n.d.

————. *We Sing Praises.* Light Records: Album LS-5825; cassette LC-5825.

————. *We're Waiting.* Newbury Park, CA: Lexicon Music, 1986.

Crouch, Sandra and friends. *He's Worthy.* Light Records LS-582.

DjeDje, Jacqueline Cogdell. Musical arrangements for "God's Trombones," by James Weldon Johnson. 92pp.

Douroux, Margaret. "Deep Water." Los Angeles (4629 S. Figueroa St., 90037): Rev. Earl A. Pleasant Publishing Co., 1975.

————. "Give Me a Clean Heart." Los Angeles: Pleasant Publishing Co., n.d.; *Songs of Zion.* Nashville, TN: Abingdon Press, 1981: 182.

————. "God Is Not Dead." Los Angeles: Los Angeles: Pleasant Publishing, 1973.

————. "God Is Passing Out Blessings." Los Angeles: Pleasant Publishing, n.d.

————. "God Made a Man." Los Angeles: Pleasant Publishing, 1975.

————. "Holy," "Somebody Touched Me," "Until I Reach My Home," "Do Something," "When I See Jesus," "Easy This Morning." *A Special Collection.* Los Angeles (Box 3247, Thousand Oaks, CA 91359): Pleasant Publishing, 1980.

————. "I'm Glad." (sacred song) Los Angeles: Earl Pleasant, n.d.

————. "I'm Gonna Take My Burdens." Los Angeles: Pleasant Publishing, n.d.

————. "Let It Be" and "Hold On." Thousand Oaks, CA: N.p., 1983.

————. "Love Song." Los Angeles: Pleasant Publishing, 1975.

————. "My Help Cometh from the Lord." Los Angeles: Pleasant Publishing, n.d.

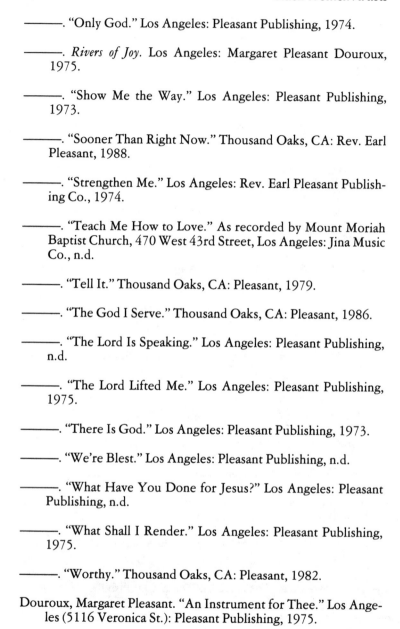

————. "Only God." Los Angeles: Pleasant Publishing, 1974.

————. *Rivers of Joy.* Los Angeles: Margaret Pleasant Douroux, 1975.

————. "Show Me the Way." Los Angeles: Pleasant Publishing, 1973.

————. "Sooner Than Right Now." Thousand Oaks, CA: Rev. Earl Pleasant, 1988.

————. "Strengthen Me." Los Angeles: Rev. Earl Pleasant Publishing Co., 1974.

————. "Teach Me How to Love." As recorded by Mount Moriah Baptist Church, 470 West 43rd Street, Los Angeles: Jina Music Co., n.d.

————. "Tell It." Thousand Oaks, CA: Pleasant, 1979.

————. "The God I Serve." Thousand Oaks, CA: Pleasant, 1986.

————. "The Lord Is Speaking." Los Angeles: Pleasant Publishing, n.d.

————. "The Lord Lifted Me." Los Angeles: Pleasant Publishing, 1975.

————. "There Is God." Los Angeles: Pleasant Publishing, 1973.

————. "We're Blest." Los Angeles: Pleasant Publishing, n.d.

————. "What Have You Done for Jesus?" Los Angeles: Pleasant Publishing, n.d.

————. "What Shall I Render." Los Angeles: Pleasant Publishing, 1975.

————. "Worthy." Thousand Oaks, CA: Pleasant, 1982.

Douroux, Margaret Pleasant. "An Instrument for Thee." Los Angeles (5116 Veronica St.): Pleasant Publishing, 1975.

Douroux, Margaret Pleasant, words and music. "Tree." N.p.: Margaret Pleasant Douroux, 1979; *Songs of Zion.* Nashville, TN: Abingdon Press, 1981.

————. "Whatever It Takes." Thousand Oaks, CA: Pleasant Publishing, 1979.

Fitzgerald, Ella, and Al Freeman. "A-Tisket A-Tasket." New York: Robbins Music Corp., 1937.

Fitzgerald, Ella, and Kenneth Watts. "Oh, But I Do." New York: Leeds Music Corp. 1945.

Gadling, Betty. "He's Alice Today." Berkeley, CA: Betty Gadling, n.d.

————. "Sweet Communion." Berkeley, CA: Betty Gadling, 1979.

Gadling, Betty, words and music. "Just You, Lord." N.p.: Betty Gadling, 1979.

————. "Thy Grace" (recorded by William Collins, as sung by Mary Bolden) and "Just You, Lord" (as sung by Billie Poole). N.P. Betty Gadling, 1979.

————. "Wonderful Savior Is He." San Francisco: DeKay's House of Music, n.d.

Lutcher, Nellie. "He's a Real Gone Guy." N.p.: Criterion Music Corp., n.d.

————. "Hurry On Down." N.p.: Criterion Music Corp., n.d.

Martin, Sallie. "Great Day". N.p.: Kenneth Woods, Jr., 1961.

Martin, Sallie, and Thomas Dorsey. "Wonderful Is His Name." N.p.: N.p., 1957.

Savage, Rowena Muckelroy. "Heart Stones, U.S.A." Musical drama presented by the Citizens of Greater Los Angeles at Patriotic Hall, 19 Oct. 1975.

Webster, Censa Faye, words and melody. "By the Spirit of God." Walter M. Walker, harmony. Bakersfield, CA: Censa Faye Webster, 1976.

———. "The Debt I Owe." Sylvia Woodgate, harmony. Bakersfield, CA: Censa Faye Webster, 1977.

———. "Without God." Sylvia Woodgate, music. Bakersfield, CA: Censa Faye Webster, 1977.

White-McCrae, Janis. "The Last Day." Copyrighted by Janis McCrae, 1972.

———. "The Lord Is Coming Back Again." From the musical *Maranatha, The Lord Is Coming,* by Larry and Janis McCrae-White. Performed by the combined Seventh Day Youth Choirs, Richmond, CA, Auditorium, 1983.

Music History and Criticism

Bonds, Margaret. "A Reminiscence." *The Negro in Music and Art. International Library of Negro Life and History,* vol 5. Ed. Lindsay Patterson. New York: Publishers Co., 1968.

Caldwell, Hansonia. "A Perspective on Graduate Music Education." A position paper presented to the Commission on Graduate Music Education of the Music Educators National Conference, Nov. 1977.

———. "Afro-American Music Resources." Published through California State College, Dominguez Hills, Oct. 1975.

———. "Conversations with Hale Smith: A Man of Many Parts." *The Black Perspective in Music* (Spring 1975): 58–76.

———. "Music in the Lives of Blacks in California: The Beginnings." *Black Music Research Bulletin* 10.1 (1988): 5, 6; *The Triangle of Mu Phi Epsilon* 82.4 (1988): 10, 18.

———. "The Plight of the Black Composer of Opera." *American Society of University Composers* Proceedings 9/10 (Spring 1976).

Cole, Maria, and Lovie Robinson. *Nat King Cole.* New York: William Morrow, 1971.

Cox, Bette Y. "A Selective Survey of Black Musicians in Los Angeles, 1890–1945." *Black Music Research Bulletin* 10.1 (1988): 7, 8.

——. "Black American Music: The Beginning." *Black Art* (An International Quarterly) 1.1 (Fall 1976): 53.

Cuney-Hare, Maud. *Negro Musicians and Their Music.* Washington, DC: Associated Press, 1936; New York: DaCapo Press, 1974.

DjeDje, Jacqueline Cogdell. "A Historical Overview of Black Gospel Music in Los Angeles." *Black Music Research Bulletin* 10.1 (1988): 1–5.

——. *African Music: A People's Art,* by Francis Bebey, trans. from French to English by Josephine Bennett. *The Black Perspective in Music* 4.3 (1976): 332–334.

——. *American Black Spiritual and Gospel Songs from Southeast Georgia: A Comparative Study.* Los Angeles: UCLA Center for Afro-American Studies, 1978. (105 pp)

——. "An Expression of Black Identity: The Use of Gospel Music in a Los Angeles Catholic Church." *The Western Journal of Black Studies* 7.3 (1982): 148–160.

——. "Black Gospel Music in Los Angeles." *Center for Afro-American Studies Newsletter,* UCLA (forthcoming in Summer 1989).

——. *Black Music of Two Worlds: From Africa, Middle East, West Indies, South America and the USA,* comp., annot. John Storm Roberts. *Ethnomusicology: Journal of the Society for Ethnomusicology* 22.3 (1978): 561–564.

——. *Black Religious Music from Southeast Georgia.* Birmingham: Alabama Center for Higher Education, 1979. (30 pp. includes cassette tape)

——. "Change and Differentiation: The Adoption of Black American Gospel Music in the Catholic Church." *Ethnomusicology: Journal of the Society for Ethnomusicology* 30.2 (1986): 223–252.

————. *Discourse in Ethnomusicology II: A Tribute to Alan P. Merriam.* Ed. Caroline Card et al. *Ethnomusicology: Journal of the Society for Ethnomusicology* 29.1 (1985): 118–121.

————. "Distribution of One String Fiddle in West Africa." Los Angeles: UCLA Program in Ethnomusicology Monograph Series, 1980. (43 pp)

————. "Gospel Music in the Los Angeles Black Community: A Historical Overview." *Black Music Research Journal* 10.1 (Spring 1988): 35–79.

————. *Let the Inside Be Sweet: An Interpretation of Music Event among the Kpelle of Liberia,* by Ruth M. Stone. *Ethnomusicology: Journal of the Society for Ethnomusicology* 26.2 (1982): 544–546.

————. "Performance Practice." *Ethnomusicological Perspective.* Ed. Gerard Behague; *The Mandinka Belafon: An Introduction with Notation for Teaching,* by Lynne Jessup; *Musicmakers of West Africa,* by John Collins; *The Trinidad Calypso: A Study of the Calypso as Oral Literature,* by Keith Q. Warner. *The Black Perspective in Music* 14.3 (1986): 306–309.

————. "Song Type and Performance Practice in Hausa and Dagomba Possession (Bori Music)." *The Black Perspective in Music* 12.2 (1984): 166–182.

————. "The Concept of Patronage: An Examination of Hausa and Dagomba One String Fiddle Tradition." *Journal of African Studies* 9.3 (1982): 116–127.

————. "The Interplay of Melodic Phrases: An Analysis of Hausa and Dagomba One String Fiddle Music." *Selected Reports in Ethnomusicology.* Eds. J. H. Kwabena Nketia and Jacqueline Cogdell DjeDje. Los Angeles: UCLA Program in Ethnomusicology, Department of Music 5 (1984): 81–118.

————. "The Role of the Mass Media in the Development of Urban African Popular Music: A Case Study in Abidjan, Ivory Coast." *Occasional Papers: Proceedings of the African Studies Conference* (Post-Independence Africa: Its Problems and Prospects). Ed.

Skyne Uku-Wertimer. Long Beach, CA: California State University Press, 1985.

——. *Tiv Song,* by Charles Keil; *African Rhythms and African Sensibility: Aesthetics and Social Action in African Music Idioms,* by John Miller Chernoff. *UMOJA: A Scholarly Journal of Black Studies* 4.3 (1980): 60–68.

——. *Women and Music in Cross-Cultural Perspective.* Ed. Ellen Koskoff. *Ethnomusicology: Journal of the Society for Ethnomusicology,* 1978.

——. "Women and Music in Sudanic Africa." *More Than Drumming: Essays on African and Afro-American Music and Musicians.* Ed. Irene Ve. Jackson. Westport, CT: Greenwood Press, 1985.

DjeDje, Jacqueline Cogdell, and Carol Merrill-Mirsky. *Remembering Kojo: A Celebration of the Maroon People of Accompong.* Jamaica: N.p., 1987.

DjeDje, Jacqueline Cogdell, and Nketia J. H. Kwabena, eds. *Selected Reports in Ethnomusicology: Vol. V: Studies in African Music.* (387 pp, includes cassette tape) Los Angeles: UCLA Program in Ethnomusicology, Department of Music, 1984.

DjeDje, Jacqueline Cogdell, ed., and William G. Carter, assoc. ed. *African Musicology: Current Trends.* Vol. 1. A Festschrift Presented to J. H. Kwabena Nketia. Los Angeles/Atlanta: UCLA African Studies Center/*African Arts Magazine* and Crossroads Press/African Studies Association, 1989.

Headlee, Judith Anne Still. "Musical Dreamer," Rpt. of "A Voice High-Sounding" and "From Composer to Composition." *Keyboard Classics* 5 (July-Aug. 1985): 6, 8–9.

——. "Turning Pages." *The Sounding Board, Marina-Westchester Symphony Society Newsletter* (Apr. 1982): 2.

Nketia, J. H. Kwabena, and Jacqueline Cogdell DjeDje, eds. *Selected Reports in Ethnomusicology: Vol. V: Studies in African Music.* Los Angeles: UCLA Program in Ethnomusicology, Department of Music, n.d. (387 pp., includes cassette tape)

Recordings

Composite of Black Religious Songs. (includes 14 7" reel tapes) Los
Angeles: UCLA Ethnomusicology Archive, n.d.

DjeDje, Jacqueline Cogdell. *Black American Religious Music from
Southeast Georgia.* Folkways Records FS 34010.

————. *Traditional Women's Music from Ghana.* Recorded by Verna
Gillis. Ethnic Folkways Records FE 4257, 1981.

Fitzgerald, Ella. *Ella Fitzgerald Sings the Duke Ellington Song Book.*
HMV CLP 1213–14.

Martin, Sallie. *The Living Legend—Sallie Martin and the Evangelical
Chorale Chapter.* Savoy MG 14242.

New Inspirational Soul. Newbury Park, CA: Lexicon Music,
n.d.

Sandra Crouch Choral Arrangements. Newbury Park, CA: Lexicon
Music, 1986. (SATB)

The Singers: 1840s. Columbia CK 40652. (Sarah Vaughan, Mildred
Bailey, Maxine Sullivan)

These Are the Blues. (Ella Fitzgerald) Verve 829-536-2.

Verrett-Carter, Shirley. *Lucrezia Borgia,* Gaetano Donizetti. Libr.
Felici Romani, based Victor Hugo's play *Lucrezia Borgia.* RCA
Victor LSC 6176. 6s, 12 in., 33-⅓ microgroove, stereophonic.
Also Montserrat Caballe, Alfredo Kraus, and Ezio Flagillo.
RCA. Italian Opera Orchestra and Chorus, Jonel Perlea, Cond.
1967.

————. *Shirley Verrett Carnegie Hall Recital.* RCA Victor LM 2835.
2s, 12 in., 33-⅓ rpm, microgroove. 1965.

Waites, Althea. *Althea Waites Performs the Piano Music of Florence Price.* Cambria Records (Box 374, Lomita, CA 97017),
n.d.

Althea Waites

Choreography

Furie, Sidney, Dir. *The Young Ones,* prod. Associated British Motion Picture Corporation. Additional dance sequences by Cristyne Lawson. Chor. Herbert Ross, 1963.

Lawson, Cristyne, chor. (dance) Chor. and perf. *The Art of Cristyne Lawson,* solo concert, at the California Institute of the Arts, 1977.

Lawson, Cristyne. *Danscape* (dance and graphic animation). Conceived, produced, directed, choreographed in collaboration with Jules Engel. Performed in The Modular Theatre, California Institute of the Arts, 1985.

————. *Jargon.* Suite of dances based on Brazilian music, 1979.

Lawson, Cristyne, chor. *Dogone.* Solo based on the emotional states of a repressed woman. Music by Lukas Foss. Chor. and performed by Lawson, University of California, Santa Barbara, 1975.

————. *Echo,* by Lukas Foss. Filmed in Buffalo by Jonathan Blair, *National Geographic* Magazine. Designed by Linda Swiniuch. Ed. Blair/Lawson, 1970–71.

————. *Linea,* music by Berio. Featuring Rebecca Bobele, Kurt Weinheimer, Donna Wood, Laurence Blake, George de la Pena, and Rebecca Wright, performed in The Modular Theatre, with space design by Robert Benedetti, music performed by the E. A. R. Unit, 1986.

————. *Nine Ladies on a Bench.* For the CalArts Dance Ensemble, 1982.

————. *Sixteen Dances,* by John Cage (five sections). Performed as part of the Contemporary Music Festival at The Japanese American Theatre as a birthday tribute to John Cage. Cond. Lucky Mosko. Perf. by 20th Century Players, 1987.

————. *Sweet Sweat.* For CalArts Dance Ensemble, 1980.

———. *The Double Life of Amphibians,* by Mort Subotnick (solo for Rebecca Bobele). Performed at Olympic Arts Contemporary Music Festival, Los Angeles, 1983.

———. *Who Cut the Cheese.* For Tina Yean, Rebecca Bobele, and Sandra Neels, 1981.

Lawson, Cristyne, dir. and chor. Ballet based on *War of the Worlds,* by Orson Welles. For the multi-level Modular Theatre, 1978.

Millsap, Ruby. *Because My Feet Are Dancing.* Music, William Grant III and Ruby Millsap. Performed by Ruby Millsap Dance Theatre. University of California, San Diego, Mandeville Auditorium, 1976.

———. *I Live in Music.* Text, Ntozake Shange. Music, Sheila E. Performed by Pilgrim Dance Ensemble at Pilgrim School, Los Angeles, 1989.

———. *Numberless Are the World's Wonders.* Music, J. D. Steele Singers, L. Breur, B. Tolso: *West Side Story,* prologue. Music, Leonard Bernstein. Performed by Pilgrim Dance Ensemble, Pilgrim School, Los Angeles, 1979.

———. *Sometimes They Seemed to Want to Cry* (suite): "Sail Away Ladies," "Have You Ever Seen the Blues?" "The Last of the Blues," "The Last of the Silk with the Paris Label." *Sometimes They Seemed to Want to Sing* (suite): "Because My Feet Are Dancing," "Walk in Jerusalem," "Upper Room," "He Calmed the Ocean," "Nobody Knows." Arr. Joe Clark.

———. *Souvenir.* Dancers, Forrest Gardner and Ruby Millsap. Japan American Theatre, Ford Theater, 1984 Olympic Arts Festival.

———. *Spell.* Music, Coleridge Taylor-Perkinson. Vocal, Leon Ware. Performed by Ruby Millsap Dance Theatre, Los Angeles Theatre Center, 1985; Wiltern Theater, 1985.

Washington, Lula. *Let Their Voices Be Heard.* Performed by Washington and the Contemporary Dance Theatre, El Camino College, Los Angeles, 21 Apr. 1989.

Ruby Millsap

Dancers Forrest Gardner and Ruby Millsap of the Ruby Millsap Dance Theatre performing in "Souvenir." The performance took place at the Japan America Theatre.

Lula Washington—Artistic Director.

LEFT TO RIGHT: Ken Morris and Michael Lee perform in "Urban Man" (choreographed by Lula Washington) at the Los Angeles Contemporary Dance Theater.

————. *Market Day.* Performed at Fifth Avenue Dance Studio, San Diego, CA.

————. *Women in the Street.* Featured by Los Angeles Contemporary Dance Theatre at University of Southern California's Bing Theatre, 11 Feb. 1989.

Audio-Visual

Lawson, Cristyne, chor. *French Dressing,* dance sequences. Dir. Ken Russell. Prod. Associated British Motion Picture Corporation, 1964.

————. *The American Crucifixion.* (sections) Filmed by Pidgeon Productions. Musical score by Julius Eastman. Principal artists of the Company of Man, 1971–72.

VISUAL ARTS

Artists

An Exhibition of Black Women Artists, May 5–17, 1975. Designer Shirley Kennedy. Santa Barbara, CA: Black Culture and the Center for Black Studies, University of California, Santa Barbara, 1975.

Beasley, Phoebe. *Zora and Langston.* (Collage, 36 x 36) From the collection of Ron and Charlene Hunter-Gault, New York, NY. 1988.

Black Angelenos: The Afri-American in Los Angeles, 1850–1950. (catalogue of exhibit showing 6 Mar.–11 June) Los Angeles: California Afro-American Museum, 1988.

Blocker, Melonee. "Constant Battle." *An Exhibition of Black Women Artists, May 5–17, 1975.* Catalogue, University of California, Santa Barbara, 1975.

———. "Untitled." (oil on canvas) Brockman Gallery (4334 Degnan Blvd.), Los Angeles, CA.

Bohanaon, Gloria. "Peace and the Child," "Mother Image." *An Exhibition of Black Women Artists, May 5–17, 1975.* Catalog, University of California, Santa Barbara, 1975.

Coustaut, Carmen, dir. *Extra Change* (film, 16mm, color, 28 min.) Writer, prod., ed., Carmen Coustaut. 1987.

———. *Justifiable Homicide* (film, 16mm, b/w, 5 min.) Writer, prod., ed., Carmen Coustaut. 1981.

Phoebe Beasley

Carmen Coustaut—filmmaker. (Photo courtesy of James Jeffrey)

Cremer, Marva. "Strange Journey," "Do You Know What I'm Doing?" (lithographs). *Black Artists on Art.* Eds. Samella Lewis and Ruth C. Waddy. Vol. 1, Rev. ed. Pasadena, CA: Ward Ritchie, n.d.: 94.

Dumetz, Barbara. "Black Woman." *An Exhibition of Black Women Artists, May 5–17, 1975.* Catalog, University of California, Santa Barbara, 1975.

Fakeye, Brenda. "The Curse of Noah." *An Exhibition of Black Women Artists, May 5–17, 1975.* Catalog, University of California, Santa Barbara, 1975.

Farrell, Duneen. "Fertility." *An Exhibition of Black Women Artists, May 5–17, 1975.* Catalog, University of California, Santa Barbara, 1975.

Gafford, Alice T. "Champagne Break" (oil). Permanent collection, Howard University Art Gallery, Washington, DC.

————. "Still Life with Antiques." Permanent collection, Charles Bowers Memorial Museum, Santa Ana, CA.

————. "Tea Party" (oil). Permanent collection, Long Beach Museum of Art, Long Beach, CA.

Grant, Coot (Liola Wilson), and Socks Wilson. "Do Your Duty," "Down in the Dumps," "Gimma a Pigfoot," "Take Me for a Buggy Ride." Recorded by Bessie Smith, *Bessie Smith: The World's Greatest Blues Singer.* Columbia GP 33.

Hildebrand, Camille. "Psalm 1 and Urn". Collection of the artist, Long Beach, CA.

Honeywood, Varnette. "Africa Woman" (acrylic on canvas). Brockman Gallery (4334 Degnan Blvd.), Los Angeles, CA.

————. "Birthday," "#3, Tub Saturday Night." *An Exhibition of Black Women Artists, May 5–17, 1975.* Catalog, University of California, Santa Barbara, 1975.

Humphrey, Margo. "Zebra Series" (lithograph). *Black Artists on Art.* Eds. Samella Lewis and Ruth C. Waddy. Pasadena, CA: Ward Ritchie, n.d. Vol. 1, rev. ed.: 9.

Lane, Artis. *Release* (bronze, 26 in.).

LeFalle, Lizetta. *Home and Yard: Black Folk Life Expressions in Los Angeles.* Exhibition catalog, 1987.

————. "Sunday Morning, Friendship Baptist Church," "Sunday Morning, Newspapers, "Red Hots." *An Exhibition of Black Women Artists, May 5–17, 1975.* Catalog, University of California, Santa Barbara, 1975.

————. *The Portrayal of the Musician in American Art.* Exhibition catalog, 1987. (video tape forthcoming)

LeFalle-Collins, Lizetta, and Leonard Simon. *The Portrayal of the Musician in American Art.* Catalog of exhibit at California Afro-American Museum, 7 Mar.–14 Aug. 1987. Exposition Park (600 State Drive), Los Angeles, CA.

Lewis, Samella. "20th Century Nefertiti," "Colonial Scene," and

Alice Taylor Gafford, artist, at age 80 in 1966.

Artis Lane and her bronze work entitled "Release."

"Migrants." *An Exhibition of Black Women Artists, May 5–17, 1975.* Catalog, University of California, Santa Barbara, 1975.

———. "Royal Sacrifice" (oil, 36 x 24). Cover, *Art: African American.* New York: Harcourt Brace Jovanovich, 1978.

Meo, Yvonne. "Ancient Wisdom Energized" (mixed media and collage on canvas). Copyright, Yvonne Meo, 1980.

———. "Sun Dance" (serigraph). Copyright, Yvonne Meo, 1985.

Middleton, Roberta B. *Chocolate Icing, Fish,* and *Painting by Roberta* (papier maché).

Montgomery, E[vangeline]. J. "Black Jade Ancestral Box." (Sterling silver cast ancestral box, 2″ x 2″), 1973. Collection of the artist, San Francisco Art Commissioner.

———. "Silver Bowl." (Sterling silver raised bowl with purple heart and silver-plated steel turned base, 6″), 1973. Collection of the artist, San Francisco Art Commissioner.

Mungen, Donna. *A Telephone Call* (video, 13 min.). 1985.

———. "Affairs of the Political Heart." (film, 16mm., 25 mins.) Bottom Line Productions, 1988.

———. "Affairs of the Political Heart". (film, 16mm, 25 min.) 1985. Premiered 23 Oct. 1988, Gallery Theatre, Barnsdall Art Park, Los Angeles.

O'Mare, Mikele Egozi. "The Story Teller." *An Exhibition of Black Women Artists, May 5–17, 1975.* Catalog, University of California, Santa Barbara, 1975.

———. "The Black Madonna." *Black Artists on Art.* Eds. Samella Lewis and Ruth C. Waddy. Pasadena, CA: Ward Ritchie, n.d.

Patterson, Roberta. "Butterfly Magic." (Water color, 22 x 30), 1986.

———. "Night Flowers." (Oil cray-pas, 22 x 30).

———. "Silent Snow." (Charcoal, 12 x 15).

Roberta Middleton

Donna Mungen—filmmaker.

Sandra Rowe

Pecot, Monica D. "Untitled," and "T. Sphere World." *An Exhibition of Black Women Artists, May 5–17, 1975.* Catalog, University of California, Santa Barbara, 1975.

Perkins, Angela. "From Reflections to Reality" (acrylic on canvas). Brockman Gallery (4334 Degnan Blvd.), Los Angeles, CA.

Rowe, Sandra. "Series: The Same Day Relative to the Same Day #1."

Saar, Betye. "Forget Me Not" and "Assemblage Box." 1976.

Sedwick, Judith. *Women of Courage: A Photographic Exhibit.* Shown at California Afro-American Museum, 600 State Drive, Exposition Park, Los Angeles, 12 Oct.–30 Nov. 1986.

Sharp, Saundra. *Back in Herself.* Prod. Sharp. (available 16mm film or videotape)

———. *Back Inside Herself.* First place in 1985 San Francisco Poetry Film Festival and in Black American Cinema Society's competitions, 1984.

———. *The Way It's Done.* (30-min TV script for *Our Street* series, prod. WMPB for PBS, Baltimore, MD, Summer 1973)

Simmons, Donna. "Untitled." *An Exhibition of Black Women Artists, May 5–17, 1975.* Catalog, University of California, Santa Barbara, 1975.

Simmons, Gloria Brown. "Detail: Plant Life".

———. "Horizon." *An Exhibition of Black Women Artists, May 5–17, 1975.* Catalog, University of California, Santa Barbara, 1975.

———. *Kiss the Sun, Largest Sphere,* and *Rain Lips.* 1' dia.

———. *Porcelain Teapot and Warmer.* 13".

———. Untitled ceramic. 20"–22".

Skinshegun, Riva. Untitled ceramic.

Tolliver, Teresa. "Fetish Series Animal". (mixed media, 5' x 6' x 2')

———. Untitled. (clay, 30")

Waddy, Ruth G. "Daisies" (oil). 1966.

———. "The Fence" (linocut). 1969.

———. "The Key" (linocut). 1969.

White, Cynthia. "Untitled." *An Exhibition of Black Women Artists, May 5–17, 1975.* Catalog, University of California, Santa Barbara, 1975.

Woodard, Beulah. Sculptor with some of her works. Collection of Miriam Matthews.

———. "Bad Boy." (cast in bronze). Collection of Miriam Matthews.

———. "Chuck." (bust of Charles H. Matthews, Jr., cast in stone) Collection of Miriam Matthews.

———. "Creation" (orange wood). Collection of Miriam Matthews.

———. "Libyan Mother (mahogany). Permanent collection of Bowers Museum, Santa Ana, CA.

———. "Masai Warrior" (terra cotta, 13"). 1937. Golden State Mutual Life Insurance Company, Los Angeles, CA.

———. "Maudelle" (terra cotta, 13"). Collection of Miriam Matthews.

———. "She" (terra cotta). Collection of Miriam Matthews.

———. "The Sharecropper." Collection of Miriam Matthews.

———. "Travail" (Korean mother and daughter, camphor wood, 32"). Permanent collection, Los Angeles City Art Department.

History and Criticism

Coustaut, Carmen. "Africans and Latins Lay Groundwork for Cooperation." *Black Film Review* (Spring 1986).

Doktorcyk-Donohue, Marlena. "The Soul of Artis Lane: Portraits of the Mind, Scultures of the Heart," *American Visions* (April 1990): 22–28.

Fanaka, Marie. "Penny." Based on Fanaka's family history. Forthcoming.

Lewis, Samella. *Art: African American.* Foreword Jacob Lawrence. New York: Harcourt Brace Jovanovich, 1978.

———. *Jacob Lawrence: A Retrospective.* Catalog, Santa Monica College.

———. *The Art of Elizabeth Catlett.* Los Angeles: Museum of African American Art, New Orleans Museum of Art, 1984.

———. *The Media, Style and Tradition of California Artists.* Catalog, California Museum of Afro-American History and Culture, Los Angeles.

———. "The Street Art of Black America." *Exxon, U.S.A.* (Third Quarter 1972): 2–9.

———. *Wildlife Sculpture: A Bayou Heritage.* Catalog, California Museum of Afro-American History and Culture, Los Angeles.

Lewis, Samella, contrib. *Arts and Esthetics: An Agenda for the Future.* Ed. Stanley S. Madeja, Cemrel, Inc. Based on a conference held at Aspen, CO, June 1976. Co-sponsored by Cemrel, Inc., and the Education Program of the Aspen Institute for Humanistic Studies.

Lewis, Samella, and Ruth Waddy. *Black Artists on Art.* 2 vols. Los Angeles: Contemporary Craft Publishers, 1969, 1971; Ward Ritchie Press, 1976.

Montgomery, E[vangeline]. J. *California Black Craftsmen.* Catalog of exhibit held 15 Feb.–8 Mar. 1970. Oakland: Mills College Art Gallery, 1970.

———. "Exhibition Chart." Presented at Black Museums Seminar, African-American Historical and Cultural Society, Inc. San Francisco, 14 Jan. 1977.

———. *Sargent Johnson, 23-Feb.–21 Mar. 1971.* Oakland: Oakland Museum of Art, 1971.

Montgomery, E[vangeline]. J., ed. *New Perspectives in Black Art, 5–26 Oct., 1968.* Oakland: Oakland Museum Art Division, Kaiser Center Gallery, 1968.

CULINARY ARTS

Bailey, Pearl. *Pearl's Kitchen: An Extraordinary Cookbook*. New York: Harcourt, 1973.

Clark, Libby. "Food for Thought." *Los Angeles Sentinel* (13 July 1989): C6-C7.

Coleman, Beverly. "The Nutrition Tune-Up." Los Angeles: Coleman, forthcoming.

————. "The Safe Use of Herbs: How to Use Ordinary Kitchen Herbs to Help You Stay Well." Los Angeles: Naches, forthcoming.

Garvin, Gladys M. *Food and Nutrients for All Ages*. Pomona, CA: The Little Informant, 1978.

Holdredge, Helen, comp., ed. *Mammy Pleasant's Cookbook*. Illust. James Beauchamp Alexander. San Francisco: 101 Productions, 1970.

Inge, Arline. "Maya Angelou Prepares a Joyous West African Feast." *Bon Appetite* (Mar. 1978): 74–77.

Lewis, Edna. *In Pursuit of Flavor*. New York: Knopf, 1988.

————. *The Taste of Country Cooking*. (recipes and narrative about appropriate seasons and other exposition) New York: Knopf, 1986,

Lewis, Edna, and Evangeline Peterson. *The Edna Lewis Cookbook*. New York: Ecco, 1979; 1983.

Negro Culinary Art Club. *Eliza's Cookbook*. Organized by Beatrice Hightower, Caterer, in 1934. N.p: n.p., 1936.

"Recipes." *Precinct Reporter,* San Bernardino, CA.

The Episcopal Church Women of Christ the Good Shepherd Episcopal Church, Los Angeles. *A Book of Favorite Recipes.* Leawood, KS: Circulation Service, 1968–1988.

The National Council of Negro Women. *The Historical Cookbook of the American Negro.* Ed. Sue Bailey Thurman. Washington, DC: Corporate Press, 1958.

Turner, Mrs. Bertha L. *The Federation Cook Book: A Collection of Tested Recipes* (Contributed by the Colored Women of the State of California). Pasadena, CA: n.p., ca. 1910.

Vence, Flossie. "Flossie's Hush Puppies." *Women Chefs: A Collection of Portraits and Recipes from California's Culinary Pioneers.* Illust. Jim Burns and Betty Ann Brown. Introd. Madeleine Kanman. Berkeley, CA: Arris Books, 1987.

View Park Section of the National Council of Negro Women, Inc. *Favorite Recipes from Our Best Cooks.* Olathe, KS: Cookbook Publishers (2101 Kansas City Road), 1985.

PART IV: OTHER RESOURCE LISTS

TOP: Dr. Hansonia Caldwell directing the Jubilee Choir, California State University, Dominguez Hills. BOTTOM: Lorenza Jordan Coles (on the far right), Musical Director of the Belvedere Junior High School Orchestra, Los Angeles, CA.

BLACK WOMEN MUSIC DIRECTORS
AND CONDUCTORS

antley, Mrs. Lillie. Minister of Music, El Bethel Baptist Church, San Francisco, CA.; Director of the Nazarene Spiritual Singers, San Francisco, CA.

ooks, Mrs. Eunice. Choir Director, Guidance Church of Religious Science, Los Angeles, CA.

ooks, Mrs. Rose. Founder, Rose Brooks School of Performing Arts, Pasadena, CA; Founder-Director, Rose Brooks Singers (toured Europe 1970), Pasadena, CA.

ldwell, Ms. Cherry. Choral Director, Washington High School, Los Angeles, CA.

ldwell, Dr. Hansonia. AKA Chorus, Los Angeles, CA.; Founder/ Director, The Jubilee Choir, California State University, Dominguez Hills, Los Angeles, CA.

les, Mrs. Lorenza Jordan. Belvedere Jr. High Orchestra, Los Angeles, CA.

wart, Mrs. Faye. Rosemont Public School, Los Angeles, CA.

x, Mrs. Bette. LaCienega School, Los Angeles, CA.

wson, Ms. Mary Cardwell. Conductor-Founder, National Negro Opera Company.

Veux, Mrs. Romaldo. Founder-Director, Overtones, Washington, DC.

naldson, Mrs. Shirley. Director of Music, Bible Fellowship

Baptist Church, Oakland, CA; Gospel Choral Instructor, St. Luis Bertane and St. Benedict Catholic Schools, Oakland, CA.

Ellison, Mrs. Elizabeth Balfour. Choir Director, Virginia Union University Choir (ca. 1947), Richmond, VA.

Freeman, Ms. Evelyn. Musical Director, Bell Choir, Holman United Methodist Church, Los Angeles, CA.

Gilmore, Dr. Jane Murray. Director, The Children's Choir, Tindley Temple, Philadelphia, PA.

Hackley, Ms. Emma Azalia (1867–1922). Organized community choirs throughout the country.

Jackson, Mrs. Gladys Childress. Founder-Director, 1980–89 Collegiate Chorale, West Los Angeles College, Los Angeles, CA.

Jessye, Dr. Eva (Died, February 21, 1992). First internationally known Black woman director of a professional Black choir: Founder-Director, Eva Jessye Chorus, New York/Sumter, SC.

Johnson, Ms. Doris. Director of the Chorus, Sunshine District Association of Missouri and Kansas; Founder and Director, Doris Johnson Singers, Kansas City, MO; Director, Kansas Musical of the General Baptist Convention; Minister of Music, Mt. Vernon Baptist Church, Kansas City, MO.

Johnson, Mrs. LoWanda. Choral Director, North Oakland Baptist Church, Oakland, CA.

Joseph, Mrs. Danellen. Choir Director, Delta Choraliers; Chairperson, Music Department, Dorsey Junior High School, Los Angeles, CA.

Kinard, Camilla. Youth Choir, Guidance Church of Religious Science, Los Angeles, CA.

King, Ms. Betty Jackson. The Grace Notes (female sextet), Roosevelt University, Chicago, IL; Pre-Professional Choral Ensemble, Chicago, IL; Dillard University Choir, New Orleans, LA; Quinn Chapel A. M. E. Church Choir, Chicago, IL; Congregational Church of Park Manor Choir, Chicago, IL; Wildwood High School Choir, Wildwood, NJ; Riverside Church School

Examples of West Coast Visual Arts

[A] "The Tea Party" (oil painting), by Alice T. Gafford in the permanent collection of the Long Beach Museum.

[B] TOP: Fish papier-maché, by Roberta Middleton. BOTTOM: "The Key," by Ruth Laddy.

[C] Chocolate Icing papier-maché, by Roberta Middleton.

[D] **TOP:** "Silent Snow" (charcoal study), by Roberta Patterson. **BOTTOM:** "The Sun Dance" (serigraph), by Yvonne Cole Meo, an exhibit at Sorbonne University, Paris. (Photo courtesy of Yvonne Cole Meo. Copyright © Yvonne Cole Meo.)

[E] **TOP: "Zora and Langston," (collage) by Phoebe Beasley from the Collection of Ron and Charlayne Hunter-Gault, New York. BOTTOM: "The Series: The Same Day Relative to the Same Day = #1," by Sandra Rowe. (Photo courtesy of Photo Technical Art Services)**

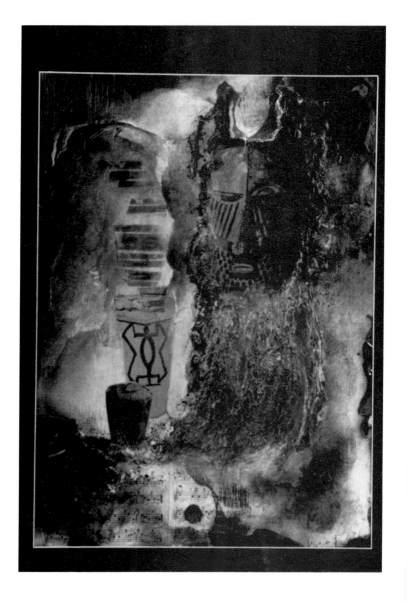

[F] "Ancient Wisdom Energized," (mixed media and collage on canvas) by Yvonne Cole Meo. (Photo courtesy of Yvonne Cole Meo)

[G] **Portrait by Roberta Middleton.**

[H] **Fetish Series Animal (mixed media) by Teresa Tolliver.**

[I] "Forget Me Not," by Betye Saar. (Photo courtesy of Lezley Saar)

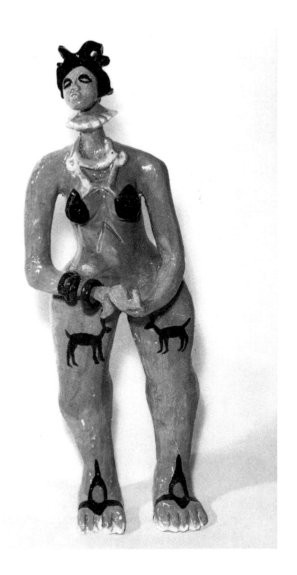

[J] **Work in clay by Teresa Tolliver.**

[K] Beulah Woodard, sculptor, shown with some of her work.
(Photo courtesy of the Collection of Miriam Matthews)

[L] "The Sharecropper," by Beulah Woodard. (Photo courtesy of the Collection of Miriam Matthews)

[M] "She," by Beulah Woodard. (Photo courtesy of the Collection of Miriam Matthews)

[N] "Chuck," a bust (cast in stone) of Charles H. Matthews, Jr., by Beulah Woodard. (Photo courtesy of the Collection of Miriam Matthews)

[O] "Creation," (carved from orange wood) by Beulah Woodard.
(Photo courtesy of the Collection of Miriam Matthews)

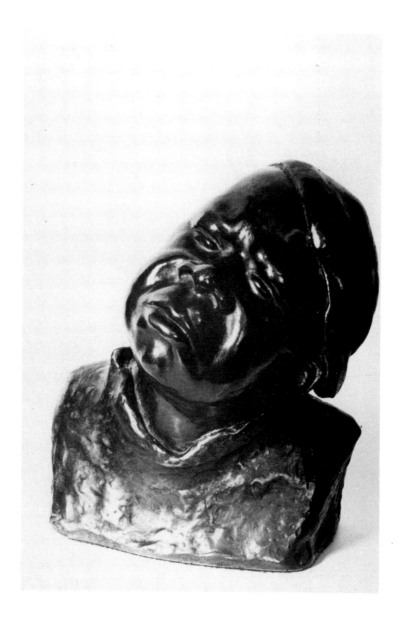

[P] "Bad Boy," (bronze) by Beulah Woodard. (Photo courtesy of
the Collection of Miriam Matthews)

Choirs (Children and Youth), New York, NY; The King Singers, New York, NY.

Mabrey, Ms. Marsha. Conductor, University of Oregon Symphony Orchestra, Eugene, OR (appointed 1982).

Moorehead, Ms. Consuela Lee. Founder/Director, Spring Tree/ Snow Hill Institute for the Performing Arts, Snow Hill, AL; Assistant Music Supervisor, *School Daze* (movie by Spike Lee).

Rhoten, Mrs. Louise. Leneicia Weems Elementary School Chorus, Los Angeles, CA.

Roberts, Ms. Kay George. Professor of Music and Conductor of the University Orchestra, University of Lowell, MA; Former Music Director and Conductor, Cape Ann Symphony, Gloucester, MA; Guest Conductor, Bangkok Symphony Orchestra (Aug. 1986).

Robinson, Dr. Gertrude Rivers. Founder-Conductor, Gamalan Ensemble, Loyola-Marymount University, Los Angeles, CA.

Selnouri, Ms. Marie Lenoi. Chorale, Los Angeles, CA.

Shambray, Ms. Celeste. Founder-Director, Shambray Chorale, Los Angeles, CA.

Sherrill, Ms. Barbara. Founder-Director, Samuel Coleridge Taylor Singers, Los Angeles, CA.

Smith, Mrs. Ethel Hardy. Director, Tuskegee Institute Choir, Tuskegee Institute, AL (1953–54).

Smith, Mrs. Willie Eva. Music Clinician's Director (conducts music workshops nationally, internationally), San Francisco, CA.

Vaughan, Dr. Beverly. Choir Director, Stockton State College, Pomona, NJ.

White-McCrae, Mrs. Janise. Founder-Director, Afro-American Ensemble, Los Angeles, CA.

Williams, Ms. Barbara. Choir Director, Sixth Street Baptist Church Junior Choir, Lakewood, NJ.

TOP: Celeste Shambray. BOTTOM: The Shambray Chorale.

Williams, Ms. Thelma O. Cleveland Public School Choir, Englewood, NJ (1961–69); Englewood Public School Choir, Englewood, NJ; Lincoln Public School Choir, Englewood, NJ.

Wyatt, Mrs. Gwen. Choir Director, Hawthorne Middle School Glee Club, Beverly Hills, CA; Founder-Director, Gwen Wyatt Community Choir, Los Angeles, CA; Former Choir Director, Holman United Methodist Church Choir, Los Angeles, CA.

Young, Ms. Laura. Choral Director, Banning High School, Wilmington, CA.

Youngblood, Ms. Marjorie. Washington Chapel A. M. E. Church, Tuskegee Institute, AL.

BLACK WOMEN COLLEGE PRESIDENTS

Barnett, Dr. Marquerite Ross. University of Houston, TX. (Died, February 1992).

Carroll, Dr. Constance M. Saddleback Community College, Mission Viejo, CA.

Cobb, Dr. Jewell Plummer. California State University, Fullerton, CA.

Cole, Dr. Johnetta B. Spelman College, Atlanta, GA.

Cook, Dr. Mattie. Malcolm-King: Harlem College Extension, New York.

Cooper, Dr. June. Interim President (1988), California State University, Long Beach.

Cross, Dr. Delores. Chicago State University, Chicago, IL.

Farris, Dr. Vera. Stockton State College, Pomona, NJ.

Harris, Dr. Zelma. Pioneer Community College, Kansas City, MO.

Jenkins, Dr. Sebetha. Jarvis Christian College. Hawkins, TX.

Kennedy, Dr. Yvonne. S. D. Bishop College, Mobile, AL.

McLean, Mrs. Mable Parker. Barber-Scotia College, Concord, NC.

Owens, Dr. Jerry. Lakewood Community College, White Bear Lake, MN.

Randall, Dr. Wueen F. American River College, Sacramento, CA.

Scott, Dr. Gloria. Bennett College, Greensboro, NC.

334

Sudarkasa, Dr. Niara. Lincoln University, Oxford, PA.

Taylor, Dr. Yvonne Walker. Wilberforce University, Wilberforce, OH.

Tucker, Dr. Norma Jean. Merritt College, Oakland, CA.

Ward, Dr. Arnette S. Chandler-Gilbert Education Center, Ext. Mesa Community College, Mesa, AZ.

Wilson, Blenda, President, California State University, Northridge, CA.

Wolfman, Dr. Brunetta Reid. Roxbury Community College, Boston, MA.

BLACK JOURNALS, NEWSPAPERS, PERIODICALS

American Visions. Visions Foundation, Frederick Douglass House-Capitol Hill, Smithsonian Institution, Washington, DC 20560.

BEEM Foundation Newsletter. 3864 Grayburn Avenue, Los Angeles, CA 90008.

Black Academy Review. Black Academy Press, 135 University Avenue, Buffalo, NY.

Black American Literature Forum. Parsons Hall 237, Indiana State University, Terre Haute, IN 47809.

Black Art: An International Quarterly. 137-55 Southgate St., Jamaica, NY 11413 (212-276-7681).

Black Art Now: International Review of African-American Art. 1237 Masselin Ave, Los Angeles, CA 90019.

Black Enterprise. 130 Fifth Avenue, New York, NY 10011.

Black Film Review. National Writers Union, 13 Astor Place, New York, NY 10003.

Black Lines: A Journal of Black Studies. Box 7195, Pittsburgh.

Black Music Research Journal. Center for Black Music Research, Columbia College, Michigan Ave, Chicago, IL 60605.

Black Perspectives in Music. Drawer 1, Cambria Heights, NY 11461.

Black World: An International Journal of Black Thought. 1580 Avon Avenue, SW, Atlanta, GA 30311.

Callaloo: A Journal of Afro-American and African Letters. The Johns

336

Hopkins University Press, Journals Publishing Division, 701 W. 40th Street #275, Baltimore, MD 21211.

Class. 27 Union Square, New York, NY 10003.

Con Brio: A Newsletter of the National Black Music Caucus. University of Michigan School of Music, Ann Arbor, MI 48109.

Conditions. (Emphasis on writing by lesbians) Box 56, Van Brunt Station, Brooklyn, NY 11215.

Crisis. 1970 Broadway, New York, NY.

Dasein: The Quarterly Review. G. P. O. Box 2121, New York, NY 10001.

Drumvoices REVUE: A Confluence of Literary, Cultural & Vision Arts. Department of English, Box 1431, SIUE, Edwardsville, IL 62026-1431.

Ebony. 820 South Michigan Avenue, Chicago, IL 60605. (September 1963—Black women's issue)

Emerge Magazine. 170 Varick Street, NY 10023.

Essence. 1500 Broadway, New York, NY 10036.

Essence. Ed. Marcia Gillespie. 102 E. 30th Street, New York, NY 10016.

Films and Video for Black Studies. Audio-Visual Services, Special Services Building, Pennsylvania State University, University Park, PA 16802. (814-863-3103)

First World, An International Journal of Black Thought. 1580 Avon Avenue, SW, Atlanta, GA 30311.

Free Lance: A Magazine of Poetry and Prose. 6005 Grand Avenue, Cleveland, OH 44104.

Homecoming: The Historically Black College Alumni Campus Newspaper. c/o Tinsley Communications, Inc., 101 N. Armistead Ave. #208, Hampton, VA 23669.

Howard University Alumni News. Department of Alumni Affairs, Howard University, 2900 Van Ness Street NW, Washington, DC 20008.

Interracial Books for Children Bulletin. The Council for Interracial Books for Children, 1841 Broadway, New York, NY 10023.

Journal of Afro-American Issues. Summer 1974; Vol. 3, Summer/Fall 1975, devoted to Black Women in America and to contemporary research on Black women.

Journal of Black Poetry. 922 Haight St, #B, San Francisco, CA 94117.

Journal of Black Studies. Sage Publications, 2111 West Hillcrest Drive, Newbury Park, CA 91320.

Journal of Religious Thought. Howard University Divinity School, 1240 Randolph Street NE, Washington, DC 20017.

Liberator. 244 E. 46th St., New York, NY 10017.

Muhammed Speaks. 2548 S. Federal Street, Chicago, IL.

Negro Educational Review. Box 2895, General Mail Center, Jacksonville, FL 32203.

Negro History Bulletin. 1401-14th Street NW, Washington, DC 20005.

Network: A Pan-African Women's Forum. Box 648, Avondale, Harare, Zimbabwe.

New Directions. Department of Publications, Howard University, 2900 Van Ness Street NW, Washington, DC 20008.

Neworld: A Quarterly of the Inner City Cultural Center. 1008 South New Hampshire Avenue, Los Angeles, CA 90006. (213-387-1161)

Nkombo. Box 51826, New Orleans, LA 70150.

Nommo: The Journal of the Obac Writer's Workshop. 77 East 35th Street, Chicago, IL 60616.

Obsidian. Department of English, Box 8105, North Carolina State University, Raleigh, NC 27695-8105.

Our Voice. 901 College Street NW, Knoxville, TN 37921.

Patterns: Newsletter of the Institute for Black Studies. 3026 Wellington Road, Los Angeles, CA 90016.

Phylon. Atlanta University, 223 James Brawley Drive SW, Atlanta, GA 30314.

Phylon. 223 Chestnut Street SW, Atlanta, GA 30314.

Présence Africaine: Revue Culturelle du Monde Noir. 24 bis rue des Ecoloes, Paris (5e), France.

Rhythm. 859 ⅓ Hunter Street NW, Atlanta, GA 30314.

Sage. Box 42741, Atlanta, GA 30311-0741.

Sepia. c/o Tommy Thompson, 28 West 44th Street, New York, NY 10036.

Shooting Star Review. Shooting Star Productions, 7123 Race Street, Pittsburgh, PA 15208.

Sisters. National Council of Negro Women, 1211 Connecticut Avenue NW, Suite 702, Washington, DC 20036.

Soulbook. Box 1097, Berkeley, CA 94701.

Take Five. Publ. by New World Creative Concepts, 3207 Washington Ave., St. Louis, MO 63103.

Tan. 1820 S. Michigan Ave, Chicago, IL 60616.

The Black Collegian. 1240 South Broad Avenue, New Orleans, LA 70125.

The Black Scholar. 485 65th Street, Oakland, CA 94609.

The CAAS Newsletter. UCLA, Afro-American Studies, 3111 Campbell Hall, Los Angeles, CA 90024.

The Crisis. 186 Remsen Street, Brooklyn, NY 11201.

The Journal of Negro Education, Box 311, Howard University, Washington, DC 20059.

The Journal of Negro History. 1538 Ninth Street NW, Washington, DC.

The NCBA News (The National Caucus on the Black Aged). Ms. Penny Lichlebury, Director of Public Relations and Publications, National Center for Black Aged, 1725 DeSales Street NW, Washington, DC 20036.

The Negro History Bulletin. 1538 Ninth Street NW, Washington, DC 20001.

The Philadelphia New Observer. 511 North Broad Street, Philadelphia, PA 19123.

The Review of Black Political Economy. Transition Periodicals Consortium, Rutgers University, New Brunswick, NJ 08903.

The Southern Register: The Newsletter of the Center for the Study of Southern Culture. The University of Mississippi, University, MS 38677.

The Urban League Review. Transaction Books, Rutgers University, New Brunswick, NJ 08903.

The Western Journal of Black Studies. Heritage House, Washington State University Press, Pullman, WA 99154-3310.

The Zora Neale Hurston Forum. Box 751, Morgan State University, Baltimore, MD 21239.

Theatre of Afro Arts. Box 94, N. W. Branch, Miami, FL 33147.

Tiger Lily Magazine. Division of Williams-Wallace Publishers, Inc., 2 Silver Avenue, Toronto, Ontario M6R 3A2 Canada.

Umbra. Box 374, Peter Stuyvesant Station, New York, NY 10009.

Vibration. Box 08152, Cleveland, OH 51108.

Virginia Union University Today. 1500 N. Lombardy Street, Richmond, VA 23220.

BLACK PUBLISHERS

African World Distributors, 28 ½ E. 33rd St #2A, New York, NY 10016.

Afro-Am Publishing Company, 1727 South Indiana Ave, Chicago, IL 60616.

Associated Publishers, 1538 19th Ave NW, Washington, DC 20001.

Black Academy Press, 135 University Ave, Buffalo, NY 14214.

Black Classic Press, Box 13414, Baltimore, MD 21203.

Black Star Publishers, 8824 Finkle Street, Detroit, MI 48200.

Broadside Press, 12651 Old Mill Place, Detroit, MI 48239.

Buckingham Learning Corporation, 75 Madison Ave, New York, NY 10016.

Drum and Spear Press, 1902 Belmont Road NW, Washington, DC 20009.

Edward W. Blyden Press, Box 621, Manhattanville Station, New York, NY 10027.

Emerson Hall Publishers Company, 209 West 97th St, New York, NY 10025.

Free Black Press, 7850 S. Cottage Grove Avenue, Chicago, IL 60619.

Free Lance Press, 5000 Grande Avenue, Cleveland, OH 44104.

Free Southern Theatre, 1716 N. Miro Street, New Orleans, LA 70119.

Ishmael Reed Publishing Co. P. O. Box 3288, Berkeley, CA 94703.

Jacksonian Press, Inc., P. O. Box 1556, Wildwood, NJ 08260.

Jihad Productions, Box 663, Newark, NJ 07103.

Johnson Publishing Company, 1820 S. Michigan Avenue, Chicago, IL 60616.

Journal of Black Poetry Press, 922 Haight Street #B, San Francisco, CA 94117.

Julian Richardson Associates, 540 McAllister St, San Francisco, CA.

Kitchen Table: Women of Color Press, Box 908, Latham, NY 11110.

Lotus Press, Box 21607, Detroit, MI 48221.

Mar-vel Publishing Co., C/O Roland Carter, 835 Oak Street, Chattanooga, TN 37493.

Oamuru Press, Inc., 161 Madison Avenue #2A, New York, NY 10016.

Oduduwa Productions, Inc., University of Pittsburgh, Black Studies Department, Pittsburgh, PA 15213.

The Third Press, 444 Central Park West, New York, NY 10025.

Third World Press, Box 730, Chicago, IL 60619.

Third World Press, 7850 S. Ellis Avenue, Chicago, IL 60619.

COLLECTIONS, RESEARCH AND RESOURCE CENTERS

African-American Institute, 866 United Nations Plaza, New York, NY, or 1201 Connecticut Avenue NW, Washington, DC.

Afro-American Collection, Temple University, Sullivan Hall, Philadelphia, PA 19122.

Afro-American Museum, 1553 W. Grand Blvd., Detroit, MI.

Alice Dunbar-Nelson Papers, Special Collections, The University of Delaware Library, Newark, DE 19717-5267.

Archive of New Orleans Jazz, Tulane University, New Orleans, LA.

Armistead Research Center, Tulane University, New Orleans, LA 70118.

Association for the Study of Negro Life and History, 1407-14th Street NW, Washington, DC 20005.

Black Music Center, Virginia State College, Petersburg, VA.

Black Music Center, Yale University, New Haven, CT.

Black Research Center, Bilbrew Library, Los Angeles County Library, 150 E. El Segundo Avenue, Los Angeles, CA.

Black Sheet Music and Piano Memorabilia, The Sheet Music Center, Box 367, Port Washington, NY 11050.

Black Women Oral History Project, Arthur and Elizabeth Schlesin-

344

ger Library on History of Women in America, Radcliffe College, Harvard University, Cambridge, MA.

Brockman Gallery, 4334 Degnan Blvd., Los Angeles, CA 90008.

Bronxville Public Library, 201 Pondfields, Bronxville, NY.

Center for African and African-American Studies, Afro-American Music Center, Atlanta University, 223 Chestnut Street SW, Atlanta, GA.

Center for Black Music Research, Columbia College Chicago, 600 S. Michigan Ave., Chicago, IL 60605-1996.

Collection of Afro-American Literature, Mildred F. Sawyer Library, Suffolk University, Boston, MA.

Collection of Black Arts and Letters, Wilberforce University Library, Wilberforce, OH.

Daisy Bates Papers, Special Collections Department, University of Arkansas Libraries, Fayette, AK.

Detroit Public Library, The Azalia Hackley Room, 3201 Woodward Avenue, Detroit, MI.

District of Columbia Public Library, Martin Luther King Branch, Black Studies Division, 9th and G Streets NW, Washington, DC.

DuSable Museum of African-American History, 740 East 56th Place, Chicago, IL 60637.

Ebony Museum, 582-14th Street, Oakland, CA 94612.

Ebony Museum of Arts, 1034-14th Street, Oakland, CA 94607.

Eva Jessye Collection, Clark College, Atlanta University, Atlanta, GA.

Eva Jessye Collection, Pittsburg State University, Pittsburg, KS.

Eva Jessye Collection, University of Michigan, Ann Arbor, MI.

Fay M. Jackson Memorial Collection. c/o Fay M. Jackson House, 1325 S. Van Ness, Los Angeles, CA 90019.

First National Black Historical Society of Kansas, 601 N. Water, Wichita, KS 67201.

Florence Price Musical Scores and Other Materials, Special Collections Department, University of Arkansas Libraries, Fayetteville, AK.

Funn, Carlton A., Teacher and Human Relations Resource Consultant with collection on Afro-American Experience and Other Minorities, 1214 Oronoco St., Alexandria, VA.

Hampton Institute Library, Hampton, VA.

Harriet Tubman Gallery, United Southend Settlement, 366 Columbus Avenue, Boston, MA 02118.

Hatch-Billops Collection, 491 Broadway, New York, NY.

Hollis Burke-Frissell Library, Tuskegee Institute, Tuskegee Institute, AL.

Howard University, The Center for Ethnic Music, Department of Music, The Moorland Room, Founders Library, Washington, DC.

Ida B. Wells Papers, Rengenstein Library, University of Chicago, Chicago, IL.

Indiana University, Black Music Center, Terre Haute, IN.

Johnson Publications, 820 South Michigan Avenue, Chicago, IL.

Karamu House, 2355 E. 89th Street, Cleveland, OH 44106.

Katherine Dunham Museum, East St. Louis, IL / St. Louis, MO.

King Library and Archives, Martin Luther King, Jr. Center for Non-Violent Social Change, 503 Auburn Avenue NE, Atlanta, GA 30314.

Library of Congress, Music Division, 1st Street between E. Capitol and Independence SE, Washington, DC 20540.

Lillie Carol Jackson Museum, Inc., Civil Rights Museum, 1320 Eutaw Place, Baltimore, MD.

Madame C. J. Walker Papers and Estate, Indiana Historical Society, William Henry Smith Memorial Library, 315 West Ohio Street, Indianapolis, IN 46202.

Mary Church Terrell Papers, Library of Congress, Washington, DC. (See also Robert H. Terrell Papers, Library of Congress, Washington, DC.)

Maryland Historical Society, 201 W. Monument St., Baltimore, MD.

Moorland-Spingarn Research Center, Howard University, Washington, DC.

Museum of African American Art, 4005 Crenshaw Blvd., Los Angeles, CA 90008.

Museum of African Art (Smithsonian), 318 A Street SE, Washington, DC.

National Afro-American Museum and Cultural Center, Wilberforce University, Wilberforce, OH.

Negro Bibliographic and Research Center, Inc., 11 R Street NW, Washington, DC.

Nettie J. Asberry Papers, Manuscript Division, University of Washington Library, Seattle, WA.

New Marcus Garvey Library, The, Box 476, Canton, MA 02021.

New York Jazz Museum, 236 West 54th Street, New York, NY.

New York Public Library, Research Division and Branches, 5th Avenue & 42nd Street; Schomburg Center for Research in Black Culture, Mid-Manhattan Division, 103 West 135th Street, New York, NY.

North American Black Historical Museum, 277 King St., Amherst-
burg, Ontario, Canada.

Paul L. Dunbar and Alice Dunbar-Nelson Papers, Ohio Historical
Society, Columbus, OH.

Philadelphia Free Library, Main Branch, Fleisher Collection, 19th
and 20th on Vine, Philadelphia, PA.

Rhode Island Black Heritage Society, One Hilton Street, Providence, RI.

San Francisco African American Historical and Cultural Society,
Inc., 680 McAllister St., San Francisco, CA 94102.

Sandy Moss Transcripts, Oral History Collection, Washington State
Archives, Olympia, WA.

Smith, Jessie Carney. "Developing Collections of Black Literature." *Black World* 20 (June 1971): 18–29.

————. "Research Resources in Negro Life and Culture." Paper
presented at and published in proceedings of workshop on
Social Sciences Approaches to the Study of the Negro, Fisk
University, 1968.

————. "The Research Collections in Negro Life and Culture Fisk
University." Paper presented at workshop on Bibliographic
Resources for a Study of the American Negro, Howard Uni-
versity Library, Washington, DC., 22–26 July 1968.

Smithsonian Institution, Constitution Avenue at 10th Street NW,
Washington, DC.

Southern Folklore Center, Box 4081, 1216 Peabody Avenue,
Memphis, TN.

Studio Museum in Harlem, 144 West 125th St., New York, NY
10027.

Talladega College Library, Talladega, AL.

Thomas F. Holgate Library, Bennett College, Greensboro, NC.

Tougaloo College Library, Tougaloo, AL.

Western States Black Research Center, 3617 Montclair St., Los Angeles, CA 90018.

Women's Research and Resource Center, Box 362, Spelman College, 350 Spelman Lane SW, Atlanta, GA 30314.

SOME IDEAS AND ACHIEVEMENTS
OF AFRICAN-AMERICAN WOMEN

This listing of significant ideas and achievement of American Black women is a challenging one for the stimulating information it provides. The women whose ideas and achievements are presented here are from the past and present and from all walks of life.

ANGELOU, MAYA (author, civil rights worker, dancer, lecturer, performer) became the first Black woman to create a movie screenplay when she produced *Georgia, Georgia.*

BAKER, ELLA (civil activist) has been described as "undoubtedly one of the great Black female figures of all times." Mrs. Baker is credited with organizing SCLC; is called the "mother of SNCC"; and was an important field worker for the NAACP, building chapters throughout the South.

BAKER, JOSEPHINE (1907–1975), star of the *Folies Bergere* during the 1920s and 1930s, legally adopted 12 children from various races to prove that people of all races and colors can live together harmoniously.

BARRETT, JANIE PORTER (first superintendent of the Virginia Industrial Home for Colored Girls) organized the Locust Street Social Settlement in her Hampton home so that young boys and girls could be kept off the streets. Through a variety of activities, young people learned "thrift, happiness, and healthy social contact." As superintendent of the Industrial Home, Mrs. Barrett employed new methods for rehabilitation. Girls were made to feel that they were beginning life anew at the home and that they could become the best women in the world. Mrs. Barrett considered the home to be a "moral

350

hospital where each girl was studied and given individual treatment" with the intention of rehabilitation and building character.

BETHUNE, MARY McLEOD was another Black woman who had many dreams which she carried out admirably. She wanted to start a school for youth. With $1.50 she started a school on what had been a dump. The school is now Bethune Cookman College, Daytona, Florida. Because there was not one hospital within 200 miles on the Atlantic Coast where Blacks could receive medical treatment, she started an infirmary which grew into a hospital and training school for nurses. In her last will and testament she left part of her dream to succeeding generations: Love, Hope, Confidence in one another, Respect for the uses of power intelligently directed, Faith, Racial dignity, a Desire to live harmoniously with other men.

BOWEN, UVELIA (organizer, social-service worker, teacher) has created, with the help of her family and friends in Philadelphia, a personal resources agency which has as its purpose giving everyone an equal opportunity and letting the integrity and ability of the individual decide the choice of occupation and position in life.

BROOKS, GWENDOLYN, LUCILLE CLIFTON, and **PINKIE GORDON LANE** are poet laureates of their states: Illinois, Maryland, and Louisiana, respectively.

BURROUGHS, NANNIE (educator, author, organizer, lecturer) organized the Harriet Beecher Literary Society as a vehicle for literary expression; organized the Woman's Industrial Club, which provided low-priced and wholesome meals to a "select group of office people"; fostered the idea of a national training school for girls in need of help. The school, opened in 1907, was called the three "B's": the Bible, the Bath, and the Broom, representing "clean lives, clean bodies, and clean homes." In her early endeavors, Miss Burroughs insisted that people valued that for which they paid. (*Women Builders,* Sadie Iola Daniels)

CATLETT, ELIZABETH (painter, printmaker, sculptor) was the first female professor of sculpture and head of the department at the National School of Arts of the National University of Mexico.

CHAMBERLAIN, NAOMI (educator) has developed a series of innovative health religious education programs. One series, which is based on scriptures from the Bible, is called "Reach Out and Touch Program." This particular program has a religious format and includes a mass that Miss Chamberlain wrote about lead poisoning.

CHINN, DR. MAY EDWARD (medical doctor) was the first Black woman graduate from Bellevue Hospital Medical College, the first Black woman interne at Harlem Hospital, and the only Black women on the Harlem Hospital staff for many years.

CHISHOLM, SHIRLEY (politician and first Black woman to sit in Congress) decided that she had the qualifications to run for the highest office in the land. She did; and although unsuccessful in her bid to win the Democratic nomination, inspired other women with the idea that a woman could become President of the United States.

CLAYTON, MAYME (librarian) founded the Western States Black Research Center in Los Angeles. The center houses more than 30,000 books, magazines, records, films, and letters by and about African-Americans.

COLE, DR. REBECCA was the first Black woman physician in the United States, practicing from 1872 to 1881.

COLEMAN, BEVERLY (poet, teacher) founded a health center in Los Angeles called Natches, for the purpose of effecting a preventive approach to health care. Her activities attempt to validate Afro-Asiatic ideas as models to prevent diseases and synthesize the arts of healthful living.

COLTRANE, ALICE (Turiya Aparna—widow of John Coltrane—harpist, organist, pianist) is also a jazz luminary who combines African and Asian mysticism with Western sounds.

COPPIN, FANNIE (educator, trained in Latin, Greek, and mathematics) believed in the training of hand and mind, a theory she executed at the Institute for Colored Youth, Philadelphia, after becoming principal of that school in 1866. She organized a home for girls and young women, and the Colored Women's Exchange; wrote a new constitution for the 1892 General Conference of the A. M. E. Church; and decreed that methods of instruction should include certain philosophies: the word "dumb" should never be used in a classroom; a child's lunch should never be taken from him, for there is no use in trying to teach a hungry child; improper ventilation of a room often contributes to sluggish children; teachers should always remember that they are dealing with a human being, whose needs are like the teacher's. She maintained that reading and writing should be taught through sentences; and that writing should be taught through letter writing.

DELTA SIGMA THETA SORORITY decided to counteract the Black exploitation films of the 1970s with a positive film, *Count Down at Kusini.*

DERRICOTE, TOI coordinated a first for Rutgers University when she arranged the University's first Black Poetry Festival, April 1977.

DICKERSON, M. ASHLEY was the first Black president of the National Association of Women Lawyers.

EDELMAN, MARIAN WRIGHT, author of *Families in Peril: An Agenda for Social Change,* President of the Children's Defense Fund, and the first African-American woman admitted to the Mississippi Bar, recently received a MacArthur Foundation Prize Fellowship of $100,000 to be awarded over a 5-year period.

FORTEN, CHARLOTTE (abolitionist, author, educator)

was one of the first individuals to analyze Negro spirituals, which she heard while teaching during the Civil War in the Sea Islands of South Carolina.

FRANCIS, DR. EDITH V., former Superintendent of Schools for Ewing Township, New Jersey, was one of the first six Black women superintendents (K-12) in the United States. She was born in Harlem and educated in the New York public schools.

HACKLEY, E. AZALIA, for whom a collection in the Detroit Public Library has been named, traveled throughout the United States' holding folksong festivals through which she taught Black communities to sing and appreciate Negro folksongs. Miss Hackley, who had been a concert singer, had a music store and publishing house in Chicago in 1918. At that time she encouraged the Black community to give Black compositions as Christmas presents or to rent musical instruments from her store.

HALE, DR. LORRAINE, co-founder of Hale House Center, a home for children of addicted mothers, did her doctoral research on children in the Hale House program. Her study is said to be one of the first "long-range" ones of its kind.

HAMER, FANNIE LOU (devoted civil rights worker, former field secretary for SNCC, politician) helped to organize the Mississippi Freedom Democratic Party and was one of its spokespersons at the Democratic Convention in 1964. At that time the newly-formed party challenged the legality of the all-White Mississippi delegation. Later, she was one of three Black candidates to run for Congress. On one occasion when she had been jailed for her civil rights activities, she was stripped to the waist, held by a Black man, and beaten by White men until she bled profusely. It was at that time that Mrs. Hamer came to understand that the Black man must be praised and reinforced to neutralize the dehumanization he experiences from White America.

HANDY, D. ANTOINETTE (author, concert flutist, educator, flute clinician, lecturer) organized and manages the Trio Pro Viva, an American-based group that has toured the Southern college circuit. Miss Handy performs and is constantly looking for compositions by contemporary Black composers.

HEWETT, MARY JANE (author, lecturer, educator) is examining the Black experience in the New World through the prism of Black women because she sees women as culture bearers. Mrs. Hewett is using Louise Bennett of the West Indies and Zora N. Hurston as her prime subjects for this study.

HOUSTON, DRUSILLA DUNJEE (author) was well known during the Twenties for her writings on African civilization. At that time, she had three volumes entitled *Wonderful Ethiopians;* two additional volumes were entitled *Ethiopians of the New World.*

JACKSON, FAY M. became the first Hollywood correspondent for the Associated Negro Press in the 1930s.

JEMISON, MAE CAROL (chemical engineer and medical doctor) is scheduled to become one of 14 women to join the astronaut corps since 1959.

JOHNSON, MRS. FREDA SHAW, Los Angeles, who studied music in Paris, formed and directed the Etude Ethiopian Choir, which sang in motion pictures and backed such singers as Lawrence Tibbett, Grace Moore, and Richard Bonelli. Mrs. Johnson also became the Director of the Los Angeles Bureau of Music.

JOHNSON, GEORGIA DOUGLAS (1886–1966) (poet, playwright, teacher, musician) christened her home in Washington, DC "Halfway House." For 40 years she used Halfway House as a meeting place for such African-American artists and intellectuals as Langston Hughes, Owen Dodson, Sterling Brown, and May Miller.

JOHNSON, JEFFALYN (public administrator, political scientist, educator, psychologist, consultant) brings together her education and experience in a number of fields to provide expertise in personal and organization development in government and private organizations. She focuses on administrative structures of organizations and the roles individuals play in order to improve their effectiveness and increase their productivity. More specifically, Dr. Johnson applies her training and experience as a public administrator and political scientist to working with top-level Federal career executives in development management systems and solving management problems. She draws from her background as an educator and psychologist to assist in developing effective interpersonal relations skills and methods of integrating personal goals and objectives with those of the organization. Dr. Johnson's primary goal is to bring about organizational changes that result in more effective delivery of goods and services to people.

JORDAN, BARBARA (Congresswoman from Texas) sponsored the first piece of major legislation to pass the Texas Senate in 1960 and also the first legislation from the Texas Legislature in 12 years to increase workers' compensation.

LAMONT, BARBARA is the only known Black woman owner of a television station—CCL-TV 49, New Orleans, LA.

LLOYD, WANDA S. became Senior Editor for USA TODAY.

MCGINTY, DORIS EVANS, professor of musicology at Howard University and author, was the first American woman to receive a doctorate in musicology from Oxford University.

MANLEY, DR. AUDREY F. is the first Black woman appointed Assistant Surgeon General of the United States.

MASON, BIDDY (former slave, midwife, nurse, philanthropist) opened her downtown Los Angeles home to newcomers

Miriam Matthews—librarian, historian, consultant, and community activist.

in need of assistance. Mrs. Mason, who also helped found the first African Methodist Church in Los Angeles, gave great financial assistance to White and Black churches; she visited the prisons, and she paid the grocery bills for flood victims of 1880.

MATTHEWS, MIRIAM (bibliographer, historian, photographer, private collector, and retired librarian) has accumulated several thousand photographs of Blacks in California. Miss Matthews, concerned about the preservation of accurate records, has identified most of these pictures and has written biographical sketches about some of the subjects.

MITCHELL, ELLA PEARSON is the first woman Dean of the Sisters Chapel at the all-female and primarily African-American Spelman College, Atlanta, GA.

MOSIKA, AMINATA (Abbey Lincoln—actress, playwright, singer) was one of four producers of a tribute to Black women at the Shrine Auditorium, Los Angeles, January 1977.

MOTEN, ETTA (former concert singer) is one of the persons who popularized African art in the United States when she and friends promoted an Afro-Arts Bazaar in New York City.

NICKERSON, CAMILLE (composer, concert pianist and concert singer, educator) toured the country, giving recitals which included Creole songs, many of which she had arranged and harmonized. Miss Nickerson gave great authenticity to the works when she dressed in "historic native costumes."

NORTON, ELEANOR HOLMES (former head of the New York Human Right Commission) includes sex as one of the irrational factors sometimes causing discrimination.

PATTERSON, EDDIMARIE (historian and truth seeker) is actively involved in planning a trip to the Nile Valley in search of Black Man's ancient history, so that Black children can re-identify with their own ancient history.

POWELL, GLORIA (psychiatrist, researcher) has published a book entitled *Black Monday's Children: The Effects of School Desegregation,* which concludes, among other things, that integration is more difficult for Black girls than for boys—if the home life and community life of the children have not been kept intact.

PRICE, LEONTYNE (opera star) became the first African-American woman to be acclaimed "prima donna assoluta."

RICHARDSON, PRINCESS MAE, whose father, Dr. R. C. Richardson, is credited with making the first credible movie of African-Americans in Philadelphia, has just celebrated her 65th year of successfully playing the harp. In addition to playing the harp, Richardson has written her story in *Jazz Harpist.* Her works are available on the album *Priere.*

RUSH, GERTRUDE, a founder of the National Bar Association, was the first Black woman to practice in Iowa.

SMITH, VICTORIA YOUNG was the first Black woman to hold a first-degree black belt in judo.

SPURLOCK, JEANNE (psychiatrist) found that Black women have not been as domineering as portrayed by social scientists.

STOUT, JUDGE JUANITA was the first elected Black woman judge and first Black woman to serve on a state supreme court.

TEMPLE, DR. RUTH (first woman graduate of Loma Linda Medical College California, and the first known Black woman to practice medicine in California) conceived the idea of a total health program which had four aspects: (1) The first phase of the program was a health study club which would offer health training courses and positive health action projects. (2) The second phase was a health information center strategically placed. (3) The third aspect was an inner city block-to-block plan of community work. (4) The fourth phase

Dr. Ruth T. Temple, M.D., first African-American woman to practice medicine in California.

was a community health week—now observed in the Los Angeles area and state-wide. The purpose of the total health program is three-dimensional: "To prepare, train, and motivate people to have new faith in God, country, fellowmen, and in that faith to prevent preventable problems, such as diseases, disorders, tragedies, violence, and crime; to conserve energy and meet basic health needs; and to go forward together and reach the highest realizable goals in happiness, development, service, and in maximum total health or wholeness of body, mind, and soul." So sound and innovative is her health program that Presidents Kennedy, Johnson, and Nixon endorsed it, commending Dr. Temple for her remarkable achievements in the field of public health education.

TERRELL, MARY CHURCH (author, champion of women's rights, educator, civil rights advocate, lecturer) was a woman of many great ideas and deeds. When invited to the International Congress of Women in Berlin, 1904, she gave her speech in fluent German, then in fluent French, and last in fluent English. Years later, using an old forgotten law that had been left on the books, she filed a discrimination suit against a number of Washington, DC, restaurants. Her efforts resulted in ending segregation in Washington's public accommodations. Another of Terrell's achievements was becoming the first president of the National Association of Colored Women.

WALKER, MADAME C. J. (1869–1919) invented a hair softener and the straightening comb. She then founded a business which included assistants, agents, schools, and a manufacturing company.

WALKER, MAGGIE L. (1867–1934) originated the first known plan by which school children could open and make regular contributions to savings accounts in the St. Luke Penny Savings Bank, Richmond, Virginia. The Virginia State Federation of Women decided to build a home, with a school and farm, for neglected girls when a judge sentenced an eight-year-old girl to jail. Some of the women who were instrumental in establishing the Virginia Industrial School for Colored Girls were Mrs. Maggie Walker and Mrs. Janie Barrett.

WELLS, IDA B. (teacher, journalist, lecturer, social service worker, and anti-lynching crusader) began documenting and publishing lynching incidents after Northern newspapers refused to give full or objective treatment of lynchings. Her works, *Southern Horrors* and *A Red Record,* were the first documented works on lynching. Mrs. Wells also encouraged Black women to organize. The Ida B. Wells Club, which she founded, was the first organization of Black women in Chicago. She was convinced that the NAACP fell short of meeting its goals because of limitations of some of the White leadership. She also led a delegation to see President McKinley about the lynching of a Black postmaster.

WELSING, FRANCES (educator, lecturer, psychiatrist) has formulated the Cress Theory, which says, in part, that the White need to feel superior to non-Whites is actually "compensation for a sense of inadequacy and inferiority."

WILLIAMS, BARBARA ELIZABETH (public school music teacher, pianist, painter) introduced her very highly successful string method, called the Williams String Method, to the Hopewell Valley, New Jersey, School System.

WILLIAMS, FRANCES, who played Miss Marie in *Frank's Place,* established a Native American theatre and the East West Players. She converted her three-car garage to house the Frances Williams Corner Theater in Los Angeles. Williams, who is also active politically, insists that women and men must work together for the liberation of the oppressed third world and of all working people.

WILLIAMS, DR. LORRAINE A. was the first female Vice-President of Academic Affairs at Howard University, Washington, DC.

WILLIAMS, RUBY MCKNIGHT, Pasadena, California, realtor, became the first Black kindergarten teacher in Topeka, Kansas.

INDEX

Letter page references (A–P) refer to the sixteen-page photo insert. All other page numbers refer to the frontmatter or the main body of the book.

NOTES ABOUT THE CONTRIBUTOR

HELEN H. BRITTON who contributed the Foreword, "Dorothy Porter Wesley: A Bio-Bibliographic Profile" in Part I, holds an A. B. in Ed., Leland College, now closed; M.A., University of Iowa; M.A.L.S., University of Michigan and is librarian emerita, California State University, Long Beach. She has been a college English instructor and assistant professor; a public librarian, and a university librarian, who has served in a variety of positions, including administrative appointments. She has practiced librarianship in the Free Library of Philadelphia; Louisiana State Library; the Thompson Memorial Library, Ohio State University; the Sterling C. Evans Library, Texas A & M University; the M. D. Anderson

Library, University of Houston; and the University Library, California State University, Long Beach, where she had positions in the latter library, as a reference librarian, an assistant library director for reference and instructional services, and an associate library director. Among her publications is "Interactions: A Library Faculty Matrix Organization and a Public Policy and Administration Program." *The Reference Librarian* 20 (1987): 187–204.

ABOUT THE AUTHOR

ORA WILLIAMS (B. A., Virginia Union University; M. A., Howard University; Ph. D., University of California, Irvine) is Professor Emerita, the Department of English, California State University, Long Beach. She taught English at Southern University, Tuskegee Institute, and Morgan State College. From 1965–1968, she was a program advisor at the national headquarters of Camp Fire Girls, Inc. She has taught in several Upward Bound programs at California State University and in 1968–69, helped establish the Black Studies Program there. In 1990, she was a Visiting Professor at her alma mater, Virginia Union University. A member of College Language Association and the advisory boards of the Inner City Cultural Center and the BEEM Foundation (the Black Experience as Expressed Through Music), she is a frequent presenter at professional and cultural meetings. In 1985, she organized an interinstitutional, intercounty, and interdisciplinary conference honoring the life and work of former choral director Dr. Eva Jessye. Williams has a number of articles and reviews published in professional journals. She has had two previous editions of *American Black Women in the Arts and Social Sciences* published by Scarecrow Press, one in 1973, and the second, in 1978. She is currently working on the biographies of Charles William Williams, New Jersey entrepreneur and civil rights activist; and Dr. Eva Jessye, choral director, actor, poet, and journalist.